Jesus and the Peasants

MATRIX
The Bible in Mediterranean Context

·

Richard L. Rohrbaugh
The New Testament in Cross-Cultural Perspective

Markus Cromhout
Jesus and Identity:
Reconstructing Judean Ethnicity in Q

Pieter F. Craffert
The Life of a Galilean Shaman:
Jesus of Nazareth in Anthropological-Historical Perspective

Douglas E. Oakman
Jesus and the Peasants

·

FORTHCOMING VOLUMES

Stuart L. Love
Jesus and the Marginal Women:
Healing in Matthew's Gospel

⊠ Jesus and the Peasants

DOUGLAS E. OAKMAN

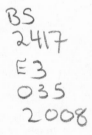

CASCADE *Books* · Eugene, Oregon

JESUS AND THE PEASANTS

Matrix: The Bible in Mediterranean Context 4

Cascade Books
A Division of Wipf and Stock Publishers
199 W. 8th Ave., Suite 3
Eugene, OR 97401

ISBN 13: 978-1-976752-275-5

Cataloging-in-Publication data:

Oakman, Douglas E.

    Jesus and the peasants / Douglas E. Oakman.

    Matrix: The Bible in Mediterranean Context 4

    xii + 336 p.; 23 cm.

    Includes bibliographical references (p. 313–336).

    ISBN 13: 978-1-976752-275-5 (alk. paper)

    1. Bible. N.T. Gospels—Social scientific criticism. 2. Bible. N.T. Gospels—Criticism,
interpretation, etc. 3. Jesus Christ. 4. Palestine—Economic conditions. I. Title. II. Series.

BS2417 .O34 2008

Manufactured in the U.S.A.

Dedicated to

the memory of my grandparents, Milos and Milka Rastovac

and

the members of The Context Group,
living interlocutors and ever-helpful critics

Do you not say, "Four months more, then comes the harvest"? But I tell you, look around you, and see how the fields are ripe for harvesting. The reaper is already receiving wages and is gathering fruit for eternal life, so that sower and reaper may rejoice together.

—John 4:35–36

Contents

PART III: THE PEASANT AIMS OF JESUS

Figures

Acknowledgments

Chapters 2, 4, 9, 16, and 17 have not previously been published. The following chapters are revised versions of previously published articles and are reprinted with permission of the publishers. The author and publisher gratefully acknowledge the cooperation of these publishers.

Chapter 1, "Jesus and Agrarian Palestine: The Factor of Debt," first appeared in *Society of Biblical Literature 1985 Seminar Papers,* edited by Kent Harold Richards, 57–73. Atlanta: Scholars, 1985.

Chapter 3, "The Buying Power of Two Denarii: A Comment on Luke 10:35," was first published in *Foundations and Facets Forum* 3,4 (1987) 33–38.

Chapter 5, "The Ancient Economy," was first published as "BTB Readers Guide: The Ancient Economy in the Bible," *BTB* 21 (1991) 34–39; then republished as "The Ancient Economy," in *The Social Sciences and New Testament Interpretation,* edited by Richard L. Rohrbaugh, 126–43. Peabody, MA: Hendrickson, 1996.

Chapter 6, "The Ancient Economy and St. John's Apocalypse," was first published in *Listening: Journal of Religion and Culture* 28 (1993) 200–214.

Chapter 7, "Money in the Moral Universe of the New Testament," was first published in *The Social Setting of Jesus and the Gospels,* edited by Wolfgang Stegemann, Bruce J. Malina and Gerd Theissen, 335–48. Minneapolis: Fortress, 2002. It has also been published in German and Italian.

Chapter 8, "Economics of Palestine," was first published in *Dictionary of New Testament Background,* edited by Craig A. Evans and Stanley E. Porter, 303–8. Downers Grove, IL: InterVarsity, 2000.

Chapter 10, "Rulers' Houses, Thieves, and Usurpers: The Beelzebul Pericope," was first published in *Foundations and Facets Forum* 4,3 (1988) 109–23.

Chapter 11, "'All the Surrounding Country': The Countryside in Luke-Acts," was first published in *The Social World of Luke–Acts: Models for Interpretation,* edited by Jerome H. Neyrey, 151–79. Peabody, MA: Hendrickson, 1991.

Chapter 12, "Was Jesus a Peasant? Implications for Reading the Samaritan Story (Luke 10:30–35)," was first published in *BTB* 22 (1992) 117–25.

Chapter 13, "Cursing Fig Trees and Robbers' Dens: Pronouncement Stories Within Social-Systemic Perspective (Mark 11:11–25 and Parallels)," was first published in *Semeia* 64: *The Rhetoric of Pronouncement,* edited by Vernon K. Robbins, 253–72. Atlanta: Scholars, 1993.

Chapter 14, "The Lord's Prayer in Social Perspective," was first published in *Authenticating the Words of Jesus,* edited by Bruce Chilton and Craig A. Evans, 137–86. New Testament Tools and Studies 28.1. Leiden: Brill, 1999.

Chapter 15, "Models and Archaeology in the Social Interpretation of Jesus," was first published as "The Archaeology of First-Century Galilee and the Social Interpretation of the Historical Jesus," in *Society of Biblical Literature 1994 Seminar Papers,* edited by Eugene H. Lovering, Jr., 220–51. Atlanta: Scholars, 1994; it then was published in slightly altered form in *Social-Scientific Models for Interpreting the Bible: Essays by the Context Group in Honor of Bruce J. Malina,* edited by John J. Pilch, 102–31. Biblical Interpretation Series 53. Leiden: Brill, 2001.

Introduction

ONE CENTRAL IDEA GUIDES the essays in this volume: Late-twentieth and early-twenty-first-century readers of the gospels, by and large, have had insufficient social experience to understand Jesus of Nazareth properly within his first-century agrarian world. Even in 1900, when only about 13% of the global population lived in cities and towns, Jesus scholarship was largely captivated by European theological interests and especially German idealism. This situation perdured through much of the twentieth century, as evidenced by Schweitzer's apocalyptic Jesus who advocated an interim ethics devoid of this-worldly care or Bultmann's existentialist Jesus who spoke only individualistic truths about authenticity.[1] The twentieth century witnessed the expansion of global capitalism and urbanism and the transformation almost everywhere of traditional peasantries.[2] By 2005, nearly 50% of the global population lived in cities, and the populations of the United States and Europe were overwhelmingly urban.

Yet the vast majority of human beings since the Neolithic have lived either as cultivators or within "peasant societies." In the early 1980s then, when I first began the line of thinking documented in this book, it seemed promising to explore the theme that the largely urban experience of modern Jesus-scholars did not prepare them properly to conceptualize his context or the meaning of his historical activity.[3]

---

1. Schweitzer, *Quest*; Bultmann, *Jesus and the Word*.

2. United Nations, "World Urbanization Prospects"; and idem, "UN Report Says World Urban Population of 3 Billion," both accessed June 10, 2007; see also Plattner, ed., *Economic Anthropology*.

3. Though grasped to some degree by earlier scholars (e.g., Weber, Theissen, Horsley, de Ste. Croix), this agrarian approach to the historical Jesus (drawing explicitly on resources of the social sciences) was first consistently stressed in Oakman, *Jesus and the Economic Questions of His Day*; Hanson and Oakman, *Palestine in the Time of Jesus* provide further perspectives on the differences between ancient agrarian and modern urban experience.

Max Weber, the Chicago School, the form critics, and others, of course, set the stage for the social study of Jesus already about a century ago. Current methodological developments, however, began in the 1960s as theological syntheses based in German idealism began to lose hold, as Liberation Theology emerged, and especially as an international group of scholars noticed the embeddedness of biblical theological perspectives within social matrices. Work of such scholars set out to correct what Robin Scroggs referred to as "methodological docetism."[4] The efforts of the 1970s—carried on among others by Elliott, Gager, Gottwald, Malherbe, Malina, Scroggs, Smith, and Theissen—were experimental and exploratory. Several of us in the early 1980s began to pose social questions regarding the historical Jesus that became a prominent focus of both the Third Quest of the Historical Jesus and the Social-Scientific Criticism of the Gospels as these emerged by 1990. This work would never have been possible without the explicit integration of the social sciences and the development of second-order reflection and models based in cultural anthropology or macrosociological theory.

Attention to cross-culturally informed models and theory has been especially important in mitigating the ethnocentric and anachronistic problems of modern urban-industrial consciousness. Cross-cultural study of the Bible, like ethnography in general, has stressed the ethnocentric and anachronistic in previous approaches. Bruce Malina once characterized the general procedure this way, "The goal of the social-scientific approach is to outfit the contemporary reader with scenarios that befit the alien texts that he or she seeks to understand."[5]

The reader will indeed find in the present volume emphasis on the importance of cross-culturally informed models and theory for formulating new questions and perspectives regarding Jesus of Nazareth. Furthermore, the reader will find numerous ideas and results that deserve further inquiry.

THE ORGANIZATION OF THIS VOLUME

The chapters of this book are organized into three interrelated parts—1) political economy and the peasant values of Jesus; 2) the Jesus traditions within peasant realities; and 3) the peasant aims of Jesus. Within each

4. Scroggs, "Sociological Interpretation," 165.
5. Malina, "Interpretation," 255.

part, the chapters are aligned in order of chronological appearance (not necessarily publication date). This will allow the reader to trace somewhat the development of interconnected ideas. First publication data is given on the Acknowledgments page; republications of several essays (or publications of mine not included in this volume) are indicated further in the comprehensive bibliography at the end. No effort has been made to revise essays substantially, to correct contested terminological usages (e.g., the occasional use of "Jew" for the first century), or to update edition-references within essays (the first citation in a chapter will make clear which edition is in view).[6] The assembly of the collection has made possible corrections where necessary, and several essays appear here in forms slightly more original than the published versions.

It might be worth pointing out that in several major respects this author's mind has changed since 1985. At that time I was still seriously willing to consider the idea that Jesus of Nazareth was preoccupied with agrarian millenarianism, though with strong, this-worldly entailments. After all, Jesus had been a disciple of John the Baptist—at least for a while. However, I came to reject the idea that Jesus followed John's apocalyptic fantasies. Like Paul Hollenbach and John Dominic Crossan, I concluded that Jesus' ideology is quite worldly in contrast with John the Baptist or the Qumran sect. Already in the Appendix to my doctoral dissertation, I saw the radical incompatibility of a positive theological wisdom based upon natural reflection ("the rain falls upon the just and the unjust," "the birds of the air") with acosmic commitments rooted in apocalyptic revelation. For a variety of reasons, I now consider the apocalyptic eschatology of the gospels to be entirely secondary.

In the beginning, I followed Joachim Jeremias and especially Norman Perrin regarding authentic Jesus material. Within the last twenty years, however, the tradition criticism of Q and the Gospel of Thomas has reshaped my thinking about the historicity of various Jesus traditions. As the last essays of this volume will show, a major social and religious matter is raised by a serious consideration of questions like, how did Jesus come to be written down (or perhaps "written up")? Or why, in fact, would literate, first-century scribes have recorded sayings and memories of a crucified, illiterate peasant? That such questions have social implications is rather obvious, but these implications are only just beginning to be investigated.

---

6. On the difficulties surrounding terms like "Jew" or "Christian," see Elliott, "Jesus the Israelite was Neither a 'Jew' nor a 'Christian.'"

Writing in the ancient world was mostly a political act, and it is clear that Jesus only appears in Josephus because of the political situation under Pontius Pilate. Moreover, the scribal interests that shaped perspectives about Jesus need to be surfaced (as the form critics first rightly insisted). The scribes of the Jesus traditions introduced various ideological colorings, and these distort our understandings of Jesus himself.

I began with investigations of Jesus and economic life, but I have come to realize that ancient economy likewise was deeply implicated in ancient politics (which K. C. Hanson and I defined as "how elite families treated everybody else"). One must speak of Jesus in relation to political-economic questions and not just economic questions. As the reader will see in Part 3, my sociological imagination is given rather free reign in relation to the political question. The peasant aims of Jesus were profoundly political—encompassed symbolically under an image about God's power—and entirely social as might be expected of a peasant sage and reformer.

INDEBTEDNESS AND GRACE

This volume thus traces both an intellectual odyssey and an adventure of ideas. The discovery (or perhaps better rediscovery) of the agrarian Jesus has had powerful resonance within my own experience. I derive from humble families on both sides. My mother's parents were Orthodox Serbian im-migrants. My maternal grandfather was a coal miner and common laborer all his life. My father's parents were farming people in rural Illinois. Only a few of my mother's sisters went to college. My father was the only college graduate in his immediate family. As far as I know, I am the only person in my entire family on either side to enter ordained (Lutheran) ministry or achieve a doctoral degree.

I did not have to theorize the existence of peasants; I directly ex-perienced the honor-shame, strong-group, gender-stratified, limited-good world of Mediterranean peasantry within the home of my maternal grand-parents. My grandmother, a loving and compassionate woman, never learned to read or write and could speak only broken English; my grandfa-ther, a tough and self-confident man, taught himself with only a primary-school education to read and write (both English and Serbo-Croatian). He used to tell me about "what God loved," which is where the immediacy of peasant religion first presented itself to me. He certainly loved his home-stead, having built his own house, and kept the traditional peasant staples until well into my teenage years. At my grandparents' home, I could visibly see self-sufficiency and limited good—orchard, vineyard, stand of corn, and garden. This is one important reason why I have dedicated this collection to their memory.

Out of that experience, however, has come for me lengthy study of the comparative literature of economy and world peasantry as well as social theory. This scholarly work has been supported and sustained by long association with The Context Group, to whom this volume is also dedicated. In the beginning, I was especially encouraged by Robert N. Bellah, Marvin L. Chaney, Robert B. Coote, Mary P. Coote, Frederick W. Danker, John H. Elliott, Victor Gold, Norman K. Gottwald, Everett R. Kalin, Edgar Krentz, Bruce J. Malina, Jerome H. Neyrey, George W. E. Nickelsburg, John J. Pilch, Richard L. Rohrbaugh, Robert Smith, Herman C. Waetjen, Antoinette Clark Wire, and Edward Wilson. Along the way, I came into fruitful conversations with Mordechai Aviam, S. Scott Bartchy, Alicia Batten, Marcus J. Borg, John Dominic Crossan, Dennis C. Duling, Douglas Edwards, Philip F. Esler, Craig A. Evans, Robert W. Funk, Ralph Gehrke, Gildas Hamel, William R. Herzog II, Paul Hollenbach, Richard A. Horsley, Richard Kibbey, John S. Kloppenborg, Stuart Love, Halvor Moxnes, Jack Olive, J. Andrew Overman, Stephen J. Patterson, John Petersen, Walter Pilgrim, Ronald Piper, Peter Richardson, Ekkehard W. Stegemann, Wolfgang Stegemann, Leif Vaage, Harold van Broekhoven, and numerous others. K. C. Hanson and I had an extremely fruitful scholarly collaboration during the 1990s. It was at his suggestion as editor-in-chief of Cascade Press that I assembled these essays.[7] It is indeed a pleasure to recall significant intellectual conversations with so many fine scholars over the years. To all of these specific colleagues, and to many more who could be named, I acknowledge my intellectual gratitude. My Religion Department too at Pacific Lutheran University has provided a congenial home for academic work for nearly twenty years, and my beloved wife Deborah has persevered with me through many scholarly deprivations. Thanks to all.

---

7. I am also grateful to the fine staff of Cascade Books, particularly K. C. Hanson, Heather Carraher, and Chris Spinks, who assisted with the production of this volume.

PAST MEANING AND FUTURE HOPE

What finally is the significance of such study? For some, such recontextualizing labor is sufficient in itself. It represents intellectual and moral
liberation, signifying *freedom from* "biblical authority" (even "biblical tyr-
anny") or simplistic Jesus-idolatries, and consequently much recent Jesus
scholarship has been devoted concomitantly to a critique of biblicism or
fundamentalism. Early forms of cross-cultural study of the Bible, like ethnography in general, stressed the ethnocentric and anachronistic in previous approaches. This work has been both necessary and salutary.

Nevertheless, significant hermeneutical and philosophical questions
remain. My own efforts, as stated, have been driven by the idea that the
contemporary urban context of academic biblical studies does not provide
the necessary social experience to understand traditions of early Christian
origins that emerged under prevailing peasant and agrarian conditions.
I still consider this idea valid, but have emphasized more recently that
investigation of the emic and socially peculiar in the New Testament must
also be balanced and complemented by a hermeneutics informed by larger
social-theoretical understandings of human interests and human values.
For if cross-cultural understanding is in fact possible and real, then there
is a universal basis for both understanding and human development. If
I could once bask in the loving warmth of my illiterate grandmother or
appreciate the sharp-witted, earthy humor of my grandfather, then even
partial understandings signify something of a commonality, a common
human bond.

Here we confront central questions of truth and method: Are biblical
studies simply an ethnographic endeavor or merely ideological tools for
emancipation of present-day thought and culture from the Bible? Are the
results of the social-scientific criticism of the Bible finished when clarity
is reached about the social and cultural distance of these alien materials? How conversely do biblical studies help us to connect to the past, to
each other, or to the future? What are the cognitive and moral bridges?
The universalist questions press in, increasingly as biblical studies become
international and ecumenical.[8] Why continue this work? What is biblical
study's deepest significance?

Perhaps it is more credible, on the one hand, to speak of some type
of cultural localism or relativism as the final truth. After all, sacred catego-

8. Räisänen, *Marcion*; idem, ed., *Reading the Bible in the Global Village*.

ries build rather discriminatory social and cultural worlds (as first clearly argued by Emile Durkheim, then carried further by students like Mary Douglas or Peter Berger). In this perspective, the historical Jesus has only accidental cultural importance. Considerations of New Testament christology describe, with no surplus of meaning, the contest of shame and honor around the historic figure of Jesus. This is, as it were, a strong nominalist position: General categories exist in name only. Biblical culture offers only relative truth value, with perhaps some suggestive analogies. And our best contemporary hope lies within some self-created spirituality.

Yet such perspectives are not completely satisfactory in intellectual terms. They do not explain why we study history, the Bible, or other cultures with interest. What draws us to history, to others, or to our world? Is it really disinterested interest? And must we always reformulate society and culture from scratch? In contrast to the nominalist view, on the other hand, could stand a strong realist position. While not denying certain relative features, this position argues for substantial truth contents that can communicate from particular cultures across cultures. Robert N. Bellah, for instance, has pondered the truth of religion in "symbolic realist" terms.[9] Bellah works out this intuitive position in relation to the history of reductionistic treatments of religion by the social sciences (where religion is seen merely as legitimation of political regimes, or ideological superstructure, or psychological projection). He is inspired by Augustine's intellectual search for faith (or faithful search for understanding: *credo ut intelligam*, "I believe in order that I might understand") and Tillich's preoccupation with ontology and the depth dimension of experience.[10] Indeed, Pierre Grondin claims that the key to Gadamer's hermeneutic also goes back to Augustine's *verbum interius* (the "inner word").[11] This strong realism, however, does not mean that all cultures have univocal meaning. Serious concern with context and cultural relativities undoubtedly complicate any cross-cultural concern.[12] This realist position attempts to understand the depth of culturally constitutive symbols, and their ability to transcend local culture with broad appeal. Concern with Jesus' central symbol "the kingdom of God," leads to understandings of it as "world-

---

9. Bellah, "Between Religion and Social Science," 251.

10. Ibid., 237–59.

11. Grondin, *Introduction to Philosophical Hermeneutics*, xiv, 119, 138.

12. Cf. Esler, "Models, Context and Kerygma."

reshaping power" or "God's eminent domain" in matters of larger human welfare.

If biblical studies is not simply antiquarian, then hermeneutical consciousness considers that transcendent meanings arise out of particular social systems—that is, are built ritually and symbolically out of peculiar experiences and cultural purity constructs—but also considers how they are not entirely constrained by them and how they have social and cultural resonance beyond their original contexts. New Testament christology, in this view, begins in the contest around Jesus' honor or dishonor, but is rooted in deeper questions about human dignity more broadly conceived— and perhaps the social and cultural arrangements, or the economic and political bases for such dignity. A detailed concern with the Jesus honored within those ancient traditions can have surprising relevance. Such study may in fact give clues as to what we might essentially be *freed for*.

Though there is estrangement from the biblical world today, as well as uncritical allegiance, critical scholars remain attracted to and fascinated by that world of traditions. The core symbols of the Bible (since not everything there is equally profound in a human or a divine sense) can continue to communicate as they give voice to "general human concerns." In any case, reader and biblical text stand within the same continuum of possible experiences (despite differing interpretations) that not only make interhuman communication possible, but also give rise to profound religious symbols.[13]

The realist position I have depicted, and am increasingly committed to, posits something in biblical experience and symbols that speaks about the essentially human. This realism is both a constructive quality and a standpoint for evaluation and conversation. For its serious students today, there is something in the Bible that is not just relatively true, but true against the widest possible horizon. Bellah speaks of such "compact symbols" that orient people within the world. Grounded in the historical Jesus and his concern for the power that shapes the world, we see within the New Testament precisely the basis for confession of the human and cosmic significance of Jesus as the Christ. But this development need no longer be understood as a legitimation of anachronistic ethnocentrism or absolutely exclusive statements of theological truth; it may be rather an invitation to an inclusive "gentle Truth" that welcomes and embraces the fullness of the human. May city and country, sower and reaper, rejoice together indeed!

13. See the discussion of Cassirer, *Language and Myth*.

PART 1

Political Economy *and the*

Peasant Values *of* Jesus

CHAPTER 1

Jesus and Agrarian Palestine: The Factor of Debt

THIS CHAPTER EXPLORES, THROUGH a variety of evidence and with the help of conceptual models and comparative study, the social dynamics of debt in early Roman Palestine. The chapter further attempts to assess whether the ministry of Jesus formulated a response to widespread indebtedness in that environment.

The value of utilizing conceptual models in the study of the past is that of allowing the known to illuminate the unknown, of testing how things were on the basis of how the modern student conceives they might have been. The model makes explicit the assumptions and judgments of the student and helps to trace the connections between bits of evidence in the effort to eliminate unserviceable interpretations. The model also helps to build the big picture, much like a mosaic. The study of history in this way becomes a history of interpretive "successive approximations."[1]

In a similar way, comparative study lends precision and focus to the kinds of questions the historian brings to this task. Employment of social scientific studies in various ways can contribute to a more adequate interpretation of particular aspects of the past.[2]

PRELIMINARY CONSIDERATIONS ABOUT DEBT IN ANTIQUITY

Debt was often in antiquity a formal expression of relations of dependency and (perhaps irredeemable) obligation. The ideals of reciprocity and social equality in the Graeco-Roman and Jewish traditions encouraged hopes for more "horizontal" relations in society, but more often than not imbalances

1. The work of Carney, *Shape of the Past*, has broadly influenced this essay.

2. This methodology might be characterized as Weberian, in view of the fact that Max Weber was its greatest practitioner. However, it should be noted that nearly all historical work assumes at some level analogical thinking, as Ernst Troeltsch noted long ago.

of power and wealth led in fact to "vertical" relations of dominance and subjection.[3]

For the Greeks, the most fundamental debt was that to one's parents. So Plato writes:

> Next comes the honour of living parents, to whom, as is meet, we have to pay the first and greatest and oldest of all debts, considering that all which a man has belongs to those who gave him birth and brought him up . . . .[4]

Aristotle also speaks of this primal debt:

> This is why it would not seem open to a man to disown his father (though a father may disown his son); being in debt, he should repay, but there is nothing by doing which a son will have done the equivalent of what he has received, so that he is always in debt.[5]

Aristotle further considers in the *Ethics* how essential reciprocity is to friendship, and whether it is better to return a favor (and thus stay out of debt), or to accept such as something which cannot be paid.[6]

The socio-political aspect of debt is expressed well by Thucydides in the mouth of Pericles:

> In generosity we [sc. the Athenians] are equally singular, acquiring our friends by conferring, not by receiving, favours. Yet, of course, the doer of the favour is the firmer friend of the two, in order by continued kindness to keep the recipient in his debt; while the debtor feels less keenly from the very consciousness that the return he makes will be a payment, not a free gift.[7]

On the Roman side, the vertical and political realities of debt were frequently evident. Cicero criticizes Sulla and Caesar for having expropriated property in order to bestow (politically useful) benefits on others. For Cicero, "liberality" in this sense is not just.[8] Plutarch tells how Caesar ran

---

3. For a useful way of looking at these issues, see Gouldner, "The Norm of Reciprocity"; Nicholas, *An Introduction to Roman Law,* 149–53, 158ff, offers a useful treatment of the law of obligations and debt in Roman legal tradition.

4. Plato, *Laws* 4.717 (Jowett); for other Greek material, see Hauck, *"Opheilō, ktl."*

5. Aristotle, *Nicomachean Ethics* 8.14, 1163b19 (Ross).

6. Ibid., 8.13, 1162a34–1163a23; 9.2, 1165a3 respectively.

7. Thucydides, *Peloponnesian War* 2.40.2 (Crawley–Feetham).

8. Cicero, *De officiis* 1.43; 2.84.

up huge debts for the purpose of sustaining his own political position and agenda.[9]

It is in this context that the whole subject of clientage needs to be mentioned. In the late republic and early empire, political networks were established, maintained, or destroyed by the bestowing of political favors, loans of money, or other social goods. This is well illustrated, for instance, in the affairs of Roman *socii* like the Herods. To give just a few examples, Antipater quickly won Caesar's friendship in Egypt by supplying a small army to support the actions of Mithridates. This gained high honors for Antipater (that is, Caesar cancelled his obligation to Antipater and made him a client).[10] Herod was unable to hide the support he had given to Antony when he presented himself to Octavian at Rhodes.[11] With his usual boldness, Herod made a point of his former loyalty to Antony as a potential asset to the new *princeps*. To this appeal, Octavian was favorably inclined: "So staunch a champion of the claims of friendship deserves to be ruler over many subjects."[12]

If debt was at times the bond of friendship or the cement of political relations in Graeco-Roman antiquity, for "little people" it was more often than not brutal compulsion and oppression. The abolition of debt was frequently encountered as a revolutionary slogan of the disenfranchised, usually accompanied by a demand for the redistribution of land.[13]

In the century and a half immediately preceding the birth of Jesus, the cases of Tiberius Gracchus, Aristonicus, and Lucullus, to name just three, give evidence of attempts to reverse or escape altogether Rome's imperialistic and exploitative agrarian policies, as well as evidence of the socially disruptive effects of debt. Tiberius, witnessing the decline of a Roman peasantry long burdened by the Punic wars and many of whose lands were in the hands of the wealthy, passed an agrarian law designed to restore

9. Plutarch, *Caesar* 5. Finley discusses this kind of politics in *Ancient Economy*, 53–54, 143, and 187 nn. 47, 55.

10. Josephus, *War* 1.187, 193–94, and cf. 199.

11. Ibid., 1.386ff.

12. Ibid., 1.391 (Thackeray, LCL).

13. See Rostovtzeff, *SEHRE*, ch. 1; also, de Ste. Croix, *Class Struggle*, 298, 608–9 n. 55 (citing references to Aristotle, Plato, Plutarch, and others); Austin and Vidal-Naquet, *Economic and Social History of Ancient Greece*, have a good discussion of Greek developments down to the fourth century and translations of several important passages; Brunt, *Social Conflicts*, 74ff treats agrarian problems in the late republic.

expropriated lands to their former owners.[14] Tiberius was murdered. His aims were carried forward without ultimate success by his brother Gaius. The social order of Rome became dominated, again as of old, by a landed aristocracy.

Almost contemporaneously with the death of Tiberius (133 BCE), Attalus III bequeathed his kingdom to Rome. Before a final settlement could take place, a great "slave" revolt erupted under the leadership of Aristonicus (132–129).[15] This revolt, according to Strabo and Diodorus Siculus, had a manifestly utopian aim—the foundation of an egalitarian state. The Hellenistic kingdoms of Asia Minor had exploited its agricultural peoples to the hilt. Rome could be expected to follow similar policies, as was evident to the insurgents from events in Greece. The insurgents had nothing to lose and everything to gain by revolt.

Plutarch makes the agrarian aspect of this revolt plain by connecting the aims of both Aristonicus and Tiberius Gracchus with the Stoic philosopher Blossius: Freedom was only guaranteed by equalitarian arrangements in property.[16] A Pergamene inscription (*OGIS* 338) indicates that a belated attempt was made to co-opt the insurrection by offering elevated status to the slaves involved. Though the insurrection eventually was crushed, the initial success of Aristonicus shows how powerful the hope for freedom could be for enslaved or indebted people. Several decades later, the lower classes of Asia Minor were still ready to risk all by supporting Mithridates.

After the defeat of Mithridates, the Roman general Lucullus found the population of Asia in terrible straits because of debts owed to Roman *publicani*. The fears of the movement associated with the name of Aristonicus were realized! Lucullus opposed the interests of these "capitalists" and implemented measures to alleviate the sufferings of the province: (a) Interest was lowered to 12 percent per year, (b) interest in arrears was remitted, and (c) creditors could take annually no more than one fourth

14. Plutarch, *Tiberius Gracchus* 13; cf. Brunt, *Social Conflicts* 78–80.

15. On the social breadth of this revolt, including not only slaves but also bondmen and the urban proletariat, see Rostovtzeff, *SEHHW,* 2:757, 807–11.

16. The revolutionary actions of Mithridates several decades later were apparently modeled after those of Aristonicus, which allows more precise inference about their nature. They included remission of debts and taxes, as well as promises of land redistribution: Rostovtzeff, *SEHHW,* 2:938, 943. In addition to Rostovtzeff, Dickey, "Some Economic and Social Conditions," 396–98. Also, Tarn and Griffith, *Hellenistic Civilization,* 40–41, 125.

of a debtor's income.[17] Plutarch says that these measures were successful in alleviating the crisis, but within a few short years the *publicani* and the evils associated with them were back.[18]

In the Graeco-Roman world, then, debt and related agrarian problems played a crucial role in historical developments. The same can be said on the Jewish side. A long biblical tradition recognized and attempted to limit, if not completely eradicate, the disruptive socio-economic effects of debt. Prescriptions or problems related to debt are mentioned in all of the major divisions:[19] Legislative (Exod 22:25–27; Lev 25; Deut 15; 23:19–20), prophetic (Isa 5:8; Hab 2:6), historical (1 Sam 22:2; 2 Kgs 4:1; Neh 5:1–5), and wisdom writings (Prov 22:7). The tradition uniformly opposes usury and the permanent transfer of real property (Exod 22:25; Lev 25:13; Deut 15:2).

The basic presupposition for the biblical view of debt was the equality, with various qualifications, of each member of Israel before Yahweh. This meant equality of access to the goods of life as well. Hence, the vociferous opposition in the tradition to disruptions of the social order from economic causes. The emergence of the Israelite monarchy and the concomitant social stratification gave fuel to the tradition of protest and legislation.[20] The interesting post-exilic episode recorded in Nehemiah 5 gives explicit detail about how the tradition might be actualized to counter agrarian problems.

DEBT AND A GENERAL MODEL OF SOCIAL STRATIFICATION IN EARLY ROMAN PALESTINE

The early Hasmonean epoch seemed to some like a return to the glorious days of Israel (1 Macc 14:4–15). The internal political struggles and agrarian unrest under Jannaeus effectively destroyed this illusion.[21] The exorbitant exactions and suffering accompanying the Roman civil wars, the fratricidal strife of the factions of Hyrcanus and Aristobulus, the rise of Antipater and Herod—all confirmed the uncertain political status of

17. See the discussion of Plutarch, *Lucullus* 20.23 in Rostovtzeff, *SEHHW*, 2:953–55.

18. Rostovtzeff, *SEHHW,* 2:965.

19. Unless otherwise noted, all biblical citations are according to the text of the Revised Standard Version.

20. See the article of Brueggemann, "Trajectories."

21. On the agrarian aspect of this struggle, see the discussion in Applebaum, "Economic Life in Palestine," 635.

the Jewish commonwealth and a new order of economic exploitation. Although peace came with Augustus, Palestine was unquestionably an occupied country. A legacy of social disruption and hardship remained. Was this situation further exacerbated by debt?

In looking at the issue of debt in the first half of the first century CE, what actual evidence is available for assessing its historical importance? For the purposes of this essay, a distinction needs to be kept in mind between the situation in Judea and that in Galilee. Furthermore, direct and particular evidence concerning debt must be distinguished from indirect general evidence that, though it cannot prove, seems to point to the existence of a debt problem. Students of this period must appeal to both types of evidence.

Two pieces of direct evidence for a debt problem in Judea are offered here.[22] First, Josephus tells us that one of the initial actions of the Jewish insurgents in the war was the burning of the office where debt records were kept. A quotation of this passage is instructive:

> [The rebels] next carried their combustibles to the public archives, eager to destroy the money-lenders' bonds and to prevent the recovery of debts, in order to win over a host of grateful debtors and to cause a rising of the poor against the rich.[23]

Josephus records another such incident at Antioch, undertaken by people under pressure from debt (*War* 7.61).[24] The motive given by Josephus for the action of the Jerusalem insurgents parallels that of Simon ben Giora, who somewhat later offered liberation to slaves so they would support his cause (*War* 4.508). These recall similar revolutionary actions taken by Aristonicus in the late second century BCE (see above).

Following the notice just cited, Josephus refers to the archives or record office as the "nerves" or "sinews" (*neura*) of the city. In another place, Josephus uses this same expression to refer to stockpiles of food which the

---

22. For a slightly different perspective, see the excellent article by Goodman, "The First Jewish Revolt." Though I had not seen this article before the first draft of this text was finished, I was pleased to note the convergence of our thinking on the direct evidence. Goodman appeals to evidence of (a) the flouting of usury laws, (b) the *prozbol*, and (c) the burning of the archives. I was also pleased to discover at the end of Goodman's article (p. 427) a different kind of model for the dynamics of debt in Judea. In subsequent revisions of this essay, Goodman's work has encouraged me to try to distinguish more clearly the debt situation in Galilee.

23. *War* 2.427 (Thackeray, LCL).

24. Cf. the discussion in Brunt, "Josephus on Social Conflicts," 151.

competing factions are burning up to their own destruction in the besieged city (*War* 5.24). The record office, then, is seen by this former aristocrat of Jerusalem as necessary for the very sustenance of the city. Debts assure the dominance of the city over the countryside supporting it (cf. *Life* 38).

The second piece of evidence here offered is the *Mishnah*'s narrative concerning Hillel's "*prozbul*":

> A *prozbul* is not cancelled [sc. in the sabbatical year]. This is one of the things which Hillel the Elder instituted; when he saw that the people refrained from giving loans to one another and transgressed what was written in the Law, "Take heed unto thyself lest there be a base thought in thy heart, etc.," Hillel established the *prozbul*.[25]

According to *m. Git.* 4:3 and *b. Git.* 36a (etc.), Hillel implemented through the "*prozbul*" a humanitarian judicial proceeding to insure the availability of loans at the end of the sabbatical cycle. The talmudic tradition uniformly identifies the *prozbol* (a) as a formulaic statement (*m. Sheb.* 10:4), (b) made before a court, that (c) circumvents the usual cancellation of a debt in the sabbatical year.[26]

A number of points need to be discussed with regard to the tradition. To start with, the Hebrew text is not pointed *prozbul*, but rather *perôzbôl* (i.e. *ḥōlem*, not *shûreq*). This philological detail does not support the usual interpretation of the word, as meaning "to the council" (i.e. *prosboulē*). Hans Kippenberg, following Ludwig Blau, has argued that behind the Hebrew word lies the Greek *prosbolē*, a word encountered in Hellenistic juristic documents. The Greek word refers to the act of distraining on the property of a defaulting debtor and disposing of it through auction.[27] *Mishnah Sheb.* 10:6 supports such an interpretation of the *prozbol*: According to this passage, a *prozbol* can be written only on immovable property (*qarqaʾ*).

25. *M. Sheb.* 10:3 (Blackman); the Scripture quoted is Deut 15:9.

26. The following material in the *Mishnah* refers to the *prozbol*: *m. Peʾah* 3:6; *m. Sheb.* 10:3–7; *m. M. Qaṭ.* 3:3; *m. Ketub.* 9:9; *m. Giṭ.* 4:3; and the doublet *m. ʿUq.* 3:10. See also other tannaitic traditions in the Talmuds and Tosephta. The difficulty of interpreting this material is here acknowledged. The traditions were written down in final form long after their origin. The point at issue in many discussions is obscure and at times perhaps idealistic. Furthermore, the *Mishnah* was not written to give the kind of information we are asking about.

27. See *prosbolē* in LSJ, 1504. The meaning of the word is illustrated, for instance, in Ptolemy II's instructions to the *oikonomos* of Syria and Phoenicia, ET in Bagnall and Derow, *Greek Historical Documents*, 96.

The Talmud mentions other types of debt documents, and it is useful to try to distinguish them from the *prozbol. Mishnah Sheb.* 10:1 speaks of loans made with or without a "bond" *(shatar).* Both types of loan are cancelled by the sabbatical year. In apparent contradiction to this, *m. Sheb.* 10:2 says that loans given on pledge or bonds delivered to the court are not cancelled. In these passages, the bond stands in contradistinction to pledges and perhaps simple verbal agreements. The pledge and the third-party surety were older means of guaranteeing repayment of a loan.[28]

Mishnah Sheb. 10:5, in which *shatar* is qualified by the noun *ḥôb,* suggests that such documents simply record a debt and the terms of repayment. The bond represents perhaps the emergence of an impersonal system of contractual or written guaranties, in place of the traditional securities. Furthermore, the bond, like the *prozbol,* is not necessarily cancelled in the sabbatical year. The reference in *m. Sheb.* 10:2 to bonds conveyed to the court suggests delinquent loans that were due prior to the onset of the sabbatical year. The debts are still due.

It has been thought that the *prozbol* was simply a clause added to a debt document, to allow the debt to be collected in the sabbatical year (and perhaps stipulate that it is secured by real estate via a mortgage or lien). Kippenberg thinks that this interpretation is mistaken, because it adopts uncritically the later rabbinic view of the *prozbol.* He points out that a debt contract recovered from Wadi Murabbaʿat, Mur 18 (54–55 CE), does not contain any formula like the *prozbol.*[29] *Mishnah Sheb.* 10:4, however, does seem to lend support to the "clause interpretation." It states that the purpose of the *prozbol* is to ensure "that every debt due me I may collect whensoever I desire." This formula (especially "whensoever") could conceivably refer to the waiving of the sabbatical year forgiveness, but it can also be understood to refer to an aspect of the just-mentioned Hellenistic procedure of attaching land. The phrase "whensoever I desire" then points to the significant amount of extra-judicial power vested in the creditor. He can move against the debtor's property without further reference to the court.[30] This feature, not to speak of conveyance of land

28. See Barrois, "Debt, Debtor," 809; Prov 6:1; 11:15; 17:18; 20:16; and 22:26 suggest why the wealthy may not have wanted to stand surety for impoverished Jewish peasants.

29. Kippenberg, *Religion und Klassenbildung,* 139 attributes such a view to Dietrich Correns (*Schebiit*) in the latter's commentary on *Mishnah Shebiʿit;* cf. *b. Giṭ* 37b.

30. Possible evidence for this is preserved in *Numbers Rabbah* 19:9: A creditor hauls away a debtor's, as well as the neighbor's, granary! Cf. *b. Giṭ.* 37a, which indicates that at

to cover a debt, was foreign to traditional Jewish law. For this reason, the later rabbis had a difficult time assessing the meaning of the innovation attributed to Hillel. Understandably, they made their interpretation along traditional lines.[31] Some authentic memory of the meaning of the *prozbol* is retained nonetheless in the talmudic material.

It is interesting to note what look like post-70 CE "codicils" to the *prozbol* regulations—R. Huspith permitted loan arrangements to be made on a wife's or guardian's property (*m. Sheb.* 10:6) and R. Eliezer declared a beehive to be immovable property (10:7, against the Sages). These apparently expanded the scope of the law. Are we to infer that lands were mortgaged to the hilt after 70, and new securities needed to be found?

The direct evidence for first-century Galilean debt, as far as I know, is found only in the Gospels. The discussion of that material is logically deferred to the next section.

Turning now to the general, indirect considerations, three will be offered. These are in turn: (1) fiscal pressure, (2) population pressure, and (3) popular unrest in the pre-70 period.[32]

F. C. Grant, over fifty years ago, argued that two competing taxation systems—the Jewish and the Roman—placed an almost intolerable burden upon the agriculturalist in the early first century.[33] This has become pretty much the standard view, even though ancient historians have not as yet achieved a comprehensive picture of Roman taxation in Palestine.[34] Gildas Hamel, in a dissertation presented to the University of California (Santa Cruz), has questioned this standard view and argued that since the Romans initially depended upon the local aristocracies for tax assessment

---

a later time only the Beth Din could seize property; Nicholas, *Introduction to Roman Law*, 149–153, discusses legal procedures available to Roman creditors.

31. Kippenberg, *Religion und Klassenbildung*, 138–39. For evidence of rabbinic debate on the meaning of the *prozbol*, see *b. Giṭ.* 37a; on the Murabbaʿat material, see n. 58 below.

32. Theissen, *Sociology*, 40, lists the following "socio-economic factors" as significant in the context of Jesus' ministry: (1) natural catastrophes, (2) over-population, (3) concentration of possessions, and (4) competing tax systems. Goodman, too, notes high taxation, increasing population, and bad harvests as potential explanations for the debt problem in Judea: "Problem of Debt," 419. He downplays all of these, however, and lays emphasis upon the great influx of wealth into Jerusalem after Pompey.

33. Grant, *Economic Background*, 89.

34. Freyne, *Galilee*, 183; Theissen, *Sociology*, 44; Jones, "Taxation in Antiquity," 151–85.

and collection (cf. Josephus, *War* 2.405), it is probably better to think that each system of taxation took account of the other.[35]

Against Hamel's view, however, can be set the evidence in Josephus and Tacitus for repeated requests for relief from tax burdens.[36] Almost in the same breath can be mentioned the message of the embassy to Augustus (*War* 2.85–86) and the petitions to Archelaus (*War* 2.4). These latter expressly mention reduction of taxes and people imprisoned (for debt?). Tacitus tells us (*Annals* 2.42) that Tiberius received requests from the provinces of Syria and Judea for the reduction of tribute (tax on the ground). With this it is to be noted that Tiberius lengthened procuratorial tenure, in order (as Josephus, *Ant.* 18.172ff. tells us) to reduce extortionate exploitation of the subject peoples.[37]

Population pressure in Roman Palestine at the turn of the eras is easily inferred by looking at the expansion of the number of villages, towns, and cities of that time compared with other periods. One may also consider the archaeological and historical evidence for extensive and intensive farming.[38] Josephus speaks of both aspects—the number of villages and intensive farming—in his description of Galilee (*War* 3.42–43).

Along with such physical evidence, one must mention the social evidence for population pressure, namely, the numerous landless who are encountered in the sources. These were excess peasant children without inheritance, expropriated smallholders, and anyone who had been deprived in one way or another of access to the land. Many of these emigrated in

---

35. Hamel, "Poverty and Charity," 281; compare Theissen, *Sociology*, 42–43.

36. Cf. Theissen, *Sociology*, 43, who cites Josephus, *Ant.* 15.365; 16.64; 18.90; 19.299. Goodman, "Problem of Debt," 419 n. 15, thinks all such statements are "ideological" and points to the wealth of Judea. However, one must remember who controlled the wealth and out of whose "pockets" the taxes were paid. Invariably the burden fell upon the lower classes—those who controlled the least amount of wealth. If they were pressed too far, they might "bite back." The aristocracy knew this, hence the petitions for lowering the tax burden.

37. Baron offers further evidence, *Social and Religious History,* 1:264 and n. 20.

38. See Monson, et al., *Student Map Manual,* comparing Maps 11–1 and 12–1. Cf. the views of Avi-Yonah, *The Holy Land,* 219–21, who places the population around 2.5 million. Hamel convincingly disputes this number in his dissertation, "Poverty and Charity," 264–65. By considering the amount of food the country could have produced maximally, Hamel arrives at a figure of around one million people. Numbers should not, however, obscure the fact that the population had probably risen to a level near the maximum that the land would support under ancient technological and social conditions. On intensive and extensive farming, see Applebaum, *Economic Life,* 646, and Hamel, "Poverty and Charity," 474 n. 245.

search of better economic opportunity.[39] Such elements apparently supplied the labor pool for Herod's building projects, as well as the discontents met in the pages of Josephus as bandits or messianic pretenders.[40] Here too are to be classed beggars, orphans, tax collectors, prostitutes, hired laborers, petty artisans, and the like.[41] Applebaum has called attention to the expropriations of Jewish agriculturalists in the final years of the first century BCE that swelled the ranks of these people.[42] Lack of land led to conflict, especially in Upper Galilee and Perea, between Jewish and Gentile cultivators. We also remember the hostility exhibited by the Galileans during the War toward Sepphoris and Tiberias—both with pro-Roman sentiments and at one time or another seat of the debt archives.[43] It is highly probable that other social mechanisms, like persistent indebtedness, were systematically adding to this pool of the disenfranchised.[44]

Consider the model sketched in Figure 1. The model is designed to show, in a general way, the pressures imposed by debt upon the lives of the lower social strata of ancient Palestine. In the lower part of the model, two continua are employed. The dependency scale marks a social continuum from a relatively independent status to a dependent status. The property scale represents an economic continuum from direct control and access to the land ("ownership") to indirect or no access to the land ("expropriation, dispossession"). The scales are oriented so that the greatest condition of dependency or lack of access to land is farthest from the upper part of the model—representing the upper social stratum.[45]

39. See the material collected by Theissen, *Sociology*, 34–35, 41, on Galilean emigration and Transjordanian resettlement.

40. Ibid., 35–36.

41. See the discussions in Schottroff and Stegemann, *Jesus*, 15–28; and Stegemann, *The Gospel and the Poor*, 13–21.

42. Applebaum, *Economic Life*, 660.

43. Josephus, *Life* 38–39, 123ff, 375, 384. See Freyne's discussion of the Galileans in *Galilee*, 166.

44. Brunt thinks so too, "Josephus," 151.

45. For the notion of dependent labor, see Finley, *Ancient Economy*, 69 and passim. Also, de Ste. Croix, *Class Struggle*, 205ff.

Figure 1: Social Dynamics of Debt in First-Century Palestine

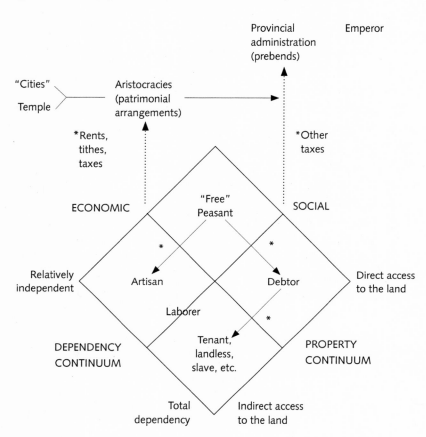

(*Various kinds of indebtedness)

The dotted lines connecting the two major sections of the model display the flow of rents and taxes upward.[46] These place a heavy burden on the peasantry. In addition, "acts of God" contribute to the pressure toward debt and foreclosure. A variety of such factors can be mentioned here, though for lack of space they cannot be indicated in Figure 1. Insufficient rain or drought, insects, crop diseases, and other pestilences make their contribution. The degree to which the Palestinian economy was monetized would affect the rate of insolvency. Trade and surplus funds to loan

46. Cf. the diagrams in Kippenberg, *Religion und Klassenbildung*, 92, 114, 127.

are an important ingredient in the rise of indebtedness. Opposed to "acts of God" would be "acts of Men"—greed, speculation, and power struggles all play a role in the concentration of property, which is the reverse of the coin of debt and insolvency.[47]

The top of the model indicates the oligarchic structure of Roman Palestine, as it was also articulated with the centralized state of the empire. The basic "polarity" of the top part of the model is the opposition between decentralized aristocracy and centralized ruler (with bureaucratic apparatus).[48]

The debate surrounding Grant's thesis has already been mentioned. The model suggests that not two, but three contending taxations burdened the producer in this period. In addition to the needs of the state and the old aristocracy (the priests), the needs of the new aristocracy (Herodians) and prebends for the Roman officials (procurators) must be kept in mind.[49] These may at times, as Hamel has suggested, have complemented each other. Yet one suspects that for the most part the old and new aristocracies competed for the same territory.

Debt probably was most thoroughly exploited by those aligned with Rome. This is basically a surmise, of course, but the previous discussion of the Hellenistic legal basis for expropriation of land would certainly point to such an alignment. It may also point to strong economic reasons for the secularization of the high priestly office and the upper priestly crust. In order for these to effectively compete, they would have had to adopt the methods of the new order.[50]

Bonds and pledges as guaranties for loans have already received some attention. Mishnaic laws, though mostly concerned with movable or im-

---

47. Theissen, *Sociology*, 41; cf. *Ant.* 17.307, 355; 18.2 on Herod's possessions. Stegemann's comment is instructive *Gospel and the Poor*, 19: "Herod the Great's expropriation of enormous stretches of farmland which were then sold to wealthy landowners . . . led to huge concentrations of land in the hands of a few . . . This in turn created great numbers of dependent tenant farmers."

48. On this polarity, see Lenski, *Power and Privilege*, 229ff. For discussions of the notions of "patrimony" and "prebend," see Max Weber, *Economy and Society*, 1:222 (prebend = benefice), 231ff.; further, Wolf, *Peasants*, 50ff.

49. See Baron in n. 37 above.

50. Consider Josephus' remark about slaves of the high priests seizing produce destined for the lower orders of priests in *Ant.* 20.181, 206; see Jeremias, *Jerusalem*, 181. Consider also the role that lower orders of priests played in the Jewish Revolt.

movable securities, speak also about limited periods of debt bondage.[51] Limited debt bondage is very much in the spirit of Old Testament laws forbidding interest, prohibiting the alienation of property, and protecting any necessary of life (Deut 23:19; Exod 23:26). This type of security is to be distinguished from unlimited debt slavery—a possibility under Roman law. In fact, the Roman law of debt was extremely harsh by comparison (see further the next section).[52]

As Figure 1 shows, "free" peasant smallholders—not, of course, free of taxes and religious dues—could become dependent upon some creditor without initially losing direct access to the land. They would remain on their ancestral plot with the legal status of "debtor," which at some point crossed over into tenancy.[53]

The model suggests the following possible scenario:[54] A bad harvest or excessive taxation, coupled with the need of the Jewish peasant to feed his family and set aside grain for animals or the next crop, led to arrears. When this was compounded with low productivity or successive bad years, default ensued.[55] The tax collector, or a wealthy man advancing credit, might insist on securing a fiscal debt through property. The peasant, obviously, would try to secure it with the labor power of his offspring or something less valuable. Besides "legal processes," there were even dishonest machinations: *y. Ta'an.* 69a tells how the people of Beitar rejoiced over the fall of the wealthy in Jerusalem who had defrauded them out of their ancestral lands.[56]

51. On this point, Goodman, "Problem of Debt," 423 n. 40 follows Urbach; see *m. 'Ed.* 8:2; also, Kippenberg, *Religion und Klassenbildung*, 143.

52. On the Roman law of debt, consult Finley, *Ancient Economy*, 40, 69, and de Ste. Croix, *Class Struggle*, 165ff.

53. See Freyne, *Galilee*, 195.

54. See a similar scenario in Freyne, *Galilee*, 195: "Indeed many tenants may have originally been owners of their own plots, but in a bad year had had to barter their land in order to pay tribute or buy grain for the following season and even feed their families."

55. Josephus, *Ant.* 18.274 is noteworthy in this connection. Applebaum, *Economic Life*, 660 n. 3 gives some evidence for how this might have worked: When Jews after the War could not pay their taxes in kind to the imperial granary in Jamnia, they were forced to borrow the next year's food. A comparative instance from modern Puerto Rico shows how debt through the "advance system" contributed there to the concentration of land ownership: See Wolf, "Hacienda System," 175–76.

56. Applebaum, *Economic Life*, 663 and n. 2.

The overall result of escalating debt, whether its nature was private or fiscal, was the growth of tenancy and the landless class.[57] Conversely, more and more land came under the control of fewer and fewer landowners. Of both phenomena in first-century Palestinian society, there are numerous indications.[58]

DEBT IN THE GOSPEL TRADITION

A number of methodological problems in dealing with the New Testament material must at least be acknowledged before proceeding. Is it appropriate to use the parables, as I am about to do, to consider Jesus in his socio-historical context? Do the parables convey direct or indirect information about social conditions in first-century Galilee? Or was Jesus' speech focused in other directions, on stock images of the oriental world with little connection to actual circumstances? Was the "real world" simply a take-off point for the essential element in the parables, their alternate "narrative world"?

The hermeneutical stance adopted in the present chapter has two elements. In the first place, it holds that public speech in an oppressive and conflicted political situation—like that of Jesus in Roman Palestine—cannot address any serious problem in material, social, or power relations without a certain indirection. The parables represent Jesus' attempt to publicly express critical truths in such a repressive political context. For this reason, they can always with probability be made to mean something else. This was the way Jesus protected himself. However, the basic meaning of the parables must always be assessed vis-à-vis their original audience and socio-political context.

57. A general view of the growth of tenancy in this period is given by Rostovtzeff, *SEHRE*, 1: 99–100, 291, 344f.

58. In addition to the previous discussion and notes: The wealthy men of the immediate post-70 period—R. Tarfon, R. Eliezer, R. Gamaliel II—did not acquire their possessions overnight. See Büchler, "Economic Conditions," 33, 36, 37. Boethus b. Zonen acquired Jewish property through default on debt: *m. B. Meṣ.* 5:3. See Büchler, ibid., 39. The loan contract from the Wadi Murabbaʿat, Mur 18, is instructive on pre-70 realities (54–55 CE). It attests to a lien on (movable?) property in case of default. Mur 22 (131 CE) documents the sale of property to cover a debt. Translations and commentary on these documents in: Benoît et al., *Les Grottes de Murabbaʿat*, 100–4, 118–21. Kippenberg, *Religion und Klassenbildung*, 139ff. Koffmahn, *Doppelurkunden*, 81–89, 159–62. On the mishnaic evidence for lease of fields, see *m. B. Meṣ.* 9.

Secondly, the hermeneutical stance of this essay stems from the recognition that, if the parables are true parables (accounts of real, one-time events), their narratives will self-evidently provide source material for social history, providing one looks for overarching themes. If the parables are similitudes (typical occurrences) or even stock images, there is nevertheless an alignment between their subject matter and the interests of Jesus, as well as a convergence with the interests of the social historian. In any case, it is believed, the parables do convey information about first-century Galilee.[59]

A further set of questions then arise: What is the nature of the concern with socioeconomic realities often evidenced in the parables? Is this concern incidental or essential for understanding the ministry and message of Jesus? These questions are now taken up here in terms of the particular issue of debt.

A comparison of Matt 18:23–35 and Matt 5:25/Luke 12:58 is instructive.[60] Three different situations are envisioned in which a debtor has defaulted. The two images in Matt 18 give dramatic testimony to the realities of one Hellenistic-Roman procedure for dealing with insolvency. Both are cases of "execution against the person" of the debtor.[61] In the one instance, however, the debtor and his whole family are going into slavery for fiscal default. In the other, the debtor is simply clapped into prison for a private debt. Sherwin-White has seen here the stock image of a Hellenistic king, though he orients his discussion to the "little kings"—including the Herods—who operated as vassals of the Romans under the early empire.[62] G. E. M. de Ste. Croix too sees in the parable something that might happen in the family of Herod.[63] Perhaps we are

---

59. This belief places me generally in the camp of the historical exegetes of the parables—Dodd, Jeremias, Perrin, and most recently Bailey. I differ from them in a direct concern with the socio-economic dimension of the parables. For the distinction between "parable" and "similitude," see Smith, *Parables*, 17. All such distinctions, as Jeremias points out in *Parables*, 20 are subsumed under the *mashal* speech form.

60. I am indebted at numerous points in this analysis to Kippenberg, *Religion und Klassenbildung*, 141ff. G. E. M. de Ste. Croix has a similar analysis, *Class Struggle*, 164.

61. On this "personal execution," see especially de Ste. Croix, *Class Struggle*, 164, 240.

62. Sherwin-White, *Roman Society*, 134ff.

63. G. de Ste. Croix, *Class Struggle*, 164.

to think specifically of Herod Antipas, who exemplified such behavior in Jesus' immediate environment.[64]

The picture in Matt 5:25 and par. is somewhat different. Here a judicial proceeding is imminent. "Making friends" with the plaintiff thus means settling the debt out of court. This suggests a private debt is in view. If there is no settlement, the debtor is in danger of imprisonment. What is different here over against Matt 18 is the court proceeding before imprisonment. Jeremias does not believe this is a Jewish court.[65] Sherwin-White as confidently asserts that the "judge" here is a native magistrate.[66] Kippenberg tries to show that imprisonment for insolvency was enforced by Jewish courts, if the debtor had no real property to offset the debt (see below).[67]

Whatever the historical reality, the court of Matt 5:25 and par. had jurisdiction over those Jesus was addressing. The legal basis for its proceedings perhaps lay in part in Hellenistic-Roman jurisprudence. While the transactions of the royal house in Matt 18 might have seemed remote, in Matt 5:25–26/Luke 12:58–59 the experience of Jesus' audience was directly engaged.

These three New Testament depictions suggest the model in Figure 2.[68] The plight of the defaulting debtor is contingent upon his landed status. If the debtor has land (assuming it has secured the loan), then property is sold at auction or even transferred to the creditor to settle the debt. If the debtor does not have land, imprisonment or possibly slavery are in store.

64. Cf. the thoughts of Jeremias on Matt 18, *Parables,* 212: "The punishment of torture was not allowed in Israel. It is again evident (see v. 25, 30) that non-Palestinian conditions are described here, unless the parable is referring to Herod the Great, who made abundant use of torture, heedless of Jewish law—but could he have been credited with the generosity of v. 27?"

65. Jeremias, *Parables,* 180.

66. Sherwin-White, *Roman Society and Roman Law,* 133.

67. Kippenberg, *Religion und Klassenbildung,* 142–43; his evidence is Matt 18, Matt 5:25, and Josephus, *War* 2.273.

68. Though Kippenberg does not explicitly lay out this model, all of its ingredients are present in his book, 141–142, 143.

Figure 2: Procedures in Case of Insolvency (After Kippenberg)

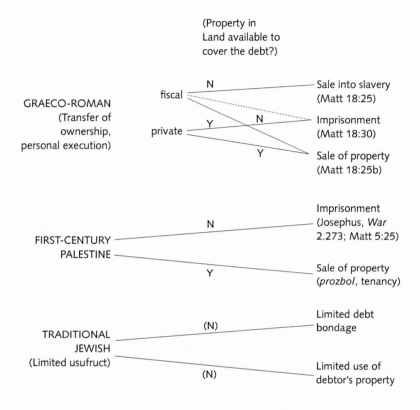

Such imprisonment probably had the purpose of forcing the debtor to cough up hidden wealth or compelling his family to redeem him. Might a public auction of a debtor's property (i.e., the *prozbol* institution) have had a similar purpose, since Jewish families would have been under pressure to "keep land in the family"? Without property, imprisonment of the debtor was more prevalent than debt bondage, both because slaves were readily and cheaply available and because there was a large labor pool of the landless. The worth of labor thereby was debased![69]

Turning to the much-discussed parable in Luke 16:1–9, a few observations about the transactions there are in order. First of all, the debts are paid in kind. Secondly, the size of the debts is remarkable. One hundred

---

69. Kippenberg, *Religion und Klassenbildung*; Goodman, "Problem of Debt," 423 n. 40; cf. M. Finley, *Ancient Economy*, 70 on the worth and supply of labor.

cors of wheat would feed 150 people for a year.[70] Similarly, the 100 *batous* (= "baths," ca. 400 liters each) amounts to a very large quantity of oil.[71] What is the nature of this debt?

Since there is nothing to indicate in the parable that the *plousios anthropos* is a royal figure, it is unlikely that such large debts in kind imply arrears in taxes. These were probably paid in money under the early empire.[72] The debtors of Luke 16 may be single tenants far in arrears on their rent.[73] The best assumption, however, would seem to be that the parable envisions a man who owns whole villages. These tenant villages, through representatives, pay a yearly produce rent on their agricultural lands. The rich man, then, sells these goods (oil and wheat would be negotiable) and/ or provisions his own household. The debt in any case is a private debt. This interpretation finds support in v. 4: *hotan metastathō . . . dexontai me eis tous oikous autōn.* By defrauding the master, the steward has made many "friends," whole villages in fact.

Of particular in Matt 18:23–35, Luke 16:1–9, and also in the brief story of Luke 7:41–42, is the aspect of debt forgiveness or remission. In Matt 18 and Luke 7, a petty king or a (wealthy) money-lender supply the examples. Such things happened in the "real world," according to these similitudes. Yet as we have seen, remission of debts was a revolutionary slogan in agrarian antiquity, and such tales on the lips of a Galilean prophet probably sounded subversive.

The case of Luke 16 is somewhat different. There an underling (cf. the contrary behavior of the underling in Matt 18) reduces the indebtedness, though not entirely. The limited nature of the reduction, nonetheless, points in the same general direction as the other two stories. The betrayal of the master's trust, along with the debt transactions, suggests an abroga-

70. This figure is derived from the following calculation: About 200 kg of grain will keep one person alive at a subsistence level for a year; on this see, Hamel, "Poverty and Charity," 472 n. 233, based upon the work of Clark and Haswell, *Economics of Subsistence Agriculture,* 58. If the Talmudic cor was around 400 liters in volume, equivalent to 11 bushels, and an average density of wheat today is around 27 kg/bu., then 100 x 11 x 27/200 = ca. 150.

71. Variant readings in D, of course, offer the smaller unit "qab," = 1/6 of the bath; compare the discussion in Jeremias, *Parables,* 181: 100 cors = yield of 100 acres. 100 baths = yield of 146 olive trees.

72. According to Rostovtzeff, *SEHRE,* 1: 208–9, and as in Matt 18; but see n. 56 above.

73. Rents were normally about 10 cors a year: *m. B. Meṣ.* 9:7. Applebaum, *Economic Life,* 659.

tion of the then-current social mores of fidelity in such relations and the rigorous exaction of debt.[74]

This point has not gone unnoticed by New Testament commentators, of course, but they have rarely made out of it any social conclusion. One final bit of the tradition will suggest strongly the need to make more out of the concrete social implications in these parables.

The Lord's Prayer has, together with the parables, been considered bedrock of the Jesus tradition.[75] Yet even so, the prayer comes to us in twofold form in the tradition. Which of the two presents the more authentic form? This question is not easy to decide. The Lukan *form* is probably closest in length to the original. However, editorial work of both evangelists can be detected. Therefore, the original form would have to be reconstructed in any case.

Fortunately, a discussion of particular points does not have to await the reconstruction of the whole. Of concern here will be only the petitions for bread and forgiveness (Matt 6:11–12/Luke 11:3–4).

Starting with the forgiveness petition first, how is it to be taken? Underlying the Greek word *aphiēmi* and cognates is the notion of both cancellation of debt and metaphorical forgiveness.[76] Behind *opheilēmata— hamartias* (Matt 6:12/Luke 11:4 respectively) probably lies the Aramaic *ḥôbâ*. This word had in Galilean Aramaic the meaning of either sin or debt.[77] Matthew's understanding of the petition is indicated by the supplemental condition in v. 15 *(paraptōmata)*. Luke has supplied the word "sins" instead of "debts." Yet it is most interesting that Luke continues with a material application —"as we ourselves forgive all in debt to us" (11:4b). The Matthean form of this comparative clause could also formally refer to actual debtors who are "forgiven" (though the above consideration argues against Matthew having so understood the clause).

Admittedly, the metaphorical use of the Aramaic word *ḥôbâ*, "debt," is well attested in the rabbinic material.[78] So also is the petition for release from "debts" owed to ("sins" committed against) God. Here may be recalled the sixth benediction in the Shemoneh Esreh and especially Akiba's prayer in *b. Taʿan.* 25b: . . . "according to thy great mercy remit

74. Recall again the passage in Cicero, *De officiis* 2.84.

75. Norman Perrin, *Rediscovering,* 47.

76. Bultmann, "*Aphiēmi, ktl.,*" 509–10.

77. Dalman, *Die Worte Jesu,* 334–35 is helpful; further, Perrin, *Rediscovering,* 151.

78. In addition to Dalman, see Hauck, "*Opheilō, ktl.,*" 565 n. 1.

[all] our promissory notes (*kol shiterê ḥōbōthênu*)."[79] However, it is to be suspected that these references, like those regarding the *prozbol,* reflect concerns and socio-economic conditions quite different from the pre-70 realities of Roman Palestine.

The basic structure of the Synoptic tradition's interpretation of this petition—apparent in both Matthew and Luke—is "forgiveness" requested in the context of a vertical relationship to God (in line with the later rabbinic viewpoint), as compared with "forgiveness" practiced in the context of a horizontal relationship to the neighbor. In this latter practice, Matthew seems to metaphorize debt to cover all kinds of social obligations, while Luke retains the literal meaning. In the former practice, neither Matthew nor Luke reads the petition other than as a request for forgiveness for infractions (debts = trespasses, sins respectively) against God.

Is it possible to see the meaning of the prayer within the context of Jesus' ministry? It is suggested here that that meaning becomes evident in the conjunction of the petition for forgiveness with the petition for daily bread.

What needs to be seen in this conjunction is the *material* link between the two petitions, a synonymous parallelism, if you will. Indebtedness threatens the availability of daily bread. Conversely, the petition for daily bread is at the same time a petition for a social order that will supply such basic human needs in a regular and consistent manner. Thus, the succeeding petition for forgiveness can be seen to address just such a social concern. Indebtedness disrupts the ability of a social order to supply daily bread. Therefore, rather than infractions against God, Jesus primarily asked through this petition for release from the earthly shackles of indebtedness. Even if one adopts an eschatological hermeneutic framework for this prayer, as for instance does Jeremias, one must still see in such an eschatology this material expectation. The material link between lack of bread and debt calls into question, therefore, the "spiritualizing" interpretations of the prayer evident already in the Synoptic tradition.

The suggested interpretation urges itself on the basis of another consideration. Jesus' ministry appealed particularly to the landless, that is, those forced for one reason or another into beggary, prostitution, tax collection, or other occupations not directly linked to working the land.[80] It

79. Quoted from Hauck, ibid., 562.
80. The works of Schottroff and Stegemann cited in note 41.

may be surmised that many of these people knew the reality of indebtedness. Perhaps they had not been able to get out of debt, and so had been
driven from "normal" social ties for this reason. Would such people have
made no connection between their material need, and the most profound
expression of the aims of the Jesus movement—the Lord's Prayer?

In conclusion it must be said that, if the interpretation advanced
is sustainable, Jesus' ministry takes on an explicitly revolutionary aspect
according to the canons of antiquity. From one side, his ministry can be
seen to have advocated the dissolution of the material mechanisms of social stratification and power. From another side, the political authorities
undoubtedly would have perceived, even in the hint of a public proclamation of the abolition of debt, a subversive, revolutionary agenda. Jesus did
not have to advocate armed insurrection to be branded a revolutionary. In
fact, he did not advocate armed insurrection. However, his vision of the
liberation coming with the reign of God directly attacked a principal element of the Roman order in Palestine and attracted a following of people
victimized by debt.

CHAPTER 2

Jesus and the Problem of Debt
in Ancient Palestine[1]

MANY OF JESUS' FELLOW Jews labored under a crushing load of indebtedness (including taxes, tributes, tithes and religious dues, land rents, as well as "borrowed money").[2] The problem of debt exacerbated the quality of relations between the owning class of agrarian, first-century Palestine and those who were forced for one reason or another into tenancy or wage labor. Debt was one of the major mechanisms whereby the rich kept getting richer and the poor, poorer. Through debt, ownership of the patrimonial land of the Jewish peasantry could be, and was, wrested from them. The "rights" of the creditor were only a manifestation of an insensitive egoism that demanded security and securities to the detriment of the well-being of all.

Debt was always a formal expression of relations of dependency and (perhaps irredeemable) obligation. The ideals of reciprocity and social equality in the Graeco-Roman and Jewish traditions encouraged hopes for more "horizontal" relations in society, but more often than not imbalances of power and wealth led in fact to "vertical" relations of dominance and subjection. For this reason, "release from debts" and "redistribution of land" were standard demands in the revolutionary movements of antiquity.[3]

---

1. This previously unpublished article, composed in 1985 for a clergy group, both draws from and amplifies points in chapter 1. In these first two chapters, the reader can perceive ideas developed at greater length in "The Lord's Prayer in Social Perspective" (chapter 14, originally drafted 1988).

2. Von Kippenberg, *Religion und Klassenbildung*; Theissen, *Sociology*; Freyne, *Galilee from Alexander the Great to Hadrian.*

3. De Ste. Croix, *Class Struggle*, 298, 307, 357, 609 n. 55, and 611 n. 14.

If in the Graeco-Roman world debt and related agrarian problems played a crucial role in historical developments, the same can be said on the Jewish side. A long biblical tradition recognized and attempted to limit, if not completely eradicate, the disruptive socio-economic effects of debt. Prescriptions or problems related to debt are mentioned in all of the major divisions: Legislative (Exod 22:25–27; Lev 25:36–37; Deut 15; 23:19–20), prophetic (Isa 5:8; Hab 2:6), historical (1 Sam 22:2; 2 Kgs 4:1; Neh 5:1–5), and wisdom writings (Prov 22:7). The tradition uniformly opposes usury and the permanent transfer of real property (Exod 22:25; Lev 25:13; Deut 15:2).

The basic presupposition for the biblical view of debt was the equality, with various qualifications, of each member of Israel before Yahweh. This meant equality of access to the goods of life as well. Hence, the vociferous opposition in the tradition to disruptions of the social order from economic causes. The emergence of the monarchy and the concomitant social stratification gave momentum to the tradition of protest and legislation.[4] The interesting post-exilic episode recorded in Nehemiah 5 gives explicit detail about how the tradition might be actualized to counter agrarian problems. Similar problems under the Seleucids probably added fuel to the Maccabean uprising. In the Roman period, Palestinian Jewish society again was troubled by agrarian problems and indebtedness leading to the Jewish War.

Since debt played a major role in the troubled social relationships of Jesus' day, it is not surprising that he addressed the problem. In Matt 18:12–35, set by Matthew in the context of a discussion of forgiveness, a Hellenistic monarch is portrayed as a model of the mercifulness required in the act of forgiving. The monarch summons a slave who is to render account for a loan (*daneion*, v. 27). The debtor, not able to pay, is to be sold into slavery along with his entire family (the normal course in these "executions").[5] Upon the slave's petition the king is moved with pity (*splangchnistheis*, v. 27) and releases (*apolyō*) the man from his obligation. This magnanimous gesture is placed in the starkest contrast by the slave's subsequent behavior. When he encounters a fellow-slave owing him a very minor sum (compared with his own previous debt), the man has the other slave thrown into debtor's prison. What callousness! This obviously is the

---

4. Brueggemann, "Trajectories."

5. St. Croix, *Class Struggle*, 163.

reaction the parable was intended to elicit. The slave who had the huge debt did not appreciate the magnanimity and generosity shown to him, at least not enough to see some claim upon his own conduct. The rage of the monarch (*orgistheis*, v. 34) issues in swift punishment of this callous man.

A positive version of this parabolic point is preserved in Luke 7:41–43. In this case the response of the "forgiven" is measured by their response of love toward the merciful creditor. Response is the *tertium comparitionis* in both Matthew 18 and Luke 7. The direction of the response, whether love toward creditor or mercy toward debtors, should not be allowed to obscure the underlying point of a response that is commensurable to the experience of forgiveness or release ("love," equal generosity shown to others). "Grace" in these two stories does not come without strings attached; rather forgiveness paradoxically lays an even greater burden of responsibility upon the recipients.

Response to generous forgiveness is also the desideratum of the steward's actions in Luke 16:1–8. Verse 9 is usually attributed to Luke (cf. the tale of Zacchaeus, Luke 19:1–10, where "unjust mammon" does indeed make friends). As for verse 8, it is debated whether the *kyrios* is the wealthy man of v. 1 (cf. v. 3) or Jesus. Jeremias' observation regarding Luke 18:6 seems decisive here: The Lord is Jesus in both this parable and that of the Importune Widow. Jesus himself, then, commends the behavior of the manager who rips off his master (the *oikonomos* is a slave) in order to insure his own future security.

A comparison of this parable with that of the Wicked Tenants illustrates the reversal that has taken place. There (in Mark 12:1–12) the intermediaries between owner and tenants (equivalent to Luke's *oikonomos*) are abused and even murdered when they try to collect on the rent. Here the *oikonomos* violates that normative order and exercises some "enlightened self-interest." The normal course for a deposed functionary of the elite is indicated in v. 3: the lot of the disenfranchised laborer or beggary. Inasmuch as these intermediaries are the enforcers of an oppressive agrarian social order, they are hated by the peasantry.

Perhaps the steward's actions are to be understood as a typical occurrence, when possible. The political astuteness of the move is, from an agrarian perspective, self-evident. Through the mechanism of releasing debtors from their obligations, the steward creates some positive alternatives for himself. Yet it cannot be overlooked that there is, from the viewpoint of the dominant culture, *adikia* involved (cf. v. 8 *oikonomon tēs adikias*). Why does Jesus then praise the man? Is he siding with the oppressed peasantry against the rich? To do so would not change the dominant ethos of self-sufficiency that Jesus opposes in both the landlord class and the peasantry. No, the story would seem to be aimed at the rich themselves (as Luke has well understood). What is laudable about the steward's behavior is his generosity (and with others' goods!)—a generosity certainly motivated by self-interest, but with particularly salutary effects. This is a generosity that not only mitigates oppressive circumstances, but creates the basis for a new relationship to the peasantry. To borrow terminology from Eric Wolf, a single-stranded relationship between exploitative elite and oppressed peasantry is modified by the addition of some new strands. However, the steward will no longer stand above the peasantry, but will be reduced to their level—otherwise, lower still!

Other passages in the tradition also play upon the theme of debt or debt remission. In the parable of the Talents, Matt 25:14–30/Luke 19:11–27, the master commends slaves who have increased his wealth. This is the conventional expectation—money will be put out on loan for interest. The slave who does not utilize his master's capital to acquire more is in trouble, even though hoarding a treasure was also a socially acceptable way of handling capital.[6] In a way, this parable, like that of the Wicked Tenants (Mark 12:1–12), graphically portrays the new order of things that has come under the Romans.

The example story of the prodigal son (Luke 15:11–32) explores the problem of moral debt. The son violates conventional mores by asking for his inheritance before his father's death. In effect, the son acts as though the father is dead.[7] Yet the father's subsequent behavior violates customary mores that would consider the son also as dead. The father forgives the son's grievous social sin and restores his status. In the violation of the customary rules, Jesus sees new possibilities for life.

The importance of this theme of debt and debt remission has not gone unnoticed by New Testament commentators, of course, but they have rarely attempted to explore the material significance of the theme within Jesus' ministry. Examining a central text of the gospels will permit a further demonstration of the crucial need to investigate the Jesus tradition in these terms.

6. Finley, *Ancient Economy.*
7. Bailey, *Through Peasant Eyes.*

The Lord's Prayer has, together with the parables, been considered bedrock of the Jesus tradition.[8] The question of original form is, nonetheless, problematic. Luke probably retains the form closest in length to the original. However, editorial work of both Matthew and Luke can be detected. Therefore, the original form is not identical with either extant version. Jeremias writes: "The Lucan version has preserved the oldest form with respect to *length*, but the Matthaean text is more original with regard to *wording*."[9]

The purpose here is not to reconstruct the original form of the prayer, but to concentrate on the petition for forgiveness. It will be necessary in addition to refer to the petition for daily bread. Starting with the forgiveness petition first, how is it to be taken? Underlying the Greek word *aphiēmi* and cognates is the notion of both cancellation of debt and metaphorical forgiveness.[10] The word *aphesis* appears in the important text of Deut 15:2 (LXX). The word is regularly employed in the Egyptian papyri to denote waiving a debt or releasing someone from debt. The Aramaic underlying the verb in the petition was perhaps *shebok*.[11] Behind *opheilēmata— hamartias* (Matt 6:12/Luke 11:4 respectively) probably lies *hôbâ*. This word had in Galilean Aramaic the meaning of either sin or debt.[12]

Matthew's understanding of the petition is indicated by the supplemental condition in v. 15 (*paraptōmata*). Luke has supplied the word "sins" instead of "debts." Yet it is significant that Luke continues with a material application—"as we ourselves forgive all in debt to us" (11:4b). The Matthean form of this comparative clause could also formally refer to actual debtors who are "forgiven" (though the above consideration argues against Matthew having so understood the clause).

The basic structure of the Synoptic tradition's interpretation of this petition—apparent in both Matthew and Luke—is "forgiveness" requested in the context of a vertical relationship to God (in line with the later rabbinic viewpoint), as compared with "forgiveness" practiced in the context of a horizontal relationship to the neighbor. In this latter practice, Matthew seems to metaphorize debt to cover all kinds of social obligations, while Luke retains the literal meaning. In the former practice, neither Matthew

8. Perrin, *Rediscovering*.

9. Jeremias, *Prayers*, 93.

10. Bultmann, *"Aphiēmi, ktl."*

11. Dalman, *Die Worte Jesu*; Jeremias, *Prayers*.

12. Dalman, *Die Worte Jesu*; Jeremias, *Prayers*; Perrin, *Rediscovering*.

nor Luke reads the petition other than as a request for forgiveness for moral infractions (debts = trespasses, sins respectively) against God.

How did Jesus intend this petition to be understood? What did it mean within the context of his ministry? First of all, the parallelism between the semicola of the forgiveness petition is important. The parallelism suggests that there must somehow be a connection (not necessarily causal) between the "small" forgiveness/release practiced by Jesus' disciples and a "large" forgiveness/release that only God can wield. The small forgiveness of the second semicolon is related to actual debt (as both Matthew's and Luke's versions reveal), but can easily be extended to moral debt too. One would suspect that the same logic originally governed the first half of the petition as well. Therefore, rather than release from infractions against God, Jesus primarily asked through this petition for release from the earthly shackles of indebtedness. The problem of debt, oppressing the people of Palestine and controlling their lives, is so vast that only God's power can effectively remove it.

It is important to notice, secondly, a *material* link between the petition for forgiveness and the preceding petition for daily bread. These two petitions form a synonymous parallelism, if you will. Indebtedness threatens the availability of daily bread. Conversely, the petition for daily bread is at the same time a petition for a social order that will supply such basic human needs in a regular and consistent manner. Thus, the succeeding petition for forgiveness can be seen to address in another way this same concern: Indebtedness disrupts the ability of a social order to supply daily bread. God is petitioned to remove the oppressive power of debt in people's lives.

The suggested interpretation urges itself, finally, on the basis of one other consideration. Jesus' ministry appealed particularly to the landless, that is, those forced for one reason or another into beggary, prostitution, tax collection, or other occupations not directly linked to working the land.[13] It may be surmised that many of these people knew the reality of indebtedness. Perhaps they had not been able to get out of debt, and so had been driven from "normal" social ties for this reason. The Lord's Prayer, through these petitions, directly addressed such people's needs.

The material parallel between the semicola of the forgiveness petition, the link between lack of bread and debt as the "horizon" against which to

---

13. Schottroff and Stegemann, *Jesus von Nazareth = Jesus and the Hope of the Poor*; W. Stegemann, *The Gospel and the Poor*; Gerd Theissen, *Sociology*.

view the bread and forgiveness petitions, and sociological considerations about the religious interests at work in Jesus' ministry, call into question, therefore, the "spiritualizing" interpretations of Jesus' prayer evident already in the Synoptic tradition. These interpretations could only conceive of the petition to God for forgiveness in moral terms.

To conclude, if the interpretation of the above material is sustainable, Jesus' ministry takes on an explicitly revolutionary aspect according to the canons of antiquity. From one side, his ministry can be seen to have advocated the dissolution of the material mechanisms of social stratification and power. From another side, the political authorities undoubtedly would have perceived, even in the hint of a public proclamation of the abolition of debt, a subversive, revolutionary agenda. Jesus did not have to advocate armed insurrection to be branded a revolutionary. In fact, he did not advocate armed insurrection. However, his vision of the liberation coming with the reign of God directly attacked a principal element of the Roman order in Palestine and attracted a following of people victimized by debt.

CHAPTER 3

The Buying Power of Two *Denarii* (Luke 10:35)[1]

INTRODUCTION

O NE OF THE TEXTS that has received some discussion in the Social
Facets Seminar of the Westar Institute is the story of the Good
Samaritan. In Luke 10:35 the Samaritan gives two *denarii* to the innkeeper
for the maintenance of the man beaten by robbers. The distance of moder-
nity from antiquity, both in terms of time and in a social sense, obscures
our understanding of the value of this amount of money. In such a simple
but critical detail, our ability to evaluate the meaning of Jesus' story is
hindered.

Exactly how much money was a *denarius* and how much would it
buy? Standard commentaries and marginal notes in reference Bibles offer
us only limited help here. For instance, the annotators of the New English
Bible and the New Oxford Annotated Bible, as well as the short article
"*Denarius*" in the *Interpreter's Dictionary of the Bible,* tell us on the basis
of Matt 20:2 that the *denarius* was a day's wage. However, this reference
point really gives us no indication as to whether the *denarius* was a living
wage for the ancient worker. Was a *denarius* per day adequate, in other
words, to feed wife and children, purchase clothing and other household
necessities, get next year's crops out, take care of any family livestock, pay
taxes, Temple dues, rents, and so on?

Walter Bauer, in the entry "*Dēnarion*" (the New Testament Greek
word for the Roman coin in question), tries to give us another yardstick
for the value of the *denarius*: The first-century *denarius* was worth eighteen

---

1. This was my first publication in a peer-reviewed journal, which I owe to the invitation
of Robert W. Funk.

cents.[2] As we shall see in a moment, this is not a very helpful measure of the worth of *denarius* either. Such a measure does not truly give us an indication of the buying power of the *denarius* in a preindustrial and agricultural society like that of Roman Palestine. Eighteen cents does not go very far today. The more important question is, "How far would the *denarius* stretch in the first century?"

RELATIVE MEASURES OF THE VALUE OF THE DENARIUS

An investigation of the places in the New Testament where *dēnarion* appears helps us to get a feel for the typical situations in antiquity where this coin might find use. A Greek concordance to the New Testament enables us to identify all of these passages. Here is a brief itemization of the occurrences of *dēnarion*:

Matt 18:28	The story of the Wicked Servant
Matt 20:2, 9, 10, 13	The Laborers in the Vineyard
Matt 22:19; cf. Mark 12:15; Luke 20:24	The Question about Tribute
Mark 6:37; cf. John 6:7	It would cost 200 *denarii* to feed the crowd of 5000
Mark 14:5; cf. John 12:5	The oil used to anoint Jesus cost 300 *denarii*
Luke 7:41	The debts of 500 and 50 *denarii*
Luke 10:35	(The passage under consideration)

For the sake of completeness, the two other places where the word *dēnarion* occurs are in the Apocalypse: Rev 6:6 depicts famine conditions when either a *choinix* of wheat (about a quart of wheat) or three *choinikes* of barley sell for a *denarius*.

Looking at these passages, we are able to say a few things about the ancients' sense for the relative value of the *denarius*. Mark 6:37; 14:5; and Luke 7:41 would seem to show that the ordinary person in antiquity looked at *denarii* in the hundreds as a lot of money. Furthermore, Jesus in the synoptic story about tribute may not be crafty when he asks whose likeness and inscription is on the face of the *denarius*. Does Mark 12:15 perhaps indicate that many common people were somewhat unfamiliar with this silver coin? Certainly Matt 20:1–15 speaks against this inter-

2. BAGD, s. v.

pretation. However that issue is decided, Mark 12:15 does tell us that the *denarius* was a coin used for paying taxes. *Denarii* could be lent: Matt 18:28 and Luke 7:41. And of course *denarii* could be used as a medium of payment or exchange, as in Matt 20:1–15; Mark 14:5; and Luke 10:35.

In modern practice a person often assesses the value of a coin in relation to other coins of a monetary system. A quarter is worth so many dimes and nickels. A dollar is worth so many quarters. Seeing what something is worth in relation to something else gives one a sense of the compared item's value. This approach can also be utilized to gain a relative understanding of ancient money values.

The silver *denarius* was part of the imperial Roman system of coinage. This three-metal system also included gold and bronze coins. Charts showing the relationships of imperial coinage are readily available.[3] The money situation in Roman Palestine of Jesus' day was complicated by the fact that many other types of coins with Greek or ancient Near Eastern historical lineage were still in use. The need for professional money changers is attested in the gospel tradition: Matt 21:12; Mark 11:15; John 2:15.[4] Money changers apparently also loaned money at interest in some parts of first-century Palestine (Matt 25:27; Luke 19:23).

A rough coin equivalence was the Roman *denarius* and the Greek *drachma* mentioned in Luke 15:8 and 9. A double *drachma* coin is referred to in Matt 17:24, the temple tax account (Matt 17:24–27). A Greek *stater,* evidently equal to four *drachmas* in the story of Peter's pence, appears in Matt 17:27 and in a variant reading to Matt 26:15. Lesser denominations are also known in the gospels. A widow's poverty is indicated by her possession of two bronze coins known as *lepta* (Mark 12:42; see also Luke 21:2). Mark explains that these two coppers were equivalent to the Roman *quadrans* (the Roman "penny"). The minuteness of the *lepton* is brought out by Luke 12:59; note that the parallel in Matt 5:26 has the slightly larger Roman *quadrans*.

Comparing the uses of the word *denarius* in the synoptic tradition or investigating the various types of ancient coins and coinage systems thus does not get us much closer to answering our initial questions. Some other measuring stick needs to be found—something that will offer us an

3. Koester, *Introduction to the New Testament,* 1:90; reproduced in Funk, *New Gospel Parallels,* 2:330. See also the article by Hamburger, "Money, Coins."

4. A computer program relating some of the major coinages with one another can be found in Oakman, *Jesus and the Economic Questions of His Day,* Appendix 2.

"absolute" basis for assessing value. Money in modern economies is often valued in real terms, by seeing what it will buy or by finding some material equivalent such as real estate or natural produce (grain, for instance). It is possible to gain this type of information from comparative studies of the ancient economies.

THE BUYING POWER OF THE DENARIUS

The normal money exchange rate for wheat in the first century, determined from ancient sources, was Roman 2–4 *sesterces* (= 0.5–1 *denarius*)/*modius* or Jewish 1 *sil'a* (= 4 *denarii*)/4 *seahs*.[5] Two *denarii* then had a real buying power of 2 *seahs* (Jewish) or between 2–4 *modii* (Roman) of wheat.

The *modius* had a capacity of around 0.25 American bushels, while the average Jewish *seah* (there were several different *seah* measures) held perhaps 0.37 bushels. Thus, both measurement standards give about the same result: two *denarii* would acquire around 0.75 bushels of wheat (3 *modii* x 0.25 bu/*modius*, 2 *seahs* x 0.37 bu/*seah*).

The food value of this amount of wheat can also be assessed: By modern measurements, 0.75 bushels of unprocessed wheat (around 20 kg or 9 lbs) has around 64,300 calories.[6] This would give an average-sized person 3000 calories/21 days (an adequate energy level for agricultural laborers) or 1800 calories/36 days (a marginal energy level for agricultural work).[7] In broad terms, this represents around a month's worth of food, perhaps longer if supplemental sources of protein and calories were utilized.

Normally in ancient Palestine, figs, olives, grapes, barley, pulse, and a variety of other fruits and vegetables supplemented the people's diet. Of items for which prices can be assessed, one *denarius* might also purchase 4 liters of wine, or 2–40 liters of olive oil, or 190–640 figs (a range depending upon whether these items were plentiful or scarce).

As we have seen (Matt 20:2), the *denarius* was a standard day's wage at the turn of the Eras. This money would, under ideal circumstances, go to feed a family of two adults with probably a minimum of four children (Mark 6:3). This family might be represented by 3–4 adults' equivalence.

5. Duncan-Jones, *Economy of the Roman Empire*, 4; Jeremias, *Jerusalem*, 122.

6. The capitalized word "Calorie" in technical nutritional literature represents the Kilocalorie (1000 calories).

7. Studies have been done on the energy levels needed for various tasks. For representative figures and the basis for these assertions, see Clark and Haswell, *Economics of Subsistence Agriculture*.

Under this model, two *denarii* would supply 3000 Cal/5–7 days or 1800 Cal/9–12 days. Two *denarii* would stretch a week to a week and a half for a family; one *denarius* would supply 3–6 days for a family.

The New Testament story of the Feeding of the Five Thousand supports the results of these calculations. If 200 *denarii* was adequate to feed at least 5000 people, then one *denarius* could be expected to provide a meal for at least 25 (5000/200). One *denarius* would, therefore, supply 2 meals for around 12 people at the minimum or 2 meals to one person for 12 days. Again assuming a family of 4 (adults' equivalence), one *denarius* would supply them with food for 3 days. Two *denarii* would double this to 6 days. These values are in line with the above figures. A year's-supply of food for a family required between 60 and 122 *denarii*.[8]

Neither of these calculations takes into account other needs like clothing, taxation, religious dues, and so on. Ramsay MacMullen, the ancient historian, has calculated that 250 *denarii* was a poverty-level income for an ancient family.[9] The ancient economist F. M. Heicheiheim thought that a minimum allowance for one person was around 100–140 imperial *denarii*.[10] As a point of comparison, the minimum census for a person of the Equestrian Order was 100,000 *denarii* and of the Senatorial Order was 250,000 *denarii*. R. Duncan-Jones has estimated the real worth of the equestrian census as between 700 and 1,400 metric tons of wheat; that of the senatorial census 2,100–4,300 metric tons.[11] In real terms, the Equestrian held between 2,550 and 5,100 years' worth of the minimum yearly amount of subsistence grain (275 kg); the Senator held between 7,600 and 16,000 years' worth.[12] These figures should illustrate the great disparities in first-century wealth and the significant social stratification of the early empire.

Two *denarii*, in summary, represent around three weeks' worth of food for one person or about 1 per cent of an ancient Palestinian family's annual budget.

---

8. See a similar use of this feeding story by Jeremias, *Jerusalem*, 123.

9. MacMullen, *Roman Social Relations*, 183 n. 1.

10. Heichelheim, "Roman Syria," 4:180.

11. Duncan-Jones, *Economy of the Roman Empire*, 5.

12. Oakman, *Jesus and the Economic Questions of His Day*, 78.

CONCLUSION

The implications of this little investigation for understanding Luke 10:35 may now be briefly stated. The two *denarii* of the Samaritan might feed the wounded man for around 24 days (two meals a day "board"). If other inn costs were involved ("room"), then the stay would have to be shorter. Nevertheless, the two *denarii* represent a substantial value—clearly worth more than thirty-six cents today. Moreover, the Samaritan also offers the innkeeper a blank check, "whatever else I owe you." The impression given by the narrative is one of an extremely generous person—one who does not mind sharing valuable commodities (in ancient terms: wine and oil [v. 34], silver *denarii* [v. 35]) with a complete stranger.

The story must have raised in the ancient hearer's mind the question of whether the Samaritan was somewhat foolish to be giving so much away. In line with this, perhaps a greater scandal and stumbling block than a Samaritan taking care of a Jew was evident here to Jesus' contemporaries: the Samaritan valued something higher than money or worldly goods, so that he was able to treat an historical enemy like a member of his own family. In terms of modern anthropology, the Samaritan practiced "general reciprocity" (the gift-giving reserved for the most intimate family member or acquaintance) toward a hated foreigner.[13] Negative reciprocity (something like what the priest and Levite do) would have been the normal behavior expected from the Samaritan. Jesus' story, then, graphically subverts conventional morality by depicting the Samaritan as more "family" to the wounded man than the true Israelites.

13. Oakman, *Jesus and the Economic Questions of His Day*, 78.

CHAPTER 4

How Large Is a "Great Crowd"? (Mark 6:34)[1]

SALO BARON ONCE CITED the historian Cippola to the effect that "[de-mography is] too vital for the understanding of all other socioeco-nomic, political, and even intellectual developments for scholarship to be satisfied with a resigned *ignoramus et ignorabimus*" ("we are ignorant and we shall be ignorant") and further the Spanish sociologist Almanza that "history without demography is an enigma, just as is demography without history."

More recently Yigal Shiloh: "The size of the population and its den-sity, its distribution among urban and rural settlements, the differing sizes of the settlements and the interrelation between them, the urban planning methods—all these constitute important components when we attempt to define the economic, political, and cultural resources of an ancient society."

There would seem to be a need for those who are attempting to un-derstand the social matrix out of which early Christianity and Judaism emerged to have a clear grasp of the facts of ancient demography and

1. This previously unpublished presentation was given at the national 1987 Society of Biblical Literature Meeting and draws upon the following resources: Amiran, "The Pattern of Settlement in Palestine"; Avi-Yonah, *The Holy Land*; Baron, "Population."; Broshi, "La Population de L'Ancienne Jerusalem"; idem, "The Population of Western Palestine in the Roman-Byzantine Period"; Broshi and Gophna, "The Settlements and Population of Palestine During the Early Bronze Age II–III"; idem, "Middle Bronze Age II Palestine: Its Settlements and Population"; Byatt, "Josephus and Population Numbers in First Century Palestine"; Geertz, "Village"; Hamel, "Poverty and Charity in Roman Palestine"; Hopkins, "The City Region in Roman Palestine"; Jeremias, *Jerusalem*; idem, *Parables*; McEvedy and Jones, *Atlas of World Population History*; Oakman, *Jesus and the Economic Questions of His Day*; Poole, ed., *Practical Basic Programs*; Rapoport, "Rank-Size Relations"; Sjøberg, *Preindustrial City*; Spiegel, *Probability and Statistics*; Zipf, *Human Behavior and the Principle of Least Effort*.

settlement distribution, but rarely if ever are these important facets of sociological thinking addressed.

My own interest in this subject emerged somewhat as a tangent to other work. I discovered I had only vague and imprecise ideas regarding the size of the ancient Palestinian population, the population of Jerusalem, and the sizes of smaller settlements. Indeed if one were to ask oneself, could one specify the size of the smallest typical village in Jesus' social environment? Or how would one resolve the discrepancy between Pseudo-Hecateus's third-century BCE notice that Jerusalem had 120,000 people and Jeremias's modern estimate that Jerusalem had 25,000–30,000 in Jesus' day?

Modern estimates of the population of ancient Palestine based upon literary sources, especially Josephus, diverge widely. Byatt has collected many of these estimates: They range from 500,000 to 6 million. Baron and Avi-Yonah both conclude that Palestine around the turn of the eras had 2.5 million people.

These estimates on the whole can be questioned on the basis of several considerations: a) The food-growing potential of Roman Palestine, at the time of maximum population expansion, can have supported no more than one million according to Hamel and others. b) The water resources of ancient Palestine, little different from today, probably cannot have supported so many. c) Comparative studies of preindustrial cities, like Sjøberg's, have tended to urge much smaller population estimates. Most importantly, d) the literary estimates are shown to be questionable by the archaeological method increasingly being employed to estimate ancient population.

This method depends upon a very simple assumption: the population of ancient settlements can be assumed to have been proportional to the settlement area. More precisely, the population of the settlement is estimated by multiplying the settlement area (alternatively the number of settlement dwellings) by a density coefficient. The determination of this coefficient can be checked against old cities of the Near East today. A coefficient often encountered in the literature is 250 persons/hectare = around 100 persons/acre.

Unfortunately, there is not yet a firm archaeological census of sites for Roman Palestine. The most accurate work to date has been done for the Bronze and Early Iron Ages. Amiran long ago noted that there are over 3,000 historic settlements in Palestine. Not all of these have been continuously inhabited. Nearly 2,200 were abandoned when Amiran wrote in the early 1950s. The archaeologist must ascertain, on the basis of artifactual remains at a given site, whether that site was occupied during a specific historical period.

The best single survey to date done by Israelis has located some 400 early Roman sites within Judea, Samaria, the Judean desert and the Golan. The Student Map Manual Index lists 376 Herodian sites and 551 Roman and Byzantine sites for all of Palestine. Avi-Yonah treats only the largest settlements for Roman Palestine; he lists around 200 sites. Our mathematical modeling will have to take this uncertainty into account because this is a key variable in the work.

Describing the method: The rank-frequency relation, which in a computer application is the basis for the present study, was first formulated by a mathematician, George K. Zipf, in the late 1940s. Zipf noted that there is a regular relationship between the rank and frequency of certain phenomena. Applied to demographic realities, Zipf observed that often the product of the population size of a human settlement and its rank in a series of regional settlements approaches a constant. This mathematical relation in various forms has come to be known as Zipf's law in the social scientific literature.

The mathematical form of Zipf's law is given in Figure 3. Note that the constant C equals the largest settlement population. The value of the largest settlement population mathematically approaches 10–12% of the total population. The translation of Zipf's law into BASIC computer code is also given in Figure 3.

Figure 3: Zipf's Law

George K. Zipf noted that rank and size are often interrelated:

Rank x Size = Constant C   (1)

Otherwise written for population studies:

Size = C/Rank   (2)

Hence

Total Population Size = C/Rank 1 + C/Rank 2 . . . C/Rank N   (3)

or (factoring out C)

Total Population Size = C(1 + 1/2 + 1/3 + 1/4 . . . 1/N)   (4)

Two BASIC programs can put the rank-size relation to work:

```
PROGRAM ONE
10 REM ENTER POPULATION OF SMALLEST VILLAGE SETTLEMENT
20 INPUT "SIZE OF SMALLEST SETTLEMENT POPULATION";SMALLEST
30 REM ENTER TOTAL NUMBER OF SETTLEMENTS
40 INPUT "TOTAL NUMBER OF SETTLEMENTS";SITENO
50 REM TOTAL = TOTAL POPULATION AFTER SUMMING OF ALL SITE
POPULATIONS
60 REM LARGEST = SIZE OF LARGEST SETTLEMENT
70 LARGEST = SMALLEST*SITENO:TOTAL = 0
80 FOR CNT = 1 TO SITENO
90 TOTAL = TOTAL + LARGEST/CNT
100 NEXT
120 PRINT "TOTAL POPULATION = ";TOTAL
130 PRINT "LARGEST SETTLEMENT POPULATION SIZE = ";LARGEST
140 END
```

```
PROGRAM TWO
10 REM ENTER POPULATION OF LARGEST SETTLEMENT
20 INPUT "SIZE OF LARGEST SETTLEMENT POPULATION";LARGEST
30 REM ENTER TOTAL NUMBER OF SETTLEMENTS
40 INPUT "TOTAL NUMBER OF SETTLEMENTS";SITENO
50 REM TOTAL = TOTAL POPULATION AFTER SUMMING OF ALL SITE
POPULATIONS
60 TOTAL = LARGEST:CNT = 2
70 TOTAL = TOTAL + LARGEST/CNT
80 CNT = CNT + 1
90 REM HAVE ALL SITE POPULATIONS BEEN INCLUDED IN TOTAL?  YES:
100 IF CNT > SITENO THEN 200
110 REM NO:
120 GOTO 70
200 PRINT "TOTAL POPULATION = ";TOTAL
210 PRINT "SMALLEST SETTLEMENT POPULATION SIZE = ";LARGEST/SITENO
220 END
```

Testing the model: I tested the validity of applying Zipf's mathematical law to the ancient Palestinian population by using it to describe the population for periods where the archaeological method was also available. Using information developed by Broshi and others, I had lists of settlements and their sizes. Using the Method of Least Squares and the

Chi-square Test developed by statisticians, the theoretical curves predicted by Zipf's law were fitted to and mathematically tested for goodness of fit against the hard archaeological data. Tests were done on the data for all of Palestine with equally good results. For most tests rank-frequency curves correlated well with the observed settlement data.

The computer modeling process was applied to the question of the population of Roman Palestine. Figure 4 indicates some of the results of this work. Modeling of the total population and the largest settlement population was done by plugging in plausible total settlement numbers and smallest village settlement sizes.

Figure 4: Results of Sample Computer Runs

SITENO = Total Settlements, independent variable
SMALLEST = Population of the Smallest Villages, independent variable
LARGEST = Population of the Largest Settlement, dependent variable
TOTAL = Total Population, dependent variable

SITENO	SMALLEST	LARGEST	TOTAL
400	25	10,000	65,700
400	50	20,000	131,400
400	75	30,000	197,000
400	100	40,000	262,800
400	125	50,000	328,500
400	150	60,000	394,000
400	175	70,000	460,000
400	200	80,000	525,600
500	25	12,500	84,900
500	50	25,000	170,000
500	75	37,500	255,000
500	100	50,000	340,000
500	125	62,500	425,000
500	150	75,000	509,000
500	175	87,500	594,000
500	200	100,000	679,000
600	25	15,000	105,000
600	50	30,000	209,000
600	75	45,000	314,000
600	100	60,000	419,000
600	125	75,000	523,000
600	150	90,000	628,000
600	175	105,000	732,000
600	200	120,000	837,000

700	25	17,500	125,000
700	**50**	**35,000**	**250,000**
700	75	52,500	374,000
700	100	70,000	499,000
700	125	87,500	624,000
700	150	105,000	749,000
700	175	122,500	873,000
700	200	140,000	998,000

Results: Figure 5 indicates the general results of this computer modeling—suggesting an abstracted model for relative population scale in Roman Palestine. Population estimates of over 1,000,000 should be ruled out for good. More importantly, the model indicates how ancient social aggregation tended to be arranged on a scale ordered in powers of ten.

Figure 5: Model of Relative Population Scale for Roman Palestine

TYPE OF POPULATION AGGREGATE	POPULATION SIZE	ORDER OF MAGNITUDE
Province, Region	100,000s	10^5
"City," Polis	10,000s	10^4
Town	1,000s	10^3
Village	100s	10^2
Hamlet, Small Village	10s	10^1

Figure 6 shows what this scale predicts for numbers of settlements and how it tests out generally against the current archaeological record for Roman Palestine.

Figure 6: Numbers of Settlements per Settlement Category Predicted by Rank-sized Modeling

(Assuming SITENO = 700, SMALLEST = 50, LARGEST = 35,000 and TOTAL = 250,000 for Roman Palestine)

Cities	3
Towns	32
Villages	315
Hamlets	350

Numbers of Settlements per Settlement Category Observed in the Archaeological Record[2]

Cities	4
Towns	29
Villages	168
Hamlets	300–500?

2. Sources: Avi-Yonah, *The Holy Land*, 127–80; Hopkins, "The City Region," 24.

Figure 7 translates into the terms of this scale Mark's notice in 6:34ff about what he imagines the size of a large crowd to be. As the reader can see, Mark's crowd (if his estimate of the size of the crowd is accepted) is very large in terms of the relative scale of things in Roman Palestine. It is understandable, if Mark's account of the crowd has historical value, that Jesus could fall under the same suspicion that his predecessor John the Baptist did. Attracting large crowds apart from officially sanctioned events was a no-no in Roman Palestine, likely to incur the wrath of the political authorities as Josephus tells us (*Ant.* 18.116ff).

Figure 7: Applying the Results of Modeling

MARK'S "GREAT CROWD" OF 5000 (6:34) SET WITHIN THE RELATIVE
POPULATION SCALE FOR ROMAN PALESTINE

	Cities	1/2
A crowd of 5000 =	or Towns	1 – 5
	or Villages	10 – 50
	or Hamlets	100 – 500

Figure 8 is developed to show how demographic considerations may play a significant role in interpreting the synoptic tradition elsewhere.

Figure 8: Demographic Light on Luke 16:7?

The debt of 100 cors of wheat = 30 metric tons = yield of about 100 acres.[3]

The typical village family of Roman Palestine tilled between 6 and 12 acres.[4] One hundred acres could represent the holdings of 8 to 16 families.

Since ancient annual rents ran between 1/5 and 1/2, the yield of 100 acres might imply the rent for a large estate of 200 to 500 acres in size. Translating this into numbers of holdings, we obtain a range of 16 to 83 family-size holdings, or (8 to a family, Mark 6:3) 128 to 664 people.

This number of people is notably within the 10^2 order of magnitude for ancient Palestinian villages, which might suggest the grain debts being paid in Luke 16 are the annual village rents.

3. Jeremias, *Parables*, 181.
4. Oakman, *Jesus and the Economic Questions of His Day*, 61.

CHAPTER 5

The Ancient Economy

INTRODUCTION

ECONOMICS, COMMONLY DEFINED TODAY as the allocation of scarce resources to competing ends, has been a constant preoccupation of twentieth-century people in western societies. Thus, economic questions overshadow our political and domestic lives. Some modern writers (e.g., Marcuse) have highlighted *homo economicus* as a special type of human being in modern times. The modern economic system—with its networks of free markets, transportation facilities, commercial institutions, banks, monetary systems and policies, industrial and corporate organizations, Gross National Products, salaries and wages—is a social system all to itself, able to dominate other social institutions. This fact of modern experience and social consciousness is the first stumbling block for thinking about ancient economic life and investigating its manifestations within the biblical writings.

Consider for a moment the story that appears in two of our four gospels (Matt 25:14–30; Luke 19:12–27), and in another form in an early Christian work outside of the Bible. The so-called parable of the Talents (Matthew) or Minas (Luke) may strike the modern reader as an apology for capitalism. The reward of the servants who increase the master's wealth, the punishment of the servant who refuses to risk his master's wealth, can fit right in with the modern corporate value system.

Seventy years ago, during the heyday of American liberalism, Bruce Barton undertook to write a book about Jesus Christ called *The Man Nobody Knows*. It can still epitomize how modern Americans might think about economics in the Bible. Barton thought of Jesus in classic liberal terms as a man who "did not come to establish a theology but to lead a life."[1] This sentiment appears in a chapter entitled, "His Advertisements." Jesus' parables are read by Barton as illustrative of modern principles of advertising: "Every advertising man ought to study the parables of Jesus in the same fashion, schooling himself in their language and learning these four big elements of their power."[2]

In like manner, Barton approaches Jesus as "The Founder of Modern Business" (the title of Barton's chapter 6). The book's title page contains an inscription from Luke 2:49 (in the quaint language of the King James Version): "Wist ye not that I must be about my Father's business?" For Barton, this "business" has much to do with modern corporate capitalism:

So we have the main points of his business philosophy:

1. Whoever will be great must render great service.

2. Whoever will find himself at the top must be willing to lose himself at the bottom.

3. The big rewards come to those who travel the second, undemanded mile.[3]

This latter point suggests how Barton might have interpreted Jesus' story about the Talents (though Barton does not explicitly say). In the similar case of the Rich Fool (Luke 12:20), Barton concludes that the story criticizes selfish satisfaction. He thinks the problem with Judas Iscariot was that he looked out only for number one; stinginess led to his downfall. So Barton sees Jesus as an advocate of philanthropy, a picture that would have been appealing in many corporate boardrooms of the 1920s.

A very different picture of the parable of the Talents emerges through Bruce Malina's and Richard Rohrbaugh's *Social-Science Commentary on the Synoptic Gospels*.[4] They point out (regarding Matt 25:14–30) that "the elitist reading of the parable is congenial to westerners conditioned to treat gain as both legitimate and proper."[5] To ancient ears, especially those of peasants, the story speaks of something else. It highlights the shameless-

---

1. Barton, *The Man Nobody Knows,* 136.
2. Ibid., 146.
3. Ibid., 177.
4. Malina and Rohrbaugh, *Synoptic Gospels* (1992, 2003).
5. Malina and Rohrbaugh, *Synoptic Gospels* (1992), 150.

ness of a "hard man" in a world of limited good, and comments upon the dishonorable behavior of taking even more away from the many who have nothing. For the agrarian audiences Jesus addressed, the hero of the story was the servant who maintained honor in a world of shameless behavior. A very early version of the story preserved in the Gospel of the Nazoreans (according to Eusebius, *Theophania*) praised the one who hid the talent. The other two slaves were respectively rebuked and thrown into prison.[6] The economic meaning of such a story shifts within an agrarian social setting.

The work of economic historians and comparative economists within the last fifty years or so has demonstrated conclusively that ancient economics, indeed any economic life prior to the Industrial Revolution of the late eighteenth century, was a different phenomenon from what moderns have come to think of under the term "economics." Therefore, it is necessary to acquire a special set of conceptual lenses when reading ancient literature, including the Bible, in order to perceive appropriately the nature and character of ancient economics. The present essay has as its primary aim the introduction of the reader to a select number of books that will supply these conceptual tools. Secondarily, this exposition will give some brief indications of how these conceptual tools can help in seeing characteristic economic emphases in the biblical writings.

Three major areas of reading are in store for the intrepid student who ventures into what has been called the "dismal science" as it applies to the Bible: the first area is the province of a single preeminent scholar; the second the sphere of economic anthropologists; the third the world of classical historians and Bible scholars.

Karl Polanyi

Perhaps the most important thinker and writer for the present topic is Karl Polanyi (1886–1964). His importance derives from his concern both with economic history and with comparative economics—the study of economics across a broad range of societies. Probably his most representative and accessible book is *The Great Transformation*, which attempts to chronicle the rise and fall of the free market as an institution that has been nearly unknown in economic history.[7] The value of the book also extends

6. Ibid., 148–50; (2003), 384–86.
7. Polanyi, *Great Transformation*.

to the illumination of several important concepts that concern the student of ancient economics. Thus, Polanyi shows how markets, which are central in modern capitalism, played only a limited role in the economic affairs of premodern societies. There, economic activities were always socially restrained or constrained. No society before the Industrial Revolution was willing to allow markets to dominate other social institutions.

The ancient economy was also embedded in (subordinate to) other social institutions, notably political and kin institutions. The Greek words behind "economy," in fact, mean "household (*oikou*) management (*nomia*)." For this reason, one needs to speak of the ancient political economy or the domestic economy as somewhat distinct economic spheres, but not of economics per se—as a separate sphere of life with free markets, capital institutions like banks, impersonal exchange values, and so forth. Market exchange in antiquity was limited to certain special cases, usually monopolized by certain groups (Phoenicians on the eastern Mediterranean, Nabateans in Arabia), and benefited only the most powerful elements of society. Ancient monarchs in the biblical period, for example Solomon (1 Kgs 10), virtually monopolized the benefits of trade arrangements.

Polanyi also points to reciprocity and redistribution as crucial economic alternatives to the market. The two dominant forms of economic exchange in antiquity were reciprocity within kinship relations and redistribution in political economies, and it is critical to understand both. Reciprocity means exchange on a gift or barter basis. It is characterized by informal dyadic contracts—social give and take—within household and village. A gift accepted implies an obligation owed (e.g., Luke 11:8). In contrast to market exchanges (e.g., getting food for money at the supermarket) in which the transaction implies no personal obligation, reciprocity exchanges often involve a commodity for some other commodity (e.g., wine for grain) and implicit personal obligations as well. Reciprocity ensures not only that goods on the average will be equitably distributed, but also that help will be available in hard times.

Redistribution, by contrast, was characteristically observed in the institutions of state and religious taxation. It involves the politically or religiously induced extraction of a percentage of local production, the storehousing of that product, and its eventual redistribution for some political end or another. Here for illustrative purposes can be mentioned Roman taxation in Jesus' day (Mark 12:13–17), the Jewish tithe (Deut 14:22–26), and the Jewish temple considered as a redistributive institution. While the modern supermarket seems analogous to the ancient storehouse, the parallel inappropriately suggests the operation of supply and demand in ancient redistributive institutions and overlooks their politically extractive nature. The essential notion of redistribution is (en)forced collection of economic surplus to a central point and redistribution at another time or place.

Polanyi (along with other students of ancient economies) has pointed us toward some other characteristic shifts of emphasis in ancient economies. The dominant industry in preindustrial societies was agriculture. Around eighty to ninety percent of the populace was engaged in one way or another on the land. Since land was the major factor of production, control of land was the chief political question of antiquity. Consider the political direction, for instance, of the Jubilee laws in Lev 25:23, 25–28, and contrast them with 1 Sam 8:14 or 1 Kgs 21:1–29.

There was no industry as we think of it today. The division of labor had not been "rationalized" to the same degree as in modern societies. Labor, like other economic factors, was embedded in other institutions, especially kinship and household contexts. Industry was normally small-scale and conducted by families and their slaves (or "hired servants," Mark 1:20).

Money appeared in antiquity after the eighth century BCE (Lydia), but it did not have quite the same significance it has today. Ancient money was generally hoarded and had real value only for certain things: to be used to pay mercenaries or taxes, to acquire land if legally possible (from other landowners who had it), or to create new dependencies through loans. It possessed only a rudimentary form of abstract exchange value. Moreover, it did not eliminate the need for personal exchanges between trading parties. Money was mostly available to and in the hands of the political elites. They did not work for it; such capital was obtained through slave-based mining of raw materials and wars of conquest. Those who worked for a wage were regarded as dependent or degraded—a form of slave. These in turn were generally restricted in the uses they could find for money.

Money also facilitated long-distance commerce and trade. Because of its potentially disruptive social effects, long-distance trade was normally insulated from local commerce. For the sake of economic security, local oligarchs prevented the incorporation of local markets into long-distance trade networks.[8] Land, as has been said, was the most precious commodity

8. Polanyi, *Great Transformation*, 60.

for the ancient elites; for them control or ownership of land implied honorable lineage and was the material basis for household (eco-nomic) security. Thus, people in antiquity who acquired wealth through commerce or other means normally attempted to achieve respectability by investing in land. Ancient societies as a rule resisted placing a money-value upon land precisely to protect the status of long-standing elite groups and to discourage newcomers from obtaining respectability.

Two other books edited or authored by Polanyi will be found helpful for thinking about ancient economics. First, the collection of essays in *Trade and Market in the Early Empires* is the classic work that brought comparative economics to the attention of ancient historians and classicists.[9] Be prepared for some heavy reading: essays range from the economic history of Mesopotamia to Aristotle's discovery of the economy, from comparative studies of South American, African, and Indian economic worlds to the modern economic theories of Parsons and Smelser. Secondly, Polanyi's posthumously published volume on human economies summarizes his lifetime of scholarship on economic history.[10] Here one will find discussions of formal and substantive economics, of the embedded economies in archaic societies, the origin and function of markets in antiquity, trade and money in ancient Greece, and so on.

ECONOMIC ANTHROPOLOGY

General Surveys

The second major area of reading pertinent for the student of ancient and biblical economics emerges from economic anthropology. Polanyi himself gleaned numerous comparative insights from the early work of Richard Thurnwald and Bronislav Malinowski, who respectively demonstrated that the economic life of "primitives" was socially controlled in complex ways. Undoubtedly the classic study in this genre, however, is Melville Herskovits's *Economic Anthropology*.[11]

Herskovits states his objective in this book very simply: "The purpose of this book [is] to provide information concerning the economic life of

9. Polanyi et al., eds., *Trade and Market in the Early Empires*.

10. Polanyi, *Livelihood of Man*.

11. Thurnwald, *Economics in Primitive Communities*; Malinowski, *Argonauts of the Western Pacific*; Herskovits, *Economic Anthropology*.

nonliterate peoples . . ."[12] After an introductory section (Part I), which contains a very helpful essay "Anthropology and Economics," Herskovits proceeds to treat "Production" (Part II), "Exchange and Distribution" (Part III), "Property" (Part IV), and "The Economic Surplus" (Part V). Herskovits finds that the differences between modern and preindustrial economy types are in degree, not in kind, because "practically every economic mechanism and institution known to us is found somewhere in the nonliterate world."[13] Nevertheless, special approaches need to be designed to study economic processes and institutions not clearly differentiated from other social phenomena. Herskovits pays special attention to the questions of economic determinism (whether economic processes affect other social processes and values) and self-interest within the economic activity of nonliterate peoples.

Manning Nash supplies another useful summary of themes of economic anthropology in his *International Encyclopedia of the Social Sciences* article of 1968.[14] He identifies four important economic dimensions in primitive and peasant societies: 1) Technology and division of labor; 2) Structure of productive units; 3) The system and media of exchange; and 4) The control of wealth and capital. Nash's 1) and 2) correspond to Herskovits's Part II; 3) and 4) correspond to Herskovits's Part III.

During the post-war period, there has been an explosion of works on themes of economic anthropology. Some of this work has been aligned with investigation of the underdevelopment of the so-called Third World. Notable here are the books by Doreen Warriner and by Colin Clark and Maurine Haswell.[15] These show in various ways why traditional agriculture throughout the globe has resisted change ("development") and shown relatively limited productivity. Clark/Haswell also provide valuable quantitative data to reveal the conditions under which traditional agriculture operates. Stuart Plattner's collection of essays, by contrast, traces how the integration of traditional societies into global markets has modernized village life in a variety of respects.[16] Much global agriculture has been carried

---

12. Herskovits, *Economic Anthropology*, vii.

13. Ibid., 488.

14. Nash, "Economic Anthropology."

15. Warriner, *Economics of Peasant Farming;* Clark and Haswell, *Economics of Subsistence Agriculture.*

16. Plattner, ed., *Economic Anthropology.*

on by peasants, so understandably a huge literature has come into being on this subject.

Peasant and Agrarian Studies

Peasants have been the predominant social type in most of the agrarian (agriculturally-based) societies of history, including especially those of the biblical period. Robert Redfield, the dean of peasant studies because of his very early effort in this area, still deserves reading. His book *Peasant Society and Culture* illuminates the general values and outlook of peasants, as well as proposes the very influential concepts of "Great" and "Little Traditions."[17] Also helpful at getting at the social world and values of peasantry is the collection of essays edited by Jack Potter, May Diaz, and George Foster.[18] Foster's influential article "Peasant Society and the Image of Limited Good" is included in the collection. This article brings out in a very illuminating way the zero-sum nature of peasant economics. Because goods are always perceived in such societies to be in limited quantities, anyone who gets ahead is thought to have done so at the expense of everyone else. These perceptions lead to a variety of village social mechanisms designed to keep everybody more or less on the same social level. From a materialist perspective, the works of Eric Wolf have contributed a great deal to the study of peasant types, subsistence and land concerns, religious orientation, and so forth. Wolf's *Peasants* is a very accessible summary of what has been learned about a variety of aspects of peasant life.[19]

In peasant or agrarian societies, social stratification, best defined as social categorization measured by differences in social wealth and power, is very pronounced. The work of Gerhard Lenski helps us to understand why. In his book *Power and Privilege*, Lenski examines the general social makeup of the agrarian and maritime societies (among others) and shows how a variety of social phenomena are interrelated because of the techno-economic level of such societies.[20] Biblical society belongs within agrarian society; this type depends technologically upon the plow and harnessed animal energy. The work of the many (90%) supports a small (10%) ruling elite. Agricultural surpluses with this technology cannot support more people not directly working the land. Lenski's discussion thus provides an

17. Redfield, *Peasant Society and Culture*.

18. Jack Potter et al., eds., *Peasant Society*.

19. Wolf, *Peasants*.

20. Lenski, *Power and Privilege*.

evolutionary and broad, macrosociological view. This can be very useful in keeping details in perspective.

General Economic History

For those who seek a map of what has been done historically in the study of economics, there is a still-useful bibliographic essay by Hoselitz in *A Reader's Guide to the Social Sciences*.[21] He gives a rather full list (but not always much annotation) of works that deal with economic analysis through history. He also organizes his bibliography to reflect schools of economic thought. Robert Heilbroner provides a lucid survey of economic activities and organization through history and down to the present in *The Making of Economic Society*.[22] His chapter on "Pre-market Economy" is brief, but underscores many of the points emphasized throughout the present essay. V. Gordon Childe's *What Happened in History* is especially useful in tracing technical and structural factors in the economic development of ancient societies.[23] Childe gives the big picture on economics, tracing for instance the general negative impact of money on societies based upon agricultural production. His book reminds us that focus on details sometimes obscures the obvious generality.

Classical Historians, Biblical Scholars, and the Ancient Economy

Helpful summaries of results of the study of economics in antiquity will be found in several works by classical historians. Thomas F. Carney's *The Shape of the Past: Models and Antiquity* devotes a chapter to "'Economics' in Antiquity" and details the hard-won results of Polanyi's and others' work. As the subtitle of the book suggests, Carney is especially interested in developing explicit conceptual models for the investigation of significant institutions of antiquity (including the bureaucratic states of the Ancient Near East).[24] This important strength allows Carney, unlike authors who adopt purely historical-descriptive treatments, to investigate in a controlled way the extent of "marketization" and "monetization" on ancient economies. (The former refers to how far prices are set in price markets,

---

21. Hoselitz, *Reader's Guide to the Social Sciences.*
22. Heilbroner, *Making of Economic Society.*
23. Childe, *What Happened in History?*
24. Carney, *Shape of the Past.*

the latter refers to how far prices are established in money.) With a clear sense of the controlling social structures of the ancient world, Carney paints a picture of economic stagnation and gross inequality in the sharing of any economic advantages. Carney's perspective helps us to understand the moral outrage, say, of the biblical prophets or Jesus over the plight of the many.

Moses Finley's *The Ancient Economy*, by contrast, restricts attention to Greco-Roman antiquity, and while he is not as self-conscious as Carney in the development and justification of explicit models for the study of ancient societies, he does make some use of the conceptual categories and results of modern economic anthropology.[25] Nevertheless, in a preliminary discussion of "The Ancients and Their Economy," Finley takes pains to argue that modern economic conceptions are largely inappropriate. He stresses at a number of points in his treatment the irrelevance of the modern notion of economic class. He does, however, provide valuable historical sketches of agricultural production, estates, tenancy, slavery, peasants, organization of labor, banking, loans-at-interest, debts, and so on.

Older, but still of great value for a general understanding of ancient economic history, are the writings of Max Weber, who like Polanyi combined classical training with comparativist study. Weber's *magnum opus* was *Economy and Society*, posthumously pieced together from partly complete manuscripts. This massive work offers dense and highly theoretical reading on the subject.[26]

Three other works of Weber are probably more useful and accessible. His *General Economic History*, originally part of a series of lectures on universal history, is oriented to understanding the development of western capitalism and economic "rationalism."[27] While he focuses primarily on medieval and modern economic developments in Europe, the ever-thorough Weber is always attentive to their foundations in antiquity. He takes up, for example, a discussion of the ancient plantation, noting that it always depended upon slave-hunting. Weber then draws upon comparative material, for this instance examining southern U.S. slave plantations in the nineteenth century.

25. Finley, *Ancient Economy*.
26. Weber, *Economy and Society*.
27. Weber, *General Economic History*.

An equally illuminating study, full of historical detail, is *The Agrarian Sociology of Ancient Civilizations*.[28] This work, unlike *General Economic History*, gives sustained attention to Ancient Near Eastern and classical social and economic organization. Weber is primarily concerned to interpret the operation of basic social values and institutions. His rich sociological imagination often makes stunning connections that mere historical description would overlook. One example of this interpretive activity will have to suffice: Weber accurately characterizes ancient "capitalism" as relatively unproductive because of its alignment with power groups and because investments were limited only to certain socially acceptable outlets. Capital, because socially restricted, did not lead in antiquity to industrial production as the modern period has known it.

Ancient Judaism, while somewhat dated in critical detail, surveys the sociological development of Judaism—from an agricultural people of the biblical period to a "pariah," commercial people of the talmudic period. Weber is particularly intent upon showing the relationship between specific biblical traditions and particular social groups and institutions (see Gottwald's more recent work).[29]

All three of these books repay careful study and consideration, but all three require a great deal of effort on the part of the student.

More advanced students will want to know about works that make available the ancient source material for economic study. A number of these can be mentioned. A very useful treatment of classical Greek society and economics, including a substantial number of texts in translation relating to these matters, is M. M. Austin's and P. Vidal-Naquet's *Economic and Social History of Ancient Greece*.[30] Michael Rostovtzeff's two great works, *The Social and Economic History of the Hellenistic World* (1941) and *The Social and Economic History of the Roman Empire* (1957), are still unsurpassed for their thoroughness and scope.[31] The weakness of these volumes lies less in their knowledge of the ancient data than in their failure to use the results of comparative social and economic study. Both sets reflect Rostovtzeff's encyclopedic knowledge of Hellenistic-Roman realities through both text and artifact. Each set contributes to our knowledge

28. Weber, *Agrarian Sociology of Ancient Civilizations*.

29. Weber, *Ancient Judaism*.

30. Austin and Vidal-Naquet, *Economic and Social History of Ancient Greece*.

31. Rostovtzeff, *The Social and Economic History of the Hellenistic World*, 3 vols.; *The Social and Economic History of the Roman Empire*, 2 vols.

of the general social context of early Judaism and Christianity. The 1957 work especially specifies how the provinces of Judaea and Syria fit within Roman imperial society.

Richard Duncan-Jones provides a wealth of data on Roman economy in his *The Economy of the Roman Empire: Quantitative Studies*.[32] As the subtitle indicates, Duncan-Jones is concerned with prices, weights, measures, equivalent values, and so forth. Another massive collection of data, though older, is available in the volumes edited by Tenney Frank, 1933–40.[33] The sub-volume done by Fritz Heichelheim on "Roman Syria" is especially valuable for students of the New Testament. Like Duncan-Jones, Heichelheim collects very specific archaeological and textual data on agricultural production, population, wages and prices, taxation, municipal finances, industry, various kinds of crafts, etc. This data represents study only up to 1938. Heichelheim offers preliminary interpretations, but does not employ sophisticated social models.

From a thoroughgoing Marxian perspective, G. E. M. de Ste. Croix's *The Class Struggle in the Ancient Greek World* provides extremely rich fare.[34] He devotes the first part of this massive book to a discussion of the importance of Karl Marx's work for ancient historiography. As the book's title suggests, de Ste. Croix pursues the notion of "class struggle" in emphasizing how much ancient history was in fact a result of the exploitation of the many-who-labored by the few-who-enjoyed-leisure. De Ste. Croix's reading of apocalyptic literature as "protest literature" and his contextualizing of the Jesus movement as a protest of country against exploitative city present understandings of early Christianity radically different from theological approaches. *Class Struggle* offers extensive bibliographic survey and discussion—further grist for the enterprising student's mill.

For the societies of the Ancient Near East in general, Karl Wittvogel's *Oriental Despotism* shows how the construction and maintenance of large-scale irrigation works led to such societies' typical bureaucratic shape. Another incisive book explicating the relationship between politics and economy in antiquity is John Kautsky's *The Politics of Aristocratic Empires*. Kautsky is especially important for tracing the imbalance of power in traditional, agrarian societies like those of the biblical period. He analyzes,

32. Duncan-Jones, *The Economy of the Roman Empire*.

33. Frank, ed., *An Economic Survey of Ancient Rome*, 6 vols.

34. De Ste. Croix, *Class Struggle in the Ancient Greek World*.

for instance, the overall structuring of power in "aristocratic empires," showing how elites maintain their position with relatively few members in such societies and why peasant uprisings are so rare.[35]

Norman K. Gottwald has investigated economic dimensions in the formation of Israel and the Old Testament tradition generally. *Tribes of Yahweh* is a comprehensive, technical study that argues against seeing early Israel as a nomadic invasion of Canaan. Gottwald presents a convincing case for the transformation of a variety of social groups, including Canaanite peasants, into the early tribes of Yahweh. Religion here is firmly linked with subsistence agricultural concerns. Gottwald's *The Hebrew Bible*, designed for college and seminary classrooms, incorporates the insights of *Tribes of Yahweh*, then traces developments down through the period of the Hebrew Bible.[36] The Israelite monarchy represents the return to centralized state structures familiar throughout the Ancient Near East. The exilic and postexilic materials are read through the lens of colonial experience. Gottwald's works show the interrelationship of power and economy in the development of Israelite faith.

Turning to the New Testament, Bruce J. Malina in his *The New Testament World* provides many examples of how to apply cultural anthropology to New Testament texts.[37] Of special interest to the student of ancient economy is Malina's chapter "The Perception of Limited Good: Maintaining One's Social Status," which shows among other things that economic poverty was subordinate in biblical society to the concern for public reputation. There was no disgrace in poverty, but the inability to maintain one's honor was a serious liability. Not to have the means to do so would be thought of as shameful. Malina reminds the reader that economy was not a free-standing social institution in ancient societies; he points thus to the cultural meaning of wealth *within* an honor-shame framework. This meaning is not identical to perceptions within modern capitalist societies.

The collaborative work by Malina and Rohrbaugh, mentioned at the beginning of this essay, gives much attention to the ancient economy in the Bible.[38] Especially valuable are their textual notes and reading sce-

35. Wittvogel, *Oriental Despotism*; Kautsky, *The Politics of Aristocratic Empires*.

36. Gottwald, *The Tribes of Yahweh*.

37. Malina, *The New Testament World: Insights From Cultural Anthropology* (1981[1], 1993[2], 2001[3]).

38. Malina and Rohrbaugh, *Synoptic Gospels*.

narios. They devote attention to what people ate, the kinds of money they used, how taxation was organized, and how lopsided power arrangements structured most social relations. This excellent resource brings together a wealth of information about Mediterranean societies pertinent for reading the Bible.

Halvor Moxnes's *The Economy of the Kingdom* employs models from economic anthropology to explore Luke's "moral economy of the peasant."[39] Through this, Moxnes sees the Lukan Jesus as an advocate of peasant values. The Pharisees are represented by Luke as those who are in league with the forces that oppose this moral economy. My own *Jesus and the Economic Questions of His Day* carries out a similar moral economic analysis with reference to the historical Jesus.[40] I focus on production and (re)distribution from the viewpoint of the village, arguing that Jesus spoke against the exploitative political economy of Roman Palestine while advocating economic values based upon general reciprocity and redistribution under a vision of God's reign.

For Palestinian and Jewish economic history, specifically, Shimon Applebaum's "Economic Life in Palestine" gives an excellent summary of first-century Palestinian economy based upon Jewish and archaeological materials.[41] Older, but still useful, are Joachim Jeremias's *Jerusalem in the Time of Jesus* and the chapter "Economic Conditions" in Joseph Klausner's *Jesus of Nazareth*.[42] These two authors amass from rabbinic traditions a substantial amount of information about economic realities in Roman Palestine at the turn of the eras. Jeremias gives details about commerce in the pilgrim city Jerusalem during the time of Jesus and shows how this commerce was controlled by wealthy priestly interests. Klausner supplies a lengthy description of the varieties of artisans and craftsmen in Jesus' environment. While these volumes do not have explicit social-theoretical frameworks, they give the reader valuable insights into economic realities and structures in the biblical world.

---

39. Moxnes, *The Economy of the Kingdom.*
40. Oakman, *Jesus and the Economic Questions of His Day.*
41. Applebaum, "Economic Life in Palestine."
42. Jeremias, *Jerusalem*; Klausner, *Jesus of Nazareth.*

THE CONCEPTUAL PAYOFF

By reading some or all of the works of Polanyi especially, as well as the foregoing economic anthropologists and historians of ancient economy, the biblical student will be able to discern significant differences between the economies of the biblical period and the present. The major institutions of industrial or corporate capitalism are missing in the historical societies that hosted the biblical tradition. Economic issues and concerns do not have the same salience in the biblical writings as they do today. Some of these necessary shifts of perception and emphasis have already been indicated. However, a brief foray into some additional biblical material may serve to suggest payoffs from this type of study.

The narrow margin between subsistence and starvation is everywhere attested in the biblical literature (Deut15:11; Mark 14:7 and par.). Biblical laws and moral injunctions were generally phrased to preserve the status of poor Israelites or poor Christians within the total covenant community (see also Exod 20:1–17, 21–23; Deut 15:11; 2 Cor 9:12; Jas 2:6).

As already suggested above, biblical religion could function to undergird or oppose either reciprocal household economy or redistributive political economy: Throwing religious influence on the side of redistribution, Deut 14:22–29; 18:1–8; Mal 3:8–12; John 13:29; Acts 4:35; 6:1–3. Religion against redistributive economy, 1 Sam 8:10–20; Mark 11:17.

The traditions of the Old Testament laws and the prophets show a profound concern with the economic conditions of the Israelites, but within the covenant or household metaphor. Economic concerns are always embedded within a larger social framework. Moreover, the biblical concern with economics is characteristically couched in agrarian terms. The Jubilee laws of Leviticus, as we have already seen, acknowledge the preeminence of land and family (Lev 25:10). The degraded status of labor and the prevalence of slavery in ancient Israel are also to be observed (Deut 15:12, 16–17). Moreover, one of the typical paths to slavery in the absence of war is indicated. Increasingly asymmetrical power relations lead to loss of ability to maintain one's status in the community (Lev 25:39). Biblical laws attempt to counteract the corrosive social effects of debt in covenant relationships (Deut 15:1–2). Loans must never be made at interest (Exod 22:25–27). The general picture is debts should never get so large that they endanger the community fabric.

The political and redistributive economic machinery of the Israelite Monarchy is well illustrated by the deuteronomic account of Solomon's reign (1 Kgs 4:7, 22–23). The account of 1 Kings makes clear that this economy was a political economy with a domestic form. Solomon, as did all ancient monarchs, considered his kingdom his own household to do with as he pleased. He monopolized the lines of trade such that the notion of a free market applied to Solomonic commerce would be inappropriate (1 Kgs 10:2, 11, 14–25). Solomon used commercial ties for his own aggrandizement. First Kings 9:15–22 indicates the generally unfree quality of labor in antiquity and differential treatment accorded Israelites and non-Israelites under Solomon. Forced labor was reserved, according to the account, to the non-Israelites. However, the cause of the division of the monarchy was precisely the displeasure of Israelites with the Solomonic order (1 Kgs 12:1–16).

The Jesus tradition, like the pre- or anti-monarchic Israelite tradition, emphasizes reciprocity in economic exchanges and opposes or discourages a redistributive economy. So Jesus speaks of sharing freely with others (Matt 5:42; Luke 6:35) but he speaks critically of the temple institution in its economic aspects (Mark 11:17 and par.; cf. Mark 13:1–2). The rich man who seeks to found his security upon self-sufficiency and a large estate (redistributive economy) is labeled a fool (Luke 12:20). The early Christian movement itself may have lived out an economic lifestyle of familial reciprocity (Acts 4:34–35). Again we see economic exchanges embedded within other relationships and sanctioned by religious values. Debt is also abhorred in the Jesus movement, and forgiveness of debts (sins) assumes the rank of a core value of the gospel tradition (Matt 6:12/Luke 11:4; Matt 18:23–35; Luke 7:41–42; Matt 5:25–26/Luke 12:58–59).

We return, finally, to Jesus' parable of the Talents. This story illustrates as well as any New Testament text how little modern notions of capital and investment apply to ancient economics. The narrative recalls two of the three prevalent uses for "capital" in antiquity: money on loan (Matt 25:16) or money hoarded (Matt 25:18). The third regular employment for the money elites was purchase of land.[43] Narrative developments revolve around these two options. Peasants would likely relate to the servant entrusted with one talent (although no peasant would ever see such an amount). Not only should such entrustments be hidden to avoid village

---

43. On these typical uses, see Finley, *Ancient Economy*, 118.

envy, but peasants would always seek the economically secure course over risky loans. Peasant and Jewish values are trampled upon, however, when the rewards go to the two servants who brought back their trust with interest. As we have seen, interest was forbidden by Jewish law; such loans implied increasingly dependent and nonreciprocal relationships. The loans are not to help folks acquire a major appliance, but lead to dominance and control over others. Luke's version of the parable brings this out clearly: the rewards given to the "faithful" (= trustworthy) servants are to be control of ten or five cities (Luke 19:17, 19).

CONCLUSION

Where to begin? The general reader or the reader pressed for time will do well to obtain works that are easily accessible and available, like Heilbroner for the economy in history or Malina and Malina and Rohrbaugh for economics in the Bible.[44] The last two books will also orient the reader to cultural issues involved in reading the Bible.

For readers interested in the broader historical-economic contexts of the Bible, Finley and Gottwald are especially helpful.[45] These works represent a little more difficulty.

Readers intrigued by the social-theoretical questions should turn first to Childe, Carney, and Lenski.[46]

There is more to be explored than can adequately be covered in the scope of this short chapter, but the reader will begin to see how economic issues are everywhere in the pages of the Bible—embedded within political, family, or religious contexts. Our economic assumptions and experiences do not help us to read the Bible and its concerns with economy sensibly or reliably. Barton's "man nobody knows" is truly a figment of modern liberal imagination, though Barton was right that Jesus had something to do with economic life. A different kind of "commonsense" about economy needs to be acquired. For this task, a world of reading and fascinating exploration awaits the courageous.

---

44. Heilbroner, *The Making of Economic Society*; Malina, *The New Testament World*; Malina and Rohrbaugh, *Synoptic Gospels*.

45. Finley, *Ancient Economy*; Gottwald, *The Hebrew Bible*.

46. Childe, *What Happened in History*; Carney, *The Shape of the Past*; Lenski, *Power and Privilege*.

CHAPTER 6

The Ancient Economy and St. John's Apocalypse

God prompted me to say this first, how many grievous woes the Immortal devised for Babylon, because it destroyed his great Temple. —*Sibylline Oracles*, 3:300–302

However much wealth Rome received from tribute-bearing Asia, Asia shall receive three times that much again from Rome and will repay her deadly arrogance to her. —*Sibylline Oracles*, 3:350–52

INTRODUCTION

INTERPRETATION OF THE APOCALYPSE has never been easy. Many modern readers avoid this final New Testament work with its frightening and often violent images. This article is not an attempt to apply the Apocalypse's imagery to the decade of the 1990s. Clearly, as we approach the twenty-first century, interpretations of this sort will be amply available!

What this essay does attempt is to increase our understanding of the intention of the Apocalypse, in the conviction that use of it in our own time must begin with general outlines of what it meant originally.[1] Foremost in our investigation is an interest in bringing out the connections between the ancient economy and the Apocalypse.

---

1. I am indebted to my esteemed teacher John H. Elliott for the notions in this essay of situation (context) and strategy. In *A Home for the Homeless*, he employs these concepts to great effect in elucidating the communication in 1 Peter, a document that also circulated in Asia Minor about the time of the Apocalypse.

Members of the Context Group and colleagues at Pacific Lutheran University have given me helpful feedback on initial drafts of this essay. I am especially grateful to Richard Kibbey (deceased 2002), who has inspired my systems models and thinking. I, of course, am solely responsible for the use and abuse of this rich wisdom.

General Reading Models and Assumptions

In recent years, social-scientific approaches to the Bible have used explicit conceptual models to aid in understanding the text. The following model indicates our intention to read the Apocalypse as a TEXT within a specific CONTEXT, reconstructed both historically and social-systemically:

Figure 9: General Reading Model

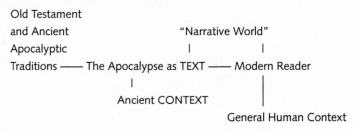

There are several interpretive ("hermeneutical") circles an investigation could pursue. One approach might examine how the Apocalypse reflects, or is influenced by, the Old Testament or ancient apocalyptic traditions. Another might consider the Apocalypse as a closed narrative world, within which the modern reader discerns various meanings. A third might reflect on what the Apocalypse means in light of universal human experience and questions. All of these approaches have been taken by scholars.[2] The method of the present essay, however, is to show how the TEXT of the Apocalypse had been formed in response to a specific CONTEXT. That is, we will see how the Apocalypse reflects and responds to disprivilege and deprivations generated by a specific type of social-economic system.

A social-science approach to John's Apocalypse needs to distinguish cultural and institutional variables within the context of John. Cultural anthropology helps to identify some distinctive values in ancient Mediterranean societies: honor/shame, for instance, was a central concern in these societies because status competition among kin groups was a central cultural dynamic.[3] Furthermore, these were highly stratified societies built upon human and animal labors invested in predominantly agricultural economies.[4] Because production was laborious and difficult,

2. Jeske and Barr, "The Study of the Apocalypse Today."

3. Malina, *The New Testament World* (1981¹), 25–48, (2001³) 27–57; Neyrey, ed., *The Social World of Luke-Acts*.

4. Oakman, "'All the Surrounding Country,'" orig. 154–55 [chapter 11 below].

the ancients tended to see the goods of life available only in sharply limited supply.

Ancient institutions tended to be built around family and politics (how one "family" dealt with others). Roman civil law, for instance, gave significant space to inheritance laws; the Romans, along with other imperial powers of antiquity, devoted enormous attention to problems of administering subject populations.[5] Religion tended to be practiced within domestic or political contexts, and economic activity was conducted within the household or subject to political control.

SPECIFIC ASSUMPTIONS IN READING THE APOCALYPSE

The socio-historical reading of the Apocalypse depends upon an accurate dating and placement of this work. While a variety of critical proposals have been offered over many years, a general consensus has come to situate its final composition in the late-first century (ca. 95 CE), reflecting conditions in the western part of ancient Turkey (Roman Asia).[6]

Thus, John seems to look back on the terrible events of 70 CE in Jerusalem. The army of Titus had first destroyed the holy place of Judea, the temple, then trampled the holy city itself (Rev 11:2). The dislocations of the Jewish War forced many to leave Palestine and settle elsewhere in the Roman Empire. A fair number would have gone to Asia Minor, since a sizeable Jewish population lived there in the centuries preceding and succeeding the disaster in Judea. Josephus gives information about this Jewish community in Asia (*Ant.* 12:125; 16:45, etc.); and an inscription from Smyrna refers to "those once Judeans."[7] John's Seven Letters at the beginning of the Apocalypse are addressed in part to such groups.

A preoccupation with temples (Rev 6:9; 8:3; 16:1) and the elaborate liturgies going on in the skies (4:8–11; 15:5) prompt one to think of Revelation's author as an ex-priest. Indeed, Eusebius knows traditions

---

5. Hammond and Scullard, *Oxford Classical Dictionary* (2d ed., 1970), s. v. "Inheritance, Law of"; s. v. "Law and Procedure, Roman."

6. A different understanding is advanced in Ford, *Revelation,* 50–56. She sees tradition in Revelation going back to John the Baptist, and, in part, reflecting conditions in Judea during the mid-first century. However, she too sees the final composition of the text connected with Ephesian churches. Compare Adela Y. Collins, *Crisis and Catharsis*, 31.

Because of the significant number of strange placenames in this discussion, the reader would do well to have access to a Bible atlas containing detailed maps of Roman Asia.

7. Hemer, *The Letters to the Seven Churches of Asia in Their Local Setting,* 9.

about the John who "leaned on the Lord's breast" (John 13:23; 18:15) having been a priest.[8] This John, then, perhaps left Judea after 70 CE and formed the center of a "circle" at Ephesus in the late-first century. However, the precise background of the author (possibly authors) of Revelation remains obscure.[9]

Fundamental to an appreciation of John's theology is the identification of his concern for God's honor. From the standpoint of the Seer, God's honor has been offended by the course of earthly developments; conversely, beings in the sky laud God's honor unceasingly. The Roman imperial cult demands such honor for Caesar. For John, Jesus' great significance lies in his courageous testimony before Roman officialdom and in his witness that God alone is worthy of honor. For his loyalty, Jesus has been supremely honored by God, and has become the Broker of God's royal patronage.[10] And it is precisely in this patronage that one significant aspect of the ancient economy reflected in the Apocalypse becomes evident. Jesus as Broker mediates everything his loyal faction members need.

An ancient treaty or covenant pattern lies behind the Seven Letters: The will of God the Sovereign is made known (through the vice-regent Jesus) in these letters.[11] The sovereign (representative) is identified (Rev 2:1); the relationship between sovereign and vassal is recounted (2:2–4); a stipulation is made (2:5a); conditions are noted (2:6); blessings are promised (2:7); a curse is hinted at (2:5b). Whoever remains faithful will receive the benefits promised in these letters. The Seven Letters represent, therefore, contractual communications from the patron-broker to the faithful of the seven churches (which include not only city members, but also members in the country territories of these churches).

8. Eusebius, *Eccl. Hist.* 3:31,3; 5:24,3.

9. Adela Y. Collins, *Crisis and Catharsis*, 25–50.

10. The analogy of patronage stands behind both the theology of the synoptic gospels and the Apocalypse; see Malina, "Patron and Client." Furthermore, John's visions of heavenly liturgies might best be thought of as "accession rites" (which happen when a king comes to the throne). Jesus, like ancient Near Eastern kings, enters into his kingship. See de Vaux, *Ancient Israel*, 1:102–3 for a description of such rites: consider Rev 5:8 ("scroll" = royal protocols); 19:11 (judgment and military leadership are royal roles *par excellence*); 19:12 (diadems); 19:12 ("name inscribed" = throne name); 5:9 and 19:13 ("robe dipped in blood" = anointing).

11. Von Rad, *Old Testament Theology*, 1:132.

General Model of Imperial Roman Economy

Rome's dominion or imperium had a profound impact on the ancient economy. Many historians have commented upon the prosperity of the Roman Empire in the first two centuries of our era (the "golden age" of Rome). What these commentaries have tended to overlook, focusing as they have on the productivity made possible by the Roman peace, is the imperium's definite skewing of economic distribution.[12]

While we cannot supply a complete account of this unequal distribution, a general model can be utilized to show how economic exploitation led to the control, hoarding, and redistribution of immense wealth by and among the relative few. The model can also help us to understand certain emphases within John's Apocalypse.

The ancient economy of the first-century Roman Empire was political in two basic respects: (1) It was based upon forced extraction of goods (taxes) that constantly drained agricultural resources out of the provinces to supply the city of Rome and its imperial bureaucracy. (2) It encouraged a movement of goods (commerce) that essentially served the elites and their delegates. For the majority of the Empire, a "trickle-down" effect from this prosperity was the best that could be hoped for. Religion had a role both in the legitimation of these arrangements and in their critique. The systems model diagramed below will serve as the basis for further reflections.[13]

---

12. Kautsky, *The Politics of Aristocratic Empires*, 38–39, 99–117.

13. Lenski, *Power and Privilege*:; Carney, *The Shape of the Past*; and Garnsey and Saller, *The Roman Empire* have been particularly influential in the formulation of this model.

**Figure 10: Roman Political Economy
(A Systems Model)**

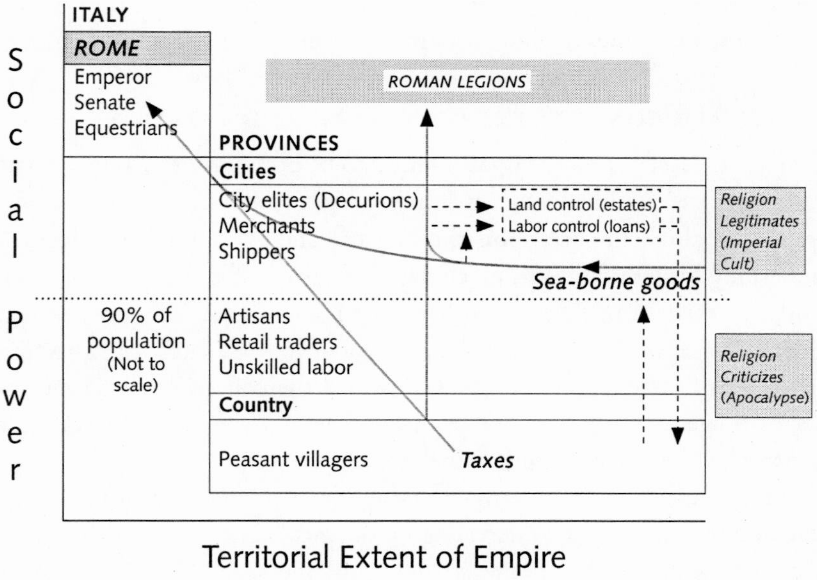

Territorial Extent of Empire

Though Rome was the economic center of the Empire, the emperors realized that Rome's privileged place could only be maintained by co-opting provincial elites into imperial service. Roman policy from Augustus onward emphasized using military force internally as little as possible (the legions were needed to defend the borders) and building up urbanized indigenous elites actually to administer the Empire for Rome. In the first century, two bureaucracies—Caesar's "family" of slaves, freedmen, and governors (in imperial provinces drawn from the Equestrian Order), together with the city elites especially in the East—shared the burden of imperial tax collection and rule. The systems model articulates how Rome's power caused goods to move "diagonally" (horizontally through space toward the imperial cities, vertically within the social structure). Commerce little benefitted the majority for two reasons: first, most had little access to free cash to enter the commodity market: the market had little depth. Secondly, overland transport was extremely inefficient and costly; for this reason, most ancient commerce in bulk commodities was water-borne.[14]

Religion under elite control tended to legitimate and reinforce these arrangements that benefitted the elites. Religion reflective of experiences

14. Carney, *Shape of the Past*, 177, 201.

at the bottom of society (such as expressed in the Apocalypse) typically offered strong critique of the Empire's arrangements of political economy and its elite religion. John's Apocalypse is one of the most exquisite and finely tuned critiques in all of ancient literature.

POLITICAL ECONOMY: THE APOCALYPSE AND TAXATION

Two interrelated aspects of taxation need to be brought into focus in order to understand its impact upon John's people (the Christian non-elites) and Revelation's impact upon the original audience. First, the Roman Imperium brought significant changes in terms of the organization of land control within Asia and other eastern provinces. This process had already begun in the Hellenistic period under the Seleucids (third-second centuries BCE). Secondly, Rome transferred the collection of taxes from her own agents (*publicani*, publicans) to the indigenous city-elites. This transfer had been completed by the first century CE.

First the Macedonian kings and then the Roman caesars fostered far-reaching social changes by encouraging the growth of cities in the eastern Mediterranean world. Under the Seleucids, the successors of Alexander who ruled Mesopotamia and parts of ancient Turkey in the centuries before Augustus, large portions of land had been taken from the ancient temple states and assigned to city foundations. The Seleucids essentially recognized royal lands and city lands. Ephesus, prior to these times, had annexed the lands of the great temple of Artemis. Pisidian Antioch held lands formerly belonging to Men (the sun god). Other temple lands were usurped as well.[15] In practice, this reorganization meant that the produce of numerous Asian villages went to cities rather than the local deity. The Romans continued this practice of "urbanization" in their conquests of Cappadocia and Pontus. Villagers were classified legally (from the urban and imperial standpoints) as "resident aliens" (*paroikoi*, parics).[16] Previously many had been royal or temple slaves. Was this a step up or a step down? Some authorities think the former, but they overlook the fact that temple slaves at least "belonged" and could count on patronage from the deity. "Aliens" had no such security.

---

15. Tarn and Griffith, *Hellenistic Civilisation*, 139; Rostovtzeff, *SEHHW*, 1:505–8.
16. See Elliott, *A Home for the Homeless*.

The religious effect of this transformation was at first politically in-choate. However, memory of suppressed temple states could feed a power-ful undercurrent of religious feeling and discontent.

The uprising of Aristonicus (133 BCE) had strongly religious over-tones and attracted a large number of disaffected peasants. As Attalus III was bequeathing his kingdom to Rome, with a sizeable number of slave-based estates, Aristonicus claimed the throne and promised his followers citizenship in a "city of the sun" ("Heliopolis"). This movement attracted a large following in the "quadrilateral eastward from Pergamum, Smyrna and Colophon (north of Ephesus) through the Caicus, Hermus and Cayster valleys to the highlands of Phrygia."[17] Whether the ideology for this move-ment was drawn from Hellenistic Utopian thought (Iambulus wrote of an island paradise where the sun was always shining), or from indigenous religious sources (a city ruled by Men, lord of justice), Aristonicus's move-ment was opposed by many urban elites of Asia, and Aristonicus himself was killed by a Roman consul in 130 BCE.

Revelation stands within a tradition that remembered similar viola-tions of divine honor. In 167 BCE, the Maccabees had risen against a Seleucid king who tried to "urbanize" Jerusalem and expropriate its temple lands. The Romans later succeeded where the Seleucids had failed. Titus razed the Jerusalem temple in 70 CE, and his father Vespasian diverted its enormous revenues into a special Roman treasury, the *fiscus iudaicus*. John alludes to the dishonorable employment of this revenue: the money was used to rebuild the Capitoline temple to Jupiter in Rome, which had been destroyed during the Roman civil war of 68–69. The "wound" on one of Rome's seven hills (the Capitol) had been miraculously healed (Rev 13:3)!

John's feelings were consonant with some eastern "Sibyls" (women oracles found in different places in the ancient world): the words quoted at the beginning of this article (Hellenistic-period, Egypt?) express outrage at the insensitive treatment of holy Jerusalem by Syrian rulers, and of prov-inces like Asia by republican Rome (first century BCE). Other utterances, contemporaneous with the Apocalypse, condemn exploitation by Rome and her agents: "Now, wretched Asia, I bewail you piteously and the race of Ionians, Carians, and Lydians rich in gold" (*Sib. Or.* 5:287–288). Like the Sibylline traditions, John designates Rome as "Babylon," establishing

17. Sherwin-White, *Roman Foreign Policy in the East*, 86.

an analogue to the archetypal temple destroyer in Old Testament tradition. God's offended honor must be avenged: "The great city was split into three parts, and the cities of the nations fell, and God remembered great Babylon, to make her drain the cup of the fury of his wrath" (Rev 16:19). Rome's rule is characterized as bloody and oppressive (9:21; 18:24). Those most liable to judgment will be Rome herself and her elite allies (Rev 6:15; 19:18).

Political Economy: the Apocalypse and Commerce

Commerce in the first-century Roman Empire did not constitute anything like "free trade." Rome controlled commerce in very definite ways: a major impetus behind all long-distance trade was the *annona*, the supply of grain to the city of Rome and to the legionary armies. Rome, therefore, organized associations of merchants and shippers (Rev 18) who did her bidding: they were hardly "free agents." Furthermore, Rome played a role in constructing facilities on the Mediterranean to conduct this trade.[18] By contrast, commerce over long distances by land—being inefficient and expensive—was relatively small.

The major items of commerce were food commodities that could be transported over long distances without spoiling (grain, wine, oil, preserved meats and fruits) and luxury items (precious metals, stones, woods,

18. *Annona* as driving force in commodity commerce and the Roman control of the associations: Rostovtzeff, *SEHRE,* 1:145 and especially 158:

> Who were the consumers of all these articles? For whom were such quantities of corn [wheat], meat, oil, and wine moved from one place to another? It must be admitted that a careful investigation of the sources shows that the largest consumer was the imperial *annona* and that most of the merchants, who frequently were at the same time shipowners and owners of store houses, worked on behalf of the emperor, that is to say, on behalf of the population of the city of Rome and the army. Such an impression is conveyed, above all, by the study of the inscriptions which speak of the *collegia* [associations] of merchants and of shipowners, the *navicularii* of the sea, and the *nautae* of the lakes and rivers. Most of the *collegia* were recognized and even favoured by the state, because they were useful or rather indispensable to it . . . It is a notable fact that the first *collegia* to be not merely recognized but also granted protection and privileges were those of merchants and shipowners.

Roman improvements of harbor facilities, Rostovtzeff, *SEHRE,* 2:615 n. 35:

> The great importance of commerce by sea is shown by the enormous sums which the emperors and the cities spent on the improvement of the old ports and the creation of new ones. . . .The greatest activity in this field was displayed by Trajan.

cloth, ivories, perfumes and spices, etc.). John knows all of these items and more (Rev 18:13).

Religion, not surprisingly, played an integral role in legitimizing these arrangements. The cult of the Emperors, which was most evident in Asia Minor, was essentially a celebration of the power that made this imperial commerce and rich urban life possible. A representative inscription from Halicarnassus (2 BCE) makes these connections clear:

> Since the eternal and deathless nature of the universe has perfected its immense benefits to mankind in granting us as a supreme benefit, for our happiness and welfare, Caesar Augustus, Father of his own Fatherland, divine Rome, Zeus Paternal, and Savior of the whole human race, in whom Providence has not only fulfilled but even surpassed the prayers of all men: land and sea are at peace, cities flourish under the reign of law, in mutual harmony and prosperity; each is at the very acme of fortune and abounding in wealth; all mankind is filled with glad hopes for the future, and with contentment over the present; [it is fitting to honor the god] with public games and with statues, with sacrifices and with hymns.[19]

The establishment of special religious rites implied the need for finances to support them. The Asian *koinon* ("commonwealth" or "league") supported imperial worship in Pergamum, Smyrna, and Ephesus. From the city elites were chosen the chief priests of these rites who also supported them out of their financial means.[20] Former slaves (freedmen) in eastern cities could be given privileges in return for serving as *Augustales*, those responsible for funding various imperial cults. *Augustales* of Asiatic origin set up a monument in Puteoli (an Italian city) to Tiberius to honor him for help given to cities of Asia Minor after three serious earthquakes.[21] Such expenses, and especially the building of temples for the imperial cult in cities like Ephesus, Pergamum, and Smyrna, would have increased the burdensome load of the cities upon the countryside.

Thus, commerce by sea and river advantaged cities on or near seacoasts. The cities and their elites served Rome as her clients in this vast movement of goods. They, of course, along with Rome, were the primary

19. Grant, *Ancient Roman Religion,* 174–75.

20. Macro, "The Cities of Asia Minor under the Roman Imperium," 681–82; Kearsley, "Asiarchs," 496a.

21. Rostovtzeff, *SEHRE,* 1:104 and 2:562 n. 18.

beneficiaries. A major transformation of the countryside took place as a result. For as the city elites gained power (through loans and other machinations) over the agricultural resources of regional lands, the productive goals of those lands were shifted to profit better from commerce.[22] The elite system thus become more effective. This did enormous harm to inland dwellers in villages, as the following illustrations suggest.

Dio of Prusa in Bithynia, a contemporary of John, can be viewed as typical of this eastern city elite. His family initially profited from holding lands sown to grain. However, as their fortunes declined, the family switched their agricultural goals. Their lands were now converted to pasture lands or sown to vines. The wealth of the family returned. Dio put this wealth into loans at interest and into "workshops" (*ergastēria*). The family of Dio thus owed elite status to control of land, but maintained this status through successful manipulation of the new commercial situation under the early Empire.[23]

The subsistence status of paric villagers on these lands grew more insecure as a result. Resident aliens ordinarily were denied the right to engage in commerce.[24] It is not likely that agricultural parics had any opportunity to do so. Through loans, villagers became more dependent upon and indebted to city landlords. Because of the shift to commercial crops (wine, livestock) villagers were now increasingly dependent upon the largesse of their city patron, the landowner. In times of famine or hardship, this largesse could become precarious. The Emperor Domitian is said to have passed laws restricting the growing of vines in the provinces because of the serious decline in grain reserves (Suetonius *Domitian* 7,2; 14,2). An inscription from Pisidian Antioch, 92–93 CE, has long been known. It tells how the Galatian procurator L. Antistius Rusticus had to force large estate owners to sell their hoarded grain to the city official in charge of grain supply (*sitones*). The price set by Rusticus: One *denarius* to the *modius*, twice the normal price in antiquity. The famine implied by Rev 6:6

22. Machinations: see MacMullen, *Roman Social Relations,* 6–7 for an example of gang violence used to acquire land in Mysia.

23. On Dio, see Rostovtzeff, *SEHRE,* 2:574 n. 10 and especially Oration 46. Though Dio was exiled, perhaps also John, for speaking against Domitian, Dio's interests were clearly with the eastern elites. The elites opposed Domitian's policies because these hurt city interests. (See the following paragraph.)

24. Elliott, *Home for the Homeless,* 37.

had driven the local price eight times the normal.[25] John speaks specifically against the political arrangements of Roman commerce, which God will overthrow when he destroys the "despoilers of the land" (Rev 11:18).

John's Vision of Renewed "Domestic" Economy

John's response to the situation just described becomes somewhat clearer. His visionary communication attacks indirectly the extractive political-economy of imperial taxation, and more directly the corrosive political-economy of commercial exploitation. His dominant theme throughout the Apocalypse is that God alone is honorable and worthy of honor, as against the religious edifice of the Imperium; that God's patronage alone is reliable and worthy of trust; and that God's vengeance upon the whole dishonorable system is sure.

John indignantly attacks the agents and primary goods of commerce up until the final visions of his work. In the Seven Letters, the poor and dispossessed are given pride of place (2:9; 3:8), while the powerful and wealthy are excoriated (3:17; 6:15; 19:18). The primary objects of contempt in chapter 18 are kings of the earth (v. 9), merchants (vv. 11, 15), and shipmasters (v. 17).

Perhaps most tellingly, John's image of God's judgment is formulated in such a way as to dishonor commerce. Joel 3:13 had provided apocalyptic tradition with a dual image for God's judgment of grain harvest and wine treading. The former became the dominant image in some traditions (e.g., Matt 13:40–42). John's Apocalypse shifts the emphasis to the latter image. Why?

In view of the oppressive effects of the shift to viticulture under the pressure of commerce in the late-first century (Rev 6:6), John's reemphasis on treading grapes and use of wine as a negative symbol in the unfolding vision makes sense. So, John speaks of the wrathful wine of Rome's fornication that all the nations have drunk (14:8; 18:3), of the worshippers of the beast who will "drink the wine of God's wrath" (14:10), of great Babylon who will be forced to drain the cup of wine of God's furious wrath (16:19), of the Harlot "with the wine of whose fornication the inhabitants of earth have become drunk" (17:2 NRSV), and of her golden cup "full of abominations and the impurities of her fornication" (17:4 NRSV). The NRSV committee may have given a misimpression of John's real meaning in 17:2,

25. Rostovtzeff, *SEHRE*, 2:600 n. 9.

since the Greek literally reads: "those who dwell (as military settlers) upon the land," perhaps a reference to the landlords whose policies produce so much wine.[26]

The major use of this image of grape treading, of course, occurs in Revelation 14:19–20 and 19:15 where the "grapes of God's wrath" get trodden. The image of "blood" from grapes seems appropriate, since John excoriates a bloody empire that has shed so much blood for the sake of its "system": "You are just, O Holy One, who are and were, for you have judged these things; because they shed the blood of saints and prophets, you have given them blood to drink. It is what they deserve!" (16:5–6 NRSV; recall the words of the Sibyls). The saints, the martyrs, ask for the avenging of their blood (6:10). The great tribulation implies a blood-bath (7:14; see 13:10). Rome specifically is accused of shedding innocent blood (17:6; 18:24), for which she will be repaid in the judgment (18:6). The harmful effects of too much wine come full circle!

The contrast in the latter part of Revelation between the status of Rome, the world's "central place" for redistributing the world's wealth (Rev 17), and the new Jerusalem, the center to which the kings of the earth bring their glory (Rev 21:24), shows strikingly the reversal of status that results from abolishing Rome's taxation rights. These rights belonged to the sovereign in the ancient world. Since God alone is worthy of honor in John's vision, God alone will be worthy of receiving tribute. This tribute will be reliably redistributed to clients. Thus, the Apocalypse promises the faithful (i.e. trustworthy clients) that all their needs will be met (2:7; 7:15–17; 21:4, 7).

The significance of the New Jerusalem for the original audience of Revelation is best seen in John's characterization of the city: It is the "holy city" (21:2). It has no temple, because God and the Lamb are its temple (21:22). Most significantly, "the city has no need of sun or moon . . . for the glory of God is its light, and its lamp is the Lamb" (21:23). John's New Jerusalem is the old Heliopolis! But John really does not have a city in mind. A "city" 12,000 stadia wide (21:16) would be as large as the Empire itself!

---

26. See also the similar constructions in 3:10; 6:10; 8:13; 11:10; 13:8, 12, 14; 17:8. Rostovtzeff, *SEHHW*, 1:477 shows *katoikia* are military settlements of the Seleucids in Asia Minor. At any rate, "More technically used, the verb [*katoikeo*] refers to the permanent 'residents' of a town or village, as distinguished from those 'dwelling as strangers' or 'sojourners' [*parics*]"; Moulton and Milligan, *Vocabulary of the Greek Testament*, 338.

Unlike 1 Peter, which uses "God's household" as the dominant metaphor, John continues to think in terms of an Asian temple state (21:22 notwithstanding). Jesus promises the faithful Philadelphians that whoever conquers will be made a pillar in the temple of God (3:12). The great multitude in chapter 7 stand before God's throne and "worship him day and night within his temple" (7:15 NRSV). God's priests (1:6; 5:10) have entered into a new domestic economy in God's presence, never again to hunger and thirst (7:16; 21:3).[27] In chapters 21–22, the security of the ancient temple state of the East has returned!

CONCLUSION

The Apocalypse was almost excluded from the canon of New Testament scriptures when later orthodoxy found its provocative criticism of earthly power inconvenient. The violent and vivid images of Revelation have continued to disturb people; the recent tragedy surrounding David Koresh is only the latest example. But it must be remarked that such a work was something of a "liberation theology" for its original hearers, or at least for those who had ears to hear. It strengthened some small group of Christians living in the eastern Roman Empire to see their resistance to oppression as meaningful in the face of overwhelming power.

Because of Revelation's strange and difficult literary form, its message is no longer easy to decipher. Yet its uncompromising insistence upon God's honor, and its unflinching critique of the "great ones of the earth" may still today challenge us as we approach a new millennium and enter a new world order fraught with danger as well as opportunity. Those who endure to the end of John's text, and who "keep the words" of his book (Rev 22:9), may still hear the ancient promise: The "leaves of the tree were for the healing of the nations" (22:2).

27. Later Christians in Asia Minor interpreted John's visions in a very literal way. Papias of Hierapolis (a city near Philadelphia and Laodicea, in the early second century CE) believed wine and grain would be magically abundant in the new age; Case, *The Millennial Hope*, 158–59.

CHAPTER 7

Money in the Moral Universe
of the New Testament[1]

You cannot serve God and Mammon. —Luke 16:13

For the love of silver [money] is the root of all evil. —1 Tim 6:10

STANDARD TREATMENTS OF BIBLICAL numismatics are rather limited as far as shedding light on the social significance of ancient money is concerned. The usual attention to art motifs and denominations is certainly useful from a historical and metrological point of view, but does very little as far as illuminating money's social place. This essay proposes an alternative approach that produces insights on a number of fronts: in relating numismatics to social world questions, in assessing the social character of the Jesus movement, in developing social indices for decisions about redactional settings in life (*Sitze im Leben*), and generally in shedding light on the origins and composition of the New Testament gospels.

The discussion is organized through four theses and two excurses. It is first suggested that standard treatments of biblical numismatics do not attain sufficient social insight. Part of the reason for this is that numismatic treatments related to the Bible have not been sufficiently in dialog with the larger field of numismatics, as Richard Oster pointed out over a decade ago. Moreover, there is palpable need for conceptual approaches informed by broader social questions and controlled through theory-informed mod-

1. Earlier versions of this material were presented to the Social Sciences and New Testament Section at the Society of Biblical Literature meeting in 1996, the Catholic Biblical Association in 1997, and an International Conference "Jesus in neuen Kontexten" at Tutzing, Germany in 1999. Also, a preliminary form of the model and discussion appears in Hanson and Oakman, *Palestine in the Time of Jesus*, 120–25.

els. For this reason, the discussion turns to the elaboration of a model regarding ancient money's social functions. This impels an analysis of descript money in the Jesus traditions, with an eye to the views of historical Jesus on the institution of money, and concluding comments about nondescript money in the New Testament outside of the gospels—indicative of increasing elite control over the early Jesus traditions.

THESIS 1:

Standard treatments of biblical numismatics either do not provide sufficient social insight or are misleading as to the social insight tendered.

Four recent publications are considered here as representative of "biblical numismatics," and I wish first to acknowledge my appreciation for and debt to them before I turn to critique. It is not that they are of poor quality, or do not present viable methodologies or results, but that they construe the work of numismatics perhaps too narrowly.

The work of Yaakov Meshorer is justifiably respected within the field of biblical numismatics. However, one may reasonably take issue with his assertion in a recent summary article that, "The dispute over the chronology of the Hasmonean coins is still the major issue in the field of Jewish numismatics."[2] Further, when he speaks of symbols on the coins of Herod the Great, he comments merely on the debate about whether they represent Jewish or pagan motifs. Certainly the chronology and symbolism of coins are important, but focusing on them without reference to the role of coinage within agrarian social relations or the politics of aristocratic empires is too constrictive.

A second recent numismatic treatment, in the dictionary of John Rousseau and Rami Arav, also illustrates the issue under consideration. The authors claim that money originated for the sake of convenience in exchange and that "the old barter system was relegated to minor local transactions."[3] They show awareness of functions of money as well as the political importance of money. However, in remarks about the Parable of the Talents, they speak of the "lack of logic in both stories," without awareness of Richard Rohrbaugh's excellent treatment of these "texts of terror"

---

2. Meshorer, "Jewish Numismatics," 212.
3. Rousseau and Arav, *Jesus and His World*, 55.

from the standpoint of Palestinian peasantry.[4] Moreover, their article assumes that the exchange utility of money was widespread and keeps the usual emphases on art motifs, weights, and denominational relationships.

A more helpful outcome is reached in a companion article by Fred Strickert.[5] Here there is a clearer statement of the relationship between interests of power and purposes of money. Strickert illustrates this social fact with reference to the images on coins, typically serving as propaganda for the powerful. In the most interesting section, a discussion of a series of coins minted by the tetrarch Philip in Northern Transjordan, Strickert traces the correlation between new coins and a series of important events in Roman Palestine. He reaches the following conclusion: "It seems that issuing coins served to publicize the legitimacy of Philip's own authority in the face of foreign domination."[6] While it is certainly possible that Philip felt challenged by the prefects to the south (as Strickert suggests; cf. Luke 23:12), it seems more likely that the coin series was intended to show Philip's loyalty to Rome as a faithful client ruler (cf. Bethsaida/Iulias, Caesarea Philippi). The prefects would be in a position to report this fidelity upon its "publication" through coinage. At least, Strickert is appreciative of the political significance of coinage, in contrast to views that might see a "free market" or freely-circulating money economy in the area.

A third example of the point under consideration is provided in *The Anchor Bible Dictionary* article on "Coinage," by John Betlyon. When Betlyon examines coinage in the Hellenistic and Herodian periods of Palestine, he observes that major mints were located in Acco and Tyre, and states "Coinage and the right to produce it were the perquisites of political and military supremacy."[7] No further inferences are made from this important statement, either about the role and function of money or about implications for social interpretation.

Most of Betlyon's comments deal with the dating of coins, brief descriptions, or historical notes. These are, again, important. However, information that could be of use for social understanding is obscured because the writer has no real sense for what "political and military supremacy" really meant for social institutions.

4. Ibid., 59; Rohrbaugh, "Text of Terror?"

5. Strickert, "Coins as Historical Documents," 61.

6. Ibid., 62.

7. Betlyon, "Coinage."

A few brief illustrations: Again and again, Betlyon observes that Hasmoneans and Herods struck bronze coins. He says, "No Hasmonean silver is known."[8] Apparently he thinks this is because silver and gold were in short supply. Rather than appeal to natural scarcity, why does he not suspect social constraints, particularly political constraints? Tyre and Acco were privileged by both Syrian and Roman interests in the minting of silver. Commerce, as well as taxation, had to do with power. Bronze coinage likewise served particular political functions within client realms, but Betlyon does not help us really to understand these dimensions.

He thinks Hasmonean coins "functioned as supplemental currency with the larger coins circulating from the major mints"; or Herod's coins "are meant to support silver from regional mints"; or "The procuratorial coinage was secondary to imperial and Herodian issues, and was used to fill out the denominational system"; or Herodian period coins "were the pocket change supplementing silver coins from imperial mints."[9]

Betlyon's statements might hold true in peculiar social contexts (cities within commercial networks like Tiberias, Sepphoris, Jerusalem, or Tyre, or farther away Pompeii), but mislead us, I would argue, as to the experience of most people. He assumes that commerce back then was like commerce now, that common folks back then had ready access to money of all denominations as now, and that money functioned then as now. These deceptive social assumptions are what social theory and models compensate for; conversely, contemporary biblical numismatics would do well to take social theory and models more seriously.

A final example derives from the recently published book of Larry J. Kreitzer.[10] This is a very fine study, with copious drawings of coins and excellent annotated bibliography, and should be of enduring value for students of the New Testament. While many of Kreitzer's chapters are devoted to studying the relationship between coin images and particular New Testament motifs (for instance, deification, triumph imagery in Paul, or Jesus' *parousia*), the first part on Julio-Claudian propaganda overlaps with our concerns. The political function of money (propaganda for the empire) is clearly in view. However, since Kreitzer is concerned with the standard art-history approach, coins are understood as illuminating history or particular textual motifs rather than as phenomena carrying significant social information.

8. Ibid., 1085.
9. Ibid., 1085–89.
10. Kreitzer, *Striking New Images*.

The limitations of standard treatments urge a search for alternative methods.

THESIS 2:

Numismatic approaches informed by broader social questions and controlled through theory-informed models can lead to important social insights.

The model that follows was suggested initially by the work of Michael Crawford, and developed in conversation with views of T. F. Carney, Karl Polanyi, Marshall Sahlins, Herman Daly and John Cobb, Richard Rohrbaugh, and William J. Booth.[11] In the background are considerations about agrarian societies, the politics of aristocratic empires, and systems sociology such as I employed in an SBL Seminar Paper a few years ago.[12] The model permits a functional analysis of money in the New Testament and raises the broader question of the function of money within societies whose key social institutions were structured through kinship and political relations.

Figure 11: Functions of Money and Barter

METAL BASIS	FUNCTION (F)
Gold, silver	F1) Storage (hoards, bullion) Mark 6:8 (Bronze As?); Matt 10:9/Luke 9:3 (Q, "Gold, silver, bronze"/ "Argyrion"); Matt 13:44/Gos. Thom. 109 (M or Q?, "Hidden treasure"); Matt 25:18/Luke 19:20 (Q, Talent/Mina); Luke 15:8–9 (L, Drachma); Matt 2:11 (M?, Gold); 23:16–17 (M, Gold); P. Yadin 5 (Mina), 17 (Denarius), 18 (Denarius), 27 (Denarius)

11. Crawford, "Money and Exchange in the Roman World"; Carney, *Economies of Antiquity*; idem, *The Shape of the Past*; Polanyi, *Livelihood*; Sahlins, *Tribesmen*; Daly and Cobb, *For the Common Good*; Rohrbaugh, "Text of Terror?" 34; and Booth, *Households*.

12. Lenski, *Power and Privilege*; Kautsky, *Politics of Aristocratic Empires*; Oakman, "Archaeology of First-Century Galilee" (chapter 15 below).

METAL BASIS	FUNCTION (F)
Silver	**F2) Measurement** Mark 6:37/John 6:7 (Denarius); Mark 14:5/John 12:5 (Denarius); Rev 6:6 (Denarius) **F3) Standard of payment** **a) Taxation** (non-elite or elite retainers > elite) Mark 12:41 (Bronze As?); Mark 12:15/Matt 22:19/Luke 20:24 (Denarius); Mark 12:42/Luke 21:2 (Lepton); Matt 17:24 (M, Tyrian didrachma); Matt 17:27 (M, Stater [Tyrian tetradrachma]); P. Yadin 16 (Mina) **b) Debt** (non-elite > elite) Matt 5:26/Luke 12:59 (Q, Quadrans/Lepton); Luke 6:34–35/Gos. Thom. 95 (L or Q?, "Money"); Luke 12:15–21/Gos. Thom. 63 (L or Q?, Chremata); Luke 7:41 (L, Denarius); Matt 18:23–25 (M, Talent); Matt 18:28 (M, Denarius); P. Yadin 11 (Denarius), 21 (Denarius, Mina) **c) Elite or estate payment** (elite > non-elite) Mark 14:11/Matt 26:15/Luke 22:5 (Silver [Stater?]); Matt 20:2–13 (M, Denarius); Matt 28:12 (M, Soldiers' pay) **F4) Exchange value orientation: M-C-M'** Matt 25:27/Luke 19:23 (Q, Talent/Mina, "Bankers")
Bronze	**F5) Use value orientation, or money barter: C-M-C** Mark 6:37/John 6:7 (Denarius); Mark 14:5/John 12:5 (Denarius); Matt 10:29/Luke 12:6 (Q, Bronze As); Matt 13:45–46/Gos. Thom. 76 (M or Q?, "went and sold"); Matt 22:1–14/Luke 14:16–24/Gos. Thom. 64 (Q, Buying fields, oxen); Luke 10:35 (L, Denarius); Matt 27:6–7 (M, Shekel?); Rev 6:6 (Denarius)
In kind	**Barter: C-C** Luke 11:5? (with intimations of F3?)

C=Commodity, M=Money medium, M'=Money increase or profit, > direction of transaction; underlining indicates database exceptions to the metal classification system (left column).

The functions have long been recognized by economic historians. Function 3 was probably the originating intent of money in seventh-century BCE Lydia. However, the model does not outline historical-genetic relations; rather, money's political-functional logic is displayed. The model in one sense extends downward from the elite household through the elite-controlled mechanisms of taxation and debt to the preferred barter exchange within peasant villages. I find it striking therefore that the Babatha Archives, containing the personal records of a wealthy woman of En-gedi from the early second century CE, consist substantially of deposit receipts and debt contracts. These important archaeological records indicate the prevalence of the first and third functions of the model, a pattern that is repeated in the Jesus traditions. These are precisely the functions one would expect in societies whose key institutions were structured by family or power: F1 represents the need for household security and F3 the need to control others, especially those outside the family.

If F1 and F3 were prevalent in antiquity, F4 is surprisingly rare in the database I have accumulated so far. This function, expressive of an exchange-value orientation, would indicate a universal utility of money: Money buying everything (including land, labor, capital) anywhere for anyone. But such utility is not much in evidence in the material I am focusing on; and F5, use-value orientation, looks more like an extension of barter than an expression of some "economic rationality" that we would be familiar with. This general picture suggests that money functioned differently in ancient agrarian societies, which follows from a very different institutional configuration.

The classified database of money references in the Jesus traditions permits the following summary observations: Mark provides 1 instance of F1, 2 of F2, each perhaps implying F5 (John and Revelation similarly attest F2/F5 in terms of money equivalencies for bread), and 4 instances of F3. Q contains 2 instances of F1, 1 certain instance of F3, 1 of F4, and 1 certain instance of F5. L represents 1 instance of F1, 3 of F3, and 1 probable instance of F5. M represents 3 instances of F1, 6 of F3, and 1 of F5. Overall, the gospels represent 7 instances of F1, 2 of F2, 14 of F3 (5 of F3a, 6 of F3b, 3 of F3c), 1 instance of F4, and 3 explicit instances of F5.

This picture compels more nuanced social conclusions. Function 1 is securely attested, though the instances of gold and silver are only in elite connections. Mark 6:8 provides perhaps the only non-elite instance. Function 2 appears directly only in Mark, John, and Revelation. This fact, and the sizable sums involved in Mark and John (200, 300 *denarii*), leaves a rather unclear picture of the social significance to be inferred. I will return to this matter in a moment in the Excursus.

F3 is most frequently attested. The many examples of money involved with taxation or in debt transactions show the reality of power behind money and the political significance of money.

F4 is rarely attested. Moneychanging is the only explicit context, with nothing in the Jesus traditions to show increase of money through commercial transactions. Only three instances of use-value operation (F5) are clearly discernable (Q/Luke 12:6/Matt 10:29; L/Luke 10:35; M/Matt 27:10). Of these, L and M demonstrate use value operating for the elite, while the Q passage alone shows the everyday use value of bronze coins. The rarity of F4 (only in Q/Luke 19:23/Matt 25:27), taken with the less rare F5, should persuade us that money did not function in the social world of the gospels as it does in the modern world (where F4 and F5 are major dimensions). How many of the instances of F2 should be understood as implying F5 is unclear. The rare appearance of a money of "general utility," and the heavy use of money for value storage (hoarding) and payment standards (taxes and debts) implies a monetary functionality in Jesus' day notably different from our experience.

Function 5 especially shows what is at stake politically even with bronze coinage: Peasants ordinarily want to see something for barter exchange. The interposition of money means that the peasant family holds a token in place of some real good; but a token cannot be eaten, so a peasant will prefer barter. Holding a token is a form of indebtedness.[13] But if political pressures impose a bronze currency and enforce its use (especially through legal debt instruments or by requiring taxes to be paid in money), then peasant exchanges based upon generalized reciprocity can be "converted" by political alchemy into exchanges of balanced reciprocity accountable in money. Thus, the political authority can better assess full agrarian production and maximize the taxation take.

Careful consideration of the functions of money in Jesus' social environment underscores how money was a crucial element in a *political* economy.[14] As evident through the analysis guided by the model, functions F1, F3, F4 are essentially available for gold or silver coinage only to

---

13. Daly and Cobb, *For the Common Good*, 420.
14. Rohrbaugh, "Text of Terror?," 35.

the elites or their agents. Function 2 is nominally available to the common person, but its utility (F5) seems rare and only appears in terms of "small change." In other words, people might estimate value in terms of hundreds of denarii, but few would actually command such sums at one time. Conversely, non-elites are primarily familiar with bronze provincial coinage, but unfamiliar with silver coinage. This sheds an interesting light on a text like Mark 12:16.

Overall, the analysis confirms Crawford's conclusions that the rural empire knew little of money as a universal medium of exchange.[15] Finley's three ordinary elite uses for money—in strongbox, in land, or on loan—are also clearly evident in the gospels.[16]

EXCURSUS I

A way to specify these insights further is in terms of "market." What was the extent or depth of ancient market relations? What was their essential social character? While a complete answer cannot be given here, a perusal of Gospel passages related to *agora* or relations of buying and selling offers some hints.

Instances of the use of *agora* in a Jerusalem setting need to be bracketed out as unrepresentative because characteristic of a city of pilgrimage (Mark 12:38 and pars.; include here Luke 11:43). Generally, "market" in our sense was developed somewhat in Roman-period cities and perhaps towns.

This leaves several passages of interest regarding the *marketplace*. Q/ Luke 7:32/Matt 11:16 shows children sitting there; however, no monied relations are indicated, children were not subject to the same social constraints as adults, and the Q tradents would have been familiar with town- and city-markets. Mark 6:56 likewise shows a place for the sick to be laid, but no monied relations are in view. Only M/Matt 20:3 depicts idle laborers, with estate-owner having access to hire them. This suggests privilege on the part of the landlord, and the vulnerability of labor is surmised. We do not have, in the canonical Gospels, an overwhelming depiction for Roman Palestine of widespread market relations in our sense.

As far as *agorazō* or *pōleō* are concerned, or the monetary relations concomitant with markets, Jerusalem passages are again bracketed. John

15. Crawford, "Money and Exchange," 43.

16. Finley, *Ancient Economy*, 116.

4:8 also shows the possibility of food purchase at Sebaste. The most signifi-cant instances seem to be these: For *agorazō* Q?/Luke 14:18–19 (buying field, 5 yoke of oxen); Q/Luke 17:28 (buying in Noah's day); M/Matt 13:44, 45 (buying field, pearl); and Mark 6:36–37 and pars. (feeding). For *pōleō* Q/Luke 12:6 (5 sparrows/2 *assaria* or 2/1); Q/Luke 17:28 (selling in Noah's day); M/Matt 13:44, 46 (selling all for hidden treasure, for pearl). Q/Luke 12:6 might reflect the experience of the average villager (but what were the sparrows for?); the reference to Noah is associated with the Q-tradents' experiences perhaps in Capernaum or Chorazin. The remain-ing instances indicate market functions that would be accessible to the wealthy, for whom we are willing to concede access to both market and the exchange value function of money.

The feeding of the multitudes also seems to presuppose the availability of bread in the market, but a comparison of Mark 6:36–37 and John 6:5, 7 suggest that irony, exasperation, and improbability may be as much the point about buying as the presumption of wide-spread market-relations.

We conclude this excursus by saying that the picture developed through the model is reflected also in a study of buying and selling: In Roman Palestine, *monetization* had proceeded apace in the service of the controlling interests of debt and taxation, while *marketization* in terms of money was limited to towns and cities, with access controlled by the powerful except for exchanges of political-economic insignificance.

A thorough-going study of the Jesus traditions through the lense of the model leads to thesis 3.

THESIS 3:

Jesus mounted a radical critique of money and Mammon.

Space permits only a statement of the broad outlines of this argument: Money in Jesus' day was an elite political tool, not a universal economic medium. It benefited the powerful inordinately, but held captive values esteemed by common folk. Money for tax collection purposes, in safety deposits, or on loan to the weak and powerless characterized money's general appearance. Jesus called these security arrangements "Mammon," from the Aramaic word at root meaning *trust*. Taxes, deposits, and loan receipts were items trusted by the powerful to provide future security. To this, Jesus responded, "You cannot serve God and Mammon" (Luke

16:13). A critique of such arrangements is still visible in Mark 10:29–31; Q/Luke 19:11–27; L/Luke 12:16–20; and L/Luke 16:1–8.

For Jesus, "God or Mammon" specifies another social modality radically independent of money. In seeing this, Luke 11:5–13 is very instructive. Luke 11:5–8 belongs to L; Luke 11:9–13 belongs to Q (Matt 7:7–11). The link seems forged by Luke. Notice, Luke's redactional framework is centered on prayer (11:1, 13). At the Lukan level, the subject matter has to do with patronage.

Despite redaction, the Friend at Midnight pericope illumines the words of Jesus in Luke 11:9–13 in a peculiarly substantive way. The neighbor's importunity is often seen as the point of the similitude, but I take the second *autou* of 11:8 to refer to the man in bed, not the man at the door. Besides, a truly shameless man would not be at the door at midnight out of sight of everyone. The meaning of the similitude does hinge upon the word *anaideian*. Egyptian papyri strongly urge the meaning "shameless desire for personal gain."[17] The point then is: The man in bed may not get up at midnight to provide for an embarrassed neighbor, but to keep the other in debt he certainly will. The "friend" will make a loan at midnight on this basis. In this vignette, relations of "balanced reciprocity," where accounting for exchanges is noted and enforceable, are prominently in view.

In Luke 11:9–13, by contrast, another sort of relations come into focus. The similitude in Luke 11:11–12 provides commentary, wittingly or unwittingly, on the Friend at Midnight story. The Jesus similitude asks whether fathers would try to meet their children's needs by offering them stones/serpents/scorpions. When the children ask for bread/fish/eggs, the natural course is to make these provisions. What does this similitude drive at?

Within a non-elite purview, Jesus asks whether money is of any real use at all. Theissen's *Lokalkolorit* method may be of assistance here: to the villager the coins are worth no more than stones.[18] Consideration of the images on Gratus or Pilate coins suggests derivation for Jesus' other metaphors: *Caduceus* or *Lituus*—emblems of numinous imperial power—were to villagers ironically suggestive of common scourges of the Galilee—serpent-ready-to-strike or scorpion's stinger.

17. Moulton and Milligan, *Vocabulary of the Greek Testament*, s.v. *anaideia*.
18. Theissen, *Lokalkolorit und Zeitgeschichte* = *Gospels in Context*.

Strikingly, the juxtaposition of Luke 11:5–8 and 9–13 illuminates the role of money as exchange "cipher." The Friend at Midnight pericope shows how debt works to control people in basic exchange relations. Money plays a pivotal role in facilitating such indebtedness. Money acquired through debt may be placed in deposit, become an object of trust and security. From the peasant villager's perspective, money barter is useless. What father would think of giving his children stones/serpents/scorpions to meet real needs? What peasant wants to hold money instead of bread? But money is now more necessary than bread.

The Lukan material reveals a connection between the critique of Mammon and a more radical (non-elite) critique of money. Jesus rarely mentions money barter (only at Q/Luke 12:6/Matt 10:29). Most often, the Jesus tradition laments the problem of indebtedness, which is really the end result for the powerless of money transactions in pre-industrial societies.[19] Important elements of the Jesus tradition shed indirect light on Jesus' hostility to Mammon, to money on deposit, or to commercial and money transactions generally (Luke 12:16–20; Mark 11:15–16).

Other elements of the Jesus tradition become intelligible in the light of a radical critique of money. There is sense in injunctions like Q/Luke 6:30/Matt 5:42/*Gos. Thom.* 95. "God" in the dilemma "God or Mammon" represents in part (not to be too reductionistic) relations of general reciprocity, wherein exchanges are gifts, accounting is forsworn, and the basic "currency" is trust itself—trust between God and humans, trust between humans.[20] Mammon as an idolatrous trust-center apart from God represents a terminal disruption in the social construction project that Jesus envisions.

The point of Luke 11:11–12 in the original setting of Jesus, therefore, had to do with a radical rejection of money in favor of the mutuality of the Kingdom of God. Luke 16:13 likewise rejected trust in Mammon in the interest of God's gracious benefactions worked out through human gift-giving (see L/Q?/Luke 6:34–36; Q/Luke 11:3; Q/Luke 12:29–31). We can understand why the one saying of Jesus preserved in the New Testament outside of the gospels was this: "It is more blessed to give than to receive" (Acts 20:35).

---

19. Childe, *What Happened in History?*, 166–68, 202.
20. Malina, "Patron and Client."

EXCURSUS 2

Something has to be said about the *glōssokomon* ("money-case" or "money box") of John 12:6 and 13:29 in relationship to what is claimed about Jesus' attitude to money. These passages, combined with the evidence of Acts 2:45; 4:32; or 4:37, might suggest less a radical rejection of the institution of money than a reconfiguration of the use of money (also in accord with Jesus' critique of Mammon). Several things in my mind speak against this interpretation: 1) A "Qumran reading" of Jesus and money has likely crept into Acts and is to be understood both as a perspective conditioned by elites and as Lukan anachronism, 2) the picture of John 12 and 13, moreover, may not depict Judas so much as "treasurer" for Jesus' followers as a security arrangement adopted by Jerusalem pilgrims (redemption money to be spent in Jerusalem?), again indirect testimony to the political nature of money.[21] We might recall in this connection the coin hoard found on Mt. Carmel in 1960, containing 4,560 Tyrian *tetradrachmas* (3,400) and *didrachmas* (1,160), it was perhaps on its way to Jerusalem but never reached its destination.[22]

A striking fact about money in the New Testament outside of the gospels and Revelation is the generic nature of its designation. Money of any specific denomination (denarius, stater, etc.) appears only in the gospels and Revelation. Paul of course refers to the collection for the poor of Jerusalem, but he refers to money only by indirection (2 Cor 8–9; 1 Cor 16:2). Later, "money" is designated either by *chrēmata* or simply under the generic labels "silver" or "gold."

FINALLY, THESIS 4:

The early Christian tradition softened Jesus' critique to focus on the moral dangers of "love of money," more apparent to those who had money than to those who did not.

Initially in Galilee, the scribes who shaped the original Q material (perhaps town accountants) reflected on the dangers of Mammon (Luke 16:13) and preserved some of Jesus' basic concerns (Luke 11:9–13). Mark's scribal tradition also incorporates non-elite perspectives to a significant degree.[23]

---

21. Brown, *Death of the Messiah*, 244.
22. Rousseau and Arav, *Jesus and His World*, 56.
23. Rohrbaugh, "Social Location"; Theissen, *Gospels in Context*, 236–49.

The views of people within the kinship networks of provincial urban elites of the empire shaped these early Jesus traditions.

While the social background of New Testament writers beyond the gospels is obscure, it is reasonable to say that many of them evidence a commercial literacy reflective of freedmen interests.[24] The greatest preoccupation with love of money appears in Acts, the Catholic Epistles, Hebrews, and the Pastorals. These documents attest to the spread of the urbanizing Christian movement throughout the Eastern empire. They show, as in James 5 or Acts 4–5, the need to reckon with moneyed interests. The interests displayed do not question the value or utility of money, only its moral place in the heart. Such sentiments fundamentally speak out of an elite consciousness: The views of people within the kinship networks of powerful urban-imperial elites now strike the dominant note in the movement. Not surprisingly, when Matthew had incorporated earlier traditions into what was to become the authoritative gospel, elite views of money came to prevail (as the M-material shows).

Conclusion

The Jesus traditions retain an echo of a vigorous critique of political economy and its exploitative monetary system in the interests of urging the alternative "network" of the Kingdom of God, with exchanges of goods organized through principles of generalized reciprocity. Outside of the gospels, with the single exception of Revelation which maintained this vigorous critique of the Roman imperial order, Jesus' negative view of money was dropped in favor of moralisms about "love of money." Such moral exhortation made sense to commercial types whose livelihoods depended upon Roman currency, but whose fidelity to Jesus needed acknowledgment as well. For Jesus, money was at the heart of evil apart from God's rule. The compromise worked out in nascent Christian tradition—seeing money's love as the danger—has maintained its salience in Western culture ever since.

---

24. Meeks, *First Urban Christians*; Rohrbaugh, "Social Location," 115–17.

CHAPTER 8

The Economics of Palestine

T HE ECONOMIC HISTORIAN KARL Polanyi noted that there have been two senses of the word "economic": 1) a substantive economics that strives to provide the necessities of life for the individual, family, tribe, or society; and 2) a formal economics that refers to rational choices between scarce means in the pursuit of human ends.

While both of these senses are applicable to antiquity, the ancients tended to think consciously about economics primarily in the first sense. For them, economics had essentially to do with the management of the household (Greek *eco/oikos*, house; *nomia*, management). "Household" could mean the family homestead, the large estate, or even the imperial realm. Since the fundament of ancient economics was agriculture, both Greek and Roman literature produced moralistic treatises on this subject (Xenophon, Cato). In NT times, the Roman Empire was managed by the imperial powers as an extended household. Easy access to the Mediterranean Sea encouraged maritime trade in the Hellenistic-Roman periods, but this was controlled by elites or their agents (Trimalchio in *The Satyricon* of Petronius).

Thus, it is equally crucial in considering the economics of Palestine in the biblical periods to keep in mind that social ends were determined at all times by powerful elites and so ancient economy was "political economy." Moreover, in the conservative, traditional agrarian societies of antiquity, individual or even group "economic choice" was a relatively limited factor in the context of larger ecological and social forces.

1. Palestine as a Region of Mediterranean Ecological Adaptation

2. Agrarian Economy and Society within the Bible

3. The Economic Values of Jesus

4. Economic Factors in Early Christianity and the Later NT Period

PALESTINE AS A REGION OF MEDITERRANEAN ECOLOGICAL ADAPTATION

Fernand Braudel referred to the Mediterranean region as the land around the Mediterranean Sea from the limit of the olive to the north to the appearance of the palm to the south. As a part of the Mediterranean littoral, Palestine has always been characterized by peculiar ecological factors pertinent to a discussion of economics. Geology and climate have unquestionably shaped ecological-economic dynamics and related human adaptations. Since the Cretaceous Period, the Mediterranean area has experienced severe faulting and on the south tectonic stresses and repeated encroachments by the sea itself. The geology of Palestine shows these features well in its abrupt transitions between lowlands and mountain, its extensive limestone formations, combined to the north with volcanic features; and its rainfall and weather patterns that produce the typical Mediterranean vegetation pattern of "evergreen thicket-woodland."[1]

The Mediterranean climate of Palestine produces rainfall in the winter and drought in the summer. With as little as 50 millimeters annually in the Negev increasing to 800 millimeters or more in Upper Galilee and the Lebanese Mountains, dry-farming methods of agriculture need to prevail. Plowing breaks only the topsoil in order to preserve the subsoil moisture; grains and trees are naturally selected that have quick growing properties or can survive the annual drought. The Bible, therefore, characterizes Canaan as "a land of wheat and barley, of vines and fig trees and pomegranates, a land of olive trees and honey" (Deut 8:8 NRSV). The difficulty of agriculture in ancient Palestine is also acknowledged (Gen 3:17–19). Biblical parables often speak through the imagery of the typical vegetation (Judg 9:8–15) or familiar agricultural operations such as sowing (Mark 4:3), harvesting grain (Mark 4:29), or gathering the vintage (Matt 20:1; see Rev 14:19–20).

The main agricultural objects of production were grain, especially barley and wheat, olives for oil, and grapes for wine. Grain, wine, and oil

---

1. Hepper, *Baker Encyclopedia of Bible Plants.*

were the staples of life (Hos 9:2, 4; Prov 9:5; Neh 5:11). Grain was harvested in late spring and early summer; grapes were gathered and processed in
summer, olives in early fall. The early rains of September–October helped
to prepare the soil hardened by drought for plowing. Once sown, growing
grain had to be weeded and was threatened by many natural predators
(Matt 13:26; Mark 4:4–7). The late rains of winter helped the cereals to
mature toward harvest in late-spring. The average yield was around five-
fold, compared to 30–40 fold today (aided by modern fertilizers). Fig and
olive trees often appear in the Bible because they, along with the grapevine,
can withstand the summer drought. Such trees have wide-spreading or
deep root systems to capture water, and pass a minimal amount of moisture to the air through their leaves. Fig and olive trees take time to come
into bearing years, and so are associated in the Bible with peaceful times (1
Kgs 4:25; Mic 4:4; 1 Macc 14:12).

Herding played an important role in biblical economy as well. Goat's
milk and cheese supplemented the proteins and calories from grain and oil.
Sheep appear in biblical parables (2 Sam 12:1–4; Luke 15:3–7). Animals
might be sacrificed for their meat, though ordinary people partook of
meat only on important occasions (Luke 15:23). The temple economy depended upon significant numbers of animal-offerings per year (Josephus,
Ant. 3.224–232).

Some generalizations can be made about the organization of production and labor, as well as distribution and consumption, in the biblical
periods. Preindustrial societies depended mainly upon human and animal
energies devoted to producing enough to eat. Such societies have been
called "agrarian societies," because they were made possible by the plow
(Lenski). In agrarian societies, a social chasm always existed between the
relative few elite urban and town dwellers whose energies were devoted
to politics or religious occupations and the many villagers who tilled the
soil. The finite surplus made possible by preindustrial agricultural placed
restraints upon the absolute size of the elite. The long sweep of ancient
Near Eastern history witnessed a succession of "world empires" whose
civilizations were dependent upon collecting the agrarian surpluses of the
sedentary agriculturalists. The earliest known writings often have to do
with accounting in royal and temple operations. Village economy in such
empires was focused on domestic need and agriculture; urban economy was
based on taxation of surplus and redistribution for elite ends. While the
Greco-Roman society of the NT period was certainly more complex than

predecessor societies, especially in the encouragement of Mediterranean commerce, its population was still divided between the majority who labored (around 90 percent) and the elite fraction of the population who did not and whose estates worked by tenants or slaves supplied the necessities of life (Matt 13:24–30; Luke 12:16–21). Strong rulers could also utilize peasant labor to build aqueducts, temples, palaces, and cities (Herod the Great: Sebaste, Caesarea Maritima, Jerusalem).

Josephus' claim that "ours is not a maritime country" (*Ag. Ap.* 1.60) rings true for the biblical literature, except that in special circumstances elites did take advantage of trading opportunities offered by caravans to the east or sea-lanes to the west. Both villager and elite citydweller sought "self-sufficiency," having all of the necessaries stored up or readily available nearby. Commercial ventures, and fine imported wines and wares, were only available to powerful elites. Pliny relates that frankincense caravan tolls for a trip from Sabota (in Arabia) to Gaza on the Mediterranean coast ran to 688 *denarii* per camel (*Nat. Hist.* 12.63–65; *denarius* a day's wage on an estate, Matt 20:2).

Villagers not only labored to raise agricultural produce, but also made their own clothing, sandals, simple tools, and even houses. Specialists, usually holding monopolistic power and controlled by powerful families, produced pottery, glass vessels, metal tools and weaponry, fine furniture, and the like. Literate elites, nonetheless, looked down on all who worked with their hands (Sir 38:25–34). Free markets hardly existed in the ancient world; participants in urban markets, except for small-value exchanges, participated on very unequal terms. Money was essentially an elite tool to facilitate tax collection or to aid elite-sponsored commerce. For the majority of the population, there was barely enough to eat after taxes.

Such an ecological adaptation encouraged certain values within biblical culture. Low productivity (and social inequities) encouraged a notion of limited good, in which the goods of life were believed to have been distributed and could not be increased absolutely (in contrast to modern, postindustrial values where productivity is ever-increasing). Biblical references to the "evil eye" are manifestations of limited-good beliefs—evil eye refers to the envious glance that would lead to seizure of what is not rightfully one's own (Prov 23:1–6; 28:22; Matt 20:15).

AGRARIAN ECONOMY AND SOCIETY WITHIN THE BIBLE

Economic justice was a constant preoccupation in biblical times. Walter Brueggemann indeed has identified a useful paradigm by which to discuss social tensions within Israelite traditions. In discussing the "royal consciousness" exhibited by Pharaoh in Egypt and again by Israelite monarchs like Solomon, Brueggemann analyzes agrarian social dynamics in terms of a politics of oppression, an economics of affluence, and a religion of immanence. Just as Rameses II, a god on earth, had conscripted the Israelites as forced labor (Exod 1:11), so Solomon was remembered ambivalently by the Deuteronomistic Historians as both wise and oppressive (1 Kgs 4:29–31; 5:13 contrasts with 9:15–22). The usurpations of Israelite kings were condemned in traditions like 1 Sam 8:11–18 or the story of Naboth's vineyard (1 Kgs 21). Conversely, Moses and the prophets appear as Yahweh's champions, as critics of a religious ideology that simply underwrites the royal arrangements. Elite economics is thus organized around the provisioning of the royal estate (1 Kgs 4:22–28) as well as the royal temple (1 Kgs 6).

Biblical law, which borrowed liberally from earlier Mesopotamian collections, is concerned with justice in economic arrangements—for instance, regarding slaves (Exod 21:2–11; Deut 15:12–18), property and damages (Exod 22), or the regulation of debt (Deut 15). The classical prophets, with varying emphasis, denounce "immanent religion" and economic injustice (Amos 5:21–24; 8:4–6; Isa 1:10–17; Mic 2:1–2). Of special concern are the widow and the orphan (Exod 22:22; Isa 1:17). Israelite wisdom too mulls over the plight of the poor and the persistence of the wicked wealthy (Prov 22:16, 22–23; Eccl 4:1–3). Poverty in the Bible means not only powerlessness and physical want, but also public disgrace and shame.[2]

The context of Jesus likewise was afflicted by social disparities and concerns (Luke 16:19–31). In his day, Palestine had been under the control of great world empires since the Babylonian Exile. Hasmonean rule (1 Macc 13:41–42) marked about a century's exception (142–63 BCE). The house of Herod the Great provided client rule for the Romans at the turn of the eras. Jesus' parables often describe the typical social features of a colonial situation with large estates controlled by absentee landlords: a landlord's departure provides the occasion for moneylending by retainers

2. Malina, "Wealth and Poverty."

(Luke 19:12–27). A landlord has to resort to violence to collect the rent (Mark 12:1–9). A tax collector secures the tax with his own body (Matt 18:23–34). Estate stewards (*oikonomoi*, household managers) and slaves make frequent appearances (Luke 12:42; 16:1–8; Mark 13:34–35).

Many of these social features are common to agrarian or peasant societies. Comparative studies have shown that preindustrial societies often have enormous social disparities and inequities, that economic phenomena are controlled by powerful centralized or urban elites, and that injustice is regularly experienced by the majority. The biblical traditions set the stage for a more hopeful type of human relations. Such hopes come into sharp focus in some of the Mosaic traditions, the prophets, and especially Jesus of Nazareth.

THE ECONOMIC VALUES OF JESUS

In the past few years, the Third Quest for the historical Jesus and Galilean studies enhanced by archaeology have reinvigorated the question of the relationship of the historical activity of Jesus of Nazareth to economic dimensions of his contemporary society. While many aspects of this discussion are as yet undecided, and debate centers especially around the social character of Jesus' environment and the movement which emerged through his activity, it is clear that Jesus paid careful attention to "economic phenomena." These were entwined with the meaning of his work, and understanding those phenomena can enhance our understanding of Jesus.

Central to the vision of Jesus of Nazareth was his conviction that the reign of God/heaven (Aram. *malkûtha' delaha/dishmaya'*) was imminent or even present in his activity. Scholars debate today the degree to which Jesus' vision should be construed through wisdom perspectives (God's reign is integral to creation or the natural order, Luke 12:22–31) or through apocalyptic Jewish elements (which surely appear in the gospels, Mark 13:26–27). The question of the meaning of the reign of God for Jesus depends upon such assessments.

There is strong evidence that Jesus associated God's reign with his own activity. It is quite likely that some aspects of this phrase resonated with the views of Judas the Gaulanite or Galilean (Josephus, *Ant.* 18.4, 23), since Jesus gained a following in the vicinity of the Galilean Lake. Jesus can refer to God's power at work in his exorcisms (Luke 11:20, alluding to

Ex 8:19). He also showed strong interest in Passover, the time for remembrance of God's liberation of the Israelites from Egyptian bondage. The Passion Narratives link Jesus' understanding of God's reign with Passover (Mark 14:22–25 and par). There are perhaps echoes of the beginning of the Passover Haggadah in Jesus' Q-Sermon:

> *Passover Haggadah* (Aramaic introduction): This is the bread of poverty which our forefathers ate in the land of Egypt. Let all who are hungry enter and eat; let all who are needy come to our Passover feast. This year we are here; next year may we be in the Land of Israel. This year we are slaves; next year may we be free men.[3]

PASSOVER HAGGADAH	Q-BEATITUDES (LUKE 6:20–21)
The bread of poverty	How honorable are you poor
Let all who are hungry	How honorable are the hungry
This year we are here	How honorable are those who mourn

Central in the early Jesus traditions is also a concern for debt and taxation. The politics of oppression familiar to first-century Galileans had to do with the Roman colonial arrangements of client rule. After Judas the Gaulanite and the revolt surrounding the census of 6 CE, questions about taxation became loaded. Jesus did not speak openly against imperial taxation (Mark 12:17), but did suggest to his disciples that the "sons are free" of temple taxation (Matt 17:26).

God's rule is related directly to release from indebtedness (and concomitant taxation) in the Lord's Prayer (Luke 11:2–4/Matt 6:9–13). While a complete analysis of the Prayer is not possible here, the petitions seem internally integrated by reference to social-systemic problems: Hunger (Luke 2:3/Matt 6:11) is a function of indebtedness (to landlord or overlord; Luke 2:4a/Matt 6:12), and the courts enforced debt contracts (Luke 11:4b/Matt 6:13) if the tradition about Hillel's *prosbol* is to be trusted (*m. Sheb.* 10:3–7; *b. Git.* 37a; Murabba'at 18, a mid-first-century debt contract from the Dead Sea area, secures a loan without the *prosbol*). Relations of indebtedness have as their social corollary that the few will have security in more than they need. Jesus' carries on a vigorous critique against *mamōnas* (Greek, from an Aramaic word), signifying stored wealth upon which one places one's trust (Luke 16:13; 12:16–20).

3. Glatzer, ed., *The Passover Haggadah.*

One of Jesus' strategies was to go to the friction point between the Greco-Roman order and the harassed producers. Jesus ate with tax collectors and "sinners" (debtors?) in order to achieve some relief for the indebted (Mark 2:15–16; Luke 18:9–14). The story of Zacchaeus (Luke 19:1–10), while likely fictional, captures the economic import of such associations.

Jesus thus spoke in behalf of a politics of liberation and compassion.[4] For Jesus, God's rule was a power opposed to the social order established by Rome. Its arrival offered the poor and lowly a vision of hope and new social possibilities (just as in the first Exodus). What did Jesus envision constructively as an expression of that rule? He offers a theology of paradoxical transcendence (*malkûtha*, reign) and immanence (*'Abba'*, Father!). God's rule overthrows the dominant political economy in favor of a fictive family. Political economy is to be transformed into domestic economy, a vision consonant with the traditions of Israel (Deut 15:2; Lev 25:35–46; Neh 5:6–13).

Relations within Jesus' entourage are to be modeled on those of close kin. Exchanges are to take place through arrangements of generalized reciprocity (Luke 6:27–36; 14:12–14; Matt 18:23–34). Generalized reciprocity, unlike the redistributive arrangements of the dominant powers, takes no accounting of exchanges. Seeking the reign of God first will bring carefree economic security and true happiness (Luke 12:22–31; Mark 10:29–30).

Jesus' vision of the reign of God, and his concomitant call for human solidarity against injustice through fictive kin relations, apparently was rejected by worldly-wise villagers. The message made sense to fishers and some alienated peasants, but Jesus' reception in Nazareth seems to have been typical (Mark 6:4). He garnered no large-scale peasant following. No vestiges of Galilean "Christianity" are apparent in the years after his death. The horizon of most peasants is limited; discontent does not often consolidate into transvillage movements. When Jesus' was crucified in Jerusalem as a "bandit," a rebel against the Roman order, not only did his popular support vanish, but also he was abandoned for a time even by his close associates. Experience of his resurrection signified a new stage of his cause, and his message would be carried beyond Palestine within a new social stratum.

4. Borg, *Jesus*.

ECONOMIC FACTORS IN EARLY CHRISTIANITY
AND THE LATER NT PERIOD

Jesus' hope for a more humane economic order did not die. The gospels continued to mediate his economic interests and values to later Christian communities, though interests appropriate to town and urban contexts also come into view. Wayne Meeks gives evidence that a substantial role was played in early Christian communities by freedmen, those former slaves who were now legally free though sometimes still obligated to former patrons. Freedmen tended to be involved in trade and commercial pursuits, a point which seems generally corroborated about leaders in the Christian circles of the eastern Mediterranean by the Acts of the Apostles (e.g., Acts 16:14–15; 18:2–3).

Such interests are already evident in the Pauline literature. Paul indicates that urban Christian groups such as in Corinth are comprised of few who could be recognized as elite (1 Cor 1:26; note that birth and power are key social variables, not economics). The Corinthian community is sundered by inequities of social power and wealth (1 Cor 11:22). It is patronized by a powerful people like Erastus, the city treasurer (Rom 16:23), but networks with others who have lesser status (Stephanus, 1 Cor 16:15). The Corinthian correspondence well illustrates that early Christian groups were organized around households, with the more powerful and wealthy as sponsors of a fictive-kinship assembly/*ecclesia* (1 Cor 16:15, 19; Phlmn 1–2). Dieter Georgi has argued that Paul's collection (1 Cor 16:1–4; 2 Cor 8–9) was an animating issue in his historical activity, both an expression of solidarity with the Jerusalem church (Gal 2:10) and a statement of conviction about the eschatological ingathering of the Gentiles anticipated in the Israelite prophetic tradition (Isa 45:14, 20, 22–25). This collection already represents an anomaly in terms of Jesus' interests, since a collection is a redistributive tax (like the temple tax sent in the first century by Diaspora Jews to Jerusalem).

In the later first century, issues of political economy present recurrent moral difficulties for the developing Christian movement. Revelation states the situation in apocalyptic terms (13:16–17; 18:3, 9, 11, 15–18). Jesus' loyal followers are those who have no truck with Roman commerce (Rev 2:9; 3:8, 17; 13:16–17). Others, however, are perceived to have been permanently corrupted (Rev 2:14–15, 20; 3:9; probably cryptic references to Christians who compromise with Greco-Roman culture in pursuit of economic interests). Acts provides a more irenic picture of the Christian position under the Roman Empire. Roman justice furthers the interests of the movement (Acts 18:15; 26:31–32). Commerce is not demonized as in Revelation (or the *Gos. Thom.* 64). Moreover, economic relations within the early Christian community are viewed in communistic terms (Acts 2:44–45; 4:32, 36–37; see 1QS 6:22).

The paraenesis of James identifies central economic problems for the future. As the Christian movement experienced success, wealth became a divisive issue (Jas 2:1–7) and social injustice emerged clearly as an intra-Christian concern (Jas 2:16; 5:4). James exhorts the wealthy to take stock (1:9–10; 5:1–6) and to practice the royal law of neighborly love (2:8; cf. 1:25). With similar moral stress, Acts reports that "[Jesus] himself said, 'It is more honorable to give than to receive'" (20:35, the only explicit Jesus-saying in the NT preserved outside the gospels; see Luke 22:26). The moral standing of wealth becomes a permanent concern of the Christian tradition, leading to later developments such as Clement of Alexandria's treatise *Quis dives salvetur?*, the Franciscan movement in medieval Italy, or the Anabaptist communities of the Reformation. Jesus' followers are still left perhaps with uneasy consciences in times that celebrate mammon and the successes of industrial and technological capitalism.[5]

5. The following works appeared in the original bibliography for this chapter: Bailey, "Agriculture," "Clothing," "Crafts," "Houses, Furniture, Utensils," "Trade and Transport"; Borg, *Jesus: A New Vision*; Braudel, *The Mediterranean and the Mediterranean World in the Age of Philip II*; Brueggemann, *Prophetic Imagination*; Countryman, *The Rich Christian in the Church of the Early Empire*; Georgi, *Remembering the Poor*; Glatzer, *Passover Haggadah*; Hanson and Oakman, *Palestine in the Time of Jesus*; Hepper, *Baker Encyclopedia of Bible Plants*; Horsley, *Jesus and the Spiral of Violence*; idem, *Galilee: History, Politics, People*; idem, *Archaeology, History, and Society in Galilee*; Kautsky, *The Politics of Aristocratic Empires*; Lenski, *Power and Privilege*; Malina, "Wealth and Poverty in the New Testament and Its World"; Matthews, *Manners and Customs in the Bible*; Meeks, *The First Urban Christians*; Moxnes, *The Economy of the Kingdom*; Oakman, *Jesus and the Economic Questions of His Day*; idem, "The Archaeology of First-Century Galilee and the Social Interpretation of the Historical Jesus"; idem, "The Ancient Economy"; Pilch and Malina, eds., *Biblical Social Values and Their Meaning*; Polanyi, *The Livelihood of Man*; Rohrbaugh, *The Biblical Interpreter*; Rousseau and Arav, *Jesus and His World*; Safrai, *The Economy of Roman Palestine*; Schmidt, "Taxes"; Theissen, *The Social Setting of Pauline Christianity*.

⌘ PART II

The Jesus Traditions
within Peasant Realities

CHAPTER 9

Social Meaning and Rural Context: The Mustard Seed Parable of Jesus[1]

THE MUSTARD SEED PARABLE, at least at the (then) most recent meeting of the Jesus Seminar in Redlands (spring 1986), was considered fundament of the parabolic bedrock of the Jesus tradition. Therefore, it is probably a good place to begin for exploring the meaning of the Jesus tradition within a rural context.

A moment must first be devoted to discussing the heuristic value of the concept "rural context." The ancient historian Geoffrey de Ste. Croix has written:

> We must begin with the central fact about Christian origins, to which theologians and New Testament scholars have never (as far as I am aware) given anything like the emphasis it deserves: that although the earliest surviving Christian documents are in Greek and although Christianity spread from city to city in the Graeco-Roman world, its Founder lived and preached almost entirely outside the area of Graeco-Roman civilisation proper.[2]

This characterization of de Ste. Croix is certainly overdrawn; but it contains a mustard seed of truth as well. The tentacles of Graeco-Roman civilization extended into the Lower Galilee of Jesus, as the work of Eric Meyers shows. Imperial bailiffs stood over the estates in the Esdraelon not far from Nazareth. Sepphoris, Tiberias, Julias (Bethsaida), Caesarea Philippi, and the cities of the Decapolis were oriented more or less toward the values of

---

1. This chapter was first presented as a paper to the late-spring 1986 Pacific Regional AAR/SBL meeting at Santa Clara University. It has not been previously published.

2. De Ste. Croix, *Class Struggle*, 427.

the empire. Antipas, Philip, and pro-Roman Herodians controlled northern Palestine for many years.

These facts, nonetheless, cannot lead us to forget that most of the
population was engaged directly in some kind of agricultural work. These
people in their villages had other interests. They tenaciously held to old
traditions. Probably they resented the presence of Hellenistic civilization.[3]
They undoubtedly resented the tax collector and worried a great deal about
where their future subsistence would come from.[4] Ramsay MacMullen has
given us a feel for some of these rural attitudes and realities in his book
Roman Social Relations. It was partly out of an analogous "potting soil" of
rural discontent and resentment that social unrest, referred to in various
ways and often quite superficially by Josephus, sprouted in early Roman
Palestine.[5]

Modern peasant studies provide yet another source of inspiration
for imagining the ancient rural context of Jesus. Robert Redfield, for instance, offers a helpful typology in distinguishing the great tradition of the
dominant civilization and the little traditions of rural areas. Jesus, to some
extent, played upon little traditions, folk traditions if you will, although
he had access of course to the great religious tradition of the synagogue.
From comparative studies in folklore, we can apprehend a range of possible meanings discerned in comparable little traditions. Frequently in such
expressions, ribald humor or serious religious utterance expresses social
discontent in some way.[6]

Certainly Jesus was a lot closer to the soil and to rural agriculturalists than to urbanites and their often far-different concerns. The agrarian
imagery of the Jesus tradition implies this. New Testament scholars have
been too quick to conform the meaning of this agrarian imagery to the
dominant interests of the urban congregations of early Christians or to the
dominant Graeco-Roman culture. So Meeks, although he notes the rural
origins of Jesus and Christianity, shows little interest in explicating the
meaning of the Jesus movement in rural context. I believe the socio-political aspect of the transition from country to city remains yet to be written,

---

3. Cf. Josephus, *War* 4.105, Kedasa vs. Galilean peasants.

4. Josephus, *Life* 38, 375, Galilean peasants' hatred for Sepphoris and Tiberias = tax
collection points.

5. Josephus, *War* 2.259–263, prophets and rebellion; Richard Horsley, "'Like One of
the Prophets of Old.'"; Hobsbawm, *Primitive Rebels*.

6. Dundes, *Study of Folklore*, 308–9.

since Meeks's view seems to pass too quickly over Ebionism and the endurance of village Christianity in Syro-Palestine (e.g., *Didache*). Theissen, Schottroff, and Stegemann have already made a start in this interpretive direction.

Assuming then a "rural context" for the speech of Jesus, what meaning or set of meanings might we be able to imagine for the Mustard Seed parable? What would a rural audience have heard in it? In terms of form, Mark's and Luke's versions of this parable are considered independent, and Matthew has conflated Mark with Q (Matt 13:31–32; Mark 4:31–32; Q 13:19).[7] I assume as the basic outline of Jesus' original speech the following: a tiny seed is sown, a mustard plant grows into a large shrub, the birds of the air find shelter in the branches of the plant.

Evidence of interpretation of the mustard plant and bird imagery by means of the Old Testament picture of birds flocking to the "tree" (Ezek 17; cf. Dan 4) is available already in Matthew and Luke. Obviously the influence of the great tradition was at work. Despite the evidence that this is a later development, scholars have frequently decided that Jesus too was alluding to the tree. Funk, however, concluded that the mustard plant was a parody of the eschatological imagery of Ezekiel. In most recent interpretations of the parable, as far as I have been able to determine, the mustard plant is thought of as a positive symbolization for kingdom or faith.[8]

A number of botanical and agronomic details urge a reconsideration of the meaning of the parable. To begin with, one must ask what setting for the sowing is envisioned. The tradition is not uniform on this point. Mark's version rather non-specifically indicates ("whenever it be sown") that the seed ends up "upon the earth." Mark's version does not otherwise make explicit the agent of sowing or the locale of the final resting place of the seed. Matthew does make this explicit: *en tō agrō* ("in [his] field"). Matthew envisions therefore a cultivated field as the scene of the parable's action. Luke's version presents a significant difference. For Luke, the seed is intentionally sown in someone's garden (*kēpon*). Jeremias already noted this difference, and even recognized in it a shift to non-Palestinian horticulture. Rabbinic tradition forbade the sowing of mustard in gardens, but not on fields.[9] *Gospel of Thomas* 20, which probably represents northern

---

7. Bultmann, *History of the Synoptic Tradition*, 172; Taylor, *Mark*, 269; Fitzmyer, *Luke*, 2:1015.

8. Funk, "The Looking-Glass Tree Is for the Birds."

9. Based on *m. Kil.* 3:2, Jeremias, *Parables*, 27 and n. 11; cf. Hunzinger "*Sinapi*," 288;

Syrian tradition, agrees with Matthew in seeing the seed sown upon a cultivated field.[10] In the light of these observations, there is good reason to believe that Jesus originally had in mind a mustard plant growing in or near a field. What kind of plant and what kind of field were these?

Pliny knew three kinds of mustard plants.[11] The *Mishnah* also distinguishes three kinds, one wild and two apparently "domesticated" (*laphsân*, *hardâl*, and *hardâl miṣri* respectively).[12] The wild and either of the domesticated varieties constitute a mixed kind, according to *m. Kil.* 1:5. It is, of course, the domesticated varieties that are not to be sown in Palestinian gardens.

Today in Palestine a number of varieties of mustard plant grow wild as weeds. These are *brassica nigra* and *sinapis alba* (the black and white mustards) and *sinapis arvensis* (charlock). The mishnaic *laphsân* probably was charlock, *hardâl* was black, and *hardâl miṣri* white, mustard. In all probability, the plant of the parable of Jesus was *brassica nigra hardâl*, which has seeds of the order of 1 mm in size and can grow to a height of two meters in Galilee.

It is of some import for the interpretation of the parable to observe that mustard plants, including *brassica nigra*, have from time immemorial been found as weeds in grain fields.[13] Pliny says regarding the fecundity of mustard:

> It grows entirely wild, though it is improved by being transplanted: but on the other hand when it has once been sown it is scarcely possible to get the place free of it, as the seed when it falls germinates at once.[14]

In this quality lies the noxiousness of mustard as a weed. For as K. D. White has noted about the varieties of rye-grass (including darnel), annual plants like these could reproduce in astonishing number and outgrow the good grain crops.[15] They were thus considered weeds and constantly

---

and Smith, *Parables*, 117–18.

10 Fitzmyer, *Luke*, 2:1016, thinks this is allegory.

11 Pliny, *Nat. Hist.* 19.171.

12 Dalman, *Arbeit und Sitte*, 2:293; Str-B. 1:668.

13 Pearson, *Principles of Agronomy*, 162.

14 Pliny, *Nat. Hist.* 19.170 (Rackham, LCL); charlock can put out 1,000–4,000 seeds: Salisbury, *Weeds and Aliens*, 186.

15 White, *Roman Farming*, 137.

attacked by the farmer through various methods of cultivation. I suspect that only Jerusalemites worried about growing enough mustard for seasoning or salad. The rural folk could find plenty growing wild and constantly endangering the crops.

Returning then to the question of setting, is the mustard plant of Jesus' parable actually a cultivated plant or to be considered an unwelcome guest among the cultivated plants? The Marcan, Matthean, and Thomas versions of the parable could support the view that the plant is a wild variety of mustard whose presence was not anticipated by the cultivator. Only in Luke is it said unambiguously that the mustard is sown for the purpose of raising a condiment. Let us examine for a moment the other versions on this point. Mark, as has been noted, refers to the sowing of the plant in a temporally indefinite manner and with passive voice. Next in Mark, the smallness of the seed is stressed through a concessive participial construction. Matthew's rendition appears to give more of a purposive aspect to the sowing by using a participle, indicative active main verb, and expressed subject: "[Mustard seed] which taking, a man sowed . . ." Then Matthew follows Mark in noting the small size of the seed. The tradition in Thomas remarks upon the smallness of the seed's size first. *Gospel of Thomas* 20 agrees with Mark about the temporally indefinite time of sowing (*hotan*), and also makes no mention of human involvement in the sowing. The Thomas version expressly states that the seed falls on cultivated field. In all three versions, therefore, the link between human intention and the appearance of the plant seems tenuous. I am inclined, therefore, to understand the reference to "cultivated field" as a grain, and not mustard, field.

The smallness of the mustard seed has agronomic implications. For the Palestinian peasantry, good seed contaminated by these very small mustard seeds meant a mustard plant surprisingly and almost mysteriously appearing around harvest time. The sower would not be aware of sowing them. As an alternative to this view of the situation, Mark and Thomas (which seem to have the earliest obtainable level of the parable on this point) perhaps simply have in mind a plant "sowing" its own seed on the grain field. Mustard seeds can also lie dormant for long periods and germinate at any time, although the plants flourish especially in springtime during the grain harvest. In any case, the result is the same. A wild mustard plant grows up above the grain to mock the cultivator and to contaminate the field with more seed.

The birds roosting in the branches underscore this reading of the import of the mustard plant. To my knowledge, no scholar has ever considered in the explication of this parable that birds are natural enemies of the sown. A humorous English saying speaks of planting, "One [seed] for the rook and one for the crow, two to die and one to grow."[16] *Jubilees* 11:13–18 tells us that Abraham had a devil of a time keeping the birds away from his seeds. Yet the danger of birds is already emphasized by the parable of the Sower (Mark 4:4b and par.)! Because many scholars have immediately made a connection in the light of the great Jewish tradition between the birds roosting in the "tree" and the gentiles, the birds have become a positive symbol.[17]

If the foregoing reading of the parable is accepted, then the power and surprising appearance of weeds amidst the grain is brought to expression. The birds follow soon after. The audience or hearer is asked to reflect upon how the reign of God is like this situation.

It is hard to escape the conclusion that Jesus deliberately likens the rule of God to a harvest time weed. The presence of the weed allows birds to roost and to meet their needs for food. Yet for the sown, the weed is no blessing. The plant promises to spoil the whole field when it reseeds itself. The birds will make off with at least part of the crop. As a metaphor for the reign of God, this "weed" stands over against the basic arrangements of civilization. It threatens the foundation of the edifice in its threat to the cultivated field. Furthermore, recalling what Pliny tells us about mustard, once it is there, one cannot be rid of it.

A consideration of the other mustard seed reference in the gospels perhaps supports this interpretation (Matt 17:20/Luke 17:5–6; cf. Mark 11:23 and *Gos. Thom.* 48, 106). There are, of course, critical problems in clarifying the interrelationship between the faith saying of Jesus and the mountain, the fig tree, and the sycamine (or sycamore) tree. This critical problem is resolved on at least one level by the question of verisimilitude. In Luke's version, where mustard seed-sized faith can remove a sycamine tree, the stress falls upon the quasi-magical dimension of faith. However, in Matthew's version there is a discernible connection with reality, though hyperbole is also present. Anyone who has concerned themselves with Palestinian archaeology will know with what surprising power "grass in

16. Salisbury, *Weeds and Aliens*, 32; birds also eat the mustard seeds, see Str-B. 1:668.

17. Fitzmyer, *Luke*, 2:1017 note *ad loc.*; Smith, *Parables*, 120–21.

the cracks" can demolish the piles of stone comprising fortified walls. It is perhaps to this power of weeds in the cracks of the walls of civilization that Jesus is referring.[18] The fact that the saying is addressed to "you" (plural) is also significant. Jesus tells the audience, "If you have the faith to act in concert, [then you can have the same power as the mustard plant growing in the cracks]." The other versions of this saying, even in Thomas, imply in one way or another the establishment of community and concerted action. Moreover, the image is complete if the "mountain" alludes to the Temple platform.

The important thing to note is that once again the destructive power of mustard seed is utilized to explicate the meaning of the reign of God or faith. This kingdom has a social dimension and even threatens the Temple edifice.

A few remarks about the general meaning of the Jesus tradition conclude this chapter. We have to be cognizant, it seems to me, of the social "tendency" in the early church's transmission of the Jesus tradition. Educated tradents tended to over-theologize. The interests of the early urban congregations tended understandably to be apolitical. Their socially-transforming interests became rather narrowly confined to the religious community. The Jesus movement addressed a total social realm—including economic institutions and political realities. The anger and hope of an oppressed rural populace comes to expression through Jesus. Rural context should prompt us to look for broader social meanings.

As hermeneutical corollary to this, the parables and sayings of Jesus can obviously be understood in several different ways. There is a multivalency in them that has led to a breakdown in Jülicher's single-point approach to parable interpretation. Recognition of Jesus' rural origin should at least lead us to suspect a bivalency and urge us to move back behind the meaning most resonant in the ancient urban context. The more it looks like the views of urban culture and literati, the less likely it will be the view of Jesus. And we cannot forget in this the oppressive political context in which Jesus conducted a "public" ministry. Anything political had to be said indirectly. Comparative studies of speech in oppressive circumstances may shed light on how to get around this significant impediment to understanding Jesus.

18. Avi-Yonah, ed., *Encyclopedia of Archaeological Excavations in the Holy Land*, 2:602 supplies a photograph of weeds growing in the cracks of the western wall of Herod's Temple platform.

CHAPTER 10

Rulers' Houses, Thieves, and Usurpers: The Beelzebul Pericope

THIS ARTICLE IS HEURISTIC and interpretive. Its focus is the socio-political situation of first-century Palestine as seen through the lens of the Beelzebul controversy. Methodologically the argument moves back and forth between the microcosm of the text and the macrocosm of Palestine under the early Roman empire; that is, the chapter adopts both emic ("insider") and etic ("outsider") viewpoints vis-à-vis the text. The emic viewpoint is informed by the gospel tradition and by ancient historians like Josephus; the etic viewpoint by comparative studies of rural peoples. Sociological imagination plays a role too, but this is not consciously an essay in sociological explanation or the testing of any general social scientific theory.

The chapter is divided into three parts. First, some general assumptions undergirding the discussion are laid out. Secondly, a brief formal analysis of Luke 11:14–26 and par. is undertaken. Finally, the chapter focuses on the meaning of the tradition in the light of other parts of the tradition and the larger sociopolitical situation.

WORKING ASSUMPTIONS

Before Q and Mark picked up their various traditions, the traditions themselves lived orally in Palestinian villages. These traditions contained meaning for people close to the soil. The village (with the single exception of Jerusalem) was also the predominant *Sitz im Leben* for the ministry of Jesus. It seems natural to assume that Jesus shared many of the same values and expectations of his peasant audiences. His ministry addressed in significant ways the needs and frustrations of his first-century rural context.[1]

Somewhere along the line, perhaps very early and certainly without supplanting the oral tradition, literate followers of Jesus arranged and recorded his words. For these followers, whose literacy and experience moved them to a greater or lesser degree out of the predominately oral culture of the countryside, the meaning of the tradition shifted. Speaking from a different social "place," these early traditors perceived the meaning of Jesus' appearance and words in more abstract and general terms (e.g., vis-à-vis the destiny of the whole people of Israel or as an appeal to the wise). Sacred written traditions and the somewhat artificial arrangement of Jesus' words began to overshadow the concrete context of first-century Palestinian villages for assessing the meaning of Jesus.

These reflections warn against reading too much popular sentiment directly out of the apocalyptic or wisdom layers of the gospels. "Popular expectations" are only available to the historian indirectly and circumstantially. Yet as has been noted by others, the Jesus tradition is one of the few extant from antiquity where the "interface" between the ancient expressions of the lower classes in the countryside and the records of the literate is still relatively close. At some points, obviously, the speech of the village resonated with and was influenced by the expectations of the apocalyptists (like Mark) and those in Israel concerned with "wisdom" (some of the framers of Q). Nevertheless, the interests of villagers were sufficiently different from those of the educated who conveyed to us these ancient traditions to necessitate analysis of meanings as well as of forms.[2] This fact compels interpretation aware of the transition from peasant to artisan, as well as oral to written culture.

Out of the preceding sociological elaboration of the form critical viewpoint emerges a simple criterion for assessing the original intention of the tradition: At the earliest levels of the tradition, two completely different or sufficiently distinct spheres of meaning can be expected to have centered on the same traditional form (or the same structure, if one

1. Gerd Theissen in several articles and in his *Sociology of Early Palestinian Christianity* was one of the first to explore the rural dimension of the Synoptic tradition. See also the remarks of de Ste. Croix, *Class Struggle*, 427ff., and the general treatment of rural antiquity in MacMullen, *Roman Social Relations*, 1–56.

2. For the background to these thoughts, see Redfield, *Peasant Society and Culture*, 41–42 on great and little traditions and Max Weber, *Economy and Society*, 1:468ff on the typical religious interests of peasants versus the ethical rationalism of the artisan classes who evidently preserved the Jesus tradition.

prefers John Dominic Crossan's view).[3] To pry out the specific meanings appropriate to the rural Jesus tradition, comparative anthropology must first give us a clue as to the customary universe of meaning shared by rural peoples. Comparative study of peasantries and other oral traditions can help in getting at the aboriginal meaning of the Jesus tradition.[4]

Two brief quotes from comparative students of peasantries will indicate some of the universe of peasant discourse and experience pertinent to this discussion:

> . . . broad areas of peasant behavior are patterned in such fashion as to suggest that peasants view their social, economic, and natural universes—their total environment—as one in which all of the desired things in life . . . *exist in finite quantity* and *are always in short supply* . . . if "Good" exists in limited amounts which cannot be expanded, and if the system is closed, it follows that *an individual or a family can improve a position only at the expense of others.*[5]

> The subject matter of [a peasant village's] evening talks embraced gossip about local events and household and community affairs, as well as 'news from the wide world'. There were also numerous tales often legendary, mystical and magico-religious in character. . . . these tales constituted an important instrument of the strengthening of the old, mystico-magical outlook. . . . A special category of tales referred to hidden treasures and benevolent robbers, who aided the poor in acts of revenge over the cruel nobles. The unusual popularity of these legends probably reflected the deep peasant desire to improve their lot, to compensate for their grief and humiliations suffered in real life.[6]

In addition to the peasant context, discussions of the Synoptic controversy stories almost entirely ignore the political situation of the villages and towns within which these conflicts took place. These literary controversies undoubtedly reflect the fact that conflict with representatives of leading Palestinian groups occurred during the ministry of Jesus (a point for which the tradition offers numerous, though stereotypical, scenes). What were the political ramifications of such controversies in the context

3. Crossan, *In Fragments*, 37–40.

4. Tools developed by folklorists, such as Thomson's *Motif-Index of Folk-Literature*, may especially be of help here. Consider the following entries: He who steals much is called king; he who steals little is called a robber (U11.2). A robber's defence: God will not permit the rich to enter into heaven unless we take their ill-gotten goods from them (J1269.8).

5. Foster, "Peasant Society and the Image of the Limited Good," 305 (his italics).

6. Dobrowolski, "Peasant Traditional Culture," 285–86.

of oriental despotism? What were the political consequences of saying or doing anything candidly, or even remotely resembling the subversive? Spies of Antipas and the wealthy landowning class (the Herodians) were ever watchful.[7] If one did not choose to take to the desert, as did the Baptist, would not one be compelled to speak indirectly? This seems to be one obvious reason for Jesus' adoption of parabolic speech, although if his activity was anywhere near as public as the tradition implies (Luke 8:16), his apparently open references to a reign of God surely could not have escaped the notice of the political authorities. Undoubtedly because of Jesus' refusal to be totally clandestine, the life of constant movement was also necessitated (as Luke 13:32 intimates). Yet neither John nor Jesus could ultimately avoid arrest and the deaths reserved for political dissidents.

So we must observe with reference to the passage under consideration: Speech could be veiled, but actions could not. What was at stake politically in exorcism? What was so offensive in the healing of bodies? Politics and religion were thoroughly confused in the ancient mind. Can we not expect to find some substantive connection between bodily exorcism and *basileia* (or *hē basileia tou theou*)? Indeed, there are overtones of the exorcism of the body politic in the exorcism of bodies. Exorcisms drew crowds. Exorcism in that context was an act with larger ramifications.[8]

ANALYSIS OF THE TEXT

The text and its parallels, as those who picked it know well, offers a fascinating collection of historical issues. At this Synoptic location, the pre-70 traditions of Mark and the pre-70 traditions of Q overlap. Both versions of the Beelzebul pericope demonstrate an interest in exorcism; both versions reveal the controversy surrounding these actions by Jesus; and both versions include similar but not identical sayings about divided kingdoms or houses.

Bultmann and Crossan concur that situation, accusation, introduction, and answer(s) supply the formal basis for this story.[9] Viewing the

7. Mark 6:14a; Luke 13:31–32; cf. Josephus, *War* 2.85. Herod built his many fortresses, according to Josephus, *Ant.* 15.291, 295, to deal with *internal* security.

8. John Pairman Brown suggested this already a decade ago, "Techniques of Imperial Control," especially 366–67; see also Horsley, "Popular Messianic Movements"; and idem, "Prophets of Old."

9. Aland, *Synopsis Quattuor Evangeliorum,* and Funk, *New Gospel Parallels,* supplied the primary instruments of study. The Q reconstructions of Robinson, "The Mission and Beelzebul," and Kloppenborg, "Q 11:14–20," have served as a point of reference. I am

pericope from the standpoint of a synopsis, aside from the fact that exorcism occasions controversy and the Beelzebul accusation, the redactional frameworks of the evangelists diverge at a number of points. It is not my intention to expound upon the significance of the redactional divergences. The present discussion will simply try to assess the pre-gospel stage of developments.

It may be of import in analyzing the traditional syzygy here that while in Mark Jesus' opponents speak only of Beelzebul (once in Mark), Jesus himself speaks of *Satan* being divided against Satan. The Q version has Beelzebul on the lips of Jesus in Luke 11:19/Matt 12:27. It is tempting to use this name-change as a criterion for a version or part of the Q tradition closer to Mark and a version or part farther from Mark. This supposition of levels in Q finds support in Matt 12:29b/Mark 3:27b, which is expanded dramatically and quite differently in Luke. Did Matthew simply follow Mark at this point? Then how to explain the sequence Matt 12:27–28 + 29b + 12:30/Luke 11:19–20 + 21–22 + 23?

Of the sayings, Luke 11:17 speaks of divided kingdoms and fallen houses (vs. division of houses in Mark). Luke 11:18 ironically asks how Satanic division will help Satan's rule. This parallels Mark. Verse 19 contains a rather cryptic reference to "your sons" as exorcists and mentions their future elevation to magistracy. Luke 11:20 then draws the connection between exorcism and God's rule coming near. Mark lacks both of these sayings. Verses 21–22 are probably two separate sayings linked somewhat artificially. The conjunction of the scene of "peace through strength" in the former verse and the scene of "the triumph of the stronger" in the latter verse highlights two very different situations. Verse 21 speaks of the "hoplite" guarding his own court (*aulēn*) and his goods thus being secure. The next verse, however, conjures up a picture of Hellenistic warfare and dividing (*diadidōsin*) the spoils of war (*skyla* = "arms stripped off a fallen enemy"), a social practice Max Weber once referred to as "booty" capitalism.[10] Mark's tradition knows only a version of the latter saying. *Gospel of Thomas* 35 is closer to Mark and Matthew than to Luke. Luke 11:23 records a commonplace about there not being a possibility for neutrality; this sentiment is turned around in another Synoptic version at Mark 9:40/Luke 9:50 (cf. POxy 1224 2). Though not considered a formal part

indebted to Crossan, *In Fragments*, 184–91 and Bultmann, *History of the Synoptic Tradition* for some observations.

10. Gerth and Mills, *From Max Weber*, 66ff.

of the Beelzebul pericope, the Q saying Luke 11:24–26 seems to take up the theme of exorcism again.

Formal analysis reveals several outcomes to parallel processes of tradition and redaction. The evangelists and Q all know a similar framework, probably authentic historical reminiscence, for a series of sayings. There seems no reason to doubt that most of the Synoptic sayings go back to Jesus, though Luke 11:21–22 is suspicious and controversy surrounding exorcism was not necessarily the actual occasion for all the sayings (e.g., Luke 11:23; cf. 9:50). One basic question of analysis is Why have all of these words been attracted to this particular context? Formal analysis must give way to some extent to a consideration of the meaning of this concatenation of sayings.

THE MEANING QUESTION

The sayings find a unifying focus in *basileia*. All imply a setting in life (*Sitz im Leben*) in the realities of unrest and fall within agrarian monarchies of the late-Hellenistic type. Luke 11:17b depicts the situation of *internal* unrest, while 11:21 evokes a picture of *external* threat. A curious connection is made in Luke 11:19 between exorcism and magistracy. By what agency or means, or on what occasion, will exorcists become popular judges? (We shall discuss this below.) Luke 11:23 is perhaps a court proverb (cf. v. 21, *aulē*), spoken from the viewpoint of the ruler. As such, this proverb contrasts with the *diadidōsin* of the previous verse. Luke 11:24–26 raises certain questions if it is simply read as what happens after the exorcism of a human body. For instance, why is *anthrōpou* definite, (not "from *a* man" but "from *the* man")? Other key words in the passage evoke political connotations (assuming they have translated the connotations of an original Aramaic): *dia anhydrōn topōn* recalls the haunt of political refugees (1 Sam 22:2; 1 Macc 2:28). In the Egyptian papyri, *anapausis* is "(temporary) relief from taxation."[11] *Oikos* is an possible metaphor for the human body, but as Luke 11:17b/Mark 3:25 demonstrates *oikos/oikia* can equally well refer to the ruling house or houses. Political allegory here might encapsulate the people's experience, say, during the time of Antigonus Mattathias and the "exorcism" of Herod (40 BCE, Josephus, *War* 1.263ff). The return of Herod brought "seven worse spirits."

---

11. Moulton and Milligan, *Vocabulary of the Greek Testament*, 36.

There are several issues of meaning, therefore, that need to be explored more deeply. These issues will be organized under the headings a) Rulers' Houses, and b) Thieves and Usurpers.

Rulers' Houses

Oriental rulers like Herod and his sons, as well as the Roman emperors, thought of their domains as "households" or by metonymy "houses." These rulers were the *patres* of their respective *familiae* and the absolute law within their realms. Furthermore, such rulers in theory held eminent domain over all of the property and even the bodies of their subjects. As Weber pointed out in his discussion of domination, however, no historical ruler in practice lasted for very long on the basis of brute force or organized robbery. Rule had to be legitimated in some way. Religion, customary rights and obligations, and laws provided serviceable tools for this purpose.[12] In early Roman Judea, the imperial administration meshed with the ruling families of priests. These collected the Roman taxes, at least in Judea (Josephus, *War* 2.405, 407), while pacifying the countryside through their religious ministrations in the Temple and their judicial preeminence in the Sanhedrin. The client realm of Antipas in Galilee was also undergirded by a landholding class, the Herodians.

The household structure of these agrarian governments meant two interrelated things—the need for a hierarchy of people to maintain the political edifice and a series of central banks or storehouses to support these functionaries and other needs of the ruling group. Sometimes functionaries were simply salaried officials as in the case of the Roman equestrians; sometimes land-grants were given as in the cases of Egyptian officials under the Ptolemies or Herod the Great's finance minister Ptolemy (Josephus, *Ant.* 17.289). Salaries weakened any internal military threat, but strengthened the possibility of disloyalty for higher gain. Land-grants were often given in military situations requiring pacification, but could engender strong aristocratic threats to the throne or weakening through assimilation. The control of land and its products (hence physical storehouses) was crucial in any agrarian monarchy.

In early Roman Palestine the competing taxation demands of the indigenous landowning class, the local procuratorial and military agents of the empire, and the Roman state itself placed great pressures upon the rural producers. The conflict surrounding Beelzebul, which immediately

12. Max Weber, *Economy and Society*, 1:212ff.

escalates into words about divided kingdoms and the plunder of the goods of the strong, underscores the political and economic dimension of demon possession. The "demons" that the *basileia tou theou* is colliding with are not just "spooks" and psychoses. There is in view here economic disprivilege, malnutrition, endemic violence, and the destruction of rural families.

A material link exists between divided houses/kingdoms and plundered goods (*skeyē*, Mark 3:27/Matt 12:29 or *hyparchonta/skyla*, Luke 11:21–22). These passages refer to the forced redistribution of what has been collected at a "central" point. Josephus gives us the ruling class view of such division and thievery at the time of Herod's death:

> Simon . . . assumed the diadem. Perambulating the country with the brigands [*lēstai*] whom he had collected, he burnt down the royal palace at Jericho and many other stately mansions, such incendiarism providing him with an easy opportunity for plunder.[13]

Such Robin Hoods were styled "brigands" by the ruling groups, and their leader could sometimes offer an alternative *basileia* to the prevailing order. What Josephus viewed as plunder, Simon and his compatriots probably thought of as their rightful due.[14]

Comparative studies of banditry suggest that peasantries are generally sympathetic with social bandits, as Eric Hobsbawm calls them.[15] Social bandits are not indiscriminate robbers, but target only the wealthy and privileged and champion the disadvantaged. Bandit leaders might claim aristocratic origin, but most of their followers will be peasants. Other peasants offer covert support to social bandits. In the face of suspicion by the ruling class, neutrality may be impossible (Luke 11:23).

The passage in Luke 11:24–26 might also refer then to these bandit-opponents of the current regime. If one bandit was exorcised (by the ruling house = the Man), the exorcised body (now = the ruling class) could surely expect seven worse spirits to come. At least, this was the prevailing pattern during the early years of Roman domination in Palestine. If it is accepted that Luke 11:21–22 are words of the historical Jesus, they assume the viewpoint either of the royal house or of aristocracy. The Markan version (3:27/Matt 12:29), of course, does not necessarily refer to a king's

13. Josephus, *War* 2.57 (Thackeray, LCL); cf. the strategy of the *sicarii*, *War* 7.254.

14. Horsley, "Popular Messianic Movements," 486: for instance, the recovery of pledges like farm tools.

15. Hobsbawm, *Bandits*; MacMullen, *Enemies of the Roman Order*, Appendix 2, has provided much comparative material on banditry in antiquity.

house. There is, however, a social analog to the royal domain, perhaps an aristocratic house or even a relatively well-to-do peasant dwelling (cf. Luke 12:39). The following diagram illustrates these analogies:

The Elite Strata

Royal House (Herod's sons)	Aristocratic House ' (Herodians, Sadducees)	Middle Peasant (*oikodespotēs* = *baʿal habayith* of the Mishnah)

Organized or Disorganized Opposition

Usurper = Social Bandit (needs to steal to support cause and gain followers)	Organized banditry, especially plagues privileged strata of social order = forced redistribution	Thief in the night (Luke 12:39)

The "binding of the strongman," then, points suggestively to another part of the Jesus tradition. There is a substantive link to the multiple "thief in the night" traditions (Luke 12:39/Matt 24:43; 1 Thess 5:2; 2 Pet 3:10; Rev 3:3; 16:15.) A further set of gospel passages will indicate that the image of the usurper/throne rival came to supply an arsenal of metaphors for the imminent reign of God in the speech of Jesus.

Thieves and Usurpers

The pivotal saying for the purposes of the present exploration is the one at Luke 12:39. It is helpful that not one, but four, sayings are linked together in Q from Luke 12:35 to 12:46. The first and fourth sayings of this group contain commonplaces that praise trustworthy slave behavior (i.e. watching at the door for the master's return and performing expected duties while the master is gone). These are, if you will, the A and A′ of a chiasm. Then, Luke 12:39 and 40 also participate in the structure of this chiasm (B and B′): the contrary-to-fact condition about the householder and the thief (*kleptēs*), and the Son of Man saying. While scholars have generally seen the parallelism here only in terms of preparedness, it will be suggested at this point that a material connection can also be made between "Son of Man" and "thief."

It is important to reclaim the meaning in what philologists of the Son of Man problem have known all along, viz., that the literal Greek for "Son of Man" reads "the Son of the Man."[16] The Greek reveals, if this expression goes back to Jesus, that there was definition in the second noun in the original Aramaic. This implies a formal title. Such definition is lacking in Daniel 7:13 and Psalm 8:4 (8:5 LXX). Nonetheless, since scholars have not been able to find extra-canonical, early Jewish parallels to the titular use of "the Son of the Man," most have begun to think this phrase on the lips of Jesus was an anachronistic projection of the earliest church based upon exegetical reflection.[17]

The suggestion that will be advanced here is that the Son of the Man was a popular village designation in the late Hellenistic period for a throne rival, who would obviously be viewed as a usurper and a bandit by the ruling class.[18] "The Son of the Man," in this view, could mean one of two things: Either a descendant of "the Man," the legitimate royal lineage—perhaps Davidic, perhaps also Hasmonean in the face of the Herodians and Rome—in which case the throne rival was a claimant of the throne by legitimate right; or one anointed by the spirit of "the Man" = God, in which case the throne rival was a throne aspirant.[19] Pre-70 expectation for this kind of aspirant is manifested both in the reports of Josephus about the activities of some of them and "through a glass darkly" in the traditions of the gospels (e.g., Mark 8:27–29 and par.; 15:26; Matt 24:23–28).[20]

Luke 12:40 then parallels the meaning of Luke 12:39 quite precisely, if we accept that *kleptēs* and *lēstēs* are virtually synonymous. The distinction between *genabh* ("thief") and *gedûd* ("robber") in Aramaic seems to consist in an individual's act of theft versus a theft committed by an organized

16. Donahue, "Origin of 'Son of Man,'" 486, refers to this expression as a "literary monstrosity in Greek."

17. Ibid., 487, 496; see also Walker, "The Son of Man," 585.

18. Josephus, *War* 2.56 also refers to the revolutionaries of 4 BCE as *tous ten dynasteian zēlontas*, "those seeking the dynasty."

19. On anthropomorphic designations for God among traditional peoples, see Leach, "Anthropomorphism"; cf. "Yahweh is a man of war," Exod 15:3. Man is synonymous with "lord" in *m. Yoma* 1.7: "My lord the high priest"; Jastrow, *Dictionary*, 60. It is not difficult to see how peasants could conceive of "a Man" above their human masters. Horsley, "Prophets of Old," 455, distinguishes, on the basis of Josephus, these activist "messiahs" from passive "prophets" who wait for deliverance from God. I think this distinction is defensible, but at root all of these movements emerged by the same kind of social power, looked for the same kind of spiritual legitimation, and aimed at similar structural changes in society.

20. The discussion of Horsley, "Popular Messianic Movements," is particularly helpful in redefining the question of such popular expectations.

band.[21] In any case, the two sayings hold similar connotations in the light of the foregoing discussion.

Upon consideration, other Son of Man sayings seem to support this viewpoint. I have divided these sayings into four tentative groups, each reflecting a stage in the process of a challenge to the incumbent ruler (or ruling class): (1) Arrival on the scene and identification as a throne rival, (2) the strategy of the throne claimant or aspirant for acquiring adherents, (3) the possible dishonor and suffering of the throne claimant or aspirant during the contest, and (4) the honor and accession of the successful rival.

Almost all of the words in category (1) have been redirected by the post-Easter church to the coming of the eschatological Son of Man. This titular use has evolved out of the original metaphor employed by Jesus. Mark 14:62 and Matt 10:23 imply a supernatural event. Luke 12:40 need not have this supramundane reference, but there seems no escaping such a meaning in Luke 9:26 (which nevertheless brings out nicely the parallel between "the Man" and "the Father") or Mark 13:26 and par. The parallel Matt 16:28 ties in the claim to *basileia* with "coming." The passage in Matt 24:23–26 is very instructive. Anointing by the spirit, authentication through *sēmeia kai terata*, and gathering of followers in the desert are all marks of throne aspirants with echoes in Josephus (e.g., *War* 2.259).[22] Verse 27b (cf. 37, 39) presupposes how critical the sudden "arrival" (*parousia*) of the royal aspirant is. Arrival demands decision by the people and presages mortal conflict. However, contrary to Jesus' original complementary and sympathetic use of the metaphor, the eschatological coming has now been turned against the aims of popular throne rivals. The Lukan parallels to these Matthean words lack *parousia*; Luke's versions hark back apparently to the "day" of Yahweh, now the "days" or "hour" of the Son of Man. Luke 17:40/Matt 24:44 both have "hour."

(2) Throne rivals had several strategies ready at hand to win adherents and sustain the cause. In addition to plundering estates and storehouses for capital to finance the struggle, the aspirant could offer to potential allies things that the present ruling house would not. A more humane and just order could be promised, one that would start with the top and reach to the bottom: This may be some of the signification behind Mark

21. Jastrow, *Dictionary*, 210, 256.

22. Horsley, "Prophets of Old," 455, denies that these are the marks of messianic aspirations. One may reflect, in this same vein, upon the meaning of the baptism of Jesus to those attuned to such realities.

10:45/Matt 20:28 (cf. 2 Sam 15:1–6). A parallel sentiment lies in Luke 19:10. Perhaps the rhetorical question on the lips of Jesus in Mark 2:10 expands upon this *exousia* of throne rivals to undermine the prevailing order. While the passage can legitimately be read and makes sense as "authority to forgive sins," if Jesus is actually alluding to the strategy options of a throne rival, he then refers to "authority to release debts." Much of the political trouble in ancient agrarian monarchies emerged out of increasingly lopsided arrangements of power and privilege that accrued to large landowners and holders of capital. It was very easy for the peasantry to get mired in debt. An aspirant to the throne simply had to offer forgiveness of debt or release from slavery to acquire any number of adherents.[23]

A throne rival must find broad-based support, so sending out messengers is a logical thing to do (Mark 6:7 and par.; Matt 13:41). The most strategic location for conflict with a central power will be where that power is weakest—on the fringes of civilization and in the wildernesses. Perhaps this is the oblique reference made in Matt 12:40b ("heart of the earth" = "not easily accessible" or "among the common people"). The three days and nights are linked by Matthew to the Jonah story (Luke equates Jonah and Jesus and makes no reference to three days and nights), but Jesus utilized the three-days time frame in another politically-weighted controversy over signs, Luke 13:32. Furthermore, the three days recalls another Son of Man saying in Luke 24:46. Mark 3:18 brings out the political connotations of *anistēmi* (= "to revolt"). "The Son of the Man [or "the Anointed"] shall rise on the third day" signified the time-table for the final push for power.

Two other strategies are adumbrated in the tradition. At first glance, it might seem difficult to fit Luke 7:34/Matt 11:19 into this schema. However, in the light of a passage like John 6:15, the connection between eating, drinking, and kingship is clear. The throne rival could also abrogate the sabbath for the larger goals of the conflict. The Son of the Man is master of the sabbath (Mark 2:28 and par.). The royal prerogative of David serves as the premise for this saying. The word also recalls actions of the Maccabees (1 Macc 2:41). There might additionally be here a hint of the larger sabbath—the sabbatical year—over which royal prerogative is additionally claimed. This meaning would mesh nicely with forgiveness of debts and provision of bread.

---

23. The case of Simon b. Giora is very instructive: Josephus, *War* 4.508; see my treatment on this subject in chapter 1 above, "Jesus and Agrarian Palestine: The Factor of Debt."

(3) Turning to the third group of sayings, Luke 9:58/Matt 8:20 reflects the forced marches of the throne rival. Once again, Luke 13:32 supplies a striking political parallel (Herod as fox, Jesus on the move).

Mark 3:28–29 belongs to the Beelzebul controversy in Mark, but not in Matthew or Luke. Once again the political angle is sustained. The throne rival *as aspirant* (i.e., as Son of the Man) may be reviled; but when the final anointing that signals accession takes place, reviling will not be tolerated. This reading assumes that the Son of the Man can easily be reviled by villagers uncertain of his chances at success (cf. 2 Sam 15:13–16; 16:5–8).

If the Son of the Man can be reviled, so also he can be tortured and executed if unsuccessful and captured. The gospel passages concerning the suffering of the Son of the Man are to be placed in this perspective. These have obviously been redacted after a knowledge of Jesus' fate, but this should not obscure their original reference to ultimate fate of many unsuccessful throne rivals in the early first century.

(4) The fourth group of sayings depict the alternative: The throne aspirant triumphs. A throne and judgment is associated with this eventuality (Matt 25:31). The followers of the new regent will receive their appropriate rewards as well (co-magistracy, Matt 19:28; intimate friendship/table fellowship [*amici, philoi*] with the king, Luke 18:30). So perhaps now the puzzle of Luke 11:19 will be more comprehensible; "your sons" work by the same anointing spirit and cannot fail to find a place in the new regime.

The foregoing does not argue that the historical Jesus was conscious of himself as a throne aspirant (*pace* Brandon), or that he considered himself to be an eschatological Messiah. Jesus drew upon a common village expectation as a metaphor for the imminent rule of God, for which the "throne rival" provides a *tertium comparationis*. From the looks of Mark 12:35–37, Jesus apparently rejected any easy accommodation between his own proclamation and the expectation of a Davidic throne claimant a là *Psalm of Solomon* 17. Of course, Jesus' peasant constituency may have had trouble making this distinction. If Jesus did see some of himself in the phrase "the Son of the Man," he did not restrict the reference to himself alone. The parallel between God as "the Man" and God as "the Father" would suggest that, as a cipher for the kingdom of God, "the Son of the Man" is more aptly parallel to "children of God." Perhaps the diagram below will serve to illustrate the relationship between metaphor and expected reality.

However the analogies are decided, there was certain to be a collision between what Jesus expected to come and the prevailing social order, just as surely as there were throne claimants or aspirants arising out of perceived injustice. Jesus gained a following in the name of the impending collision and was executed as "the King of the Jews." It is in the light of this social conflict, therefore, that the Beelzebul controversy needs to be read.

Figure 12: Rulers' Houses

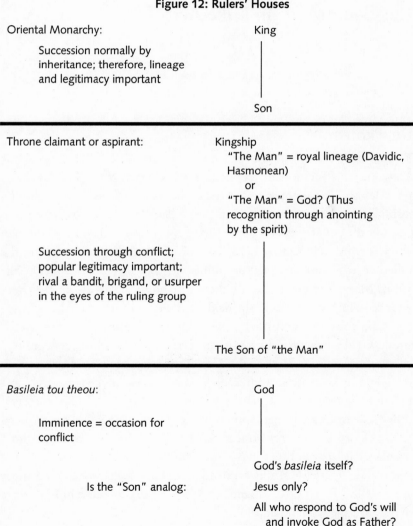

Oriental Monarchy: King

     Succession normally by
     inheritance; therefore, lineage
     and legitimacy important

         Son

Throne claimant or aspirant: Kingship
         "The Man" = royal lineage (Davidic,
         Hasmonean)
         or
         "The Man" = God? (Thus
         recognition through anointing
         by the spirit)

     Succession through conflict;
     popular legitimacy important;
     rival a bandit, brigand, or usurper
     in the eyes of the ruling group

         The Son of "the Man"

Basileia tou theou: God

     Imminence = occasion for
     conflict

         God's *basileia* itself?

     Is the "Son" analog: Jesus only?

         All who respond to God's will
         and invoke God as Father?

CHAPTER 11

"All the Surrounding Country":
The Countryside in Luke-Acts

> . . . and a report concerning him went out through all the surrounding country. —Luke 4:14

THE PROJECT

LUKE DEVOTES NO LITTLE space to the countryside in his two-volume work. This is especially apparent in the Gospel, where Luke includes much Jesus material not encountered in the other gospels. The neighborly hospitality and conviviality that suggest village locales (Luke 11:5–8 and 15:9), or the country estates of the Rich Fool (12:16–21) and the rich man who has a dishonest steward (16:1–8), provide windows directly into the milieu of Jesus' early first-century ministry. Luke also provides scenes like that of Mary's journey to her rural cousin's home (1:39–40) or the shepherds tending their flocks in the fields at the time of Jesus' birth (2:8).

Luke's vocabulary further suggests countryside as an area for investigation. Of the twenty-eight occurrences of the Greek word for "country" or "rural precinct" (*chōra*) in the New Testament, seventeen occurrences (60%) are in Luke-Acts. Admittedly, some of these are generic references to "country," as, "A nobleman went into a far country" (Luke 19:12). Other references are to agricultural locales (12:16). Luke uses a nuanced variety of Greek words for rural areas: "Field" (*agros*) appears eleven times in Luke-Acts, sixteen times in Matthew, and once in Mark. "Surrounding countryside" (*perichōros*) appears six times in Luke-Acts, twice in Matthew, and once in Mark. "Piece of land" (*chōrion*) occurs six times in Acts, once each in Matthew, Mark, and John.

An exploration of this theme, therefore, seems fully warranted. Two sets of questions will guide the ruminations of this essay:

1. Is Luke familiar at first hand with the realities of the Palestinian countryside or the countryside elsewhere in the Roman Empire? Or does Luke betray evidence of idealized or romanticized conceptions of the essentially rural milieu of nascent Christianity? How also does Luke stand with respect to important political-economic questions affecting the interests of the countryside? In other words, what is the sociology of Luke's knowledge of the countryside? To some extent, these sociological questions are a part of the traditional question regarding the life-setting (*Sitz im Leben*) of the Lukan Gospel: Where in the Roman Empire did Luke write?

2. How has Luke handled the rural Jesus traditions that form a part of his narrative world? Is there a discernable literary and thematic role for the countryside here? Or has Luke simply embraced the countryside out of necessity, because it is in the tradition? These questions are more focused upon Luke's literary conception.

Neither of these sets of questions can be adequately addressed without the broader perspectives developed in the next section of the study. In order to get at the sociological dimension, results of modern comparative studies of rural and peasant societies are drawn upon.

CONCEPTUALIZING THE COUNTRYSIDE OF MEDITERRANEAN ANTIQUITY

A General Sociological Model for the Ancient Countryside

A fundamental polarity between country and city has been noted by the modern historians of the ancient world Rostovtzeff, de Ste. Croix, and MacMullen. This conceptual polarity traces its roots back to the classical writers. So as early as the eighth century BCE, the Greek poet Hesiod contrasts the goodness of the village engaged in agricultural work with the evil of the city-state occupied by war and the shipping trade (*Works and Days* 225–247). Horace (first century BCE) sums up the Roman agrarian ideal of the late Republic when he writes:

> A man is happy when, far from the business world, like the earliest
> tribe of men he cultivates the family farm with his team, and is free
> from usury's ties . . . when he keeps away from the Forum and the
> proud doorways of influential men.[1]

While an absolute dichotomy between city and countryside in antiquity
is hardly tenable, a number of sociological indicators point to significant
differences between the two realms. The accumulating results of economic
anthropology, modern rural sociology, and peasant studies can help to
bring out these differences quite precisely.

To start with, the construction of conceptual models for the countryside in antiquity might employ either a broadly *functionalist* or a broadly
conflict approach, in view of two of the dominant paradigms in sociological
theory. Functionalist sociological theory, otherwise known as structural-
functionalism or equilibrium theory, envisions societies as systems with
needs, in the service of which social behaviors are "functional." Functional
theory often focuses on why societies remain stable over time. The alternative conflict theory looks at societies as the arena for competing groups
and interests. Conflict theory frequently attempts to understand why and
how societies change. Table 1 illustrates some of the implications of this
choice:

Figure 13: Comparison of Functionalist and Conflict Approaches

	FUNCTIONALIST	CONFLICT
1 Interests perceived as	Uniting	Dividing
2 Social relations viewed as	Mutually advantageous	Exploitative
3 Social unity achieved by	Consensus	Coercion
4 Definition of society	System with needs	Stage for class struggle
5 Nature of humanity	Requires restraining institutions	Institutions distort basic human nature
6 Inequality viewed as	Social necessity	Unnecessary, Promotes conflict
7 The State	Promotes common good	Instrument of oppression
8 Social class	Heuristic concept	Objective social groups with different interests

[Source: Sanders, based on work of A. E. Havens[2]]

1. *Epodes* 11, quoted from White, *Country Life in Classical Times*, 40.
2. Irwin T. Sanders, *Rural Society*, 9.

The *functionalist* approach will be congenial to the guardians of society, who tend to think of social order as "an organic system" and the best of all social possibilities. In terms of the countryside of antiquity, the functionalist approach will talk about the symbiosis or mutual dependence of city and country folk and will assume a stance like the following: Augustus and the armies of Rome provided order and the country people supplied the bread of empire (*mutual advantage* [2]). The Empire was in the best *interests* [1] of agricultural producers. The country people as a rule were happy, well-adjusted, and supported the status quo (*consensus* [3]). Empire required a few to govern and the many to work on the farm (*system with needs* [4]). A functionalist reading of antiquity might stress, "For rulers are not a terror to good conduct, but to bad" (Rom 13:3; cf. 1 Pet 2:14: *Human nature requires restraining institutions* [5]; *the state promotes the common good* [7]). As for *social classes* [8] in the Roman Empire, MacMullen epitomizes the functionalist views of many modern historians of classical antiquity when he writes, "The very number [of legislative and cultural social classifications] seems to have worked against class feeling."[3] MacMullen effectively denies with this statement the objective reality of social class; at most "class" can be a term of conceptual convenience.

The *conflict* (peoples) approach will tend to focus on the discontent of the subjugated and expose the harmful effects of the "system," as well as indicate its chief beneficiaries. In this view, Augustus and the ruling groups of the Empire *exploited* [2] the majority of agricultural producers (*state an instrument of oppression* [7]). The Empire was not in the best material *interests* [1] of the producer and injected deep-seated hostility and bitterness into the *social relations* [2, 4] of empire—especially between city and country. At times, this hostility broke out into open conflict. Military operations by the state against insurgents, bandits, or rebels was more often necessary than history produced from an elite perspective might lead us to believe (*coercion* [3, 7]). The rural populace in such a distorted social situation looked upon human nature as basically good when liberated from the burden of empire [5]. *Inequality and oppression* [6] were not in the original nature of things.[4] From this perspective, *social class* [8] is delineated clearly between those who have and those who have not, between those who do not toil for what they eat and those who do, between those whose who

3. MacMullen, *Enemies of the Roman Order,* 198.
4. See Hesiod, *Works and Days* 109–120.

rob and extort and those who are never adequately compensated for their labor.

Objectively speaking, though, the choice of one or the other perspectives might be made with a concern for appropriateness to the specific sociological situation. *A conflict approach is assumed in the development of the model that follows, in view of the political situation of agrarian (peasant) societies in general and of early Roman Palestine in particular.* Important terms in the discussion are underlined and defined as they occur.

The General Nature of Agrarian/Peasant Society

An *agrarian society*, typical of the majority of those in Mediterranean antiquity, is one built predominantly upon the plow and agricultural production.[5] The chief productive factor in agrarian economies is land. Control of land is one of the central political questions of agrarian societies. Furthermore, human and animal energies supply the dominant energies of such societies. Ability to mobilize these energies for useful social ends is also an important agrarian political question. Given the generally low level of technology and the meager energy resources of these types of societies, agriculture is generally of a low-yield sort. This means that as a rule there is a very narrow margin between what can be harvested and what is needed by the majority of agriculturalists for food, seed, or animal fodder. There might be just enough, but not much more. As we shall see in a moment, the social and political condition of country folk compounds this basic productive problem.

Agrarian societies can also be considered *peasant societies*, "a set of villages socially bound up with preindustrial cities."[6] These types of societies are stratified into essentially two *social classes*—a small ruling elite in the cities and a mass of toiling agriculturalists in the villages whose labor and product supports that elite. Another way to delineate "social class" within peasant/agrarian societies is to look at who controls the land and the distribution of its products. Elites will control more or most and be advantaged in the distribution. A more sophisticated analysis will discern at least two further classes in these types of societies, a service class to the political elite (priests, soldiers, merchants, craftsmen) and a service class to the village (traveling or local craftsmen, village elders, local religious lead-

---

5. Lenski and Lenski, *Human Societies*, 207; Lenski, *Power and Privilege*, 192.

6. Malina, *New Testament World*, (1981[1]) 71, (2001[3]) 81.

ers). Lenski has estimated that only 2% of the agrarian population belongs to the ruling elite, about 8% comprises the service class in the cities, and the remaining 90% or so tills the soil or services the village.[7]

Agrarian Economics

The economic aspect of agrarian/peasant societies has been described or interpreted in detail by social scientists and historians like Weber, Heichelheim, Polanyi, Wolf, Braudel, Lenski, Sorokin, and others. Rural economic realities do not comprise a separate social institution (as our notion of the family farm "business" in the Midwest might lead us to imagine). Rather, ancient economic life was normally conducted within kin or political institutions. Said in the technical jargon of cultural anthropology, what moderns think of as economic realities are in agrarian/peasant societies embedded in political or kin contexts.[8] An example will clarify this a little: In modern America, family members leave home and go to work somewhere else. During leisure time, family members may spend money in a stranger's place of business. All members know what "the economy" is, because it impersonally affects and organizes their personal lives in many particular ways. By contrast, the ancient family tilled the soil or worked together to produce some specialized product. The home was the place of work. In fact, the Greek word "economy" (*oikonomia*) means "management of the household." In the rural village money transactions were rare. The usual course was bartering something of mutual value for something else, and then only with someone who was known by the family and trusted (like family). Otherwise, the landlord or the state agent (political institutions) would compel the family to give up produce or product for rent or taxes. "The economy" as an overarching social institution did not exist for the ancient person.

Hence, agrarian *exchange* frequently takes place through non-market means. "Exchange" means the transferring of control over material or cultural goods between persons. Village exchanges are more or less rigorously accounted for. Economic anthropology, the social science subdiscipline that concerns itself with non-industrial economic systems, thus speaks of either *balanced* or *general reciprocity* as characteristic of village barter. Exchanges are balanced if done on a quid pro quo basis and when the debt

7. Lenski, *Power and Privilege*, 284.

8. Polanyi, *The Great Transformation*; Malina, *New Testament World*; and idem, *Christian Origins and Cultural Anthropology*.

is liquidated fairly quickly. A balanced exchange might be one family's receipt of three loaves of bread on Monday (consider Luke 11:5) and the repayment to the other family on Wednesday of a basket of figs. The debt is not left outstanding for very long. The valuables exchanged are of roughly equal value (in the eyes of the parties involved). Close kin in a peasant village, however, might operate on a different basis, on the basis of general reciprocity. This means that the exchange is essentially unilateral—a gift from one party to another—and that the "debt" may go uncollected for a long time if at all (Luke 11:11). The dominant form of exchange toward those distant from the kinship group or toward strangers will be *negative reciprocity*, the attempt to acquire something of value for something of less or no value.

In contrast, the basic economic structure of ancient societies from the elites' point of view was that of a *redistributive* network. This means that taxes and rents flowed relentlessly away from the rural producers to the storehouses of cities (especially Rome), private estates, and temples. This *surplus*, which might have gone to feed extra mouths in the village, ended up being redistributed for other ends by the ruling groups.[9] All ancient societies were, therefore, *political economies*, because the powerful could compel rents and taxes to support their cultured lifestyle.

In Greco-Roman antiquity, the ruling elites lived in cities. Hence, the world empire of the Romans was governed through the city-state of Rome. Cities, in addition to being centers of higher culture, were economically parasitic upon the countryside, and urbanites spent significant amounts of time engaged in activities other than agriculture. Cities could function as administrative centers or tax collection points. They could also function as commercial centers. Trade and commerce in antiquity primarily benefited cities and local or state oligarchies, but not the peasants in country villages.

"Industry" and "finance," terms which must be viewed as modern economic anachronisms, require careful nuance when applied to the ancient agrarian world. In antiquity there was no mass production based upon systematic division of labor, no broad-based free market, no credit institutions analogous to modern industrial capitalist institutions. Pottery, weapons, and other specialized goods were produced in households, not

---

9. Social scientists argue as to whether surplus is the right word under these circumstances, since "surplus" is at the expense of peasant subsistence; see Wolf, *Peasants*, 110–11.

factories. The family remained the basic unit of production in antiquity, whether on the farm or in the city. Loans and credit were available, but debt routinely functioned to create dependencies rather than to capitalize profit-making enterprises. Interest-free loans might be made between friends or near kin; otherwise, interest rates in antiquity were exorbitant and usurious (sometimes as high as 50%).

Elites conducted their political affairs in cities, but also adhered to the peasant ideal of self-sufficiency (see Typical Peasant Values below) and household economy (so as not to be politically dependent upon others) by concentrating lands into great estates. War and conquest sometimes made this task easier, as in the case of the growth of Roman magnates and latifundia (large Italian agricultural estates) during the late Republic (about a century before Luke). During normal times, peasant debt secured by land and foreclosure enforced by courts (controlled by elites) played a much larger role in land concentration in the hands of the few. Figure 14 indicates how this process worked. Elites had access to "capital" through trade, taxation, and interest on money loans. With the narrow margin between subsistence and famine, peasants did not accumulate capital and once in debt found it difficult to get out. Although Jewish law forbade loans at interest, there is evidence that certain kinds of subtle usury were practiced in early Roman Palestine. Rabbi Hillel's *prozbul*, for instance, discussed in the *m. Sheb.* 10, was a legal fiction designed to avoid the debt release in the seventh year mandated by Old Testament law (Deut 15:1–3). Ostensibly to help debtors by making credit more readily available, the *prozbul* institution worked against the long-term interests of peasant-debtors. The creditor, by turning debt contracts over to a court, could thereby sidestep the literal meaning of Deut 15:3, "your hand shall release" (i.e., in the seventh year). Furthermore, the *prozbul* debt was secured upon immovable property (houses, land). Thus eventually, the first-century creditor wrested away control of the peasant's plot by enforcing foreclosure through the courts. The peasant became the new landlord's *tenant*, liable to pay rent in the future. Unequal distribution of wealth and poor harvests for the peasant made this practice feasible, but the need for economic security and social status on the part of the elites undoubtedly fueled the escalation of indebtedness and concentration of land in early first-century Palestine.[10] Figure 14 represents a *dynamic model* of the general process, envisioned over an indefinite period of time.

10. See further Kautsky, *The Politics of Aristocratic Empires*.

Figure 14

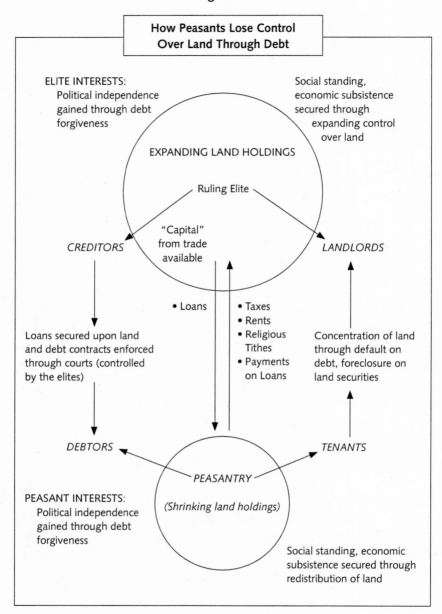

Typical Peasant Values

The chronic politically-induced poverty of peasant existence produces certain characteristic attitudes and values in peasant communities. Peasants generally view the goods of life as *in limited supply*. This view accords with the *zero-sum nature* of peasant economics: If someone gets ahead, someone else is sure to have lost.[11] A corollary of this perception is the *institutionalized envy* of the village. No one can get too far ahead of his neighbors without bringing into play village envy and inimical gossip. This gossip and envy may shame the offender into sharing (hence, gossip and envy function as a pressure toward redistribution of wealth). Peasants themselves come to expect very little out of life; any gain is traditionally carried off by the landlord. This peasant *wantlessness* coalesces with a stress in peasant life upon *self-sufficiency*. This means not only household self-sufficiency, having everything necessary for life within the productive realm of the peasant family and depending for nothing upon outsiders, but also being content with the little there is. The peasantry knows all too well what indebtedness to outsiders does to the subsistence margin (again consider Figure 14).

On the other hand, peasants will not endure exploitation beyond a certain point:

> The right to subsistence—to the preservation of one's status in all the dimensions of the ideal man's role—is the active moral principle in peasant societies. In other words, the only time our first-century villager or non-elite urbanite will rebel is when his subsistence is taken away.[12]

Given the role that debt plays in the loss of peasant control over land, it is not surprising that the two chief themes of ancient peasant rebellions were "abolition of debt" and "redistribution of land."[13] Peasant or rural radicalism does not aim at collectivization of property, as does modern industrial urban radicalism, but rather the maximum possible distribution of landed property.[14]

Elite Control Mechanisms

Understandably then, ancient elites had to develop strategies to deal with the simmering anger of the peasantry. *Patronage*—the development of in-

11. Foster, "Peasant Society and the Image of the Limited Good," 304–5.

12. Malina, *New Testament World*, (1981[1]) 77, (2001[3]) 91; see James C. Scott, *The Moral Economy of the Peasant*.

13. De Ste. Croix, *The Class Struggle in the Ancient Greek World*.

14. Irwin T. Sanders, *Rural Society*.

terpersonal bonds between social unequals—was a social institution that evolved in various forms throughout the ancient Mediterranean world in order to alleviate the otherwise harsh exploitation of the landlord and redistributive state. Through the practice of patronage, for instance through occasional remissions of overdue rent or through the sponsorship of a village festival, potentially explosive relations with peasant households might be headed off by actions designed to suggest solicitude and good will. Bonds of loyalty and gratefulness can sometimes avert the anger generated by naked exploitation. There were periods in antiquity, however, when exploitative pressures became too great and peasant banditry or revolt resulted. At such times, as during the Jewish War 66–70 CE, the ruling groups were forced to take *military action* against insurgency.

Peasant Religion

Like rural economics, the rural religion of antiquity was normally embedded within kin and political contexts. Peasant religion tends to be magical and geared to assuring the success of the agricultural work. While most peasant religion is informal and conducted within the everyday routines of the family and village, peasant "superstition" encourages a strong bond to form between peasant and religious specialist ("priest"), the latter insuring that the correct ritual actions are taken at the right times. The arrangement tends to work against the peasant economically when a priesthood becomes centralized outside the village and a strong temple organization demands frequent religious dues (another form of redistributive economy). When religious and/or political taxation pressures became too great, peasant religion can be linked with protest against exploitative temple, city, or state (e.g., as in Hesiod or the Old Testament prophet Micah). The Jesus tradition originally had strong overtones of rural protest.[15]

A Specific Model for the Countryside in the Traditions of Luke

A model of agrarian social stratification to suit Luke's Jesus traditions can be developed out of the foregoing general concepts as in Figure 15. The chief question the model answers is, Who controlled the land? The primary variables in the model are 1) the amount of land held or controlled (only in very general terms, see Who Controlled the Land? and Who Worked the Land?) and 2) the social identities of the controlling parties. Thus, the

15. Theissen, "Die Tempelweissagung Jesu"; and idem, *Sociology of Early Palestinian Christianity*.

model delineates the general pattern of social stratification as a function of land control or land tenure. It represents a *static model* and supplies a convenient map to selective social features of the ancient countryside.

Figure 15: Who Controlled the Land?
Agrarian Social Stratification Illustrated from Luke's Traditions

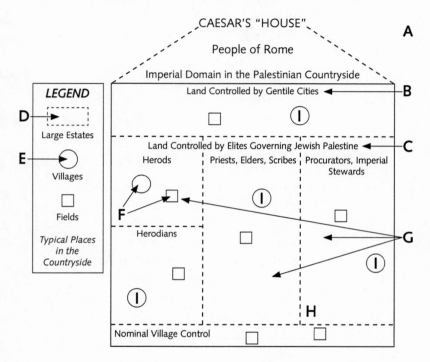

The letters shown in Figure 15 are keyed to the material in the following listing. The model can be overlaid, like a mosaic, with pieces of the rural Jesus tradition in Luke-Acts.

A. **Social Stratification**: All through Luke's writings there is evidence of the great disparities in wealth, power, and privilege present in the Roman Empire. The powerful and those who control large amounts of land appear prominently (a representative listing only): Luke 1:5 (Herod the Great); 2:1 (Caesar Augustus); 3:1–2 (Tiberius Caesar, Pontius Pilate, Herod Antipas, Philip, Lysanias, Annas, Caiaphas); 12:16 (Unnamed landlord); 16:1 (Rich man with an estate); Acts 4:36–37 (Barnabas owns land); 13:1

(Manean, member of Herod Antipas's court). The conditions of the powerless, destitute, and dishonored are also shown, even contrasted with the former group: Luke 3:11 (Sharing coats, food necessary); 6:20–25 (Beatitudes for the poor, hungry, sorrowing, but woes for the rich); 16:19–31 (Dives and Lazarus). The bitterness and anger of the oppressed sometimes shines through: Luke 1:52–53 (Mary's song, the "Magnificat"); 6:24–25 (woes for the rich); 8:18 (To him who has . . .); 16:23 (Dives in hell).

B. **Land Controlled by Gentile Cities**: Not all land in the Palestine of the Jesus tradition was under Jewish control. The presence of Gentiles and foreigners injected cultural issues into agrarian conflict: Luke 8:26, 34 (Gerasene Demoniac).

C. **Land Controlled by Jewish Elites or Roman Agents**: Luke-Acts gives information about these people in passing: Luke 1:5; Acts 23:35 (Herod the Great); Luke 3:1; 23:1 (Pontius Pilate); 3:1, 19; 8:3; 9:7, 9; 13:31; 23:7, 8, 11, 12, 15; Acts 4:27; 13:1 (Herod Antipas); Acts 13:1 (Manean, member of Herod Antipas's court); Luke 3:1 (Annas); 3:1 (Caiaphas); Acts 12:1, 6, 11, 19–20, 21 (Herod Agrippa I); Luke 7:3; Acts 4:5 (Elders); Luke 9:22; Acts 6:12 (Scribes); Luke 20:1; 22:52; Acts 4:18; 23:2 (Chief priests).

D. **Large Estates, Estate Relations, or Patronage**: From Luke-Acts we get a glimpse into relations between the powerful and the powerless, especially relations embedded in the political institution of the large rural estate: Luke 8:18 (More will be given to the rich and powerful); 12:16–21 (Rich fool); 12:33–34 (Alms); 12:42–46 (Faithful servant); 12:47–48 (Discipline of servants); 13:6–9 (Fig tree); 14:18 (Buying a field); 14:19 (Five! yoke of oxen); 16:1–8 (Unjust steward); 16:10–13 (Loyal service); 16:19–31 (Dives and Lazarus); 17:7–10 (Servant's reward); 18:18–30 (Ruler and wealth); 19:11–26 (Minas);

20:9–19 (Wicked tenants); Acts 12:20 (Herod Agrippa deprives Tyre and Sidon of "king's grain").

E. **Village Relations/Realities**: Likewise, Luke-Acts gives us a glimpse into who lives in villages, some of their physical surroundings, and social conditions: Luke 1:58 (Neighbors and kinsfolk); 4:16–30 (Nazareth); 6:1–4 (Gleaning); 7:11–15 (Nain); 7:32 (Children in the market); 8:4–8 (Sower); 9:1–6 (Disciples' mission in villages); 9:52–56 (Xenophobia of villagers); 10:38–42 (Hospitality of Martha and Mary); 11:5–8 (Importune friend); 12:6 (Price of sparrows); 12:13–14 (Dividing inheritance); 12:22–30 (On anxiety); 12:39 (Thief at midnight); 12:52–53 (Household orientation); 13:19 (Mustard plant in fields); 13:21 (Leaven); 14:28–29 (Building a tower); 15:3–6 (Lost sheep); 15:8–10 (Lost coin); 15:11–32 (Prodigal son); 17:12 (Lepers in a Samaritan village); 19:31 (Reality of eminent domain); 24:13–31 (Village hospitality); Acts 8:25 (Gospel proclaimed to Samaritan villages); 11:28–29 (Famine under Claudius).

F. **Sayings and Proverbs Reflecting Rural Realities**: This agrarian oral wisdom can directly or indirectly give us information about realities in the countryside: Luke 3:8 (Bear fruits reflecting repentance); 3:9 (axe); 3:17 (winnowing fork); 5:36 (Old garment patched); 5:37 (Old wineskins); 6:34–35 (Lending without expecting in return); 6:38 (Giving full measure); 6:41–42 (Speck and log); 6:43 (Good and bad trees); 6:44 (Figs not gathered from thorns); 6:48–49 (Building house on a rock); 7:32 (Children in market); 8:16 (Light and lampstand); 8:18 (To him who has . . .); 9:25 (Gaining the whole world); 10:2 (Harvest is plentiful); 10:7 (Laborer deserves wages); 11:11–13 (Father and gifts); 14:28 (Cost of tower building); 14:34–35 (Salt and dunghill); 16:13 (You cannot serve God and Mammon); 20:47–21:4 (Widows' houses devoured); 21:29–31 (Fig tree as a sign of the times).

G. **Economic Realities—Debt, Taxation, Oppression**: The political character of ancient economics, redistribution, and debt all come to expression in Lukan traditions: Luke 2:2 (Census of Quirinius); 3:13 (Overcollection of taxes); 3:14 (Extortion); 4:19 (hope for Jubilee release?); 5:27 (Tax office); 6:34 (Lending and usurious return); 7:41–42 (Two debtors); 8:18 ("The rich keep getting richer"); 11:4 (Forgiveness petition); 12:58–59 (Debt bondage); 19:1– 10 (Zacchaeus); 19:11–27 (Minas and lending at interest); 19:45–48 (Temple cleansing); 20:9–16 ("Wicked" tenants); 20:20–26 (Tribute to Caesar); 20:47—21:4 (Widows' houses devoured).

H. **Hunger, Robbery, Violence, and General Insecurity**: Luke-Acts reveals the general conditions of political insecurity and subsistence anxiety in the ancient countryside: Luke 1:53 (Feeding the hungry); 3:10–14 (John's words to tax collectors and soldiers); 3:19–20 (Herod imprisons John the Baptist); 4:29 (Villagers at Nazareth try to kill Jesus); 6:1 (Plucking grain on the Sabbath); 6:20–21, 24–25 (Beatitudes and woes); 9:12–17 (Feeding of the 5000); 9:52–56; 10:5–8, 10–12 (Xenophobia of villagers); 10:29–37 (Good Samaritan); 11:34–36 (Sound eye); 12:22–32 (Anxiety); 12:46–48 (Beating of servants); 12:51–53 (Division in households); 12:58–59 (Threat of prison); 13:1, 4 (Building accidents? Police actions?); 20:9–16 (Violence of tenants); 20:47—21:4 (Widows' houses devoured); 21:5–6 (Temple will be violently destroyed); 22:36, 38, 49–52; 23:19, 32, 39–43 (Robber allusions); 23:26 (Simon of Cyrene—forced labor); Acts 5:36–37 (Mention of the revolutionaries Theudas and Judas the Galilean); 11:28–29 (Famine under Claudius).

I. **Oppressed and Economically Marginalized Groups**: Many marginalized and landless people appear in the pages of Luke-Acts: Luke 2:8 (Shepherds); 2:36–38 (Widows); 4:25 (Elijah and widows); 5:12–16 (Leper); 6:20–21 (Hungry and poor); 7:11–12 (Widow at Nain); 7:41–42 (Debtors);

8:18 (Powerless, have-nots); 12:58–59 (Debtors); 17:11–
19 (Lepers); 20:9–16 (Tenants); 21:1–4 (Widows); Acts
3:2 (Lame man).

This Lukan material, along with the various dimensions of Figure 15, are
now discussed in detail.

Imaging the Countryside through the Model and Luke's Traditions
Who Controlled the Land?

The land of early first-century Palestine was directly or indirectly under the
political control of Caesar or the people of Rome. Caesar thought of his
rich empire as a large "household," but imperial taxation (through control
of land) amounted in fact to a gigantic redistributive economy. Caesar
had "inherited" lucrative estates from the Hasmoneans in the Esdraelon
Plain and the Jericho area. The rest of the land was nominally under the
ownership of the people of Rome, but in practice it was controlled by the
local elites of Palestine who acted as Roman agents of subjugation (even
if unwillingly). The major classes of these elites are indicated: Gentile cities [B] controlled land along the Mediterranean coast, in Samaria, and
in the Transjordan (Luke 8:26). The Jewish areas [C] were controlled for
the most part by the Herods, with oversight from imperial agents like
Pontius Pilate (Luke 23:1). Smaller subordinate shares went to political
subordinates—stewards of Caesar's estates and to other "secular" landowners (Herodians, Elders of the Jews, Scribes, etc.). Herod the Great is
mentioned as a chronological reference point in Luke 1:5. Herod Antipas,
the first Herod's son as well as governor of Galilee when Jesus was alive,
appears numerous times in the Gospel of Luke (3:1, 19; 8:3; 9:7, 9; 13:31;
23:7, 8, 11, 12, 15). Grandson Herod Agrippa I makes an entrance in the
pages of Acts (12:1, 6, 11, 19, 20– 21; 13:1). The Herodians, large land-
holders who were political partisans of the family of Herod, are known to
us from Matthew (22:16) and Mark (3:6; 12:13), but Luke remains silent
about them (unless Manean was one, Acts 13:1). Elders ("leading men"
of the Jewish people in the first century, possibly in part Herodians) are
mentioned in both Luke (e.g., 7:3) and Acts (e.g., 4:5). In the same breath,
Luke includes the Pharisaic leaders, the Scribes (e.g., Luke 9:22; Acts 6:12).
The high priestly families held land also, passed down from generation to
generation in the Second Temple period and perhaps increasingly augmented by land acquired through default on debts or Temple dedications.

These "chief priests" appear in Luke–Acts as leading opponents of Jesus or his followers (Luke 20:1; 22:52; Acts 4:18; 23:2). Most land tended to be under the control, therefore, of indigenous or foreign elites. It was subject at all times to rents and taxes of various sorts. Very little, if any, land was under indigenous village control during the first century ("Nominal village control" in Figure 15; see further below).

As we have seen, the landlords of Jesus' Palestine were accumulating land at the expense of the peasantry through debt manipulations. The concentration of land control in the hands of the few resulted in marked social stratification [A]. Luke's Gospel leaves no doubt that some landowners had access to more (see Luke 8:18). The Rich Fool was undoubtedly familiar throughout the first-century Mediterranean world (12:16–21; a useful comparison can be made to the famous character of Trimalchio in the *Satyricon* of Petronius). There were those who owned vineyards (13:6–9), who could buy more fields (14:18), who had many oxen (14:19). By contrast, there were those in material want who needed charity (3:11). Some in both Jesus' and Luke's audience needed to contemplate giving alms and benefactions: Luke 12:33–34; 18:22; and 19:11–26. Distribution of goods was not always done equitably (8:18). There was characteristically a political aspect to distribution. The strong and powerful could take what they needed or desired (3:14). Herod Agrippa could turn food into a political weapon (Acts 12:20). Eminent domain was a fact of life (Luke 19:31). The reality of *slavery*—unfree, coerced labor—is everywhere attested: Luke 12:42–46 and 47–48; 16:10–13; 17:7–10. Sharp social stratification is the manifest background for the Lukan beatitudes and woes (6:20–25). A most graphic picture of social division is offered, moreover, in the story of Dives and Lazarus (16:19–31). In general, wealth, land, and the subsistence security that control of land represents were not within peasant grasp.

Who Worked the Land?

The estate lands of these ruling groups were worked by peasants. Most of this rural populace, which in Palestine was predominantly Jewish, dwelt in villages. Village lands without question were subject to taxation. The level of taxation may have been as high as 50% of the total crop in some cases.[16] As a result, relations between social classes were frequently not cordial (Luke 20:9–19). Undoubtedly only a very few village parcels were

---

16. Oakman, *Jesus and the Economic Questions of His Day*, 71.

free of rent to a local landlord. These were the lands of "middle peasants," a group whose size is difficult to determine from the historical sources. The percentage of land under direct village control by "small peasants" is also uncertain from the historical record. It will have been very small. Most village lands were estate lands of the Herods and their agents or of the Jewish elders and priestly families. Furthermore, Jewish villagers needed to set aside produce or land to meet Temple obligations. This was at minimum a tenth of the harvest (tithe, Deut 14:22). Certainly some Jewish villages were the homes of priests (Zechariah and Elizabeth, Luke 1:5, 39–40; perhaps why priest and Levite were going to Jericho in 10:31–32), who received a portion of the village harvest. Other Jewish village lands may have comprised part of the Temple "estate" proper under the conviction that "the land belongs to Yahweh" (Lev 25:23—a Priestly tradition).

Character of First-Century Village Life

Besides the large estate, village [D] (despite the designation of "city": 7:11–15; 10:38) and field [E] (Luke 6:1–4) are envisioned in Luke's Gospel as the primary social settings of the ancient Palestinian countryside. The wilderness areas stand over against the sown fields and the cities as the refuge of demons and social rebels (Luke 4:2; 8:29; 11:24; Acts 21:38).

The villages of ancient Palestine seem to have been organized along kinship or quasi-kinship lines (Luke 1:58). Many villages will have been comprised of members of a single extended family. Mutual help was expected within the village community (11:5–8). Generosity in line with general reciprocity was the village ideal (6:38; 11:11–13). Frugality was a way of life, but did not preclude common celebration (15:6, 8–9, 22–23). Economic exchange within familial or quasi-familial context is evident.

Hospitality might perhaps be extended to outsiders (Luke 10:8, 38; and 24:13–31). Peasant villagers as a rule, however, tend to be suspicious and mistrustful of strangers, because outsiders so often violate the interests of the village community. This defensiveness can be seen behind Luke 9:5, 52–56; and 10:10. Recall the tendency of peasant villagers to behave toward outsiders in terms of negative reciprocity. Perceived betrayal of peasant family or village interests means ostracism or worse: Luke 4:23–29 (Jesus nearly killed by angry residents of Nazareth) and 15:19 (Prodigal Son not worthy to be called a son).

Typical Economic Experience in the Village

For the most part, peasant villagers of the first century CE were *labor generalists*, that is, proficient at a number of agricultural and domestic tasks. The peasant family normally produced and consumed most of what it needed "in-house." Simple technology and life-needs permitted most things to be built or constructed by family members, such as houses (Luke 6:48–49) or towers (14:28–29). All villages were primarily agricultural production centers, but since agriculture normally did not keep villagers occupied year around, there was opportunity for its members to adopt other economic pursuits. This incentive was increased by any surplus village children. Surplus village labor power could easily be absorbed into the labor needs of the large estates (10:2). These workers were paid wages by the day (10:7).

There is evidence outside the New Testament that Palestinian villages tended to specialize in certain much-needed crafts—notably crafts related to clothes, building, special foods, fishing, medicine, metal working, tools, etc.[17] Handicraft and small craft production was absorbed in intra- and inter-village barter, probably by the Temple economy as well (Luke 13:4). Many products of craftsmen, however, were only available to the elites. Any such economic activity was purely supplemental for the village economy. The predominant activity at all times remained agriculture.

Broad agricultural experience is attested in sayings and proverbs of the Lukan Jesus tradition [F]. First, familiarity with a variety of Palestinian flora and crops is indicated: grain (Luke 6:1; 8:5–8), weeds (6:44), grapes and wine (5:37–39; 6:44), figs (6:44; 21:29–31), orchards (6:43), condiments (11:42; 13:19). Second, farm animals—both of Jews and of Gentiles—are sometimes mentioned: sheep or lambs (2:8; 10:3; 15:3–6), swine (8:32; 15:16), a colt (19:30). The tradition is quite familiar with village or agricultural operations and tools: axe (3:9), winnowing fork (3:17), new woven cloth (5:36), broadcast sowing (8:5), oil lamp (8:16), plow (9:62), women serving guests (10:40), baking and providing hospitality to strangers (11:5–6), care of fig trees (13:6–9), use of leaven (13:21), salt and dunghills (14:35), servant plowing (17:7).

The basic economic problem of all ancient village life, as has been already stressed, was the narrow margin between subsistence and famine. Mutual help (Luke 11:5) and liberal gleaning rights (6:1–4) were nor-

17. Klausner, *Jesus of Nazareth*, 177–78.

mal institutions that carried villagers through lean periods of the year. Since peasant villagers and urban poor had little food reserves, the chief economic effects of any serious famine invariably fell upon them (Luke 15:13–16; Acts 11:28–29). Heavy rents and taxations only served to strain this narrow margin. Understandably, many peasants lived under constant anxiety over subsistence. Words of the Lukan Jesus tradition address this anxiety, admonishing disciples to trust in a providential God (Luke 12:22, 24, 29–31).

There is good reason to believe that chronic overtaxation and debts played a significant role in the unrest in Palestine preceding the Jewish War and earlier in the genesis of the Jesus movement [G]. Luke knows the paraphernalia of Roman taxation: The census (2:2), the toll collector's office (5:27), and tribute to Caesar (20:20–26). Oppressive taxation can be inferred from the tradition (3:13–14; 20:22; 23:2). Accumulated wealth, or "Mammon" (from an Aramaic word meaning "wealth"), was adjudged evil from an agrarian perspective because perceived as gained unjustly (16:9, 11). Moreover, Mammon represented an eternal threat to one's life (9:25; 12:20). While Luke's story of the Minas (19:12–27) differs in a number of details from the parallel version in Matthew 25:14–30, the general picture of loans at interest (usury) and their social consequences becomes clear. Interest violated the zero-sum sensibilities of peasant villagers. The typical peasant response to wealth—hiding it in the ground—is shamed by the story. The rewards of unjust gain are control of villages' agricultural increase. Insolvent debtors faced prison (Luke 12:58–59). Luke's version of the Lord's Prayer contains the significant fourth petition (fifth petition in Matthew's Gospel, Matt 6:12): "Forgive us our sins, for we ourselves forgive every one who is indebted to us" (11:4). Luke also expands the saying at Luke 6:32–33 (= Matt 5:46–47) with the significant statement, "lend, expecting nothing in return" (6:35). This remarkable Lukan special tradition clearly forbids usury. Elsewhere, Lukan tradition places a definite stress upon debt forgiveness and its beneficial effects (7:41–42; 16:1–8). Forgiveness or restitution can also be contemplated in the case of overtaxation (19:8).

Peasant Disaffection

Violence became a regular part of village experience and rural consciousness (Luke 1:51–52; 9:54) [H]. Violence might come in the form of extortion (Luke 3:14), of forceful removal of rent from the threshing floor (see 20:10) or of fraud (3:13; 19:8), from robbers who had left the normal courses of society (10:30; 12:39), through police actions (13:1) or through forceful imprisonment (3:19–20; 12:58–59). Estate slaves were often beaten (12:46–48). Forced labor was possible (23:26). Robbers were a fact of life (22:36, 38, 49–52; 23:19, 32, 39–43; Acts 5:36–37). These were often painted by ancient aristocrats like Josephus as self-serving and self-aggrandizing, but many were undoubtedly "Robin Hoods"—the type of peasant leaders whom Hobsbawm has called social bandits—who effected forceful redistribution of goods they believed had been robbed from the countryside by the powerful.[18] Intra-village conflict might originate because of inheritance disputes (12:13–14; 15:28, 30); or it might be provoked through some other external cause (4:29; 12:51–53).

Peasant Victims

Luke's tradition knows a host of social misfits and down-and-outers [I]. These are the victims of the Roman agrarian order. Their individual life-courses are never recounted, but their plight makes sense from the perspective of typical agrarian disorder. Given the narrow margin between subsistence and starvation, the presence of the hungry and poor is not surprising (6:20–21). The pressure toward debt has already been indicated (7:41–42; 12:58–59). Many widows appear in Luke's pages (2:36–38; 4:25; 7:11–12; 18:3; 20:47; 21:1–4). These women without a husband were particularly vulnerable to exploitation and abandonment within agrarian societies; many Old Testament passages attest to their perennial vulnerability (Exod 22:22–24; Isa 1:17; Mal 3:5). Their goods and household were prey for legal disputes (Luke 18:3; 20:47). Other have-nots were vulnerable as well (8:18). In a highly politicized, redistributive economy, the powerless were the standard victims. Loss of adequate means of subsistence meant loss of honor or status within the community.[19]

Another group of people fit within this category. They are those whose lack of physical health meant exclusion from the normal affairs of society. Lepers epitomize this ostracized group (Luke 17:12). For them, physical healing must also mean restoration of status within the community. Ill health implies undignified dependence upon others' generosity (Luke 18:35; Acts 3:2). So in Luke, Jesus restores numerous people to health

18. See implied popular support for the brigand Eleazar in Josephus, *War* 2.253. See Hanson, "Jesus and the Social Bandits."

19. See Malina, *New Testament World*, (1981[1]) 85, (2001[3]) 100.

and reinvigorates their social standing (e.g., Luke 4:39; 5:14; 7:15; 18:43). The disciples duplicate this work in Acts (e.g., 3:8; 9:40; 19:11). To some extent, eye and skin ailments in the gospel tradition might have been the product of poor nutrition (Luke 11:34). Under such conditions, there was a significant connection between Jesus' feeding work (9:17), advocacy for the hungry (6:21), and Jesus' healing work.

Luke's Jesus makes this kind of liberation and healing a hallmark of his ministry (4:18–19). Jesus' inaugural sermon recalls the Jubilee tradition of the Old Testament (Lev 25; Deut 15; Isa 61), wherein the covenant community is kept healthy by periodic redistribution of land, redemption of slaves, and abolition of indebtedness.[20] If Luke has not made this an overt program in the Gospel and Acts, his allusion to the issue of religiously mandated agrarian reform prompts the final part of this investigation.

TENSIONS WITHIN THE LUKAN CONCEPTION: HOW DOES LUKE REPRESENT THE COUNTRYSIDE?
Preliminary Considerations

Luke apportions a good deal of space to the countryside, as we have seen in the foregoing. Luke has received and chosen to leave the countryside somewhat unexpurgated in the tradition. We now turn to consider *how Luke represents the countryside* in his two-volume work. This venture both utilizes and goes somewhat beyond the traditional redaction critical method; it might better be termed *interest criticism* (pursuant to our adoption of a conflict framework for analysis). Using the foregoing sociological ruminations as a backdrop, we propose to see how Luke's conception embraces the standard interests of the countryside. Does Luke come out clearly in favor of rural interests, or does his presentation militate against those interests, or is the situation somewhat in between these two extremes? A few preliminary observations are in order.

A careful study of the word commonly translated as "city" in Luke-Acts (*polis*)—combined with information from Palestinian archaeology, Josephus, and the Talmud—will show that Luke applies the word apparently indiscriminately to places that were patently villages in Jesus' own day. This is certainly true of Nazareth (Luke 1:26) and Nain (7:11), possibly true of Bethlehem (2:4, because the appellation "city of David" was traditional). On the other hand, Luke can utilize the Greek word for vil-

20. See Hollenbach, "Liberating Jesus for Social Involvement."

lage, *kōmē*, quite appropriately (5:17; 8:1 in coordination with "city"; 9:6, etc.). This phenomenon may simply indicate Luke's unfamiliarity with Palestine, as is sometimes suggested. On the other side, Luke may have in mind a distinction for *polis* and *kōmē* that we are as yet unaware of—he may, for instance, use *polis* at times in the technical sense of "town" where a population settlement serves as an agricultural market center or tax collection point or simply as a granary for the surrounding fields.[21] *Kōmai* would then be smaller satellite settlements of *poleis*. In this scenario, Luke could perhaps locate himself quite precisely both sociologically and within the Roman Empire by his use of this terminology. It is unfortunately not possible to settle at this point whether Luke is ignorant of Palestinian settlement patterns or really better informed about such distinctions at a certain point of time than we are. Such considerations urge caution, however, in assessing Luke's representation of the countryside. Luke's use of terminology would not seem to be an easy indicator of his interests.

Perhaps more significant than terminology, Luke emphasizes again and again that the message of Jesus in the Gospel and of the various evangelists in Acts consistently reached peasants and the rural precincts. Consider the following passages: Pharisees from every village in Galilee come to hear Jesus (Luke 5:17); Jesus passes through "city and village" in his preaching tours (8:1; see 13:22); Jesus thoroughly covers Galilean villages (9:6); Jesus visits Samaritan villages (9:52, 56; 10:38?; 17:12); in Acts 8:25 the disciples evangelize many villages of the Samaritans. Even more important than these references are Luke's summaries regarding "surrounding country": Jesus' fame spreads through all the surrounding country of Galilee (Luke 4:14, 37); Luke believes Jesus' fame also reached everywhere in Judea (7:17, but Nain is not in Judea); the Hellenists are dispersed throughout the Judean and Samaritan countryside (Acts 8:1); even Paul preaches to the Judean countryside (26:20); in Acts 14:6–7 Paul and Barnabas preach to Lystra and Derbe and all the surrounding country; the Word of God spreads through the whole countryside of Pisidian Antioch (13:49); the Galatian and Phrygian countrysides receive the good news (16:6; 18:23).

Most of these countryside references occur in Lukan summaries of the gospel's progress. What the list seems to imply, then, is that Luke has at least a passing interest in the countryside as an object of evangelization.

---

21. On the use of *polis* for a chief city of a rural district, see examples from the Egyptian papyri in Moulton and Milligan, *The Vocabulary of the Greek Testament*, 525.

It remains to explore whether Luke's Gospel authentically represents rural interests.

The Politics of the Countryside: Violent Realism or Irenic Idealism?

Ramsay MacMullen begins his study *Roman Social Relations* by noting an encounter on the road between the party of young Marcus Aurelius and two shepherds. The encounter was a brief but violent one, which MacMullen observes was rather typical in rural areas during the period of emergent Christianity. According to Josephus (*War* 2.60), a Judean shepherd named Athronges declared himself king and engaged in violent brigandage at the turn of the eras. Enmity between shepherd and settled folk became a commonplace in the Tannaitic traditions of the second century CE.[22] Shepherds invariably kept flocks belonging to others; the enmity between them and settled villagers arose because mobile flocks were a grave danger to the sown fields and shepherds were careless of others' fields.

So MacMullen sums up the general character of the ancient countryside and wilderness areas in this way: "The less populated countryside throughout the empire approached a state of endemic warfare, from which only a stout cudgel, a fast horse, or a well-built little fortress gave protection."[23] The famous "Dangers" (*Peristaseis*) catalog of St. Paul in 2 Cor 11:23–27 corroborates MacMullen's view (even with allowances made for hyperbole): ". . . in danger from rivers, danger from robbers . . . danger in the city, danger in the wilderness." Characteristic of the view of an urban apostle, there is no countryside for Paul—only city and wilderness.

It is significant for our theme, then, that Luke includes the (to us) quaint story about the shepherds at the birth of Jesus. Does Luke intend that one of the more violence-prone groups of rural antiquity is the first to hear of "peace on earth," or is the countryside in Luke the place where peace is assumed to be prevalent, or where peace may get a receptive or sympathetic hearing? If so, then Luke has idealized the countryside into a region of peacefulness. Of course, this would militate against what is known of the authentic ancient countryside from historians like MacMullen and what could be predicted about the countryside by conflict theory. A genuine restoration of peace between shepherds and peasant villagers of

---

22. Goodman, *State and Society in Roman Galilee*, 24; Baron, *A Social and Religious History of the Jews*, 1:254.

23. MacMullen, *Roman Social Relations*, 4.

antiquity would have been the resettlement of shepherds upon land and the incorporation of their flocks into the rural economy.

Consideration of some other of Luke's material seems to bear out the idealizing tendency of Luke's conception. Both John and Jesus are born in the countryside proper (Luke 1:57, 65; 2:7); both John and Jesus are reared away from major cities (Luke 1:80; 2:51). John's ministry takes place in the wilderness (3:3). Jesus' temptations begin in the wilderness, but end in Jerusalem. Often Jesus escapes to a lonely place for refuge (4:42). By contrast, cities (even if some of Luke's "cities" are patently villages) are frequently the place of confrontation and conflict *over the message of peace and salvation* (Nazareth: 4:29; "One of the cities": 5:21; Capernaum[?]: 6:11; Jerusalem: 13:34; 19:42, etc.). Significant intracity conflict surrounding the message continues in Acts (5:18; 6:12; but see 7:58; 12:1–3; 13:45; 14:5, 19, etc.).

Of course, the tradition compels Luke to acknowledge conflict in the countryside and wilderness as well (Luke 6:1–5; 10:30–35). The issue, however, is how Luke understands or interprets the nature of that conflict. What does it signify? Luke has, as we have seen, several allusions to robbers and swords. The relationship between this conflict and rural oppression is not clarified by the evangelist. Luke also knows of conflict within rural households (10:40; 12:52–53), but this conflict is over Jesus rather than explicitly rural concerns. Only if Luke understands Jesus as representing rural interests, can this conflict be understood as pro-countryside.

As Figures 1 and 2 have hopefully made clear, one significant measuring stick of rural interests and cause of rural unrest in antiquity was the issue of land control. Luke's narrative gives a mixed perspective on this important rural preoccupation. Luke 4:19 might allude to the ancient Jubilee traditions of Lev 25 and Isa 61:1–4 that promised redemption of family land. However, a consideration of the one tradition in the Synoptic Gospels that seems to address radical peasant demands for land redistribution, namely Mark 10:28–30 and parallels, shows it is significantly omitted by Luke. Mark 10:29 and Matt 19:29 expressly state that Jesus' disciples have left *fields* for the gospel's sake. Luke omits the reference to fields. Furthermore, Mark 10:30 promises the disciples *fields* in the age to come. Both Matthew and Luke delete this reference in their versions. Luke also lacks the Matthean beatitude, "The meek shall inherit the land" (Matt 5:5), which might resonate with peasant radicalism. The so-called Wicked

Tenants parable (Luke 20:9–16) vividly shows the tenor of landlord-tenant relationships in the early Empire and indicates that a frequent bone of rural contention was who got the fruits of the land. As Luke has used this tradition, however, the point has been allegorized into a condemnation of the "'tenants'" (i.e., Israel's present leadership's) stewardship of the vineyard (God's people). This point becomes clear from Luke 20:19. Luke does not utilize the story in any manifest way as a critique of landed relations, nor is Luke sympathetic with the tenants. Similarly, Luke 13:6–9 plays upon such tensions, but Luke places the story in a context emphasizing accountability to God and repentance (12:47–48, 56, 58; 13:3, 5). Finally, in Acts 2:44–45; 4:32–37; 5:1–11, Luke stresses the collective holding of the early Jerusalem church's land. Such collective property would militate against peasant radicalism's demand for land redistribution.

In one critical area, therefore, Luke apparently fails to represent adequately the interests of the ancient countryside. Collective control of land, as advocated in Acts, would not "sell" with peasant villagers. For them, redistribution of land implies redistribution of heritable plots that will sustain the honor and political independence of individual families. Collective control simply substitutes one landlord for another. Luke holds up a rather idealized countryside in his narrative, out of sync with this one crucial peasant interest, but where Jesus' and the apostles' message takes root and where a more or less peaceful refuge from the violence waiting the message in the cities is possible. An investigation of Luke's handling of political economy will bear out this impression in another way.

The Economics of the Countryside:
Place of Generosity or Stinginess?

Just as control of land was a crucial question for peasants in antiquity, so also was the harsh experience of political economy in the form of debt. Luke has a significant amount of material dealing with debt, as the analysis above has indicated. However, a careful consideration of that material will also reveal that Luke has not focused on the connection between debt and loss of land or between debt forgiveness and restoration of control over land. These are the accents one would expect if Luke were overtly concerned with the interests of countryfolk. Luke's Jubilary allusion in 4:18–19 does not specifically mention debt remission or land redemption. Luke's version of the Lord's Prayer has the significant, "for we ourselves also forgive everyone in debt to us" (11:4). Taken by itself, this petition might appeal to rural folk. But they are usually *in debt* and *themselves in need of debt remission*. In its present form, the petition makes more sense on the lips of creditors—the first part, "Forgive us our sins," even suggests the Publican of Luke 18:13. A creditor-moral is explicitly drawn from Luke 7:41–42. And surely Luke 6:35 has in mind the behavior of creditors. Since it explicitly advocates loans without expecting interest or even return of principle, the passage envisions pure general reciprocity or gift. Moreover, Luke's Jesus does not limit this loan to near-kin; apparently such reciprocity is to be practiced even toward strangers. Similarly, the actions of the Good Samaritan (10:33–35) represent the practice of general reciprocity toward strangers. The restitution of Zacchaeus (19:8) and the debt forgiveness of the Unjust Steward (16:6–7) also fit this picture. Only in a partial and incomplete way can Luke's debt material be said to serve the interests of the countryside related to debt. Luke uses the material to draw morals for creditors.

Giving and sharing are certainly prominent emphases in Luke-Acts, as a series of sayings at Luke 6:34–38; in 16:9–13; and at Acts 20:35 suggest. Luke seems to have urged reciprocity exchanges as a mark of the Jesus/Christian movement. This is in line with Jesus' own message, as Luke's tradition, Mark 6:38 (Sharing among 5000), Mark 10:21 (Rich are to give to the poor), Matt 5:42 (Giving to whomever asks), and many other gospel passages would suggest. However, for Luke reciprocity does not seem to change the *political* structure of social intercourse, nor does it mark the disappearance of social hierarchy per se within the Christian community (see Luke 22:26 with its parallels). Luke 12:48 is a central text for understanding the Lukan conception of material and political stewardship. There are, of course, the excoriations of the rich and powerful (1:52–53; 6:24–26) and the "utopian" passages like 12:33 or Acts 2:44–46. Yet Luke also acknowledges that some in the early Christian movement (and in Luke's community) possessed more than others. So he mentions the wealthy women who supported Jesus during the ministry (Luke 8:3); he notes the special ministration of Joseph of Arimathea (23:53); and he acknowledges that some early Christians had special means (Acts 4:37; 12:12). Luke is impressed with their example of sharing, but he never clearly states that the whole politico-economic order of the Roman agrarian state will be dramatically altered by Jesus or the kingdom of God.

Patronage and the redistributive function of the community will still be necessary.

Leaders of the Christian community are *not to be called* "benefactors," but they *are to be* benefactors (22:25–26). That Luke has an ideology based upon the practice of Hellenistic benefaction seems clear.[24] That the country mores of antiquity could easily sympathize with this standard when generalized to all is questionable. The Prodigal Son story depicts a generous father who gives despite being wronged. Would a peasant patriarch act in this way? Perhaps. General reciprocity is normally practiced within close kin relationships. There is the somewhat parallel saying at Luke 11:11–12. Yet to give on this basis to complete strangers, as the Good Samaritan does, would be difficult to expect from a village patriarch or any normal peasant.

Recall that most peasant households strive for self-sufficiency, face narrow margins between subsistence and famine, often account for barter exchanges on the basis of balanced reciprocity, and have an oversupply of children to care for. Under the typical circumstances of first-century Palestine, most peasant fathers would not have been so generous. Children who acted in that dishonorable way were easily disowned. According to peasant norms the Prodigal's brother would be the one rewarded with the fatted calf. Peasants would feel the injustice of the father's endangering the family subsistence for the younger son's frivolity.[25]

Most villagers in Jesus' rural environment would have been stingy, as are most peasants under the pressure of subsistence and village envy. Peasants at the time of the early Empire were probably forced by heavy taxation to account carefully for everything and call in debts on a strict quid pro quo basis. If Jesus told stories like the Prodigal Son or Good Samaritan, it was to subvert traditional village morality and open the countryside up to other possibilities. It is likely that Jesus urged the practice of general reciprocity as characteristic of the kingdom of God and as radical protest against the agrarian situation in early Roman Palestine.[26] In Luke's narrative, the stories of the Prodigal Son and Good Samaritan

---

24. Danker, *Luke*, 6–17.

25. See the cultural appraisal of the father's actions in Bailey, *Poet and Peasant*, 181–82.

26. Oakman, *Jesus and the Economic Questions of His Day*, 215–16.

undoubtedly function to shame those who have amassed goods into sharing. Dives and Lazarus must serve a similar purpose.

Where Jesus envisioned the destruction of the Temple as a prelude
to a general socio-economic arrangement ("kingdom of God") devoid
of redistributive political economy, Luke plays down this element in the
Jesus tradition compared to the other evangelists (Luke 19:45–46), and
he "historicizes" the allusion to the Temple destruction (Luke 21:6, 20).
Mark 10:2 and 14 imply the Temple's destruction will accompany the
final apocalyptic events of the establishment of God's reign (Mark 10:26),
but Luke's parallel passages look back to the historical destruction of the
Temple in the Jewish War. The redistributive political economy of the
Temple is defunct in Luke's view as a divine mechanism for social justice,
probably to be replaced by a redistributive Christian community (Acts
2:44–45; 4:32–37). Redistribution by its very nature involves unequal
status and a "division of labor" (Luke 22:25–26; Acts 6:1–4). There must
be faithful overseers of the distribution and guardians of the store (Luke
12:41–48). All of Luke's incorporation of reciprocity exchanges and debt
remissions do not change this social fact.

The general impression is that Luke's reciprocity motif is operative
within a social setting still marked by unequal status and redistributive
economic mechanisms. Hence, it is still a hierarchical benefaction or patronage motif. It is not a strategy for a general restructuring of society in
the direction of primitive village exchange without redistributive institutions or patrons/landlords/creditors, as was Jesus' exclusive emphasis upon
general reciprocity toward all. Yet since Luke clearly keeps the reciprocity
motif applicable to all, so as to violate normal peasant sensitivities, he has
preserved an authentic theme of the Jesus tradition in his own limited
way.

CONCLUSION: LUKE'S ELITE-DIRECTED MORALISM

The political implication of Luke-Acts is a hotly debated topic today.[27]
The foregoing analysis has shown that this debate needs to be broadened
and deepened in its scope. Ancient politics invariably encompassed broad
social and economic questions. For the countryside, ancient politics were
invariably bad news. Redistributive economy worked against the interests

27. Cassidy and Scharper, eds., *Political Issues in Luke–Acts*.

of rural agriculturalists. Has the Lukan Gospel addressed good news to that situation? Only partially.

Luke followed Jesus superficially in urging the remission of literal debts and in retaining the necessity of the destruction of the Jewish Temple (which for Luke was an accomplished fact). Yet for Jesus debt remission and Temple destruction were bound up with an ideology of God's kingdom that envisioned the abolishment of social stratification per se.[28] So Jesus, according to Mark (10:22) and Matthew (19:22), can send the rich young man away sorrowing; this seems close to the historical meaning of Jesus' ministry. Luke's rich ruler, however, does not go away (Luke 18:23), though he is sad. Luke *must* reckon with wealth and privilege in his community , and he is strenuously trying to turn the hearts of the powerful to the powerless and dishonored poor by his discriminating use of the radical Jesus tradition (Luke 12:48; 19:8–9; 22:26).[29]

In wrestling with this persuasive task, Luke does not simply endorse the demands of peasant radicalism, as Jesus very nearly did in the name of God's kingdom. The debt petition in Luke's version of the Lord's Prayer indicates how Luke is employing material that might originally have addressed peasant hopes for debt abolition—a challenge, so to speak, is now thrown in the creditor's court. The Dishonest Steward gives some debt relief, to be sure, but he is not the landlord. Zacchaeus promises restitution for fraudulent exactions, but he is not the imperial procurator. Likewise, Luke's silence on redistribution of land control, except when land tenure is firmly vested in the Christian community as in Acts, does not provide a satisfying solution to the plight of the ancient peasantry. Luke may envision "Rich Fools" in his own community, who are more interested in stored grain than in helping the disadvantaged of the community. Luke never says *unequivocally* that the kingdom of God is incompatible with large estates whose (Christian) landlords open their hands to make friends with the unrighteous Mammon. Lazaruses may expect to become part of the estate, but not to be rid of estates altogether. Thus, Luke's "peasant moral economy" is rather limited in scope to domestic concerns. The political dimensions of rural oppression are left alone.

What was originally a radical social critique by Jesus and his followers of the violent and oppressive political-economic order in the countryside

---

28. Oakman, *Jesus and the Economic Questions of His Day*, 213–16.

29. Karris, "Poor and Rich," 120, 122–24.

under the early Empire becomes in Luke's conception a rather innocuous sharing-ethic ambiguous in its import for rural dwellers. The countryside is apparently idealized by Luke as a place particularly receptive
to this message. Cities resist God's purposes and violently kill his agents,
but nonetheless (in Luke's view) primarily urban hearts need change and
then peace (as Luke understands it) will prevail. No dramatic social reconstruction—such as the elimination of the preindustrial city or Roman
imperium—is to be expected or is necessary. Thus, while Luke has preserved much of the countryside in the early Jesus tradition for us, he has
to some extent revised the original intention of the Jesus movement. For
Jesus, the kingdom of God was world reconstruction, especially beneficial
for a rural populace oppressed by debt and without secure subsistence.
For Luke, political expediency demands that the world restructuring be
limited to alleviating the harshest aspects of political economy within the
local Christian community.

We may finally hazard an hypothesis as to Luke's "place" between
city and country: As Luke addresses his patron Theophilus (and others
like him), he stands sociologically somewhere between preindustrial city
and peasant village, without endorsing unambiguously the interests and
values of either one. Luke does not look to the countryside as one who
labors on the land. He does not share some of the core rural interests
of antiquity. He does not seem "native" to the country, at least on the
evidence of his narrative. Yet Luke cannot ignore the countryside either,
because of its prominence in the early Jesus traditions. Luke sees in certain
aspects of the peasant moral economy a solution to difficulties within his
own community.

Luke's community probably resides in a large town or city somewhere
in the Roman Empire.[30] That community undoubtedly includes landlords
who control parts of Luke's immediate countryside, and whose "estate
people" may be part of the community. The landlords control Luke's
community as well. Perhaps the country members are numerous. Their
normal environment is field and village outside of the city/town. They
are regularly seen, but rarely heard. One can envision frequent interaction
in Luke's community between city/town dwellers and country, but along
the predictable political lines of the Roman Empire. This mixed social
constitution explains the preservation of rural Jesus traditions and their

30. Early tradition traces Luke's origins to Antioch in Syria: Foakes-Jackson and Lake,
The Beginnings of Christianity, 2:233, 235; Fitzmyer, *Luke*, 1:42.

continuing significance for the community. Luke's literary work, however, addresses primarily the landlords and creditors in the interests of the well-being of the whole community. It is the behavior of the powerful and the rich that affects the quality of communal life for all.

CHAPTER 12

Was Jesus a Peasant?
Implications for Reading the Samaritan Story
(Luke 10:30–35)[1]

IT HAS LONG BEEN asserted that Jesus of Nazareth was a small-town artisan (e.g., by Max Weber). Such an assertion may lead to inappropriate social assumptions, if Jesus is thought of as "middle class" or as a cultured "urban man." Work of peasant theorists prompts a reappraisal of this definitional problem.

What difference does appropriate social characterization—in this case seeing Jesus as peasant—mean for reading the Jesus tradition? While Jesus certainly looked and moved beyond the narrow horizon of the village, many of his parables reflect the concerns and values of his peasant surroundings. It is likely that Jesus had in mind at least some of the interests of his fellow peasant villagers in Roman Palestine. An exploration of Luke 10:30–35, traditionally labeled the Good Samaritan Story, will endeavor to show this. Some of Jesus' peasant audience, if not Jesus himself, probably evaluated the Samaritan as a "fool," rather than as "good." (No attempt is made to investigate the meaning of the Samaritan Story within the Lukan

1. As indicated in the Introduction, the meaning of the Jesus tradition, especially the parables of Jesus, depends upon a world of experience, values, and institutions far different from our own. Anachronistic assumptions regarding, or inadequate understanding of, social context and audience can potentially mask the original meaning inherent in authentic Jesus material. This chapter examines conceptions of peasantry currently entertained by the social sciences. On this basis, it is argued that Jesus is best seen as a peasant artisan and that peasant assumptions and values urge a very different reading for the Samaritan Story in Luke. Like several others in this volume, the chapter originated out of discussions of the Westar Institute's Social Facets of the Ancient World Seminar (1986–1989). The original text was presented at the second meeting of The Context Group in Portland, OR, March 14–17, 1991.

164

redaction.) Yet such a determination of meaning raises further interesting questions: Was Jesus sympathetic with such foolishness? What could such a story have meant within the framework of Jesus' central proclamation of the Kingdom of God? What did the Kingdom of God imply for the majority of peasant Palestinians in Jesus' day?

WHAT IS A PEASANT?

Working toward a Definition

What is a peasant? This question immerses us immediately in one of the thorny definitional problems regularly debated by social scientists. It soon becomes evident, in the reading of studies devoted to peasantry, that peasants are neither entirely the uncultivated boors of Theophrastus's famous "Character" nor the romantic stereotypes projected in the writings of Tolstoy. Often they are somewhere in between. One of the major disputes in peasant studies is, Who belongs in the category of "peasant"? Eric Wolf, Barrington Moore, and Teodor Shanin have more or less limited this appellation explicitly to those who cultivate the soil directly for their own subsistence.[2] This definition excludes, of course, village artisans, wage laborers, beggars and disabled, rural priests, and others. Wolf's definition explicitly focuses on the agricultural surplus extracted from peasant cultivators that sets them apart from primitive cultivators of the soil.[3] Wolf's close colleague, Sydney Mintz, shares some of Wolf's exclusive concerns, but stresses that any treatment must take into account the internal differentiation of the peasantry and their relationships to non-peasant groups.[4]

Other authorities are content to leave the definition more open-ended, because they are interested especially in the interrelationships of various subgroups within a broader notion of peasantry. So, for instance, Firth's studies of groups in the Far East extended the label "peasant" to include fishermen and craftsmen. Landsberger is hesitant to promulgate a categorical definition and argues instead for a series of "dimensions" that help the student to identify a group as peasant.[5] Nonetheless, Landsberger is sympathetic to the open-ended definitional tendency, observing that

2. Landsberger, "Peasant Unrest," 7; Mintz, "Definition of Peasantries," 93.

3. Wolf, *Peasants*, 3, 10.

4. Mintz, "Definition of Peasantries," 98.

5. Landsberger, "Peasant Unrest," 8–10.

landless "peasants" have played a crucial role in rural unrest in Brazil.[6] Foster too tends toward an open-ended approach. He puts his view this way:

> It is not *what* peasants produce that is significant; it is *how* and *to whom* they dispose of what they produce that counts.[7]

Foster means by this that restricting the definition of peasantry to an occupational status ("cultivator of the soil") obscures vision of the common situation of a whole range of rural groups who are occupationally diversified. Members of these groups are compelled to give up a precious amount of their hard-earned sustenance to outsiders. Here we have arrived at a core of characteristics that might be said to represent a consensus of contemporary thought on what makes a peasant. Foster, following Wolf, puts it well:

> *Not the city, but the state is the decisive criterion of civilization* and it is the appearance of the state which marks the threshold of transition between food cultivators in general and peasants . . . We believe Wolf's recognition of outside power-holders as the key variable [sc. in determining peasantries] is correct; normally, if not always, such power is associated with the city.[8]

Robert Redfield had made somewhat the same point in 1953: "It required the city to bring [peasantries] into existence."[9]

Redfield, Foster, Shanin, and Hobsbawm, following the lead of Kroeber, have remarked upon the common cultural orientation of peasantry.[10] Peasants think of themselves as a distinctive type of humanity and have a deep distrust of those outside the village. Clifford Geertz has rightly questioned the "myth of a nearly absolute social discontinuity between the world of the ruling classes and that of the peasantry . . . ."[11] Certainly, peasant culture depends to some extent upon the great tradition of urban civilization. Often it is derivative.[12] Yet what peasants and subgroups of peasants do with that culture, what Mintz (following Wolf) has referred to

6. Ibid., 14–15.

7. Foster, "What is a Peasant?" 6.

8. Ibid., italics Foster's.

9. Quoted in ibid., 5.

10. Landsberger, "Peasant Unrest," 8.

11. Geertz, "Village," 318.

12. Foster, "What is a Peasant?" 10.

as "social manoeuvre," is very important in their self-definition.[13] There is
to a certain extent a peasant counter-culture which expresses the peasantry's
unique sense of itself and of its situation. So Wolf has developed a typology of peasant villages that distinguishes those that are more open to the
outside world from those that are relatively closed to the outside world.[14]

Putting all of this together: A peasantry is a rural population, usually
including those not directly engaged in tilling the soil, who are compelled
to give up their agricultural (or other economic) surplus to a separate group
of power-holders and who usually have certain cultural characteristics setting them apart from outsiders. Generally speaking, peasants have very
little control over their political and economic situation. In Mediterranean
antiquity the overlords of peasants tended to be city dwellers, and a culture-
chasm divided the literate elite from the unlettered villager.

What Do Peasants Value?

The typical peasant's socialization and life is molded by the agricultural
year. Mediterranean peasants have devoted the majority of their energies
toward viticulture, arboriculture, and agriculture. Vines and orchards, as
well as grain and vegetable production, provide their staples. Animals have
supplemented the vegetable diet. Inanimate energy sources are rarely tapped
and productivity is relatively low. Excess peasant labor may be devoted to
craft specialization if agricultural opportunities dwindle and tax pressures
are high. Lenski has noted that surplus children of peasant households are
often forced to leave the village in search of livelihood.[15] Jewish villages
in the time of Jesus knew such specialization.[16] An especially important
thing to note here is that peasants generally produce for consumption, not
for commercial purposes; peasants value self-sufficiency and produce for
subsistence purposes within the household (however defined).

Yet, as emphasized in the foregoing section, peasants are typically
dominated by landlords and overlords. Politics puts pressure on the subsistence margin of the typical peasant household. Therefore, peasant anxi-
eties focus around that margin. Peasants tend to see the goods of life in
limited quantities, and peasant economics are traditionally "zero-sum": If

13. Mintz, "Definition of Peasantries," 97.
14. Geertz, "Village," 320; Roseberry, "Peasants and the World," 117.
15. Lenski, *Power and Privilege*, 278.
16. Klausner, *Jesus of Nazareth*, 177.

someone's wealth increases, it must be at the expense someone else. For this reason, peasants are normally suspicious and envious of "windfalls."[17]

What Makes Peasants Mad?

Peasants become discontented when the subsistence margin is too close or when secure access to land is denied. Peasant indebtedness is usually an indication of trouble, since indebtedness leads to less secure access to produce and to land. Figure 16 presents a model of important factors that encourage rural unrest and even revolt. Landsberger has hazarded the following statement upon which the Figure is based:

> The economic integration of the society under consideration into a larger, possibly international market; the consequent drive to commercialise agriculture; and the subsequent encroachment on peasant lands and peasant rights and status in general; this sequence is certainly the most promising candidate for the position of 'universal ultimate cause' [of agrarian discontent and revolt].[18]

Figure 16: A Dynamic Model of the Causes of Agrarian Conflict

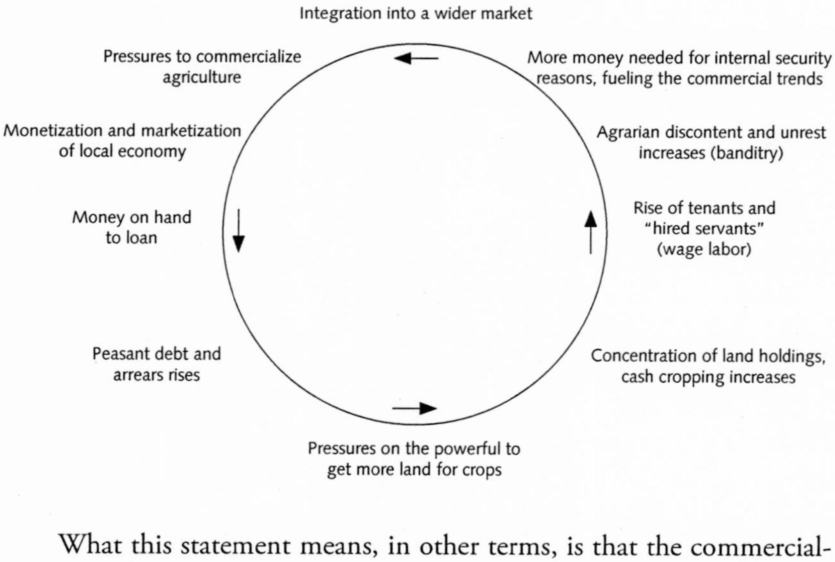

Integration into a wider market

Pressures to commercialize agriculture

More money needed for internal security reasons, fueling the commercial trends

Monetization and marketization of local economy

Agrarian discontent and unrest increases (banditry)

Money on hand to loan

Rise of tenants and "hired servants" (wage labor)

Peasant debt and arrears rises

Concentration of land holdings, cash cropping increases

Pressures on the powerful to get more land for crops

What this statement means, in other terms, is that the commercialization of agriculture and the encroachment of landlords on hereditary peasant landholdings consistently will be observed to go together. This

17. Foster, "Peasant Society and the Image of the Limited Good," 305, 311, 316.

18. Landsberger, "Peasant Unrest," 29.

generalization makes sense systemically. If there are commercial outlets for agricultural productivity, then the value of land—even marginal land—will go up. There will be the temptation to the powerful to acquire more land for the sake of gain. Usually the consumption aspirations of the powerful will rise also. One of the chief mechanisms for wresting patrimonial land from peasantry will be debt transactions. This is a rather convenient mechanism. Not only will the commercial activity of the powerful provide them with cash or commodities on hand to loan, but the pressure upon the peasantry to borrow will go up. Commercialization will bring greater monetization and marketization to the local economy in which the peasant will participate on unequal terms.[19] State taxes will doubtless rise with the expanding economic pie, adding further pressure upon the local cultivator. Borrowing will be necessitated. Unpaid debts will eventuate in the loss of the peasantry's land and the appearance of tenants and a wage labor pool. Land holdings will be concentrated in fewer hands. Agrarian unrest and discontent will cause the costs of security to rise. This will mean pressure for money to pay the troops. These developments will in turn continue to fuel the commercial revolution. This is a neat "system," but extremely disadvantageous from a peasant's point of view. The peasantry comes out the loser.

Some corollaries can be arranged beside the foregoing "general theorem." Several other factors generally contribute to peasant disaffection and possibly revolt: Large landowners can be converted into pure rent and tax collectors, not engaged directly in farming or in any other useful function apparent to the peasantry. As such, landlords fail to perform compensatory services for the peasantry (e.g., protection)—their relationship to the village becomes one of purely economic exploitation. Such situations usually imply absentee landlordism. The local aristocracy become weak in the face of a growing central government. Finally, there is a partial survival, through all of these changes, of peasant communities that are damaged but intact.[20] These societal changes induce peasant discontent when the peasantry begins to feel status inconsistency, deprivation relative to another group, or deprivation relative to a past status (or some combination of these).[21] Commercial activity, high taxation, and absentee landlordism are all mirrored in the Roman Palestine of Jesus' day.[22]

19. Carney, *The Shape of the Past*, 146–52, 201.

20. Landsberger, "Peasant Unrest," 17–18.

21. Ibid.

22. Brunt, "Josephus on Social Conflicts in Roman Judaea"; Horsley, "Popular

[]

The political response of peasantry to such changes is typically local and of limited scope. Most peasants protest or revolt in order to "remain traditional" (Wolf) or in order to eliminate specific evils and abuses
(Huntington). Most peasant uprisings or protest actions are aimed at local
landlords and officials. Rarely do peasants revolt self-consciously against
a central government.[23] Equally rarely do peasants adopt an anarchist or
utopian ideology. The political aims of peasants are manifestly parochial
and of limited scope.[24] It is difficult for peasants to unite beyond the local
level. Peasant movements on a national scale are remarkably infrequent.
Of significant interest concerning peasant radicalism is a comparative observation made by Sorokin and Zimmerman long ago:

> . . . radicalism of farmers has attempted to maintain wide distribu-
> tion of private property whereas radicalism among wage earners
> has sought to concentrate ownership of property in the state or do
> away with the institution of private property.[25]

Marx noted the "rural idiocy" of peasants and argued that peasants
are incapable of representing themselves. Hobsbawm has written:

> . . . a communally organised traditional peasantry, reinforced by
> a functionally useful slowness, imperviousness and stupidity—ap-
> parent or real—is a formidable force. The refusal to understand is
> a form of class struggle . . . .[26]

When indigenous peasant leaders have arisen to lead a movement,
the goals of the movement have generally mirrored what all peasants
value—parochial and limited ends. Radical peasant movements have typically been organized and led by leadership from outside the peasantry itself—priests, intellectuals, and so on—although these leaders often spend
their early years in peasant villages.[27]

When peasant movements or revolts have succeeded in the past, one
or more of three major social components perhaps have played assisting

---

Messianic Movements; Horsley and Hanson, *Bandits, Prophets, and Messiahs*; Oakman,
Jesus and the Economic Questions of His Day.

23. Hobsbawm, "Peasants and Politics," 13; Landsberger, "Peasant Unrest," 36–37.

24. Hobsbawm, "Peasants and Politics," 12.

25. Quoted in Irwin T. Sanders, *Rural Society*, 135.

26. Hobsbawm, "Peasants and Politics," 13.

27. Landsberger, "Peasant Unrest," 40, 47–48; Hobsbawm, "Peasants and
Politics," 12.

roles. The peasants' cause might be taken up by a central power, a king, who is believed to be (or poses as) a font of justice or who is called as an ally against the peasants' real masters, the local gentry. Religion can play a major part in peasant uprisings; here social perspectives are reversed. The bishop or priest may be seen to represent a repressive and institutionalized church remote from peasant interests, while the peasants take spiritual sustenance and guidance from saints or local holy men. Finally, a "proto-nationalism" may help groups of peasants to align themselves translocally. These factors can, of course, cross-cut or work against peasant aspirations as well.[28]

Was Jesus a Peasant?

The social delineation of Jesus of Nazareth makes a good case study in view of this theoretical debate. Was Jesus fundamentally a peasant? Or did his occupation as artisan imply some other social category? Certainly as an artisan Jesus had access to experiences denied those who remained in the village or on the land. Yet Jesus' socialization was within a village context, as the Synoptics make plain (Mark 6:1–3; Luke 2:51), and many of the scenes of his ministry and much of the content of his teaching embrace the culture and society of rural Palestine. Occupationally, Jesus is best understood as a peasant child forced to leave the village in search of livelihood (Mark 6:3).

Jesus continued to speak Aramaic in a Greek-speaking world; the language of the village marks Jesus' authentic voice and his primary world of social experience. While Jesus could probably speak some words of Greek, it is doubtful that he could read or write.[29] As his parables show, Jesus' culture was an oral culture.

Jesus' parables have long been considered to reflect the mores and experiences of the countryside.[30] It is interesting to observe that many of the parables mirror experience upon large estates, undoubtedly including those of the Esdraelon Plain near Nazareth. Do these replay Jesus' own experiences? It is probable that they do at least in the typical sense. In any case, it seems certain that Jesus was a careful observer of agrarian life.

28. For a brief discussion of these components, Hobsbawm, "Peasants and Politics," 17.

29. *Pace* Helmut Koester, *Introduction to the New Testament*, 2: 74; more probable is the view of Meier, "Jesus," 1319.

30. E.g., Smith, *Parables*.

Most importantly in this connection, Jesus stood in the same structural relationship to the powerful as other villagers and artisans of his environment. He was a peasant, because a few powerful others determined
many of the important decisions of his and others' lives. It was in the cause
of these weak and exploited that Jesus' own ministry was conducted, as
much recent scholarship is demonstrating.[31] Jesus promised his disciples
such secure subsistence in the name of the Kingdom of God (Mark 10:30;
Luke 12:22–31/Matt 6:25–33). Jesus also spoke about debt forgiveness as
an essential characteristic of the Kingdom (Luke 7:41–42; Luke 11:4/Matt
6:12). So Stegemann rightly says that the popular movement "associated
with the name of Jesus was a movement *of the poor for the poor*."[32] Peasants
constituted the majority of these poor.

Certainly all peasant societies are part-societies, as first Kroeber and
then Redfield have made clear, and people like Jesus simply underscore
this fact by moving between two worlds. Yet the very existence of people
like Jesus who mediate the larger world to the village and vice versa makes
the interpretation of peasant realities so critically interesting and difficult.
Which of those worlds is primary in the understanding of Jesus and his
activities? Later Christian interpretation, beginning with Matthew and
Luke, decided the issue in favor of the larger Mediterranean world and its
dominant Greco-Roman value system. However, the historically sensitive
student of the gospel tradition cannot make this unilateral decision.

It is accepted here, therefore, that Jesus was fundamentally a peasant, qualifying the views of Weber and a long line of interpreters who
have given Jesus' artisan side prominence.[33] Several important scholars
in Jesus studies have come to similar conclusions recently.[34] Jesus was a
rural artisan working often within typical peasant contexts. His parables
reflect these contexts. This means that while Jesus could and did move
beyond the village during his life, his fundamental world of values and
his fundamental interests and loyalties were shaped within and oriented
to the village. The interpretation of Jesus' parables must start with what
is known typically about peasant values and expectations. Indeed, many

31. Theissen, *Sociology of Early Palestinian Christianity*; Stegemann, *Gospel and the Poor*;
Oakman, *Jesus and the Economic Questions of His Day*; Borg, *Jesus*.

32. W. Stegemann, *Gospel and the Poor*, 23, his italics.

33. See Weber, *Economy and Society*, 1:481, who does admit that Jesus was a "small-
town" artisan.

34. Freyne, *Galilee, Jesus and the Gospels*; Crossan, *Historical Jesus*.

of the parables themselves urge this starting point, assuming as they do knowledge of the Palestinian countryside under the early Roman empire.

INTERPRETING THE SAMARITAN STORY

Taking into account the foregoing, we can go on to sketch a revisionary interpretation of the so-called Good Samaritan Story. The standard interpretations have generally done the following things:

- Allowed the Lukan framework to govern interpretation, neglecting the fact that the Lukan framework is secondary

- Ignored important social data in the story, such as the character of banditry in Jesus' time, the fact that the Samaritan is a trader, and the nature of public inns (*pandocheia*)

- Seen the Samaritan as self-sacrificing and "good" in contrast to the self-preoccupied priest and Levite; frequently, however, commentators note that Samaritans were hated by Jews.

The present interpretation will explore the story with the following considerations in mind:

- The Lukan framework is not original. While Bultmann and Crossan have seen v. 36 as essential for understanding the story, a recent group of Jesus scholars believes the parable ended after v. 35.[35]

- The peasant Jesus, himself engaged in a "ministry of protest and renewal,"[36] would likely have been in sympathy with the ends of social banditry, although not necessarily with its means.

- Jewish peasants were hardly in sympathy with Samaritans, especially if they were engaged in commerce.

- Inns had unsavory reputations.

I will now consider the last three points.

35. Bultmann, *History of the Synoptic Tradition*, 178; Crossan, *In Parables*, 61; Funk, Scott, and Butts, *Parables of Jesus*, 30.

36. Theissen, *Sociology*.

JESUS AND SOCIAL BANDITS

Horsley and Hanson give a good orientation to the subject of social banditry in Roman Palestine.[37] The important aspect to be understood here is that bandits in Jesus' day were perceived by the Jewish peasantry as social bandits and thus were considered heroes in the villages. They stood for a justice denied by the system.

A story in Josephus well illustrates these points:

> On the public road leading up to Bethhoron some brigands [lēstai] attacked one Stephen, a slave of Caesar, and robbed him of his baggage. Cumanus [ca. 50 C.E.], therefore, sent troops round the neighbouring villages, with orders to bring up the inhabitants to him in chains, reprimanding them for not having pursued and arrested the robbers [lēstas].[38]

The people in Jesus' story who were going down to Jericho from Jerusalem were undoubtedly understood as city-dwelling elite by villagers in the audience. The sympathies of the latter would have been with the bandits. Villagers probably evaluated the first part of the story in some such way: You see, none of them take care of each other, and they're getting what they deserve.

As for Jesus' own attitude toward banditry, he seems to have abhorred the violence of such bandits. So at one point, he implies that brigands are trying to force the coming of the Kingdom (cf. Luke 16:16/Matt 11:12; also Mark 12:1–12). On the other hand, Jesus accepts some of the basic goals of banditry—justice and the securing of subsistence that guides peasant radicalism. Ironically, Jesus is classified in Roman eyes with such bandits, mandating crucifixion (Mark 15:27 [lēstai]; cf. John 18:40).

THE SAMARITAN

The hatred of Jews for Samaritans was proverbial in Jesus' day.[39]

Luke's reading of the parable, given the framework of the lawyer's question to Jesus, has biased Christian interpreters to see the Samaritan as "good." Only the Samaritan proves to be neighbor. Yet, this reading leaves out of account the fact that the Samaritan was a merchant or a trader.

---

37. Horsley and Hanson, *Bandits, Prophets, and Messiahs*, 48–87.

38. *War* 2.228–229 (Thackeray, LCL).

39. John 4:9; see also Scott, *Hear Then the Parable*, 197–98.

The following in the story are indicators that the Samaritan is a tradesman: He journeys (v. 33) and has an animal to bear his wares (v. 34). He has at his disposal "oil and wine" (v. 34), typically items of trade at the time. The Samaritan takes the injured man to a public inn, typically the stopping places for commercial people.[40] Jeremias endorses this view of the Samaritan as well.[41]

As Landsberger's model above suggests, peasants would see a trader in oil and/or wine as a contributor to the social problem oppressing them. "Samaritan" would offend Jewish sensitivities; "merchant" would offend the peasant in Jesus' audience. As a matter of fact, commercial people were despised by elite groups as well. Elites felt their own honor and lineage threatened by "upstarts" and "new wealth."[42]

Yet Jesus is not nearly so negative about traders, using them on at least one other occasion to exemplify the Kingdom of God (Matt 13:45–46).

Furthermore, the Samaritan's behavior toward the injured man is in-line with the element of grace exhibited elsewhere in the Jesus tradition but out of line with ordinary mores. The Samaritan does not relate to the injured man as was usual in the society of Jesus. Villagers and elite alike were gracious only within the narrow confines of family. Such generosity, which Marshal Sahlins has called general reciprocity, was only practiced toward nearest kin.[43] Otherwise, careful accounting, balanced reciprocity, was the norm. Toward strangers and enemies, negative reciprocity was acceptable and even expected.

The Inn

Public inns were notorious in the ancient world for being "primitive, dirty and noisy."[44] As Frederick Danker puts it, "Inns of that time were worse than American fifty-cent-a-night hotels. And innkeepers were not noted for their humanitarian sentiments."[45] The following stories show these conditions:

40. August Hug, *"Pandokeion,"* 18.3, col. 527.

41. Jeremias, *Parables*, 204.

42. See the comments of Finley, *Ancient Economy*, 19.

43. Oakman, *Jesus and the Economic Questions of His Day*, 152; idem, "The Buying Power of Two Denarii: A Comment on Luke 10:35," 37 in original [chapter 3 above].

44. Stählin, *"Xenos, ktl.,"* 19 n. 135.

45. Danker, *Jesus and the New Age*, 132.

[Carura (between Phrygia and Caria)] has inns [*pandocheiai*] . . .
Moreover, it is said that once, when a brothel-keeper had taken
lodging in the inns along with a large number of women, an
earthquake took place by night, and that he, together with all the
women, disappeared from sight.[46]

In the Armenian tradition of Philo, extant also in Greek fragments, the
following is said:

But he who is unlike [the wise man] does not have even his own
house or a mind of his own but is confused and is treated con-
temptuously like those who, as it were, enter an inn [*pandocheion*]
only to fill themselves and vomit in their passions.[47]

The apocryphal Jesus tradition has the following:

Just then a leper comes up to him and says, "Teacher, Jesus, in
wandering around with lepers and eating with them in the inn, I
became a leper myself."[48]

Jewish tradition has equally negative things to say about inns:

Cattle may not be left in the inns of the gentiles since they are
suspected of bestiality; nor may a woman remain alone with them
since they are suspected of lewdness; nor may a man remain alone
with them since they are suspected of shedding blood.[49]

The story about Nahum of Gazmo is instructive (early second century CE?):

On the way, Nahum stopped at an inn over night. During the
night the occupants (of the inn) got up, took out everything that
was in the bags and filled the bags with dust.[50]

Ramsay MacMullen notes that "the advice of a contemporary [of
Columella, mid-first century CE] in Palestine was, if one stopped the
night at a wayside inn, to make one's will."[51] Kenneth Bailey also observes,
in *Targum Jonathan* the word "prostitute" is "regularly translated 'woman

46. Strabo, *Geography* 12.8.17 (Jones, LCL), late first century BCE.

47. Marcus translation quoted in Royce, "A Philonic Use of *pandocheion*," 193 (early
first century CE).

48 Papyrus Egerton 2, in Miller, ed., *Complete Gospels*, 415, early second century CE.

49. M. *'Abod. Zar.* 2:1 (Danby), second century CE.

50. B. *Ta'an.* 21a, trans. Malter, *The Treatise Ta'anit of the Babylonian Talmud*, 304.

51. MacMullen, *Roman Social Relations*, 4 and n. 13.

who keeps an inn.'"[52] Jastrow's dictionary shows that *pandocheion* had become a loan word with similar connotations in both Talmudic Hebrew and in Aramaic.[53]

Commentators on the "Good" Samaritan Story, like Danker, have regularly noted the negative image of inns, but have never made much of it in terms of interpreting the story.

For the Samaritan to leave the injured man at the inn seems folly in view of the evil reputations of inns. The *Mishnah* tells the following story:

> Once certain levites went to Zoar, the City of Palms, and one of them fell sick by the way, and they brought him to an inn. When they returned thither, they asked the mistress of the inn, "Where is our companion?" She answered, "He is dead and I buried him."[54]

Inns were not good places for sick people to stay.

For the Samaritan to give the innkeeper a blank check (v. 35) seems equally unwise. For peasant audiences, the Samaritan's "aid" has left the man in a worse condition than at first. Not only will the injured man in danger of his life, but he is held hostage until the Samaritan spends even more. What will the bill come to in the end?

JESUS' INTENTION IN THE STORY

How did Jesus expect his contemporaries to evaluate this story? For the ruling class in Jerusalem, the evaluation is already implied. They would endorse the actions of the priest and Levite. Not only were purity concerns in view, but also involvement could lead to unpleasant consequences if the bandits had laid a trap. The whole story has disturbing overtones for them, since traders and public inns were despised by Greco-Roman elites.[55] Tradesmen might look favorably on the Samaritan, although if the tradesmen were Jewish, this would be difficult. Yet tradesmen might also ask whether the Samaritan was a complete fool to endanger any shipment or commercial activity to help a stranger.

Jewish peasants would have multiple reasons for not being sympathetic. For them, the Samaritan is a cultural enemy, an evil man, and a

---

52. Bailey, *Through Peasant Eyes*, 53.
53. Jastrow, *Dictionary*, 1143 s.v. *pundaq*.
54. M. *Yebamot* 16:7 (Danby).
55. Hug, "*Pandokeion*," cols. 522, 526–27.

fool: an enemy because a Samaritan, evil because a trader, a fool because he treats a stranger like family and is unsavvy about the situation at the inn. Conversely, the bandits are probably viewed as "good" in the eyes of villagers in Jesus' audience. The innkeeper is one of their own. In peasant eyes, only such negative reciprocity will bring about (someday) secure subsistence. Would not peasants have laughed all the way through Jesus' story?

Very likely Jesus counted on this kind of response. He counted on positive reactions to the victimization of the Jerusalemite and the activities of the bandits; he counted on knowing nods to the behaviors of the priest and Levite; he anticipated visceral responses to the coming of the Samaritan; he "upped the ante" in showing general reciprocity and leaving the audience hanging, probably laughing, with the Samaritan's final words. How then did Jesus understand the story? Does he embrace the view of the village?

Was the story originally intended to function in a social-critical fashion (as perhaps did Mark 12:1–12 and Matt 20:1–20)? Then the story exemplifies all of the evils of the age that will see the Kingdom arrive: Brother Israelite no longer cares for Israelite; exploitation has led to endemic banditry; and the commercial activities of Samaritans make the situation all that more the worse. This interpretation, however, is not entirely satisfying, for it does not bear the surprising or radical stamp of other parables of Jesus. A deeper reading might be gained by rethinking the Kingdom connection with the Samaritan Story.

THE SAMARITAN STORY IN JESUS' MESSAGE OF THE KINGDOM

For Jesus, the question of most parables was not a general moral question about neighborliness, but rather what the Kingdom is like. Luke or pre-Lukan tradition has biased the reading of the Samaritan Story toward the development of the "example story" view (the Samaritan is simply a model of good behavior). Such a development does not take into account all of the data of the parable, especially the negative connotations of inns and the apparent foolishness of the Samaritan at the end of the story. How might this data be incorporated into a reading closer to the intention of Jesus?

Several features of the story stand out: 1) The Samaritan, practicing general reciprocity toward the injured man, shows generosity out-of-line with cultural expectations. 2) Inns and innkeepers had very low moral reputations. 3) The Samaritan—carelessly, dangerously, foolishly?—indebts himself to, and gives himself and the injured Jerusalemite over into the power of, the innkeeper. Suppose, then, that Jesus concluded his narrative not with a question about neighborliness, but with an implied, "And the Kingdom of God is like this." Similar comparisons can be found in the Jesus tradition, for instance in the Pearl (Matt 13:45–46; *Gos. Thom.* 76) and in the Feast (Luke 14:15–24/Matt 22:1–10; *Gos. Thom.* 64).

God's reign, then, is strikingly compared to the actions of a hated foreigner of despised social occupation and is revealed literally in the wilds of bandits and inns. The generosity of God is portrayed as enormous (general reciprocity toward enemies). Even more so, the generosity of God reaches the point, in the human terms of Jesus' day, of danger and folly. God, like the Samaritan, is indebted to pay whatever may be required. The innkeeper has incentive to keep the injured man alive as security and to demand even more. The Samaritan offers a blank check.

And so the story ends. That is *what* God's activity is like. The parable also implies *where* the Kingdom is found—in the most unlikely, even immoral, places! In consequence, the Samaritan Story, which we shall finally call the Foolish Samaritan Parable, is *not* an example story but does function as a parable of reversal, as Crossan sees:

> When the north pole becomes the south pole, and the south the north, a world is reversed and overturned and we find ourselves standing firmly on utter uncertainty. The parables of reversal intend to do precisely this to our security because such is the advent of the Kingdom.[56]

Crossan also correctly analyzes the process by which such parables are turned into example stories, especially in Luke.[57] Such a process domesticates the "immoral" danger of the Kingdom. Likewise, Crossan classifies the Great Supper Parable with the Foolish Samaritan. Crossan accomplished his classification with insufficient attention given to the socio-cultural framework of Jesus' parables.

In Jesus' world, peasants *always* existed with a threat from outside—that threat is what constituted their world. In the Foolish Samaritan parable, the threat is manifest in the bandits, in commerce, and in the hostile

56. Crossan, *In Parables*, 55.

57. Ibid., 56.

environment of the inn. Jesus characteristically turns that outside threat into a positive metaphor for the Kingdom of God. For some, the Kingdom is critical opportunity; for others, perhaps judgment. Jesus is like his peasant acquaintances and neighbors in promising that the Kingdom brings what all peasants want—secure access to subsistence. He moves beyond the village in seeing that those on the margins or in the interstices of society are more reflective of the coming Kingdom than conventional expectations. Jesus does not endorse violent means to the end of the Kingdom. Yet the Kingdom will more effectively turn the world upside down than all social bandits combined.

CONCLUSION

Reading the Jesus tradition against the horizon of peasant typicalities highlights aspects hitherto ignored.

Jesus, himself of peasant origins and upholding important peasant values, nevertheless found promise where most peasants would have seen challenge. In the reading of the Foolish Samaritan developed in this essay, Jesus has counted on typical peasant valuations, but has not simply identified with all peasant interests. A tension is evident. Peasant villagers may have to overcome some of their own prejudices and interests in order to see the Kingdom Jesus proclaims come near. But so also, and even more so, will the governing elites! The Kingdom represents social challenge and transformation.

A certain indeterminacy in the reading remains, of course. No interpretation of a parable of Jesus can ever be established with absolute certainty, due to the ambiguous nature of parables and to the recontextualizing nature of the tradition. It is clear, however, that there is more to the Samaritan Story than has met the eye of traditional Christian readings (beginning with Luke).

Retrojecting the hermeneutical investigation of Jesus' parables into the social setting of early Roman Palestine promises to bring new insights into Jesus' overall message. This methodology also apparently will raise many new questions, not all of which may prove answerable. Every new development in biblical studies brings its own set of problems. The employment of social scientific perspectives will be no different. Let us hope the results will outweigh in importance the problems and unanswered questions generated.

CHAPTER 13

Cursing Fig Trees and Robbers' Dens
(Mark 11:12–25 and Parallels)

R ECENT SOCIAL SCIENCE APPROACHES to the New Testament, continuing and deepening older conceptions of historical and form criticism,
have stressed that texts require social context for interpretation. These approaches have argued that grasping the meaning of biblical texts requires an
understanding of the social system or world in which they originated.[1] The
present essay explores the social dynamics behind pronouncement within
the early Jesus tradition and proposes a cluster of interrelated interpretations for the Cursing of the Fig Tree/Cleansing of the Temple stories that
depend upon an understanding of the social system encompassing Jesus
and much of the Jesus tradition up until Mark's time. The reader is urged
to appreciate the importance of the social system for understanding crucial
dimensions of the two stories. The "selectivity" of the tradition regarding
what kind of saying would be associated with a situation, especially while
the tradition was in Palestine, was governed to a significant degree by the
experienced social system of tradition's originating society (the cases of Q,
Mark, early Johannine tradition).[2] As the tradition moved away from the

---

1. Malina, *New Testament World* (1981[1]; 1993[2]; 2001[3]); Elliott, ed., *Semeia*, Vol. 35:
Social-Scientific Criticism of the New Testament and Its Social World; Neyrey, ed., *Social
World of Luke-Acts*.

2. In this essay, "Jesus" is often used interchangeably with "early Jesus tradition"
without prejudice to deciding the historicity questions. Likewise, "redaction" may imply
"composition" without prejudice to tradition critical decisions. "Jesus tradition" and
"tradition" can also be used synonymously.

The metaphors of "selectivity" and "resonance" (used at various points of this essay) are
borrowed from the realm of radio reception. Resonance is the property in tuning circuits
that allows a radio to receive a station at a precise frequency; the circuits oscillate, are
resonant, at that frequency only. A receiver with high selectivity can separate and clearly

society of origin (Matthew [in part], Luke, Johannine redactor[s]), the stories could be reworked, condensed, or even eliminated.

In each instance, a literary analysis of the texts is an essential preliminary for understanding pronouncement in social-systemic perspective. In this analysis, some sense needs to be gained of the formal structure of the units, as well as of the relation between tradition and composition or redaction. Important questions for the present essay are: Are pronouncement stories purely arbitrary creations at the stage of composition? Are they arbitrarily reformulated within early tradition? Or can some understanding of the shaping and meaning of pronouncements be gained by attention to social system? Does social system play a significant role in what pronouncements are made, and why?

THE FIG TREE EPISODE AND APPENDIX

Mark 11:12–14 and Matt 21:18–19 comprise the only Jesus traditions about the Cursing of the Fig Tree. There is a similarity between these two stories and Luke's parable about a fig tree (Luke 13:6–9). Elsewhere, fig leaves are known to herald summer's arrival (Mark 13:28). Nathaniel is marked as an Israelite by reference to a fig tree (John 1:48). Fig trees were long associated with peace and safety in Israelite tradition.[3]

In Mark, furthermore, the Cursing episode receives an Appendix (vv. 20–25) which adds a series of sayings of Jesus in response to the withered fig tree. Matthew retains the Marcan Appendix as an *immediate* response of disciples and Jesus to the immediate withering of the fig tree. The withering is only implied in Mark and separated from the Cursing by the Temple "Cleansing." Moreover, Matthew's version of the Appendix contains only three of Mark's four sayings. Matthew has the fourth saying in the Sermon on the Mount (Matt 6:14–15).

An analysis of the structure of the Fig Tree episode reveals a root similarity between the Marcan and Matthean versions. In each case, the main verbs (indicative mood, aorist tense) trace out a first-order structure and likely delineate the common tradition. Around this first-order structure, subordinate clauses make clear a second-order structure, far more

---

distinguish stations close together on the broadcast spectrum. High selectivity implies a pickiness with respect to what is received. It is argued in this chapter that the early Jesus tradition analogously was resonant to certain concerns and was picky about what it passed on. Later stages of the tradition proved resonant and selective in other ways in response to new social settings.

3. Mic 4:5; Zech 3:10; 1 Macc 14:12; see Hunzinger, "*Sykē, ktl.*," 752.

influenced by redaction. When these two orders of the structure are seen, the unique aspects of each redaction stand out.

The primary-order structure becomes clear from the following table of the main Greek verbs:

MARK 11		MATTHEW 21	
12	*epeinasen*	18	*epeinasen*
13	*ēlthen*	19	*ēlthen*
	ouden heuren		*ouden heuren*
	(*ouk ēn*)		(—)
14	*eipen*		*legei*
	(*ēkouon* [disciples subject])		(*exeranthē* [tree subject])

The basic skeleton outlined by the main Greek verbs is striking: Jesus hungered, came, found nothing, said (Matt: says). This structure seems anchored in the tradition, especially when it is noted that in the Lukan near-parallel, a similar structure inheres in the Fig Tree Parable: The owner of the vineyard came (seeking fruit on the fig tree), he did not find, he said.

At the end of the Cursing pericope, the divergence is equally striking in suggesting redactional influences. Mark has the disciples listening to Jesus. This is a theme consistent with the Marcan redaction (e.g., Mark 4:3, 9; 9:7). Matthew, by contrast, emphasizes the immediate effect of Jesus' word of curse: The fig tree dries up! Elsewhere in Matthew, the immediate effect of Jesus' word is also brought out (e.g., Matt 8:13; 9:22).

It is likely, as Bultmann thought, that Matthew preserves the more original *form* of the Cursing story (while being selective about details).[4] As the analysis shows, the traditional story ends with a pronouncement, the curse by Jesus. Since both Matthew and Mark have the Appendix, although in different configurations, Cursing – Appendix belonged together in the tradition. The Appendix, therefore, represents a development of the pronouncement that happened at a stage of the tradition prior to Mark.

The secondary-order differentiates quite distinctly the Marcan and Matthean redactions of this tradition. Three aspects are especially striking. First of all, Matthew 21:18a stresses the goal of Jesus' movement toward the *polis* (Jerusalem), while Mark notes (11:12) Jesus' departure out of the village Bethany. These characterizations localize the stories quite differently (especially in terms of the social system).

4. Bultmann, *History of the Synoptic Tradition*, 218.

Secondly, the object of Jesus' sight in Matthew (v. 19) is the fig tree by the road; Mark's object (v. 13 *echousan phylla*) is a fig tree in leaf. The motive for Jesus' approach to the fig tree is explained better by the Marcan tradition.

Thirdly, what Jesus says in each case is different. Matthew's version stresses the eternity of the curse. The emphatic *ou mēketi* ("never ever") is reinforced by the proximity of *eis ton aiōna* to the subjunctive verb ("forever"). Mark's version does not say "never . . . forever"; rather by keeping *mēketi* together with *eis ton aiōna*, Mark stresses the validity of the curse only during the present "aeon" (consonant with Mark's consistent apocalyptic outlook on his times). Mark's weaker optative mood verb ("may no one eat"), suggests also that Mark did not understand the curse in as binding a manner as Matthew (consider Matt 18:18—unique to that gospel).

A final consideration relates to the well-known difficulty in Mark's Cursing story, v. 13b "for it was not the time for figs." This gloss disrupts the first-order structure completely and betrays its redactional origin. Furthermore, the word-order of the sentence is absolutely crucial for understanding its Marcan sense. A variant reading for this sentence attempted to move the adverb and verb to the sentence beginning and to place *kairos* together with *sykōn*.[5] The undoubtedly more difficult word order in the Nestle-Aland[26] text says something peculiarly Marcan when observed. The word *kairos*, translated "time" or "season" here, appears five times in Mark, more than in any other New Testament writing. Mark 1:15 effectively marks this word as a synonym for "kingdom of God." Mark 10:13 contrasts the present *kairos* with the future age. Similarly, Mark 13:33 refers to the return of the Son of Man at an indefinite *kairos*. The usage in Mark 12:2 seems to return to the mundane referent of harvest time. These usages should alert us to the importance for Mark of the present declaration. What this importance is can only be brought out by reference to the social system.

The Appendix, briefly, consists of a response by the disciples to what has happened to the fig tree. Jesus, in turn, responds to the disciples in the form of three (Matt)/four (Mark) sayings. In Mark, the catch-words "faith/believe" have contributed to the linking of the first three sayings, while "prayer" has led to the fourth addition. In view of Matthew's form of the tradition, the Appendix followed the Cursing immediately; Mark then is responsible for separating Appendix from Cursing and probably for

5. The described changes are present in A, C (second corrector), numerous other Greek manuscripts, and some versions.

linking the fourth saying (as its lack in Matthew suggests). Whether there is a more compelling reason for the linkage of these sayings—in tradition or redaction—remains to be seen.

CURSING FIG TREES

As Figure 17 illustrates, when leaves were visible on a fig tree, fruit was normally present.[6] Jesus could reasonably expect to find fruit in various stages of ripeness on the tree. Viewed in this light, the statement of Mark 11:13b is utter foolishness *as a botanical statement.*[7] It is not necessarily foolishness as a social statement. This insight will need further exploration in a moment.

Figure 17: The Fig Production Cycle

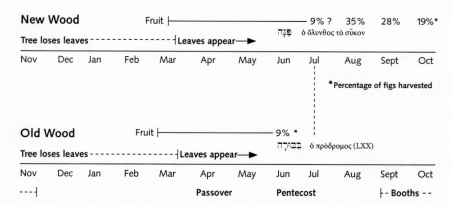

Because of the imagined botanical difficulties, the dating of the Cursing episode has long been discussed. Is this event to be associated with Jesus' entry into Jerusalem during the Feast of Tabernacles in the fall?[8] In this case, Jesus would be seeking fruit roughly in the period September to

6. Figure 17 was developed especially with the help of Childers, *Modern Fruit Science*, 489–96; Trevor, "Fig Tree, Fig," 267; and Hunzinger, "*Sykē, ktl.*" The chart represents the fig production per average year from one tree. The new wood produces in the fall the majority of the year's crop (roughly 90%). The old wood produces the early figs. Included for reference are the chief Greek and Hebrew words for these fruits and the major Jewish festivals.

7. It has been suggested that Jesus held up unreasonable expectations for fruit based upon conditions in Galilee: Near Genesareth, fig trees bear ten months of the year (Josephus, *War* 3.519; Str-B. 1:857). This interpretive option seems unlikely, however, because in either locale leaves normally appear with the maturing figs.

8. Nineham, *Mark*, 293.

October, before the leaves drop off for the winter (November). The fruit on the new wood, representing the major part of the fig harvest for the year, would be available at this time. Jewish peasants did not pick all of the fruit at once, since it was not all ripe at once.[9]

The other dating option is to place the Cursing episode in the spring before Passover. Here the leaves would be just on the tree (appearing at the end of March). The early fruit (ready by late-May) would hardly be ripe, although some fruit from the previous season might be on the tree. Mark's comment has often been taken to imply such a date, if *ho kairos* ("the season") means the late-summer fig harvest. Otherwise, Mark's comment can be referred to the June harvest of the early figs (on old wood).

In view of the previous assertion that the presence of leaves made it reasonable to expect fruit, a different line of inquiry seems warranted. The dating discussion, while important, overlooks a yet more important question: The question is not, *When* did Jesus not find fruit? but *Why* did Jesus not find fruit? Considering this story in the light of the social system, several interlocking answers emerge.

The Augustan Age and the Principate are frequently thought to have ushered in an era of peace and prosperity. It is true that Augustus brought to a conclusion the disastrous and disruptive civil strife (especially in the eastern provinces) of the late Republic. The *Pax Augusta* also encouraged commerce.[10]

Yet many citizens and subjects of the early Empire did not share in this prosperity and commerce. This is a social fact that must not be forgotten. The Herodian period in Palestine is illustrative of this fact. Herod the Great, by any standard, was a brutal dictator who established a police state, bled his subjects nearly to death through taxation, and established monuments to a prosperity shared only by the wealthy and powerful.[11]

Yet the social problem was not just the problem of a political regime that once gotten rid of would allow things to return to a more equitable ar-

---

9. Hamel, *Poverty and Charity*, 10.

10. Koester has a useful summary in *Introduction to the New Testament*, 1:322–36; see also Jeremias, *Jerusalem*, 31ff.

11. Josephus on Herod in general: *Ant.* 16.154; police state: *Ant.* 15.291, 295; heavy taxation: *War* 2.84ff. Herod's building programs are well known, especially the expansion of the Temple complex that began in 20 BCE. See also Horsley and Hanson, *Bandits, Prophets, and Messiahs*, 66.

rangement. What emerged in Herodian Palestine was a systemic problem, which undoubtedly got its start earlier in the Hellenistic Period.[12]

Figure 18 outlines the general features of the social matrix in which the Jesus tradition took shape.[13] The features of most importance here are the consolidation of judicial power in the hands of the landlord-commercial class and their religious legitimation through alignment with (or identity as) those who controlled the Jerusalem Temple, the use of debt to enlarge landed estates, and the shift to cash cropping and tenancy agriculture.

Figure 18: The Herodian Social System

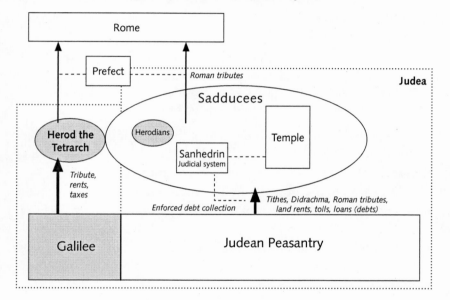

The Judean oligarchy in the early first century, ascendant over all Jews in Palestine, was comprised primarily of three groups, traditionally labeled by their religious views as Sadducees: The priestly upper crust (high priests and high priest) comprised of four major families (Boethus, Kathros,

12. Hengel, *Hellenism and Judaism.*

13. The model has been developed with the help of modern comparative treatments of agrarian societies, especially that of Lenski, *Power and Privilege.* The vertical dimension of the model represents the relative power of various groups. The groups and institutional relationships are described more closely in the text. For a similar approach to the society of early Roman Palestine, see Saldarini, *Pharisees, Scribes and Sadducees.*

An early version of this model was presented in a paper delivered at the Social Sciences and New Testament Interpretation Section of the Society of Biblical Literature, New Orleans, 1990.

Hanin [Annas], and Phabi); village and town lay nobility tracing their lineage back to important families in Israel's past (elders); and the recorders and administrators of the system (scribes).[14] Members of the Herodian family and their adherents also played a part in the elite picture.

Palestinian Judaism at this time took the ancestral law traced back to Moses very seriously, although there were disagreements about what belonged to that law and how to interpret it. The supreme court of the land, the Sanhedrin, ultimately decided how especially the civil aspects of law were to be interpreted. Before 70 CE when the Temple was destroyed, this body was controlled by the previously described Judaean elite. The court rigorously backed creditors. A first-century legal ruling attributed to Hillel reveals this quite clearly:

> [A loan secured by] a *prozbul* is not cancelled [by the Seventh Year].
> . . . This is the formula of the *prozbul*: "I affirm to you, such-a-one and such-a-one, the judges in such-a-place, that, touching any debt due me, I will collect it whensoever I will. (*m. Sheb.* 10:3–4)

By placing debt contracts with the courts, the creditor could circumvent traditional Jewish law (e.g., Deut 15:2). Jacob Neusner sees as the effect of the *prozbul* the making of debt "a perpetual burden."[15]

Debt contracts enforced through court proceedings enlarged the estates of creditors. Their control of the Temple and of "sacred" debt records also contributed to growing agrarian problems. *Mishnah Sheqalim* 1:3 relates that those unable to pay the Temple tax had to make pledges. Under such debt burdens, peasants lost their patrimonial land and became tenants on that same land (which now belonged to the creditor). Some peasants fought back as bandits. Hobsbawm's notion of social banditry is helpful in understanding the aspirations for justice of these groups.[16] Agrarian factors played a significant role in the Jewish War at the end of this period.[17] These bitter changes can only be traced in the historical

14. The New Testament Gospels, especially Mark, know the Jewish elite triad, e.g., Mark 11:27. On the four major families, see *t. Menaḥ.* 13:21.

15. Neusner, *From Politics to Piety,* 16; see also Applebaum, "Economic Life in Palestine," 662. The difficulties of applying rabbinic traditions to the period before 70 CE are notorious. The approach in this essay is to accept only those that seem appropriate to the late-Second Temple epoch.

16. Horsley and Hanson, *Bandits, Prophets, and Messiahs,* 48.

17. Kreissig, "Landwirtschaftliche Situation," 223–54; Goodman, "First Jewish Revolt."

record with difficulty. Residents of the Judaean village of Bethar celebrated the downfall of the system in 70 CE, because patrimonial land was stolen from them through fraudulent contracts (*Lam. Rab.* 2:5 19).[18]

Landlords of growing Palestinian estates understandably shifted their agricultural priorities from purely subsistence concerns to sharing in the commercial bonanza of the early Augustan period. Cash crops and other commercial agricultural investments would have grown in importance. Chief among commercial crops were wheat (primarily in local trade) and the grape and the olive (better for long distance trade because more portable as wine or oil). Nakdimon ben Gorion, Kalba Sabbua, and Ben Zizit Hakeset were remembered long after 70 CE as wholesalers who could supply the food needs of Jerusalem for ten years (*Lam. Rab.* 1).[19] Eleazar ben Harsum later controlled merchant ships, "but his family and his large estates go back to the pre-70 period."[20] These and similar merchants, who also controlled significant amounts of Palestinian land, would have played a significant role in determining agricultural production. While exact patterns are not known, there are indicators in the scanty historical record that crops of greater commercial significance were displacing subsistence crops in the pre-70 period. *Tosefta Menaḥot* 8:3 indicates that wine and grain were privileged in Judaea. Olives were cultivated everywhere.[21] *Mishnah Sheqalim* 7:4 attests to much livestock in the vicinity of Jerusalem that were used for sacrifices. According to Applebaum:

> Although it belongs to the third century, R. Johanan's advice, "Let your holdings be divided into three parts, a third grain, a third olives, and a third vines [*b. Baba Meṣiʿa* 107a]," would certainly have been accepted also in the first.[22]

Fig cultivation was consequently of much less importance, since it was ordinarily a subsistence staple. Figs, for instance, remained a part of the marriage contract provisions for Jewish women (*m. Ketub.* 5:8). Josephus (*War* 3.519) calls the fig the "royal fruit" along with the grape, but this is in reference to Galilee. While fig and vine figure prominently in the older Israelite tradition, Sirach already drops mention of the fig when

18. Applebaum, "Judaea as a Roman Province," 371.

19. Applebaum, "Economic Life of Palestine," 659, 687.

20. Ibid., 689.

21. Jeremias, *Jerusalem*, 45–46.

22. "Economic Life in Palestine," 651.

mentioning olive and vine (Sir 24:13–17). As Luke 13 clearly shows, keeping a fig tree bearing required a sizeable amount of care and labor. To the Palestinian Jew, the care required had become proverbial: "He who tends a fig tree will eat its fruit" (Prov 27:18). Commerce in figs was likely to be a purely local affair.[23] Early figs were offered as first-fruits at the Temple. Bethany and Bethphage were renowned for these.[24] It is likely that fig orchards near Jerusalem belonged to estates of the oligarchy. Bethany may in fact have meant "house of Hino" or "house of Hanan" rather than "house of unripe figs."[25] The Temple utilized fig wood for sacrifices, but significantly olive wood and the vine were not permitted (*m. Tamid* 2:3).[26]

Luke 13, therefore, implies that a dramatic shift to tenancy agriculture was underway in early first-century CE Palestine, and such a transition meant a shift away from subsistence agriculture to other crops, especially olives, grapes, and wheat, or to herding. Whether through neglect or through loss to specialized production, Judaean, and perhaps also Galilean, peasants were deprived of one of their staple crops. A rabbinic tradition implies that bearing fig trees were jealously watched by their owners.[27]

From this viewpoint, Jesus visits a fig tree that has gone to wood because of intention or neglect. The fig tree's barrenness again testifies to the shift in the agricultural priorities of the elites. By cursing the fig tree, Jesus in effect curses the social system that has led to its neglect. Understanding that fig trees might supply so much wood for the sacrificial fires, the Q word of John the Baptist (Luke 3:9) holds ominous overtones for the Temple elites!

If the fig tree were not neglected, Mark implies by, "for it was not the season for figs," then figs under ordinary circumstances could be expected from this tree. When the Jerusalem elites took all figs to the storehouse or to the local market, their policies resulted in an "artificial famine" of such staples.[28] Consequently, nothing was left for the peasant family or

23. Jeremias, *Jerusalem*, 46. Expensive figs were available in Jerusalem (*m. Maʿaś.* 2:5).

24. Avi-Yonah, *Holy Land*, 192.

25. Str-B. 1:855–56.

26. Jeremias, *Jerusalem*, 50.

27. *Y. Taʿan.* 4.4; Hamel reproduces this text in translation and has a useful discussion; John 1:48 has important significance if it corroborates this fact.

28. Note that the Jesus tradition knows this mentality: Matt 24:45. On famines, see MacMullen, *Enemies of the Roman Order*, 249–54; Jeremias, *Jerusalem*, 140ff; Hamel,

hungry passerby (consider the gleaning of Mark 2:23–28). Queen Helena had to provide Jerusalem with dried figs during the famine in the late forties CE (Josephus, *Ant.* 20.51).[29] The elite storehouse was in permanent competition with peasant subsistence. Jesus' curse, typical of Galileans,[30] was occasioned by more than just the lack of figs on a fig tree.

Will the tree be barren forever? Answering this question depends upon how *eis ton aiōna* is interpreted. Could this phrase anticipate Jesus' word at the Last Supper: "I will no longer drink of the fruit of the vineyard until that day when I drink it new in the kingdom of God" (Mark 14:25)? For Mark, the curse is effective in this aeon, not in the next. The fig tree will no longer benefit its self-aggrandizing owners. In the new aeon coming, they are out of business. At that *kairos*, figs will be freely available for human consumption.

For Jesus, the grace of the kingdom of God is especially a material grace (Q/Luke 12:22–32). The conclusion of the Cursing narrative brings this point out strongly. When Peter sees the withered fig tree (Mark 11:21), Jesus reminds him of God's faithfulness. While *pistis* in Mark usually means the subjective faith of the disciple, in 11:22 another linguistic option is possible. Most versions translate v. 22b, "Have faith in God" (objective genitive stressing the act of the disciple's belief). The imperative verb form is ambiguous here; *echete* can also be indicative. The verse can equally well be translated, "You have God's pledge."[31] This reading would strengthen the foregoing interpretation. This much is probably Marcan redaction, for it recalls Jesus' previous statement that what is not possible for human beings is possible for God (Mark 10:27).

Is the referent in Mark's mind for "this mountain" (11:23) the Mount of Olives with its specialized arboriculture or the Temple mount? In either case, Jesus' curse extends to the site of specialized production and the place of its sanctification/legitimation. God, in contrast to the current elite, is

---

Poverty and Charity, 44ff.

29. Jeremias, *Jerusalem*, 129.

30. Galileans were renowned for their swearing: *m. Ned.* 5:5 and *b. Ned.* 48a. Mark documents this elsewhere: Mark 8:12, *ei dothēsetai*, is strong enough to be translated, "I'll be damned if (a sign is given)." See further Klausner, *Jesus of Nazareth*, 231; Freyne, *Galilee from Alexander the Great to Hadrian*, 277; Goodman, *State and Society in Roman Galilee*, 99–100.

31. On this meaning of the word *pistis* see Moulton and Milligan, *Vocabulary*, 515; Acts 17:31.

a faithful patron (vv. 23–24).[32] The new distributive order of God, which Jesus calls God's *basileia* ("kingdom"), will provide adequate subsistence to the hungry and dishonored.[33] The final word of Jesus, which echoes the fifth petition of the Lord's Prayer, enjoins the need for debt forgiveness.[34] Clearly Mark is responsible for placing the saying about debt/transgressions here. The current dishonorable order derives from indebtedness. It can only be effaced by radical means, as the Temple Cleansing will show. Debt exploitation, which is unworthy of God's *basileia*, shall not be found among Jesus' disciples. The total effect of these sayings in Mark's Appendix to the Fig Tree episode is to elucidate the significance of the curse and point to its antidote in God's gracious patronage.

THE TEMPLE EPISODE

The so-called Cleansing of the Temple appears in all four canonical gospels. These are the only accounts of the Cleansing in the Jesus tradition. One recent commentator on this passage has called into question the traditional label "Cleansing" for this reported action of Jesus. E. P. Sanders thinks that Jesus' activity is best understood as a prophetic action to symbolize the Temple's destruction. Craig A. Evans, however, has recently argued against Sanders and for the traditional Cleansing understanding.[35] For the purposes of the following analysis, Cleansing, Incident, and Action will be used interchangeably without prejudicing a final conclusion about the significance of Jesus' deed.

The synoptic evangelists report the incident at the end of Jesus' ministry (Mark 11:15–19 and par.), while John places it early in his gospel

32. Malina, "Patron and Client," investigates and explains this analogy in a very helpful way.

33. As Malina, *The New Testament World*, 84–85 points out, injustice and deprivation are also experienced here in terms of dishonor.

34. The Aramaic word for debt, *ḥôbâ*, can also mean sin; see Oakman, "Jesus and Agrarian Palestine," orig. 72 [chapter 1 above]; or idem, *Jesus and the Economic Questions of His Day*, 153. Matthew 5:23, parallel to this saying in Mark, also has an economic implication: Do not give a gift to God until you have satisfied your [material] obligation to your neighbor. This also reflects Jesus' negative attitude regarding the *qorban* dedications, Mark 7:11. On *echein ti kata tinos* ("to have something against someone") as a legal phrase frequently implying court proceedings against debtors, see Moulton and Milligan, *Vocabulary*, 322, s.v. *kata* I. (2) and 544, s.v. *pros* (3) (c). Matthew 6:23–26 confirms this connection.

35. E. P. Sanders, *Jesus and Judaism*, 75; Evans, "Jesus' Action in the Temple."

narrative (John 2:13–17). Both versions agree on proximity in time to Passover.

The basic structure of the story is Action – Saying. Mark brings this out in v. 17 with *edidasken kai elegen* ("he was teaching and he said"). For Mark, Jesus' teaching often involves action (e.g., 1:27 in response to an exorcism).

A comparison of the Marcan and Johannine accounts of the Temple action of Jesus shows that the tradition agrees on several things: Both versions agree that the action of Jesus focused upon buying and selling in the Temple (John: sacrificial animals; Mark: not clear what sold), upon the activities of the money-changers (Mark: *kollybistai*; John: *kermatistai/kollybistai*), and upon the sale of doves. Mark diverges from John in alone reporting that Jesus prevented anyone from carrying vessels (*skeya*) through the Temple; perhaps the Court of Gentiles is meant, since commercial activity is known to have taken place there.[36]

Luke has only a severely truncated version of the action (19:45b). This action leads to a "judgment" that the Temple is a house of prayer.[37] Verses 47–48 extend the unit in narrative fashion to show that the Jerusalem leadership seeks a way to kill Jesus.

Matthew's version also condenses the Marcan account. However, Matthew does not see an immediate controversy with the Jerusalem leadership (as do the other three versions); rather, the blind and the lame come to Jesus to be healed. It is this healing activity and the praise of Jesus by the healed that leads to the controversy (v. 16).

Since the synoptic and Johannine versions of what Jesus said in conjunction with the Temple incident are remarkably divergent, pronouncement seems arbitrarily selected. In Mark, Jesus quotes from Isaiah 56:7 and Jeremiah 7:11. This dual quotation technique is familiar in Mark (e.g., 1:2–3, 11). Matthew and Luke, with some minor variations, follow Mark's quotations. John (2:16) diverges, however, with an allusion to Zechariah 14:21.

---

36. Eppstein, "Historicity"; Jeremias, *Jerusalem*; Evans, "Jesus' Action in the Temple."

37. On the notion of a "judgment," or legal decision, see Mack and Robbins, *Patterns of Persuasion*, 28–29.

CURSING ROBBERS' DENS

The question of arbitrariness can only be decided when the meaning of these pronouncements is evaluated. Is Jesus thought to be pointing to the need for the Temple's purification or signifying its need for removal? The cleansing view would imply to a great degree a concern by Jesus for the purity of the Temple as a religious institution. Often in the past, interpreters have thus opposed "bloody sacrifice" (implied: impure, fleshly religion) with "prayer" (implied: pure, spiritual religion). Besides the fact that this view imposes a dualism unlikely in Jesus' (admittedly Hellenized) Jewish context and an anachronistic assessment of what constitutes vital religion, it fails to take into account the role of the Temple in the wider social system.[38]

What is important to note, therefore, in both the Marcan and Johannine versions of this incident is the emphasis upon buying/selling (Mark: of sacrificial animals?) – money-changers – sellers of doves. The implications of this confluence need to be explored. The ordinary person of the time became religiously indebted to God for various reasons—through life-events, personal actions, or vows. The Temple as a religious system existed to alleviate these debts incurred to God.[39] Even if people did not perceive a debt, the system operated so as to indebt them anyway. This is especially noticeable in the case of the Temple tax. Temple scribes recorded people's indebtedness, as previously noted. These debts had real economic repercussions upon most Jews of the time.[40] Debts had to be expunged in ways acceptable to the official interpreters of the sacred traditions. Animals offered had to be ritually acceptable to the priests. Coins of payment had to be of requisite Tyrian currency (*m. Bek.* 8:7). The buying and selling, as well as the money-changers, supplied these needs. The people who controlled the Temple trafficked in goods that the Temple system mandated. Oil and livestock were central to this activity; so was the use and exchange of money. Jesus' action calls all of this into question. His action focuses attention on the visible mechanisms of the Temple and Temple elite's power.

---

38. See Evans's appropriate remarks "Jesus' Action in the Temple," 257, about inappropriate Christian assessments of the Temple cultus.

39. I am indebted to Belo for this insight, *Materialist Reading*, 38ff.

40. Priests were exempt: *m. Sheqal.* 1:3.

The sayings connected with Jesus' action explicate its social-systemic implications. While John's and Mark's pronouncements differ in specifics, they agree at least in a fundamental respect. Both sayings bring out the meaning of Jesus' action within the agrarian context of Judaea. Commerce, as Polanyi long ago noted, disrupts local agrarian economies. For this reason, medieval European aristocracies were long careful to keep local agrarian economies insulated especially from long-distance commerce.[41] Judean oligarchy, during the early first century, had not done this. For one reason, the Temple was an international focus of commerce at the time, especially for the Diaspora. For another reason, the Judean elites themselves engaged in commerce.[42] The second part of Mark's saying brings out the destabilizing effects of long-distance commerce in agrarian societies: "Den of robbers." This is a reverse social banditry practiced by the elites. "House of trade" is roughly translated in peasant eyes by "den of robbers"; Jesus expresses the view of the countryside and its exploited people.[43]

What, then, can be implied by "house of prayer"? Haenchen, despite noting that Isaiah 56 does not oppose prayer and sacrifice, takes the cleansing episode to signify (for John at least) the end of the Jewish cult.[44] Mark and Jesus may not so have understood this event. For the real problem with the Temple system, which Jesus' action exposes and opposes, is that ordinary people are deprived of their own offerings for the most part. Jesus opposes the Temple system as a system of exploitative redistribution for the benefit of the few. What would "prayer" imply in place of *this* system?

The answer to this question is suggested by a slight agreement between Mark's and John's versions of the incident. Mark: "*My house* shall be called a house of prayer." John: "Do not make *my father's house* a house of trade." The image of the Temple as God's house, familiar from the Old Testament, implies by extension God's household. A house of prayer, then, suggests a household in which petition to the householder results in the

41. Polanyi, *Great Transformation*, 64: "An increasingly strict separation of local trade from export trade was the reaction of [medieval] urban life to the threat of mobile capital to disintegrate the institutions of the town."

42. Kreissig, "Landwirtschaftliche Situation" emphasizes this; case of Baba b. Buta: *y. Yom Tob* 2.61c, cited in Haenchen, *John 1*, 182; see critical comments in Applebaum, "Economic Life in Palestine," 662.

43. A view also argued, on different grounds, by Theissen, "Die Tempelweissagung Jesu."

44. Haenchen, *John 1*, 187b; cf. 186: "'House of prayer' is thus not being contrasted here [in Isaiah] with sacrifices."

meaningful satisfaction of needs—material as well as spiritual. Jesus envisions, under the image of kingdom of God or household of God, a storehouse of blessing rather than a cave of curse. The *basileia* Jesus proclaims opens the storehouse of God's patronage (Q/Luke 12:31; Mark 10:30). The continuation of Mark's tradition with the Fig Tree revisited brings this idea out further in the sayings catena. Jesus condemns the social system of the Herodian Temple, without necessarily envisioning the end of sacrifice. Yet the sacrificial system will be one that no longer prolongs indebtedness; all will share in it as at Passover (Deut 16:11–12).

Conclusions

The foregoing literary and social analyses have suggested the need for further exploration of pronouncement within social-systemic perspective. The analyses urge moving beyond purely religious or theological inquiries into these episodes, since only in modern individualist existence are religious dimensions of life neatly insulated from other dimensions. A social-systemic analysis insists on keeping the "literal" or "mundane" situation in view, together with the Jewish context that shaped the Jesus tradition, and on conceptualizing the social system of Roman Palestine to shed light on otherwise puzzling episodes.

Furthermore, modern literary approaches to the gospels that proceed without reference to the real context of Jesus traditions will miss significant meanings in those traditions. Elizabeth Struthers Malbon rightly acknowledges in her recent discussion of Marcan characterizations of Jesus' opponents that "a literary approach to Mark . . . is bounded by our understanding of its probable historical context."[45] Malbon's otherwise excellent literary discussion still does not plumb the depths of agrarian anger that led Mark's Jesus to refer to the Jerusalem elite as bandits.

Even recent treatments that one might expect to explore or to make deeper reference to the political-economic connotations in the texts only do so in part. Both Fernando Belo and Ched Myers read the Cursing of the Fig Tree as an acted parable (with little or no meaning in itself) prefiguring the Temple's and Temple elite's doom.[46] Belo and Myers manifest the general modern exegetical tendency to take the Cursing of the Fig Tree as a figurative action, which reflects negatively upon the religious/moral

45. Malbon, "Jewish Leaders," 274.
46. Belo, *Materialist Reading*, 180; Myers, *Binding the Strong Man*, 299.

quality of Judean society. Why precisely *this* figure is used is not explained. Herman Waetjen comes closest to articulating the argument laid out in the foregoing paragraphs:

> It is [the temple] episode which makes the seemingly senseless act of cursing the fig tree intelligible, while at the same time its far-reaching significance is obviated by it. The two incidents are inter-dependent . . . . Like the fig tree, the temple is intended to serve the needs of human beings. But while a fig tree can produce fruit only in its season, the temple as an institution that mediates divine–human relationships cannot be, indeed must not be, regulated by the cycles of nature. . . . The cursing of the fig tree symbolizes the condemnation of the temple institution which, as the central systemic structure of Judaism, has been regulating the religious, political, economic, and social life of the Jewish people.[47]

The strength of the argument in the present essay is that it makes sense out of *both* Cursings and shows how the two episodes are bound together by the social system. Each pronouncement episode examined has a significant tie to first-century, Palestinian social realities. Since the originating social system did not appreciably change over the period when the Jesus tradition was being formed and integrated into, say, Mark's conception, it is quite possible to make some judgments about how the traditions reflect/react to that system. The system itself can be modeled with available historical evidence and conceptual tools offered by comparative social studies.

It has been suggested by some that the Fig Tree Incident really is a parable like Luke 13 that has been historicized.[48] Although it is difficult to see why such a parable should have been historicized, especially given the destructive nature of Jesus' action, it can now be appreciated that such a transformation at an earlier stage would not have happened arbitrarily. Since Luke's and John's compositions drop the Cursing, tradition later moved away from an account requiring a specific social setting for its comprehension. The tendency was to forget the story, not to create it.

Similarly, even though there are historical difficulties in saying precisely whether Jesus cleansed the Temple, and what he might have said on such an occasion, the incident can hardly have been concocted wholesale by the tradition. Such an arbitrary invention would be difficult to understand

47. Waetjen, *Reordering of Power,* 182.
48. Taylor, *Mark,* 459; Harrington, "Mark," 620.

at the hands of a later, apparently Temple-loyal Christian movement (Acts 2:46). The criterion of dissimilarity, therefore, suggests "authenticity" at some level for both pronouncement stories. Social-systemic considerations urge resonance in both accounts with wider social concerns as the source of this authenticity. These concerns helped the early Jesus communities in Palestine to understand and to preserve Jesus' pronouncements quite selectively. Variability within the tradition is seen to have been controlled to an important extent by the experienced social system.

Within that social system, the early Jesus tradition maintained a fairly consistent focus: The "what" of its pronouncements, and related prophetic actions, had to do with interest in the emergence of a new material order, symbolized under the umbrella concept "kingdom of God." The "why" of Jesus tradition pronouncements was given by institutions of the old order that blocked the coming of the kingdom. A fair amount of cursing was necessary to bring in the new order of blessing.[49]

49. I am grateful for having received perceptive critique on earlier drafts of this piece from John J. Pilch, Paul O. Ingram, Patricia O'Connell Killen, and James F. Sennett. These colleagues helped me immensely in formulating the argument. Vernon K. Robbins has graciously encouraged me at several crucial stages. Of course, the faults of the article remain mine alone.

CHAPTER 14

The Lord's Prayer in Social Perspective

> In the villages of Galilee, the Lord's Prayer was revolutionary "wisdom" and "prophetic" teaching . . . .[1]

INTRODUCTION

MUCH HAS BEEN WRITTEN about the Lord's Prayer during the modern era. It may seem as if everything has been said that could have been said. Learned disquisitions are available regarding the linguistic aspects (Greek, Aramaic, even Hebrew), the various forms of the Greek text and their relationship to Q, and the meaning of the Prayer or its individual petitions.[2] The voting of the Jesus Seminar has stimulated much discussion related to the words of Jesus generally, and the Lord's Prayer in particular.[3]

This essay is centrally concerned with the tradition history and social meaning of Jesus' prayer. It presumes or interacts with existing scholarship, but is not intended to offer anything dramatically new related to linguistic or textual issues. The Jesus Seminar's judgments are reviewed and in some ways endorsed, though it is argued that the Seminar incorrectly has assigned gray and pink. In their chromatic terms, we apportion red to *'abba'* and the second table of Matthew (though pink in Luke), and pink or gray

---

1. Duling and Perrin, *The New Testament* (1994), 25. Duling and Perrin offer an excellent discussion of methods that have been applied in the study of the Lord's Prayer, and a valuable beginning point for further study.

2. The recent bibliography compiled by Mark Kiley includes well over 250 items; Kiley, "The Lord's Prayer and Other Prayer Texts from the Greco-Roman Era: A Bibliography."

3. Results appeared first piecemeal in the journal *Foundations and Facets Forum*, then in Funk et al., *Parables of Jesus*, and most fully in Funk et al., *The Five Gospels*.

to the first table.[4] The canonical texts provide a starting point for inquiry into the tradition history. The social meaning is considered *pari passu* with this history, since basic impulses in the tradition derive from conflicting social interests. The meaning for the earliest Jesus movement is parsed essentially in the light of a significant "social problem" of Jesus' day, namely, the growth of indebtedness and the swelling of the ranks of those displaced from the land because of debt. As the Prayer passed into written forms, the interests of various scribes found their way, as it were by way of glosses, into the Prayer tradition. We consider two distinct settings in life (*Sitze im Leben*)—the village and town scribal settings of earliest Q in Galilee, and the Judean-oriented scribal concerns of later Q recensions. By the time the Prayer was incorporated into canonical Matthew, Luke, and indirectly John, Judean interests had come to predominate, and basic concerns of the original Jesus movement had been reworked in systematic ways.

BASIC SOCIAL MODELS OF THIS STUDY

The employment of explicit social models provides distinctive perspectives on the "trajectory" of the Prayer from Jesus up until inclusion in the canonical gospels and later Christian traditions. Since the meaning of a prayer depends significantly upon the social system and location of the petitioner, social-scientific criticism plays a prominent role in the formulation of this essay's approach, working hypotheses, exegesis, and conclusions.[5] The meaning of the text is perceived vis-à-vis a critically reconstructed social world. The approach is thereby dialectical, and if it gives a credible and reasonable accounting of the data, and can incorporate or rule out the major alternatives, it becomes persuasive.

Recent scholarship has strongly urged that religion was imbedded in politics in Jesus' Palestine.[6] Religion and theology were consequently bound up with certain kinds of socio-economic interests, and it is possible to recover some of those links through our extant textual traditions. The social model that supplies the primary working assumptions of this essay,

4. The (Lord's) Prayer, for the purposes of this study, is discussed formally in terms of an address, two "tables" of two to four petitions each, and a concluding doxology or "ascription." Table 1 = Petitions 1–3; Table 2 = Petitions 4–7.

5. Elliott, *What Is Social-Scientific Criticism?* Regarding the relation of meaning to social system, see Malina, *The Social World of Jesus and the Gospels*, 10, 17.

6. Oakman, "The Archaeology of First-Century Galilee," orig. 220–51 (chapter 15 below); Horsley, "Jesus, Itinerant Cynic or Israelite Prophet?," 80.

thus, begins with the consideration that *Jesus' religion spoke to an immediate need in concrete terms*. As with peasants generally, Jesus had little concern for priestly mediations of the divine, or purity in the priestly sense, and was paramountly concerned with the changing of material circumstances and the institutions that controlled them.[7] He spoke out of an intense election consciousness: His experience of God was immediate and in little need of mediating institutions. This characteristic could be construed by later Judean tradents of the Jesus materials as evidence of Jesus' (messianic) authority and status. While Jesus' aims have been hotly debated, he did seem to want to articulate the meaning of Israel's core traditions, especially Moses (Passover) and the prophets (justice for the powerless), for the situation of early Roman Palestine.

Social conflicts were endemic in early Roman Palestine and are presumed as concomitants to the activity of Jesus as well as the development of the gospel traditions. Such conflicts should not be construed naively as "Jesus (or Christians) versus the Jews." The Herods or the Judean elites in Jerusalem were often the object of popular enmity, as not only the gospels, but also Josephus and later rabbinic traditions show. The socio-political conflict which is the initial frame for understanding the Lord's Prayer is analogous to social phenomena familiar to us from the Old Testament and Intertestamental Jewish writings. For instance, Micah's tirade against eighth-century Jerusalem (Mic 3:9–12) or Jeremiah's later judgment against the Jerusalem temple (Jer 7:8–15) provide suggestive social parallels (involving agrarian and village discontent) to the conflicts in Jesus' day. The traditions of *1 Enoch* bespeak similar social discontent in the early Hellenistic period, and the revolt of the Maccabees, beginning in the village or town of Modein, certainly had agrarian overtones (1 Macc 2:23–30). The literature of Qumran attests for the late Hellenistic and early Roman periods that Jerusalem politics, overlaid by strong religious

7. The abductive procedure here depends upon peasant studies and readings of the Jesus tradition that are justified in the subsequent pages (see Malina, "Interpretation," 259–60). For general concerns of peasant religion, see Weber, *The Sociology of Religion*, 80, 82; Wolf, *Peasants*, 101; Redfield, "The Social Organization of Tradition," 26. Jesus of Nazareth, of course, came from the peasantry, but was not entirely limited in his own concerns to peasant horizons, as I have argued in Oakman, *Jesus and the Economic Questions of His Day*, 175–98; and idem, "Was Jesus a Peasant?" (chapter 12 above). Jesus' "brokerage" activities, moreover, had to do with transforming, not sustaining, the socio-economic order. For a very different view of Jesus' relationship to purity, see Chilton, *The Temple of Jesus*, 133, who claims that Jesus was concerned about fulfillment of the aims of Leviticus. Jesus was still in fundamental conflict with the priestly establishment (ibid., 100–2).

ideology, could become quite volatile. And Josephus amply documents the "banditry" and disorder that preceded the Judean-Roman War of 66–70 CE.[8] In striking Judean analogy to the peasant prophet Jesus of Nazareth, "Jesus son of Ananus" appeared in Jerusalem in 62 or 63 CE declaring that the temple was dishonored and the people bound for disaster.[9]

The earliest scribes of the Jesus tradition, working in villages and towns of eastern Galilee, produced the first translations of Jesus' Aramaic speech into Greek. For perceptions of the original meaning of the Lord's Prayer, some appeal must be made to the Aramaic behind the (likely) Q Greek. Nevertheless, the case made in this essay about original meaning does not depend upon a precise knowledge of the original words, but only upon probable linguistic elements conjoined with social considerations.[10] There would have been a close interface, although hardly an identity, between the early Q tradents' social interests and the interests of Jesus.[11] Q was originally compiled by Galilean scribes, probably within the Herodian administration (Mark 6:14; Luke 8:3; 13:31) and not overly sympathetic to scribal interests prevalent later in the Jesus tradition (Luke 11:39–52).[12]

Once Jesus' Prayer had assumed written form, in the language of commerce and to some extent empire, other interests would become more significant than those of the originating context. "Socialtextural" considerations (to use Vernon Robbins' language) are more important at an earlier stage, "intertextural" considerations come into play at later stages.[13] Whereas an illiterate Jesus was preoccupied with the immediate and concrete, *later tradents of the Jesus tradition become more concerned with theological (christological, eschatological) abstractions or the articulation of the Jesus material with Israel's great traditions.* Also, as the Prayer was uttered

---

8. Material discussed at length in Horsley and Hanson, *Bandits, Prophets, and Messiahs.*

9. Josephus, *Ant.* 6.300–305.

10. Some of these ideas and issues were first sketched much too simply, in Oakman, "Rulers' Houses, Thieves, and Usurpers" (chapter 10 above).

11. I consider that Jesus was an illiterate peasant, for these reasons: 1) Jesus did not leave any written record that we know of; 2) Jesus was known through oral-speech forms (parable, aphorism); 3) generally, peasant artisans would have little opportunity for education (see Oakman, "Was Jesus a Peasant?" [chapter 12 above]). Some have urged that Jesus possessed at least Torah-education, e.g., Klausner, *Jesus of Nazareth,* 234–35 (cf. 193), but this does not urge a literate education.

12. Kloppenborg, "Literary Convention" has been influential here.

13. Robbins, *Exploring the Texture of Texts,* 40, 71.

within other social locations, socio-political concerns were softened (but not completely obliterated) while socio-religious concerns came more to the fore.

In general, purity concerns and apocalyptic concerns emphasizing judgment are highly correlated; as Qumran clearly shows, apocalyptic Judean interests stood within priestly and temple concerns.[14] Similarly, apocalyptic New Testament images (Mark 13; 1 Cor 5–6; Revelation) are filled with violence and conflict, reflecting the collision of incompatible principles. These interests are marked by a concern for God's magical intervention to rectify conditions of impurity from the standpoint of priestly sensibilities. Apocalyptic "readings" of Jesus, Jesus' aims, or Jesus material will thus have depended upon Judean scribes standing within significant temple or priestly interests (late-Q, Paul, late Mark [i.e., 11–15]).

The Canonical Texts of the Lord's Prayer

The fact that there are differing forms of the Lord's Prayer provides one of the key warrants for a tradition-critical analysis and for letting "social imagination" loose in dialectic between text and social models. It is necessary at the start to examine the textual basis for the study.

There is a modern "sociology of knowledge" issue reflected in defense of harmonistic texts, glossed understandings, or the printing of both the Matthean and Lukan versions in red in Red Letter Editions. This issue is well illustrated in the history of English versions. The King James Version offers the non-specialist with perhaps the easiest access to the shape of the Lord's Prayer according to the *textus receptus*, the Greek text most common during the Middle Ages that shaped the earliest printed Greek testaments, English versions, and liturgical traditions among English-speaking Protestants. The Matthean and Lukan versions of the Prayer are printed almost identically. Missing in Luke is the final doxology; heaven and earth are reversed in Luke 11:2b; Luke's "day by day" (11:3) replaces Matthew's "this day" (6:11); Luke's "sins" (11:4a) replaces Matthew's "debts" (6:12a), and the final clause of Luke 11:4a is longer than the Matthean version (6:12b). These similarities demonstrate the well known harmonistic

14. The author is aware that this generalization glosses over some of the fine distinctions in recent studies, for instance John J. Collins, "Early Jewish Apocalypticism," 287. However, even Judean apocalyptic traditions that emphasize wisdom are probably still within the orbit of priestly interests.

tendencies of *textus receptus* (in light of numerous variants in the Greek manuscript tradition of the Prayer).

Following important textual discoveries and the critical work of scholars like Tischendorf and Westcott-Hort, the English revisions in the late-nineteenth and early twentieth centuries began to incorporate more critical readings.[15] Edgar Goodspeed's *The New Testament: An American Translation* was greeted with popular indignation based in ignorance of scholarly progress in text critical work.[16] One editorialist even suggested that the Prayer that Jesus had prayed should be left unchanged:

> Nothing stops his [Goodspeed's] devastating pen. He has even abbreviated the Lord's Prayer, a petition not so long originally but that hustling, hurrying Chicagoans could find time for it, if they ever thought of prayer. It is a petition that in its present wording has been held sacred for nearly two thousand years, for the King James translators are said to have made no changes.[17]

Goodspeed justly observed that the *English Revised Version* (1881) together with its close relative the *American Standard Version* (1901), as well as Weymouth (1903), the *Twentieth Century New Testament* (1905), and Moffatt (1913), had all printed the shortened Lord's Prayer at Luke 11:2–4.[18] The shorter Lukan text, moreover, was adopted in the Revised Standard Version, and indeed in all modern versions based upon a critical Greek text. While at least one scholar has promoted a return to something like the *textus receptus*, his arguments have not proven persuasive.[19]

Turning to the Greek text itself, eight variant readings in the Lukan prayer stem from Matthean parallels, since early copyists were often tempted to harmonize. Typical of this type of variant would be the expansion of the address in Luke: Alexandrinus and several Western manuscripts (which tend to conflate readings) have "ours in heaven." Similarly, against the majority of Greek manuscripts, Alexandrian (especially P[75]),

15. The English Revised Version appeared in 1881–1885 and its American counterpart in 1901: see *The Holy Bible Containing the Old and New Testaments* (1901). Westcott and Hort detailed many of the problems in their *Introduction to the New Testament in the Original Greek*.

16. Goodspeed, *The New Testament: An American Translation*.

17. Goodspeed, *As I Remember*, 176.

18. Ibid., 177.

19. Van Bruggen, "The Lord's Prayer and Textual Criticism," argues the case and is generally skeptical about modern text criticism, but Bandstra, "The Original Form of the Lord's Prayer," provides a thorough refutation.

Western, and pre-Caesarean types supply the Matthean third petition in Luke 11:2.[20]

The most interesting Lukan variant appears in 11:2: Several medieval manuscripts have for the second petition, "Let your holy spirit come upon us and cleanse us." This reading is attested in the East in the writings of Gregory of Nyssa and faintly in the West in Tertullian. Perhaps the reading entered the manuscript tradition out of Montanism in the second century CE and likely in connection with baptism.[21]

The longer Matthean version shows no variants of the harmonistic type. The most significant variant here is the doxology or ascription—"For yours is the kingdom, and the power, and the glory, for ever"—which also appears in the *Didache* (ca. 125 CE) but not in the best manuscripts of the Alexandrian, Western, and pre-Caesarean types. (The manuscript tradition shows a number of interesting minor variations to this reading.) It would also seem to have crept into the Matthean Prayer as a gloss encouraged by liturgical usage.[22] There are numerous other minor variations between the two forms of the Prayer as well as within the manuscript tradition, but these will not be comprehensively itemized.

The manuscript tradition of the Prayer thus shows that its text was not immune to accretions or modifications. A critical Greek text, maintaining the striking differences between Matthew and Luke, must form the starting point for a consideration of the original form and meaning of the Prayer.[23]

TRADITION HISTORY AND THE SOCIAL CONTEXTS OF THE LORD'S PRAYER

The early tradition history of the Lord's Prayer must be reconstructed primarily through canonical New Testament materials (Q through Luke, Matthew; allusions in Paul, Mark).[24] *Didache* 8 provides a point of ref-

---

20. The other parallels: Aorist *dos* for *didou* and *sēmeron* for *to kath hēmeran* in 11:3; *to opheilēmata* for *tas hamartias*, *hōs kai hēmeis* for *kai gar autoi*, *tois opheiletais* for *panta opheilonti hēmin*, and the insertion of *alla rhysai hēmas apo tou ponērou* in 11:4.

21. Metzger, *Textual Commentary*, 155–56.

22. Ibid., 16–17; Betz, *The Sermon on the Mount*, 414–15.

23. The Nestle–Aland text, 27th edition provides this basis.

24. Brooke traces allusions more extensively in Paul and John, "The Lord's Prayer Interpreted through John and Paul." Compare the chart in Houlden, "The Lord's Prayer," 357.

erence for Syrian tradition after the time of Matthew, but the *Gospel of Thomas* does not allude to the prayer or seem to offer additional insight. Several earlier stages or strata can be perceived through a tradition-critical analysis of the canonical materials. The penultimate stage corresponds with the latest form of the Q Prayer; developments from Jesus to the latest Q form are perceptible though somewhat dimly; and some proposals can be made about the form of the Prayer used by Jesus himself. We turn to an examination of these stages in reverse chronological order.

Stage 3: The Latest Setting in Q

Doubt persists as to whether the Lord's Prayer pericope belonged to Q.[25] Kloppenborg accepts the Prayer as early as Q[1], since he claims it formed the core of one of the sapiential speeches. Jacobson, however, sees the Prayer as a late addition to Q (with concerns similar to the Temptation) and follows Manson in thinking that it may have been "secret teaching" reserved for the mature. Betz also urges that the Prayer entered Q rather late in two different versions, and existed only in Greek.[26]

The most persuasive reasons for seeing a Q version behind Luke and Matthew reside in the verbatim identity of Petitions 1–2 and in the word *epiousion*. In regard to the latter, it would be very difficult for two completely independent versions of the Prayer to convey the Aramaic by a word that turns out to be *hapax legomenon* in ancient Greek. This fact seems easier to account for by means of a common Greek origin for the canonical prayers. Departures from that common form have then to be accounted for more by the evangelists' redaction than by translation, but the divergences in their language still reflect to some extent uncertainties about meaning derivative from the Prayer's earlier history.

At the latest Q stage, before the Prayer was taken up and edited by Matthew and Luke, the Q prayer had a form similar to this:[27]

---

25. Kloppenborg provides a helpful survey, *Q Parallels*, 84.

26. Kloppenborg, *Formation of Q*, 203–6; Jacobson, *The First Gospel*, 158–59; Botha, "Recent Research on the Lord's Prayer," 43. Betz, *Sermon on the Mount*, 371: "If the Lord's Prayer was part of Q, it must have become a part of it after the two versions of Q developed." He denies (375) that the Prayer ever existed in Aramaic: "no evidence suggests that the Lord's Prayer as we have it was first composed in Aramaic or Hebrew and only then translated into Greek."

27. Davies and Allison, "Excursus," 591. Duling and Perrin concur, *The New Testament*, 16.

Figure 19: The Lord's Prayer Form in Q

	Address	*Pater,*
Table 1	**Petition 1**	*hagiasthētō to onoma sou*
	Petition 2	*elthetō hē basileia sou*
Table 2	**Petition 4**	*ton arton hēmōn ton epiousion dos hēmin sēmeron*
	Petition 5	*kai aphes hēmin ta opheilēmata hēmōn, kai gar autoi aphēkamen tōi opheilonti hēmin*
	Petition 6	*kai mē eisenegkēs hēmas eis peirasmon.*

Even given a Q Lord's Prayer, the view of Jeremias that an "original Aramaic form" lies behind the Greek retains strong plausibility because of the uncertainties regarding meaning manifest in Matthew's and Luke's diverging wordings: "the Lucan version has preserved the oldest form with respect to length, but the Matthaean text is more original with regard to wording."[28] Jeremias' reasons for giving priority to the Lukan length were fourfold: 1) The strict parallelism of Matthew's version, as well as 2) Matthew's greater elaboration, suggested to Jeremias the end product of liturgical usage. Furthermore, 3) Luke's simple address "Father," in contrast to Matthew's "Our Father in heaven" (well attested in Targums and later Jewish prayer forms), seems to reflect the Aramaic address of Jesus, *'abba'*, also adopted by later Christians (Paul: Rom 8:15; Gal 4:6; *Didache* 8). Finally, 4) Jeremias noted the parallel between the Lukan version of the first two petitions of the Lord's Prayer and the *Qaddish* of the Jewish synagogue. The *Qaddish* begins (following Jeremias' arrangement):

> Exalted and hallowed be his great name in the world which he created according to his will. May he let his kingdom rule in your lifetime and in your days and in the lifetime of the whole house of Israel, speedily and soon. And to this, say: amen.[29]

On the other hand, Jeremias was forced to the anomalous conclusion that, in terms of the specific wording of the respective prayers, the Matthean version was at several points indicative of earlier understandings. What these observations imply is that a critical discussion of an "original Aramaic form" is still necessary, though in this task Jeremias' position requires some modifications. The changes and expansions evident between Luke and

28. Jeremias, *Prayers*, 93; cf. Fitzmyer, *Luke*, 2:897.

29. Jeremias, *Prayers*, 98.

Matthew are along lines governed not only by a semitic linguistic sensibil-
ity, but also by social interests operant in the tradition.

It is important to have some definite, even though general, ideas about
the social origins of the Q recensions. Kloppenborg has provided the most
satisfying proposal so far about these matters. He notes that the wisdom
interests manifested in the contents and composition of Q[1] (consequently,
"Wisdom Q") would be appropriate to town or village scribes, "the 'petit
bourgeois' in the lower administrative sector of cities and villages. It is
plain from Egyptian evidence that it is precisely within these sectors that
the instructional genre was cultivated."[30] Moreover, wisdom was usually
the concern of royal administrative personnel. And Q[1]'s metaphorical
preoccupation with an "alternate kingdom" would indicate this as well.[31]
It goes a step beyond Kloppenborg, though he sparks the thought, to suggest that Herod Antipas' administrative personnel around the Galilean
Lake probably provided the first Q draft (adumbrated by Matt 9:9?).
Kloppenborg tantalizingly suggests that the transfer of Tiberias to Agrippa
II (54 CE), and concomitantly the royal archives back to Sepphoris, left
its mark in the Q tradition in the move to prophetic forms. It certainly
makes sense, given that ancient recensions were frequently connected with
changes in political fortunes, to connect the more heavily Judean character
of Q[2] ("Deuteronomic Q") with the work of Sepphorean scribes.[32] These
considerations would urge dating Q[1] somewhere between the late 20s and
54 CE, and Q[2] somewhere in the period 54–66 CE.[33]

Zahavy has lent insight into the sociology of scribalism around the
time of the Judean-Roman War. In the immediate aftermath, he sees a
struggle between scribes who focused their ultimate concerns and piety
around the *Shema*ʿ and Deuteronomy and scribes whose interests congre-
gated in the *Amidah*. As he sees the situation:

---

30. Kloppenborg, "Literary Convention," 85. Jacobson's reservations about "wisdom"
(*First Gospel*, 257) are noted. He prefers to account for Q transformations by appeals to the
diachronic experiences (256) of a single group, while the proposal here assumes activity in
different scribal spheres.

31. Kloppenborg, *Formation of Q*, 317–20.

32. Coote and Coote, *Power, Politics, and the Making of the Bible*. On the Judean character
of Sepphoris, see Stuart S. Miller, *Studies in the History and Traditions of Sepphoris*.

33. Jacobson, *First Gospel*, 251–55 indicates that the situation was probably more
complicated than indicated in a two-stage development. For the purposes of this essay,
however, identifying the two major contexts is sufficient.

> In the crucial transitional period after the destruction of the Temple, the *Shema'* emerged as the primary ritual of the scribal profession and its proponents. The Amidah . . . was a ritual sponsored mainly by the patriarchal families and their priestly adherents.[34]

Both of these scribal groups were involved in Jerusalem-Judean affairs, but Zahavy's "professional scribes" would have been less tied to Jerusalem than families associated with the temple and priesthood. Therefore, post-temple Judaism was to be (as Zahavy sees it) a compromise between these two scribal interests, attested in the combination of *Shema'* and *Amidah* in the synagogue service. What Zahavy's work suggests about the Q tradents, assuming similar circumstances a quarter century or so before, is this: Q^1 was the product of Herodian scribes; Q^2 was the product of Judean scribes whose theological commitments were expressed through the *Shema'*. A logical line from Q^1 to Q^2 and the later synoptic tradition (in strong argument with Pharisees and post-temple developments) can begin to be traced.

Stage 2: Between Jesus and Q^2

So within years of Jesus' death, if not during his lifetime, some intrepid collector or collectors began gathering his oral legacy and committing it to writing. It is perhaps appropriate to apply the second-century word of Papias to this stage, "Matthew collected the sayings in the Hebrew language, and each interpreted them as best he could."[35] Jesus' sayings existed originally in Aramaic (Papias' "Hebrew"), but were partially in Greek as early as Q^1.

Numerous attempts at retrotranslation (from Greek to Aramaic or Hebrew) have been made over the last century. Notable are the efforts of Dalman, Jeremias, Fitzmyer, and de Moor.[36] Whereas Dalman, Jeremias, and Fitzmyer had attempted to recover the "everyday" speech of Jesus, de Moor places the Prayer within the sphere of "literary Aramaic." Here is something like the Aramaic exemplar for Q^2 (following Fitzmyer):

---

34. Zahavy, *Studies in Jewish Prayer*, 87.

35. Eusebius, *Eccl. Hist.* 3.39.16. Kloppenborg is extremely skeptical, *Formation of Q*, 51–54.

36. Dalman, "Anhang A: Das Vaterunser," in *Die Worte Jesu*, 283–365; Jeremias, "The Lord's Prayer in Modern Research"; Fitzmyer, *Luke*, 2:901; de Moor, "Reconstruction," 403 n. 17. See Davies and Allison, "Excursus," 593. For an attempt to discover a Hebrew exemplar of the Prayer, see Young, *Jewish Background*. Meier, *A Marginal Jew*, 2:291–302.

Figure 20: The Lord's Prayer in Aramaic

	Address	ʾabbaʾ
Table 1	Petition 1	ythqdsh shmk
	Petition 2	thîthî mlkûthk
Table 2	Petition 4	lḥmnʾa <u>dîmsthîʾa</u>
		(de Moor: pthgm yôm;
		Jeremias: dlmḥr)
		hb Inâ <u>yômʾa dnâ</u>
		(de Moor: byoîmiyâ)
	Petition 5	ûshbôq Inâ ḥôbînʾa
		kdî shbqnʾa lḥîbînʾa
	Petition 6	wlʾa <u>thʿalînnʾa</u>
		(de Moor: ʾithînʾa) Insiyôn

Since various assumptions have to come into play, consensus about reconstruction has not been achieved. Variations in the modern retrotranslations appear especially in the second table (the underlined words). Fitzmyer aptly writes: "The reconstruction of the original Aramaic form of the 'Our Father' will always remain problematic, conditioned above all by our knowledge of the Palestinian Aramaic of Jesus' days."[37] Not only the Aramaic, but also the meaning of the Greek controlling the Aramaic retrotranslation is obscure. Though consensus may not be possible, certain details in the tradition reach higher salience, especially related to bread and debt.

The evidence of Paul and Mark on the use of ʾabbaʾ supplies important information regarding this period of the Prayer's history. Since the Lord's Prayer inculcates an election consciousness that bespeaks immediacy with God, these two writers seem generally familiar with Jesus' characteristic understanding of God (Q/Luke 10:21–22; Rom 8:15–16; Mark 1:10–11; 14:36). Mark 11:25 and 14:36 also seem to echo the third and fifth petitions, but neither Paul nor Mark quotes the entire Prayer. How should its absence in their texts be understood?

As the Corinthian correspondence, Romans 15, and Acts make clear, Paul was widely traveled, and it would be difficult now to determine with

37. Fitzmyer, *Luke*, 2:901.

precision where he came into contact with particular streams of early Jesus traditions. By a careful study of quotes and allusions, and keeping in mind Victor Paul Furnish's observation about Paul's rare use of Jesus in contrast to the Old Testament,[38] we can make the following observations:

1) Paul seems only fragmentarily to have known Q in its distinctive Galilean form (i.e., Wisdom Q). First Corinthians 9:14 and 10:27 allude to Luke 10:7, 8 respectively. These seem to be the only places where Paul connects with Q^1. Perhaps one of the factions of Corinth possessed a copy, in view of the general concern for wisdom there. However, Paul's failure to mention the Prayer where it might be beneficial (e.g., 1 Cor 11 in reference to the communal difficulties surrounding the meal of association, when such a Prayer might be offered) seems to speak against this, or at least Paul's knowledge of it.

2) Paul otherwise is more familiar with "Judean" elements of the synoptics, as when he refers in 1 Cor 7:10–11 to something like Mark 10:11 or in 1 Cor 11:23–25 to something like Luke 22:17–19. Already in 1 Thess 5:2, 4 there is contact with Q/Luke 12:39 or Mark 13:35–36. Elsewhere (Rom 12:14, 17), Paul shows familiarity with traditions like Q/Luke 6:27, 29/Matt 5:39–44 and in a fashion that would suggest concern for Antiochene Torah interpretation. Concerns with marital purity, Jerusalem traditions of the Last Supper, Torah interpretation, and apocalyptic timetables we would expect from a former Pharisee (Gal 1:14; Phil 3:5) who received significant elements of his knowledge about Jesus from the Jerusalem church (1 Cor 11:23; 15:3).[39]

Mark, while still remaining unfamiliar with the majority of Q's contents, had more substantial contact with them (how is unclear). This can be seen, for instance, in Mark's knowledge of Q/Luke 3:2–4; 3:16–17; 4:1–2; 10:4–11 (cf. Paul); 11:14–23; 13:18–19. As in Q^2, Mark also evinces a prophet christology (e.g., Mark 1:1, 8, 10; Q/Luke 6:23; 7:31–35), shows conflict with Pharisees (Mark 2:16; Q elements of Luke 11:39–52), a heightened concern with purity issues (Mark 7:1–2, 14–15; Q/Luke

38. ". . . one must concede the relative sparsity of direct references to or citations of Jesus' teachings in the Pauline letters. The argument that he could presuppose his readers' familiarity with these because he had already passed them on in his missionary preaching is not convincing. He could and does presuppose knowledge of the Old Testament, but this in no way deters him from constantly and specifically citing it in the course of his ethical teaching," Furnish, *Theology and Ethics in Paul*, 55.

39. Compare Betz's assessment of these issues, and additional bibliography, *Sermon on the Mount*, 6 and n. 12.

11:39–41), and apocalyptic-eschatological preoccupations (e.g., "son of man" preoccupations as at Mark 14:62; Q/Luke 12:8). Paul was not familiar with the bulk of this material (absence of "son of man" material in Paul is particularly striking), so a time after Paul for Q^2 seems appropriate. Mark, however, clearly had contact with or at least shared interests with the later Q tradents.

Q^1, therefore, did not contain the Lord's Prayer, or contained the Lord's Prayer (Kloppenborg) which however remained unknown to Paul and Mark. These both were substantially linked to Jerusalem-Judean traditions. Paul remained largely ignorant of Galilean Jesus materials, though Mark had access to Galilean miracle stories and ideas similar to those of Q^2.[40] As the two-source hypothesis has long urged, extensive Jesus materials were mediated independently to Matthew, Luke, and John(?) through at least two separate lineages of Judean-oriented scribes (Mark, Q). Q was a Galilean source, but with Judean interests. Unless the "secret teaching" hypothesis is embraced, the Lord's Prayer would seem to have been largely unknown or only imperfectly known to Jerusalem-Judean sources (available to Paul and Mark) until the later first century.

Stage 1: The Setting of Jesus

The Lord's Prayer existed in a much simpler form in the context of Jesus and the earliest Jesus movement, and grew by certain measurable developments into the forms we have come to know today.[41] The differences in form are best accounted for by differing scribal traditions and interests.

Some further decisions are necessary about the form of the Prayer for Jesus. The uniformity of the first table in contrast to the second at the Q^2 stage suggests that the former was extremely conventional and perhaps extant only in Greek, while the latter offered difficulties of interpretation indicative of the earlier move from Aramaic to Greek. Besides uniformity in the Greek, various other considerations argue against the first table having belonged originally to the Prayer of Jesus; chief among them are linguistic, internal theological, and external social considerations. Linguistically, the first table adopts the more polite jussive, while the imperatives of the second table are coarse and direct. Theologically, there is great tension

40. Theissen, *Gospels in Context*, 99.

41. There are similarities between the approach of this essay and the views of Lohmeyer, who distinguished a Galilean from a Jerusalem form of the Prayer. We work with a more developed relation of the Prayer to social context.

between Jesus' own *Abba*-consciousness and Petitions 1, 2, or 3; as well, the abstractions of the first table (God's name, kingdom, and will) militate against the concrete and mundane concerns in Jesus' Prayer. Sociologically, the first table stands in clear relationship to later synagogue prayer traditions and thus is an understandable accretion.

Taussig points out that *'abba'* stands uneasily over against the first petition. He characterizes this tension as deriving from either Jesus or someone closer to Q: "The irony of an occasional juxtaposition of the familiar *'abba'* with the next phrase 'May your name be holy' certainly could have been appreciated by a witty aphorizer."[42] A comparable tension, however, is evident between the second petition and the address. An immediate consciousness of God and concern for God's direct involvement in the moment (second table) are *both* difficult to reconcile with purity (Petition 1) and eschatology (Petition 2).

Jeremias a generation ago pointed out the connection between the Lord's Prayer and the *Qaddish*. He can be criticized today for a rather anachronistic employment of this material, since there is debate as to the antiquity of the prayer.[43] Jeremias argued that the form of the *Qaddish* validated the shorter Lukan form of the prayer, even though all three of Matthew's first-table petitions are contained within the *Qaddish*:

> *Exalted and hallowed be his great name* in the world which he created *according to his will.*

> May he let his *kingdom rule (etc.)*

> [Our Father who are in heaven, let your name be *sanctified*, let your *kingdom come*, let your *will be done (etc.)*]

Clearly the *Qaddish* is related to the late-synoptic forms of the Lord's Prayer. There are also perceptible links between the Lord's Prayer and the *Amidah* (or *Shemoneh Esreh*, "Eighteen Benedictions").[44] As Zahavy's dis-

42. Taussig, "The Lord's Prayer," 33.

43. Baumgardt, "Kaddish and Lord's Prayer," 165, dependent upon Elbogen, *Der jüdische Gottesdienst*, notes that the *Qaddish* is attested no earlier than the Byzantine period. De Moor, "Reconstruction," 405 n. 26 claims that the "antiquity of the prayer is recognized by all authorities" and appeals to *b. Ber.* 3a (R. Jose b. Halaphta, ca. 150 CE) and *Sipre* 306 (132b). Lachs, "The Lord's Prayer," 118 considers that the *Qaddish* is too dissimilar to the Lord's Prayer to provide a convincing parallel and that the tannaitic "short prayer" (*tpillâ qsrâ*) provides a more appropriate genre.

44. Lachs, "The Lord's Prayer," 118 and 123 n. 1; Davies and Allison, "Excursus," 595–97.

cussion of the social origins of these materials indicates, Jerusalem-Judean
interests are in view, with the implication that the Lord's Prayer was augmented at the Q² stage for better alignment with Judean scribal interests.
Hence, the first table of the Lord's Prayer ought to be assigned pink, if not
gray, in the scheme of The Jesus Seminar's *The Five Gospels*.[45]

However, whereas Taussig and The Jesus Seminar have tended to read
Jesus too much in relation to Socrates, Jesus' concerns can with greater
historical logic be seen to stand solidly within the orbit of Israelite tradition, have much more to do with Moses than Socrates, and define Jesus as
a particular type of first-century "Jew." This is evident in a perceptible link
between the Lukan beatitudes (the first sapiential compositional unit in
Q¹) and the Aramaic beginning of the Passover Haggadah:[46]

PASSOVER HAGGADAH	BEATITUDES
The bread of poverty	How honorable are you poor
Let all who are hungry	How honorable are the hungry
This year we are here	How honorable are those who mourn

Likewise, the second discourse in Q¹/Luke 10:4 contains a possible (albeit
negative) allusion to Exod 12:11. Ezekiel the Tragedian, of the second
century BCE, already showed a concern for this text in the Hellenistic
period:

> your loins girt up and shoes upon your feet, and in your hand a
> staff, for thus in haste the king will order all to leave the land. It
> shall be called "Passover."[47]

It is clear in comparing Mark's to Q's "discourses" that the respective traditions have situated these instructions within a less focused mission for the
kingdom of God. Mark's tradition would thus seem to be closer to Jesus
given an original Passover or Passover pilgrimage setting for the material.
The injunctions about money, bag, food, and clothing suggest dependence
upon hospitality along the pilgrim's way, perhaps reflecting trust that God
will provide for the pilgrim. Galilean "Jews" seem to have been particularly
attracted to the Passover pilgrimage. Jesus alluded to Exodus imagery in

45. Funk et al., *The Five Gospels*, 36–38.

46. A fuller statement about this connection is made in Oakman, "Archaeology of
First-Century Galilee," orig. 220–51 (chapter 15 below).

47. *Ezek. Trag.* 181–84, according to Robertson, "Ezekiel the Tragedian," 816. Cf.
Mark 6:8–9 which is closer to the injunction of Ezekiel.

stating the meaning of his own healing activity (Q/Luke 11:20; cf. Exod 8:19). And Jesus' Last Supper (even if not a Passover meal) is clearly tied to the great festival within the synoptic tradition.

While this is not the place to develop a full-blown account of the "theology of Jesus," a few remarks will make intelligible the exegetical approach taken below toward the Lord's Prayer. Jesus' preaching of the kingdom is universally conceded by scholars to be the center of his historical message.[48] The interests of Jesus in Passover and Exodus, as well as the early prophet christologies, would suggest that he meant by "kingdom of God" something like the "lordship of God" over historical affairs and looked for something like an Exodus from "Egypt," representing what must have been felt to be oppressive circumstances of his first-century environment. Jesus was not a scripture specialist, however, and seemed to flesh out his theology as a kind of village wisdom preacher more with reference to the natural order of things.[49] Both aspects (concern with Moses and natural theological wisdom) allow us to understand how the peasant Jesus could inspire Wisdom Q as well as Deuteronomic Q and apocalyptic Mark.

This picture seems corroborated by indications of Josephus about typical, lower-class theological concerns around the Lake of Galilee. During the early phases of the Judean-Roman War, Jesus son of Sapphias had led an attack of the lower classes of Tiberias against Herod Antipas's palace, in which were animal representations.[50] Half a century earlier, Judas of Gamala had urged that payment of Roman taxes was a sign of servitude to alien gods.[51] If Judas of Gamala brought to expression the rage of at least some Galilean peasantry, who could be convinced that Roman Palestine might be a new Egypt, then Jesus of Nazareth operating in the vicinity naturally might have shared similar religious interests and orientations. His interests and concerns stand at the root of a complex of traditions, not only Q[1], but also Q[2], Paul, Mark, and even John. Elaborations of these traditions have to be kept in the discussion about Jesus' theological and social outlooks. The Lord's Prayer, nonetheless, can certainly be understood as an expression of familiarity with the God of Exodus.[52] Its meaning thus

48. Jeremias, *New Testament Theology*, 96. Perrin, *Rediscovering*, 47 points to the close linkage between kingdom of God and the Prayer.

49. Oakman, *Jesus and the Economic Questions*, 240–42.

50. Josephus, *Life* 65–67.

51. Josephus, *War* 2.118; *Ant.* 18. 4.

52. Cyster, "The Lord's Prayer and the Exodus Tradition," provides a rather popular

can be investigated within a developmental frame that expanded Jesus' concrete requests in definite directions.

THE SOCIAL MEANING OF THE LORD'S PRAYER

Three major stages of development of the Lord's Prayer have thus been suggested, now listed in chronological order: *Stage 1)* The form of the prayer in Jesus' own usage, consisting of the address + Petitions 4–6; *Stage 2)* the difficult-to-trace transition from oral-Aramaic to written-Greek forms of the Prayer; and *Stage 3)* the form of the Prayer reached by the latest stratum of Q (as seen in Luke), consisting of the address + Petitions 1–2 + Petitions 4–6. Matthew and *Didache*, indicative of late first-century Syrian tradition, subsequently carried things further by the addition of expanded address, Petitions 3 and 7, plus the doxology. These presumptions now come into play in pursuit of the social meaning of the Lord's Prayer, first for Jesus and then for the later tradents of the Jesus traditions.

The Address

Luke's version of the address stands closest to the actual speech of Jesus. The emphatic and simple address, in contrast to Matthew's version which reflects more nearly the formal conventions of synagogue prayer, is noteworthy.[53] Jeremias argued for the uniqueness within Judaism, as well as the intimacy, of addressing God as *'abba'*, "Papa," but both claims are disputed today.[54]

Whether intimate or simply direct, the prayer addresses as *pater familias*, "head of the household," the One who is also expected to rule as King. The petitioner acts as a royal personage and heir, a part of the royal household.[55] The generosity and benevolence of the King are invoked, who acts as Patron. This assumption of the graciousness and benevolence of God comes through at several other points in the Jesus tradition. One thinks, for instance, of the Prodigal Son/Father (L/Luke 15:11–32). There are also passages like M/Matt 5:45, Q/Luke 11:11–13, 12:30, and Mark 10:30.[56] In Jesus' context, the concern for God's patronage in relation to

treatment of this idea.

53. Jeremias, *Prayers*, 96–97.

54. Davies and Allison, "Excursus," 601–2; Barr, "Abba Isn't Daddy."

55. This will have further implications in the discussion of the bread petition.

56. Kloppenborg, "Literary Convention," 89. See Malina, *The Social World of Jesus and the Gospels*, 143–75.

concrete need was underscored by immediate transition to the petitions of the second table.

Petition 4 of the Second Table

The general concern of Jesus and the early Jesus movement for the hungry is manifest directly in the feeding narratives (e.g., Mark 6:34–44) and indirectly by a number of other gospel passages. For instance, many of the people "healed" by Jesus were perhaps suffering the effects of malnutrition. These were typically people with skin ailments or eye problems (Mark 1:40–45; 10:46; cf. 5:43 and the Q saying Matt 6:22–23)—perhaps due simply to vitamin deficiencies. Therefore, one must emphasize the therapeutic significance, in a physical as well as a social sense, of table fellowship for the Jesus movement (Mark 2:15). This fellowship was probably the primary *Sitz im Leben* of the first petition of Jesus' Prayer, a table fellowship I have elsewhere argued was tied to Passover concerns.[57]

Interpreting the petition for bread has long been vexed by the question surrounding the meaning of the word *epiousios*. Questions were already raised in the days of Origen, who believed the word was a neologism of the evangelists. On the basis of current philology, Origen's judgment appears to be correct.[58]

Four major solutions to the issue of meaning have been suggested over the centuries: 1) That of Origen, Chrysostom, and others tracing the etymology of *epiousios* to *epi* + *ousia* = "necessary for existence"; 2) that of Debrunner seeing an analogy with the phrase *epi tēn ousan* [sc. *hēmeran*], "for the current day"; 3) that of Grotius, Wettstein, and Lightfoot connecting the adjective with the Greek phrase *hē epiousa* [sc. *hēmera*], "the following day"; 4) finally, that of Cyril of Alexander, Peter of Laodicea, and others linking *epiousios* with the verb *epienai* "coming in the future."[59] There are subvarieties of these major solutions; all but 1) assume a temporal meaning of some sort.

---

57. Oakman, "Archaeology of First-Century Galilee," orig. 243–44 (chapter 15 below).

58. BAGD, 297; BDF 66 §123. See, however, the cautionary remarks of Deissmann, *Light From the Ancient East*, 78, whose experience with the papyri led him to suspect any "neologistic" approaches to biblical Greek. He offered a slightly different opinion in his *Bible Studies*, 214. Colin Hemer, "*Epiousios*," attempts to find a good Greek lineage for *epiousios*. He follows Lightfoot and argues strenuously for Solution 3, "the following day." For a thorough discussion of previous philological solutions, see Foerster, "*epiousios*."

59. BAGD, 297.

The two somewhat different solutions proposed here build upon Origen's suggestion and basic interpretation. However, the meaning is not sought in the philosophical use of *ousia*, i.e., "being, existence, substance," but in the usages attested in many of the Egyptian papyri. The word *ousia* in the papyri often means "landed estate" or "large estate."[60] This is a concrete meaning rooted in the material realities of antiquity. If *epiousios* is a neologism reflecting a semitic idiom, it makes sense to look for something in Aramaic incorporating the notion of "estate." The papyri, as purveyors of a more popular idiom, are more likely than Greek philosophy to give a clue to the meaning of *epiousios*.

Warrant for this philological procedure is given by considering the New Testament *hapax legomenon, periousios*, a word linguistically near in kinship to *epiousios*.[61] While *periousios* clearly means "chosen" in Titus 2:14, its meaning in the Septuagint is tied more literally to the Hebrew word sglâ = "possession, property" and in very late Hebrew "treasure."[62] Thus, in Eccl 2:8 (LXX) "Solomon" talks about having gathered "gold and silver, and treasures (*periousiasmous*) of kings and countries." In the Greek papyri, *periousios* means "abundance, superfluity." An excellent example of the use of this word from approximately the same time as the prayer of Jesus was being translated from Aramaic into Greek is given by the famous rescript of Claudius to the Alexandrian Jewish community (ca. 41 CE):

> I explicitly order the Jews not to agitate for more privileges than
> they formerly possessed . . . while enjoying their own privileges

---

60. Moulton and Milligan, 242, s.v. *epiousios*, and 467, s.v. *ousia*. Moulton once wrote (Moulton and Howard, *Grammar*, 2:313): "the only meaning quotable for this noun [sc. *ousia*] from NT and papyri is property or estate, which is not hopeful." Moulton could see no way to elucidate the meaning of *epiousios* from the papyri. He did, however, recognize (91) that the lack of elision between *epi* and *ousia* would constitute no barrier to Solution 1: "The Hellenistic indifference to the confluence of vowels, due to the slower pronunciation which has been already noted, is well seen . . . This feature of the *Koine* makes it very plain that classical scholars of the last generation were yielding to their besetting sin when they ruled out (e.g.) etymologies of *epiousios* that broke the laws of 'correctness' by allowing hiatus." Recently, Fitzmyer, *Luke*, 2:900, has endorsed the use of Solution 1 with these words: "After long consideration, I have reverted to the explanation given by Origen . . ."

61. Titus 2:14, quoting Deut 14:2 (LXX). Origen already noted this parallel, observing the underlying material implications of both words in ordinary speech but arguing for the "spiritual" meaning of *epiousios* in view of the use of *periousios* in Titus.

62. BDB, 688. Jastrow, *Dictionary*, 953.

> and sharing a great abundance [*periousias*] of advantages in a city
> not their own . . . .[63]

Periousias in some cases in the Septuagint and in the secular usage of the papyri occurs in contexts reflecting material abundance. A similar sphere of meaning can be suggested for *epiousios*.[64]

Thus, the first proposal offered here is that *epiousios* is simply a synonym for *periousios* as used in the papyri, which would lead to the meaning for the fourth petition, "give us today bread in abundance." The implication is that adequate bread is not available, and the Divine Patron is approached for immediate redress. Since several of the ancient Jewish apocalypses expected the end time to be a time of great abundance, it is not difficult to see how this petition might later (in Q) have connected with eschatological themes.[65]

A related inquiry (proposal two) might pursue some semitic idiom behind the word *epiousios*. Fitzmyer, presuming Origen's basic view, cites Prov 30:8 *lḥm ḥqî*, "the food I need." In the Aramaic targum this is expressed *lḥm'a <d> msthî*. Fitzmyer consequently offers as a translation for his reconstruction of the Aramaic form of the bread petition: "Give us this day our bread for subsistence."[66] This concrete meaning (as opposed to Origen's abstraction of "supersubstantial" bread) undoubtedly appealed to peasants. Again, "peasant" included not only agriculturalists, but also their impoverished relatives eking out a living in lowly building trades or the fishing syndicates by the lake.[67]

Perhaps there is yet another option related to this line of inquiry: A correspondence might be established between *epi* and the Aramaic particle *dî*. Both the Greek preposition and the Aramaic particle can serve to mark the genitive case in their respective languages.[68] Hence, there may be noth-

---

63. Hunt and Edgar, *Select Papyri*, 2:87; Moulton and Milligan, *Vocabulary*, 507.

64. *Epi* often means "in addition, above" [in a figurative sense], BAGD, 287, s. v. *epi* II.1.b.b. *Peri* in *periousios* is synonymous with *hyper*: Moulton and Howard, *Grammar*, 321. The adverb *enousios* also provides an analogy, meaning "very rich"; LSJ, 572, 1439.

65. E.g., *1 Enoch* 10; *2 Bar.* 29:5.

66. Fitzmyer, *Luke*, 2:900–901.

67. Oakman, "Was Jesus a Peasant?" orig. 117–18 (chapter 12 above).

68. "A genuine Aram. idiom," according to BDB, 1088. The corresponding particle in late Hebrew is *sh*, which shows the influence of Aramaic: "in usage limited to late Heb., and passages with N. Palest. colouring," BDB, 979. Cf. Jastrow, *Dictionary*, 1577, s. v. *shl* [= *sh*]. A literal equivalence would pair *epi* with Aramaic *'al* = "upon." Nigel Turner, *A Grammar of New Testament Greek* (Edinburgh: T. and T. Clark, 1963), 271 shows that

ing more than a simple possessive sense demanded by the *epi*: "Belonging to the estate or property." In Dan 2:15, for instance, the Aramaic reads *shlîṭ'a di–mlk'a*, "the king's captain." In the Septuagint, this is translated by a simple genitive case. However, in the case of *epiousios* a very literal correspondence between the languages has evidently been maintained. It might also be an attempt to avoid ambiguities which would result from making a genitival adjective out of *ousia*, the stem of which ends in *iota*.

Such a wooden Greek translation may have signposted a meaning integral to Jesus' understanding of *'abba'*: The patron made regular provision for those already on the estate ("the kingdom"). A suggestive late-Hebrew parallel is at hand in *Ruth Rab.* 2:14. There reference is made to *lḥm shl mlkût*, "bread belonging to the kingdom," or "the royal maintenance."[69] *Ousia* in the Egyptian papyri can signify an imperial estate. *Epiousios* with this connotation would then give the following sense for the fourth petition: "Give us the bread of the kingdom today," or perhaps "Give us the royal bread ration today." An even more colloquial rendition, taken in conjunction with the suggested interpretation of the address, might be: "Give us today bread on the house." These are words spoken by the King's own children, addressed to their benevolent Father.

(Secondary: Petition 1 of the First Table)

Abundant or "estate-bread" was of immediate concern to Jesus and his disciples, but the Q tradition moved toward greater theological abstraction. If the Lord's Prayer belonged to Wisdom Q, then the concrete concerns above were still evident in Q/Luke 11:9–13 (better preserved at the end in Matt 7:11). A later concern about idolatry in Deuteronomic Q (Q/Luke 4:3–4, 7–8) pushed the meaning of the Prayer toward a concern for purity of the name (Q/Luke 11:2) and eventually the doing of God's righteous will on earth (Matt 6:10). Q and Mark would then align Jesus' interests more clearly with the prophetic traditions of Israel, and this also involved the purity and eschatological concerns evident in later first-century Jewish prayers.

A general distance, though clear connection, between Jesus and the interests of Judean-Jerusalem scribes can be traced. Careful study

---

during the New Testament period *epi* was fast becoming a marker of the accusative case rather than the genitive case. The ratios for various bodies of literature (taken from Turner) are: (Papyri) 4.5 [gen.]::2.5 [acc.], (NT) 1.2::2, (LXX) 1.4::3.8.

69. Jastrow, *Dictionary*, 704.

of *hagiazein*, which appears in the New Testament in 1 Thessalonians, 1 Corinthians, Romans, Matthew, Luke, John, Acts, Ephesians, 1–2 Timothy, Hebrews, 1 Peter, and Revelation, shows that the word signifies New Testament materials with clear links to temple or Judean-Jerusalem interests (Paul, later gospels and Acts, Deutero-Paulines, Hebrews, and Revelation). The lack of such links in early Q (Q¹), and the unlikelihood of such interests for peasant Galileans, is therefore worth note.[70]

The accretion of Petition 1 by the time of later Q (Q²) moves the Prayer more tightly into the orbit of Judean interests. What is meant by sanctification (*hagiasthēnai*) of the name in early Judaism? Jeremias connects this petition (and the second) with the previously mentioned Jewish *Qaddish* prayer and believes that both prayers make entreaty for

> the revelation of God's eschatological kingdom. . . . They seek the hour in which God's profaned and misused name will be glorified and his reign revealed, in accordance with the promise, "I will vindicate the holiness of my great name, which has been profaned among the nations . . . ." (Ezek 36:23)[71]

Jeremias' understanding, however, does not go far enough. For Jeremias and for many twentieth-century commentators, the first petition is only a prayer bidding God to sanctify his own name in an eschatological sense.

Yet even the *Qaddish* suggests a more extended significance: "Exalted and hallowed be his great name *in the world* . . ." *Who* it is who will "sanctify the name," and *where* this will happen, are the critical questions. The *Qaddish* implies that human, in addition to divine action, and actions in the world, are critical for the issue of sanctification.

This impression is borne out by a study of the idiom "sanctify the name" in rabbinic traditions.[72] The Piel form of the Hebrew verb *qdsh*, just as the Pael in Aramaic, can specify human activity as sanctification of the name. *B. Soṭa* refers to Joseph's sanctifying deed; *Sipra* 18, 6 (339a) refers to Israel's obligation; and the third benediction of the *Amidah* enjoins such human activity without specifying precise content. Later midrash

---

70. Meier, *A Marginal Jew*, 2:295–98, notes that "The idea of hallowing (sanctifying, making holy) the name of God is totally absent from the rest of the Synoptic sayings of Jesus . . ."

71. Jeremias, *Prayers*, 99.

72. In addition to what is laid out here, see the material gathered in Str-B. 1:411–18 ("Menschen als Subjekt des Heiligens").

is rich in illustration. In *Genesis Rabbah* Abraham says, "I will go forth and fall [in battle] in sanctifying the name of the Holy One, Blessed be He."[73] The Levites were believed to have given their lives slaughtering the unfaithful to sanctify the name.[74] The suffering of the exile is an occasion for sanctifying the name.[75] God's name can also be sanctified when justice is accomplished in human affairs.[76] Most of these instances illustrate *in extremis* that fidelity unto death or punishment by death can sanctify the name. This observation is documented perhaps most completely by a midrashic passage about the martyrs at the time of the Bar Kochba revolt (132–35 CE):

> The Rabbis say: He [*sc.* God] adjured them by the generation of the great persecution. They are called *zebaoth* because they carried out My will (*zibyoni*) in the world and through them My will was executed; and HINDS OF THE FIELD because they poured out their blood for the sanctification of My Name . . . R. Ḥiyya b. Abba said: If one should say to me, "Sacrifice your life for the sanctification of God's name," I am ready to do so, on condition only that they slay me at once, but I could not endure the tortures of the great persecution.[77]

Other lesser human actions can sanctify the name of God. Blessing is one such action. In the Babylonian Talmud we read, "A benediction which contains no mention of the Divine Name is no benediction."[78] The Passover Meal begins with a blessing of the name: "Blessed art thou, O Lord our God, creator of the fruit of the vine."[79] This connection between human

---

73. *Gen. Rab.* 43:2 (1: 352) [Numbers in parentheses refer to the volume and page in Freedman and Simon, *Midrash Rabbah*]. Abraham in the fiery furnace, *Gen. Rab.* 63:2 (2: 557); *Lev. Rab.* 11:7 (4: 144); *Num. Rab.* 2:12 (5:43); *Eccl. Rab.* 2:14:1 (8: 64). Jastrow, *Dictionary*, s.v. *qdsh*.

74. *Num. Rab.* 1:12 (5:19–20); *Num. Rab.* 4:6 (5:100).

75. *Num. Rab.* 13:2 (6:501); cf. *Gen. Rab.* 98: 14 (2:964).

76. David wipes out Saul's family: *Num. Rab.* 8:4 (5: 219). Punishment of the unfaithful of Jerusalem by Nebuchadnezzar: *Lam. Rab.* 2:1:3 (7:155).

77. *Cant. Rab.* 2:7:1 (9: 113). Incidentally, the parallel between God's will and sanctification of the name is again established. On the date of the great persecution, see *Cant. Rab.* 2.5.3 (9: 106 n. 2). However, compare *Cant. Rab.* 2.7.1 (9: 115) where "great persecution" refers to days before "Ben Koziba."

78. *B. Ber.* 40b, quoted. in Smith, "Lord's Prayer," 155.

79. A reading from Genesis is placed just before this blessing when Passover coincides with the Sabbath: See Glatzer, ed., *The Passover Haggadah*, 17.

blessing and divine sanctification is further cemented by the *Qaddish* at the beginning of the Sabbath service in the Jewish Prayer Book:

> Glorified and *sanctified* be God's great name throughout the world which he has created according to his will. May he establish his kingdom in your lifetime and during your days, and within the life of the entire house of Israel, speedily and soon; and say, Amen.
>
> May his great name *be blessed* forever and to all eternity. Blessed and praised, glorified and exalted, extolled and honored, adored and lauded be the name of the Holy One, blessed be he, beyond all the blessings and hymns, praises and consolations that are ever spoken in the world; and say, Amen.[80]

Many other such blessings—and the firm connection between blessing and God's name—can be seen throughout the devotional literature of the Jewish people. Furthermore, the Mishnah gives a rather detailed picture of the events and situations that elicit blessings.[81] Many of these blessings are connected with food and the meeting of material need.

The first petition of the first table is secondary, therefore, though in some senses it forms a logical development out of the bread petition. If the fourth petition prayed for the concrete situation that would evoke such blessings of the name, then blessing God for the reception of food can be one of the concrete meanings of "sanctifying the Name." This may indeed be one understanding of the tradition in the synoptics (heavily influenced by Judean-Jerusalem scribal interests), as evident in Jesus' words around bread-breaking (Matt 14:19; 26:26; and par.) and *Didache's* association of the Prayer with the Lord's Supper. Q² played a significant role in these developed meanings of the Lord's Prayer, for while it does not directly mention a concern with the *Shema'* (as Mark 12:29–30), it does show concern with Israel's integrity and fidelity to God (Q/Luke 3:8; 4:4):

---

80. Birnbaum, editor, *Daily Prayer Book*, 50 [italics mine].

81. *M. Ber.* 6–9.

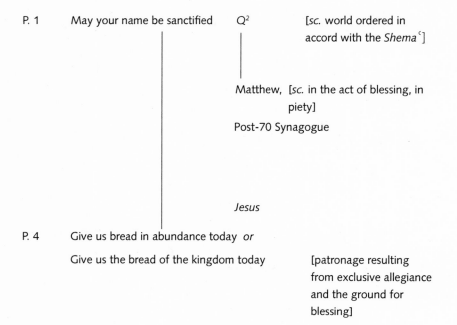

P. 1   May your name be sanctified   Q²   [*sc.* world ordered in
                                                         accord with the *Shema*ᶜ]

                                             Matthew, [*sc.* in the act of blessing, in
                                                         piety]
                                             Post-70 Synagogue

                                             Jesus

P. 4   Give us bread in abundance today *or*

           Give us the bread of the kingdom today   [patronage resulting
                                                         from exclusive allegiance
                                                         and the ground for
                                                         blessing]

Petition 5 of the Second Table

The fifth petition of Jesus' Prayer gives a critical clue as to what brought about this situation of want and hunger (not to mention we surmise the cursing of God's name because of physical deprivation). An agrarian context in which indebtedness prevails is a social context that will be characterized by an increasing level of impoverishment and hunger. Lack of bread coupled with debt presented a familiar constellation for Jesus and his peasant contemporaries.

Agrarian debt was pushing peasantry of Jesus' day either entirely off the land (wage labor on estates) or into client-dependency relations on the land vis-à-vis the Roman overlord (e.g., Caesar's large estates in the Esdraelon Plain or the land controlled by Judean-Herodian aristocrats in Sepphoris–Tiberias). The insecurity of the tenant or wage laborer was evidenced in the increase in beggary and brigandage.[82] Brigands perhaps would have been more impressed by a zealot-like religious movement, but the ministry of Jesus, which clearly shows concern for the beggar and dis-

---

82. See Horsley and Hanson, *Bandits, Prophets, and Messiahs*, 52–85.

advantaged, sought alternate ways to resolve class tensions and reconcile class interests.[83]

The Jesus tradition reveals an intimate acquaintance and concern with debt in the first half of the first century CE.[84] Q material alluding to debtor's prison (Luke 12:58–59/Matt 5:25–26), the story of the Unforgiving Servant (M/Matt 18:23–35), the parable of the Two Debtors (L/Luke 7:41–42), and the Widow's *lepta* (Mark 12:41–44) suggest this. The parables of the Talents (Q?/Luke 19:12–27/Matt 25:14–30) and the Unjust Steward (L/Luke 16:1–8) relate the oppressiveness of the creditor.

Outside of the New Testament, historical data for a debt problem in early Roman Palestine are supplied by the so-called *prozbul* of Hillel and an important passage in Josephus. One of the first acts of the insurgents in 66 CE was the burning of the record office where debt contracts were kept:

> [The rebels] next carried their combustibles to the public archives, eager to destroy the money-lenders' bonds and to prevent the recovery of debts, in order to win over a host of grateful debtors and to cause a rising of the poor against the rich . . . .[85]

In the same context, Josephus refers to such archives as the "sinews" (*ta neura*) of the city, a telling metaphor.

The precise significance of the *prozbul* is not easily established. The *Mishnah* indicates that Hillel's measure was supposed to make credit easier to obtain. Loans were not being given on account of the seventh-year release, so Hillel ostensibly permitted a practice that would alleviate the cash flow crisis. According to *m. Sheb.* 10:2 and *b. Giṭ.* 37b, loan contracts "delivered to the court" are not canceled according to the seventh-year prescriptions of Deuteronomy 15. The "logic" behind this is that the letter of the law in Deut 15:3 demands, "your hand shall release," but if the bonds are with the court, the letter does not apply. The development of this legal maneuver apparently resulted in the interpretation "before the court" commonly placed upon *prozbul* in later rabbinic tradition.[86]

---

83. Oakman, *Jesus and the Economic Questions*, 210, 215.

84. See also my "Jesus and Agrarian Palestine: The Factor of Debt" (chapter 1 above); *Jesus and the Economic Questions*, 72–77; and Goodman, "The First Jewish Revolt."

85. Josephus, *War* 2.427 (Thackeray, LCL).

86. Again *b. Giṭ.* 37b. Cf. Blau, "Der Prosbol," 111.

Work of Ludwig Blau years ago offered a different insight into the meaning of *prozbul*. The Hebrew in the *Mishnah* in fact is *prôzbôl*, sometimes *prôsbôl*.[87] Blau traced the etymology of the word back to the Greek *prosbolē*, which according to Egyptian papyri was the "knocking down" of mortgaged property. Blau's view has recently been revived by Hans Kippenberg.[88] Furthermore, form-critical study of the Hillel legislation by Neusner has led him to believe that Hillel's name and scriptural warrants were only later attached to a legal institution firmly established prior to the second century CE. Debt documents from the Judean desert, for instance, show no knowledge of a stipulation along the lines of the later rabbinic view of the *prozbul*, but they do reveal that loans were secured by various kinds of property:

Murabbaʿat Contract 18 (ca. 55 CE):

> [On . . . of the month . . . in] the second year of Caesar Nero in Siwaya, Absalom, son of Hanin, from Siwaya agreed that he borrowed from him in his presence: I, Zechariah, son of Johanan, son of . . . resident in Chessalon, have received the money [as a loan] of 20 denarii. I will repay it on . . . and if I do not restitute it by this term, then it will be paid to you with a fifth, and it will be completely repaid on this sabbatical year ([alternately] though a sabbath year intervene). And if I should not do it, there will be a substitute for you out of my goods, and to that which I shall acquire, you have right of appropriation.[89]

Murabbaʿat Contract 22 (132 CE):

> On the fourteenth of Marḥeschwan, Year One of the liberation of Israel . . . [the sum] of 50 [denarii] in coins according to the assessed valuation. This piece of ground of Chizqia is security for the payment [of the debt] to the value of . . . .[90]

It can be concluded that the *prozbul* originally was a legal device whereby debts were secured by means of immovable property and foreclo-

---

87. Jastrow, *Dictionary*, 1218.

88. Von Kippenberg, *Religion und Klassenbildung*, 139. Cf. Preisigke, *Fachwörter*, 149; also LSJ, 1504.

89. Benoît et al.. *Les Grottes de Murabbaʿat*, 1:100ff; Koffmahn, *Die Doppelurkunden*, 80–1. Cf. Neusner, *From Politics to Piety*, 17 n. 2.

90. Benoît et al., *Les Grottes de Murabbaʿat*, 1:118ff; Koffmahn, *Die Doppelurkunde*, 158–59. Kloppenborg indicates that the "execution clause" here was a standard feature of Greco-Roman legal contracts (private communication).

sure accomplished through a court proceeding. This practice went against the letter of the Mosaic law, which viewed the patrimonial lands of the clan as a permanent trust (Lev 25:23). Any land that had to be sold had to be redeemed under the old Israelite law (Lev 25:25–28). If the *prozbul* measure was "good" for urban artisans like the Pharisees and later rabbis, it could not have been as sympathetically perceived by rural folk.[91]

The fact that a Greek legal institution is here in view suggests three possible "entry points" into the legal practice of early Judaism: Ptolemaic Palestine, the later Hasmoneans (perhaps Jannaeus), or Herod. This legal institution, in any view, was a part of the social fabric of Jesus' period. Passages like 1 Macc 14:8 and 14:12 seem to indicate that the Maccabees were "pro-peasant." The picture in *Aristeas* (esp. 107ff), if it is to be dated around 100 BCE, confirms the agrarian prosperity of the early Hasmonean years. If under the first Hasmoneans the ancient Jewish peasantry was in relatively good shape, by the second century CE its condition had deteriorated dramatically. There is evidence throughout the *Mishnah* of a large pool of "free" labor. Martin Goodman's book on Roman Galilee provides a start at analyzing the second-century social situation behind the tannaitic material.[92]

Stresses on rural déclassés (including artisans and fishingfolk) were on the increase in turn-of-the-eras Palestine. In place of traditional peasants holding patrimonial land, tenants and wage-laborers were appearing, on the one hand, and large landed proprietors, on the other. For these social realities the parables of Jesus give ample evidence. One of the chief mechanisms fueling this process of agrarian destruction was the burden of debt. Roman taxation (including the building programs of the Herods) and population increase contributed to this problem.

In a milieu in which debt of one sort or another was compromising the viability of life for many, the fifth petition of Jesus' prayer takes on a special vibrancy and urgency. The meaning of the petition assumes a "horizontal" and a "vertical" aspect. The horizontal meaning is concretely perceptible in both the Matthean and the Lukan versions of the second half of the petition:

(Matt) as we have released (or forgiven) our debtors.

---

91. Neusner, *From Politics to Piety*, 16: "Debtors . . . were here given a good motive to dislike Pharisees, who now rendered their debts into a perpetual burden."

92. Goodman, *State and Society*.

(Luke) for we ourselves are releasing (or forgiving) everyone in
debt to us.

The meaning "release" for *aphiēmi* (Matt perfect tense, Luke present tense)
in a literal or concrete sense is clearly attested by Deut 15:3 (LXX).

How is the vertical aspect to be understood? It must be noted that
Matthew has "Forgive us our debts," while Luke has "Forgive us our
sins." The literal or concrete material understanding of the petition is not
thwarted, because in Aramaic the same word means sin or debt (*ḥôbâ*).
Also, the dative plural *hēmin*, "for us," can best be understood as the dative
of advantage (indicative of the general thrust of the original Aramaic).

There were perhaps two concrete situations in which God might be
petitioned to achieve debt forgiveness for the advantage of the petitioner:
1) A court-system, perhaps one in which the *prozbul* held sway, and 2) the
temple debt-system. Q/Luke 12:58–59 likely refers to the courts within
the jurisdiction of Herod Antipas. The passage makes clear that the debtor
goes to court at a great disadvantage (ironically, petitioning the creditor as
patron provides better "justice") and indicates that prisons stood ready to
effect execution (cf. M/Matt 18:30, 34). Josephus and Philo show clearly
how this mechanism worked: Debt prison forced the debtor's family to
pay up![93]

The temple also imposed indebtedness upon Jews. The temple tax
was levied on all Jewish males over twenty years of age. The *Mishnah* indicates that ability to pay was not considered:

> On the 15th thereof the tables [of the money-changers] were set
> up in the provinces; and on the 25th thereof they were set up in
> the Temple. After they were set up in the Temple they began to
> exact pledges.[94]

M/Matt 17:24–27 certainly depicts a post-70 CE situation (v. 27a), but
the pronouncement of v. 26 likely goes back to Jesus himself and fits well
with the notion of debt forgiveness. In such a case, then, the fifth petition
could request of the "owner of the house" (i.e., the temple) for release from
the onerous obligations requisitioned each year by Judean authorities.

93. Consider for instance the behavior of Albinus, Josephus, *War* 2.273. Philo, *Spec.
Laws* 3.30 recounts the depredations of an early first-century tax collector who laid hands
on family members to force payment; see Lewis, *Life in Egypt Under Roman Rule*, 161–
62.

94. *M. Sheq.* 1:3 (Danby).

Another significant index of a concern about debt appears in the attention Jesus gives to disadvantaged groups—children (Mark 9:36), women forced into degrading social situations for economic reasons ("impure" Mark 5:25; prostitutes, Matt 21:31; widows, Mark 12:41–44), and others economically marginalized.[95] The case of the widow in Mark 12:41–44/ Luke 21:1–4 is especially illuminating for the connection between economic marginalization and indebtedness. Why was the widow putting her money in the box at the temple? And was Jesus praising her generosity or lamenting her misfortune?[96]

There is compelling evidence that the widow's deposit in the temple was reason for lament. As Wright has convincingly observed, to think that Jesus praises the widow for depositing her "whole life" in the temple coffers directly contradicts Jesus' censure of the Pharisees over Qorban vows (Mark 7:11–12). The principle enunciated there by Jesus brings out the priority of human need over temple piety. The same logic can be expected to apply in the case of the widow's *lepta*. Whatever she may be doing for God by her temple sacrifice, she is thereby depriving herself and her orphaned children. Furthermore, Wright points out the significant connection in the synoptic tradition between this story and Jesus' saying immediately preceding it: "Beware of the Scribes . . . who devour widows' houses and for a pretext make long prayers" (Mark 12:38, 40).

Wright might have gone farther with this connection between "devouring widows' houses" and the widow's *lepta*. There may in fact be grounds for restoring to some extent an aspect of praise in Jesus' word, although lament will also remain apparent, for there is another legislative tradition attached to the name of Hillel that perhaps brings a direct light upon the widow's action in Mark 12:41–44:

> If a man sold a house from among the houses in a walled city, he
> may redeem it at once and at any time during twelve months. . . .
> Beforetime the buyer used to hide himself on the last day of the
> twelve months so that [the house] might be his for ever; but Hillel
> the Elder ordained that he [that sold it] could deposit his money

---

95. For a discussion of the connection between these groups and economic marginalization, see Schottroff and Stegemann, *Jesus von Nazareth*, 15–28 (see *Jesus and the Hope of the Poor*).

96. Wright, "The Widow's Mites."

in the [Temple] Chamber, and break down the door and enter, and that the other, when he would, might come and take his money.[97]

This tradition seems to pit Hillel against the scribes "who devour widows' houses," but it supplies a possible context for the widow's behavior and rationale for Jesus' observation as a mixture of lament and praise. The widow was demonstrating fidelity to her obligations to keep the house (which perhaps included land) in the family. Her deposit was, in this view, redemption money of some sort.

(Secondary: Petition 2 of the First Table)

In framing possible understandings of God's kingdom and will in the first table, emphases at the penultimate stage of the synoptic tradition indicate how Q and Markan prophetic understandings would flesh out the Prayer of Jesus. Q^2 held a general concern for Israel's prophets, and linked John the Baptist and Jesus with their fate. John had been active at one point in Batanea, within the tetrarchy of Philip.[98] John was also associated with Perea and Herod Antipas's territory. Elijah had originated from Gilead (1 Kgs 17:1), and an Elijah-John the Baptist association came to be made at least in Mark (Mark 1:6). Since the Elijah-Elisha traditions had also showed concern for miraculous feedings (1 Kgs 17:6,16) and demonstrated special concern for widows (1 Kgs 17:8; 2 Kgs 4:1–7), these aspects of Jesus' activity were also highlighted by Mark (Mark 6:15; 8:28; 9:4, 11–13) and later Luke (4:26).

The precarious legal position of the widow in the ancient Near East was long recognized, especially in the wisdom tradition and the promulgations of kings.[99] Unlike the Greeks, many peoples of the ancient orient believed that God or the gods and the powerful on earth had a special obligation toward widows and orphans. Thus, in the Old Testament:

> You shall not afflict any widow or orphan. If you do afflict them,
> and they cry out to me, I will surely hear their cry; and my wrath

97. *M. 'Arak.* 9:3–4. This tradition is discussed in detail by Neusner, *From Politics to Piety*, 18–19. On temples as depositories for money preserving redemption rights, see Ginzberg, *Studies in the Economics of the Bible*, 62–63.

98. Riesner, "Bethany Beyond the Jordan," 704.

99. Especially helpful in understanding the widow's plight is the article by Stählin, "*xēra.*"

will burn, and I will kill you with the sword, and your wives shall become widows and your children fatherless.[100]

The Ugaritic story of Aqhat praises the wise man Daniel:

> Straightway Daniel the Rapha-man, Forthwith Ghazir [the Harna]miyy—[man], *Is upright*, [sitting before the g]at[e, Un]der [a mighty tree on the threshing floor, Judging] the cause [of the widow, Adjudicating] the case [of the fatherless.][101]

Hammurabi boasts that he has protected the rights of widows and orphans.[102] In Egyptian wisdom tradition, the "Instruction for King Meri-Ka-Re" admonishes:

> Do justice whilst thou endurest upon earth. Quiet the weeper; do not oppress the widow; supplant no man in the property of his father; and impair no officials at their posts.[103]

The connection of widow, property, and officials is significant. For, the "ancient oppression of widows at law may be seen in their frequent sale as slaves for debt," and "the main plight of widows was in the legal sphere."[104]

Much-later Jewish traditions continue to validate this picture quite precisely. The Judean Qumran material shows acute awareness of this problem:

> Unless they are careful to act in accordance with the exact interpretation of the law for the age of wickedness: to separate themselves from the sons of the pit; to abstain from wicked wealth which defiles, either by promise or by vow, and from the wealth of the temple and from stealing from the poor of the people, from making their widows their spoils and from murdering orphans . . . .[105]

Goods of orphans might be valued by a Jewish court to meet their father's debt.[106] The property of widows was similarly vulnerable. A wid-

---

100. Exod 22:22 (RSV).

101. Pritchard, *The Ancient Near East*, 126.

102. Stählin, "*xēra*." 443 n. 31 for other ancient Near Eastern references.

103. Pritchard, *Ancient Near Eastern Texts*, 415.

104. Stählin, "*xēra*," 443, 445 respectively.

105. CD VI 14–17, according to García Martínez, *The Dead Sea Scrolls Translated*, 37.

106. M. 'Arak. 6:1.

ow's *kethûbâ*, her marriage contract, could be compromised if her husband dedicated his property to the temple. However, the rabbis stipulated that when the property was redeemed, the proceeds must go to meet the former contractual obligations of the husband to the wife. Debts and obligations, whether inherited from her former husband or forced upon her by circumstance, could seriously undermine the economic security of the widow in antiquity.

Numbers Rabbah 21:12 relates that the inheritance of a woman changes hands only through judges.[107] The control of property in antiquity was a man's game. *Numbers Rabbah* 10:1 tells how a widow is forced to bring suit against her own son, although the precise issue at law is not clear.[108] Undoubtedly, the dispute is over property or the widow's maintenance—which are also concerns of tannaitic discussions.[109] *Exodus Rabbah* 31:5 shows clearly that widows are oppressed by the lending at interest.[110]

The second petition now links Jesus' immediate and concrete concern for the oppressive affliction of little people with the sphere of royalty and the long–standing ancient Near Eastern traditions to place the weak under royal justice. As has been suggested on the basis of the *Qaddish*, the second petition for the coming of the kingdom of God emphasizes the (eschatological) hope for the manifestation of God's rule in the world. *'abba'* and the direct, second–person imperatives of the second table of the Prayer indicate God's immediacy to the needs of the petitioners. Wisdom Q also shared a much stronger sense of God's presence in Jesus' context. This immediacy is compromised a bit by a stronger eschatological sense of kingdom, which develops in the decades prior to the Jewish-Roman War and is evident in Q² and Mark. Whereas Jesus and followers had requested release from immediate ties of indebtedness, eschatology might prolong the wait for release or convert literal debt into sin (e.g., Luke 12:33–34).

---

107. Freedman and Simon, *Midrash Rabbah*, 6:840.
108. Ibid., 5:333.
109. *Mishnah Ketuboth.*
110. Freedman and Simon, *Midrash Rabbah*, 3:397.

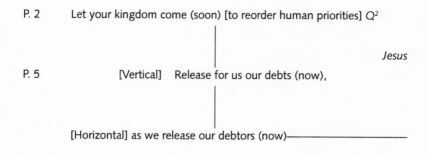

P. 2   Let your kingdom come (soon) [to reorder human priorities] Q²

Jesus

P. 5   [Vertical]   Release for us our debts (now),

[Horizontal] as we release our debtors (now)—————————

To ask God to release debts is to ask in the name of God's rule that human oppression through debt machinations cease. Many of these machinations are abetted by the courts and other "legal" means. This leads logically into Jesus' final petition.

Petition 6 of the Second Table

Most commentators consider the sixth petition in the light of Jewish eschatology, as a request for the ultimate defeat of evil.[111] This might be close to its meaning at the Matthean or Lukan stages of redaction, but for Jesus the meaning of the sixth petition was far more mundane and pertinent to the concerns being traced up to this point. It brings into focus the subornation of justice for the weak and appeals directly to God for redress.

The Unjust Judge parable (Luke 18:2–5) links nicely the situation of the lowly, issues of indebtedness, and courts of law.[112] While nothing directly states that the widow's cause pertains to debt, the word used of her unnamed adversary at law, *antidikos* appears in another significant text, Q/Luke 12:58–59. The widow's opponent at law is likely a creditor. This picture coheres with what we previously learned about the plight typical of widows in antiquity.[113]

The twice–repeated phrase about the judge, who "neither feared God nor regarded man" (vv. 2, 4 RSV), offers another key linkage. The general meaning of the phrase is already suggested in 18:6 by "unjust judge," *ho kritēs tēs adikias*. Fitzmyer translates the phrase "neither feared God nor cared about human beings," citing a parallel from Josephus about King

---

111. Typical are Viviano, "The Gospel According to Matthew," 645 [42:39] *ad* v. 13; or Stendahl, "Matthew," 778–79. Cf. Str-B. 1:422.

112. Helpful in reading this parable is Derrett, "Law in the New Testament." The parable is prefigured in Sir 35:12–18. See also Manson, *Sayings of Jesus*, 305–8.

113. And cf. Derrett, "Law in the New Testament," 187.

Jehoiakim, "neither reverent toward God nor fair toward human beings."[114]
Irreverence captures only part of the issue. The first half of the description
needs to be considered from the fact that "fear of God" for a Jew would
imply doing what God wants, hence, doing the will of God: From the
wisdom tradition of the Old Testament comes the sentiment, "The fear
of the Lord is the beginning of knowledge" (Prov 1:7). Sirach explicitly
connects fear of God, God's law, and wisdom:

> The man who fears the Lord will do this, and he who holds to the
> law will obtain wisdom. (Sir 15:7)

It is likely, then that the judge's problem in this story, and the source of his
adikia, is his lack of respect for the will of God. After all, he does not seem
to take Exod 22:22 seriously.

What then might we make of the second part of this phrase, "does
not regard or care for human beings." Perhaps all that needs to be said is
that this expresses in concrete form how the judge lacks fear of God. He
cares not for the widow's plight. On the other hand, this is a rather bland
result for such a colorful expression. There is reason to suspect some sort
of idiom, undoubtedly a semitic rather than a Greek idiom. Furthermore,
we can suspect a synonymous parallelism to "not fearing God."

Some help seems afforded by a regular idiom in Old Testament
Hebrew that is carried over into rabbinic usage. In the Old Testament "to
lift up the face," *nsh'a pnîm* is "to show favor, respect, or partiality to."[115]
The Greek verb *entrepomai* in Luke's text also means "respect."[116] In the
Old Testament showing partiality in judgment was considered heinous.
"Turning one's face to silver" (i.e., accepting gifts or bribes) was thought to
be synonymous with thwarting justice (Prov. 6:35). In later Jewish tradi-
tion we encounter what was undoubtedly typical:

> The usual experience is: Two men go before a judge, one of them
> poor and the other rich; towards whom does the judge turn his
> face? Is it not towards the rich man?[117]

---

114. Fitzmyer, *Luke*, 2:1178

115. BDB, 670; Jastrow, *Dictionary*, 937.

116. A study of the translation of the Greek verb *entrepō* in the Septuagint shows that
on several occasions the underlying Hebrew text has an idiom involving "face" (e.g., Exod
10:3; 2 Kgs 22:19).

117. *Lev. Rab.* 3:2 (4:37).

This idiom helps to understand *entrepomai*, but the unjust judge is said *not* to show respect to human beings. Can we suspect here an ironic narrative device to emphasize the fact that the judge *does* show partiality to the more powerful cause? Jesus' audience could then be expected to laugh (bitterly) at the judge's self-deception in Luke 18:4. Perhaps there is double meaning, too, if the judge "neither feared God nor was partial to humane considerations." He shows partiality to the powerful who can pay, but the widow has nothing to offer except her obnoxious persistence. Sirach was aware of just this sort of situation:

> Do not offer him [sc. God] a bribe, for he will not accept it . . . for the Lord is the judge, and with him is no partiality. He will not show partiality in the case of a poor man
> . . . He will not ignore the supplications of the fatherless, nor the widow when she pours out her story. Do not the tears of the widow run down her cheek as she cries out against him who has caused them to fall? (Sir 35:12–15; cf. Prov 6:35)

If in the *Sitz im Leben* of Jesus' own ministry the meaning of the Unjust Judge was to indict those who devour the houses of widows, then the final comment of Jesus (Luke 18:7) means something other than Luke thought (18:1). This story is not so much an example story encouraging prayer, as it is a warning to judges not to oppress the widow. Jesus promises that the God who shows great compassion for the fatherless and widow will be vindicating their cause quickly.

What then does the sixth petition mean? Its rather crude attribution of cause to God stands in good stead with previous comments about peasant sensibilities (immediacy, direct address). The *crux* of the matter has to do with the meaning of *peirasmos*. Derived from a root *peir-*, with cognates in the Latin *experiri* and English "experience," this noun is extremely rare in non-biblical Greek.[118] Verbal forms appear with the basic senses of "to attempt" or "to put to the test." Since Homer, *peira* conveys the notion of "to test the value of something." In the Hellenistic-Roman period, the word can be associated with imperial or royal contexts in the sense of "loyalty test."[119] *Peirasmos* translates an Aramaic noun *nsiyôn* from *nssî*, Hebrew *nsâ*. Manifesting a field of meanings similar to the Greek *peira*, the biblical word, for instance, can refer to the testing of or attempting

118. Appears only three times, BAGD, 640; J. Seesemann, "*peira*," 23.

119. Egyptian papyri: Moulton and Milligan, *Vocabulary*, 501, s.v. *peira*; Plutarch, *Brutus*, 10.

to use military equipment (1 Sam 17:39). Perhaps the most significant occurrence appears in biblical wisdom: Job 9:23–24 links the "trials" of the innocent (if indeed the root there is *nsâ*) with the flourishing of the wicked and the "covering of judges' faces" (i.e., the denial of justice). In later rabbinic usage, the standard understanding of "temptation" comes to the fore.[120]

Matthew's seventh petition may confirm these tentative expositions if it is seen as "epexegetic" of the meaning of Petition 6. The "evil one," then, refers to the corrupt judge who presides over a court prejudiced toward the collection of debts and rigged in favor of royal or imperial interests. The sixth and seventh petitions vividly request deliverance from suborned legal proceedings before evil judges.

In light of this discussion of the second table, it is highly probable that Jesus' Prayer originally expressed a concrete and tight-knit integrity: It is a vivid request for deliverance from hunger, debt, and trials in rigged courts before evil judges. The social system of Roman Palestine, with debt relations reinforced by temple religion, had left many hungry and marginalized. Jesus' Prayer directly addressed their plight, and held out hope that God would hear their prayer as God had heard the cry of the Israelites in Egypt.

The presence of the kingdom's power (Q/Luke 11:20) has profound implications for human institutions and action. Many of the parables of Jesus refer to this reordering power. It is a power as effective as yeast (Q/Luke 13:20–21 parable of the Leaven) or a tiny seed to grow into a towering mustard shrub in a field (Mark 4:30–32 and par.). In terms of human affairs, the reign of God disorients and reorients like the sudden discovery of a priceless pearl (Q/Matt 13:46). The reign of God leads to surprising actions, perhaps foolish from the standpoint of conventional wisdom (the Good Samaritan, L/Luke 10:29–37, or the Prodigal Father, L/Luke 15:11–32). The third petition of the first table develops this line of understanding even further.

(Secondary: Petition 3 of the First Table)

The word "will" in "will of God," *thelēma tou theou*, often translates in the Septuagint (LXX) the Hebrew word for "pleasure" of God, *ḥpṣ*.[121] Another

---

120. Str-B. 1:422.

121. Schrenk, "*thelēma*," *TDNT* 3:52–62. Cf. idem, "*boulomai*," *TDNT* 1:629–37. S. V. McCasland, "Will of God," *IDB* 4:844–48.

significant Hebrew word for "will" is *rṣôn*. In either case, the emphasis in the semitic mind is upon the objective ethical content of God's will and its concrete performance.[122] This can be seen from a few of the Old Testament occurrences of either word:

> [The Lord] says of Cyrus, "He is my shepherd, and he shall fulfil all my *purpose*.[123]

> The Lord loves him; he shall perform his *purpose* on Babylon . . . .[124]

> I *delight* to do thy will, O my God; thy law is within my heart.[125]

The Psalmist brings together will and delight in the last quotation, and the parallelism between "will" and "law" is particularly noteworthy. While many of the occurrences of *ḥpṣ* (verb) and *rṣôn* are in priestly or cultic contexts, there are also a significant number of occurrences of *ḥpṣ* (verb and noun forms) in contexts that emphasize that justice and mercy are qualities pleasing to God:

> . . . let him who glories glory in this, that he understands and knows me, that I am the Lord who practice steadfast love, justice and righteousness in the earth; for in these things I *delight*, says the Lord.[126]

> For I *desire* steadfast love and not sacrifice, the knowledge of God, rather than burnt offerings.[127]

Perhaps the most important passages from the Old Testament for the purposes of this discussion lie in Malachi. Various words for God's pleasure or displeasure occur frequently here. Furthermore, the hope of the return of Elijah—which colors at a number of points the gospel accounts of John the Baptist's and Jesus' ministries—is brought to expression in this book. Finally, the critical stance of Malachi toward the cultus suggests some striking parallels to the Jesus traditions:

---

122. McCasland, "Will of God."

123. Isa 44:28 (RSV). "Purpose" = LXX *thelēma* = *ḥpṣ*.

124. Isa 48:14 (RSV). "Purpose" = LXX *boulē* = *ḥpṣ*.

125. Ps 40:8 (RSV) = 40:9 (MT). "Will" = LXX *thelēma* = *rṣôn*.

126. Jer 9:24 (RSV) = 9:23 (MT).

127. Hos 6:6 (RSV).

I have no *pleasure* (*hps*) in you, says the Lord of hosts, and I will not accept an offering from your hand.[128]

You have wearied the Lord with your words. Yet you say, "How have we wearied him?" By saying, "Every one who does evil is good in the sight of the Lord, and he *delights* in them."[129]

Behold, I send my messenger . . . the messenger of the covenant in whom you *delight* . . .[130]

Then the offering of Judah and Jerusalem *will be pleasing* to the Lord . . . .[131]

The "will" of God, that is, what is pleasing to God, is not only cultic in Malachi, but also ethical:

> For the lips of a priest should guard knowledge, and men should seek instruction (*torah*) from his mouth, for he is the messenger of the Lord of hosts. But you have turned aside from the way; you have caused many to stumble by your instruction (*torah*); you have corrupted the covenant of Levi . . . and so I make you despised and abased before all the people, inasmuch as you have not kept my ways but have shown partiality in your instruction (*torah*). (2:7–9)

> I will draw near to you for judgment; I will be a swift witness against the sorcerers, against the adulterers, against those who swear falsely, against those who oppress the hireling in his wages, the widow and the orphan, against those who thrust aside the sojourner, and do not fear me, says the Lord of hosts. (3:5)

These passages are addressed to the sons of Levi (2:8; 3:3). They reflect old Israelite conceptions of the role of the Levites, who were both cultic figures and judges rolled into one (cf. *torah*). Where might such traditions have been preserved? Malachi is generally dated to the early fifth century BCE—prior to the work of Nehemiah and Ezra.[132] The nature of the criti-

---

128. Mal 1:10 (RSV); cf. Mark 7:6–7; 12:32–34; Matt 9:13; 23:23.

129. Mal 2:17; cf. Mark 3:4; Matt 23:27–28.

130. Mal 3:1; cf. Mark 9:11–13; Matt 23:30, 34; Luke 4:18–19 (+ Isa 42:1).

131. Mal 3:4; Mark 11:15–19.

132. For the historical situation of Malachi, see Eissfeldt, *The Old Testament*, 442–43. Nehemiah's dates are fairly certain: 446–434 BCE. Ezra's mission has been variously dated: The two most likely dates are 458 and 398 BCE (depending upon which Artaxerxes is meant in Ezra 7:1). Cross, "Reconstruction of the Judean Restoration," 14 n. 60, sees 458 BCE as the more likely date. Consult Eissfeldt, *The Old Testament*, 554–55 for the

cism of the cultus evident in the document suggests a writer among the priests, but not among the upper echelon. In the post-exilic situation, families descended from Aaron were the dominant figures in the Jerusalem cultus. Furthermore, the address in Malachi to the sons of Levi perhaps reveals the interest of the author in this second-class group of priests. The book of Ezekiel tells us that the Levites or families tracing their lineage back to Levi had fallen into disfavor during the period immediately after the exile (Ezek 44:10–31). Ezekiel, in fact, relates that the Aaronides, who supplant the Levites,

> shall not marry a widow, or a divorced woman . . . They shall teach my people the difference between the holy and the common, and show them how to distinguish between the unclean and the clean. In a controversy they shall act as judges, and they shall judge it according to my judgments.[133]

These are the very issues that concern Malachi, so it is not entirely clear whether Malachi is thinking of the Aaronides under the more comprehensive designation "sons of Levi." In any case, Malachi is written from a critical, not sympathetic, point of view. The writing insists that the priests must attend both to cultic and covenantal concerns. Its author is probably a lower division priest knowledgeable regarding the Old Israelite legal traditions (which combined covenant-ethical and cultic concerns). As proof of this orientation, the figure of the Old Israelite charismatic prophet, Elijah the Tishbite, appears in the final chapters of Malachi.

The later tradition about Elijah presents fascinating material for study.[134] There are tantalizing glimpses of apparently widespread popular beliefs about Elijah. The impression given is of expectations forged in conformity with specific needs of diverse groups.

Thus, Mal 3:2 envisions the work of the Messenger (Elijah according to Mal 4:5) as "purification." Furthermore, as the passage quoted above indicates, Elijah will restore the integrity of judgment for those who are legally at a disadvantage (3:5–12). Mal 4:5 adds that Elijah will "turn the hearts" of fathers to their children. Sirach (ca. 200 BCE) adds to this list the restoration of the tribes of Israel (Sir 48:10). According to rabbinic

---

opposing arguments.

133. Ezek 44:22–24.

134. Lightfoot, *Commentary*, 2:243–47 (*ad* Matt 17:10). Jeremias, "*ēl(e)ias*," (+ bibliography). Billerbeck, "Der Prophet Elias," Appendix 28 Str-B. 4:764–98.

tradition, Elijah will decide disputed questions of law.[135] On the more popular side, and reflecting traditions of Northern Israel, Elijah will anoint the Messiah and set up the symbols of the messianic age—the three bowls of manna, purificatory water, and oil.

> Thus Elijah prepares the people of God for the last time. When peace has been restored, the community reconstituted, Antichrist overcome and killed and the Messiah anointed for His kingly office, then the great final age of grace begins.[136]

Elijah comes, therefore, to seal the eschatological will or pleasure of God. The third petition of Jesus' Prayer came to evoke this matrix of expectation, and in conjunction with the other petitions to ask for the concrete observance of God's will among humankind. This point is underscored by the expansion of the third petition's probably original form in Matthew by "on earth as it is in heaven." This parallel may have been intended to go with the entire first table rather than just the third petition.[137] It certainly would be appropriate as an explicit conclusion to what is implied in the other petitions. Furthermore, there is latent in the third petition the intimation that those who guarantee the observance of God's will—the interpreters of the law or torah, i.e., priests, levites, scholars of Q²'s day—must come in for blame. If God's will is not now being observed as it should be, then the guarantors have failed (cf. Q/Luke 11:52).

This petition articulates quite concretely what is implied already in the sixth petition (and likely the seventh):

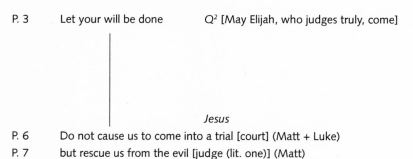

| P. 3 | Let your will be done | Q² [May Elijah, who judges truly, come] |

Jesus

| P. 6 | Do not cause us to come into a trial [court] (Matt + Luke) |
| P. 7 | but rescue us from the evil [judge (lit. one)] (Matt) |

---

135. Jeremias, "ēl(e)ias," 934.

136. Ibid.

137. Origen long ago suggested this: Smith, "Lord's Prayer," 156.

Originally these latter petitions articulated the immediate concerns of people threatened with foreclosure or imprisonment through court action. These sentiments were also felt to be appropriate to the agony scene in Gethsemane. There Jesus prays words quite similar to the third petition. The prayer is offered up immediately before Jesus is arrested and taken to the suborned Sanhedrin. He is being arrested precisely because he has openly criticized in his teaching (Mark 12:40) and in his actions (Mark 11:15–17) the mechanisms proliferating debt and misery in Roman Palestine around 30 CE. For Mark, Jesus is about to suffer for doing the work of Elijah.

CONCLUSION

The Lord's Prayer, when viewed in its original connection to the work of Jesus, displays a concrete, immediate, and consistent this-worldly concern. While we may still speak (as older scholarship does) of its basic framework of meaning as "eschatological," in the sense that it hopes for ultimate and final changes in human affairs and conditions, nevertheless, the Lord's Prayer is surprisingly more concerned with specific problems and human welfare in the here and now than might have been suspected.

This essay has argued that Jesus' original prayer consisted in the distinctive *'abba'* address and Petitions 4–6; the seventh petition repeats Petition 6 in synonymous parallelism. These petitions centered around the constellation of social problems bound up with court–enforced debt collections and resulting lack of adequate bread (whether substantial, subsistence, belonging to the estate, or "daily"). The first table of the prayer in the Q tradition elaborates on the basis of the great traditions of Israel, and reflects more abstract theological interests of these early scribes of the Jesus traditions.

The two tables of the Prayer, thus, are organically related and internally unified to a degree. Where the second table delves into specific human needs and expresses values peculiar to Jesus' Galilean movement, the first table articulates the general care of God and parameters of faithful human action. Each petition of the earlier second table correlates in some definite respect with the parallel member of the later first table:

	Table 2 *Primary (Jesus, Q¹?)*		Table 1 *Secondary (Q², later evangelists)*
P. 4	Petition for daily bread	P. 1	Sanctifying the name in blessing
P. 5	Request for the removal of debt	P. 2	Request for the arrival of God's kingdom
PP. 6–7	God to deliver from rigged courts and evil judges	P. 3	God's will to be done

Central to the concerns of Jesus' original Prayer was the reality of oppression, indebtedness, hunger, and social insecurity. When early Christian groups moved out of the immediate context of such social realities, the concrete and immediate meaning of Jesus' prayer was led in the direction of theological abstractions and aligned with Israelite traditions and early Jewish forms of prayer. Late twentieth-century Christian communities might reflect on the meaning and consequences of that transition as they confront social and economic crises at the threshold of a new millennium.[138]

138. I am grateful to Jerome H. Neyrey, Dennis C. Duling, and John S. Kloppenborg for astute comments on earlier drafts of this study. They, of course, cannot be held responsible for the views promoted here.

PART III

The Peasant

Aims *of* Jesus

CHAPTER 15

Models and Archaeology
in the Social Interpretation of Jesus

> The conflict between Jesus and his Jewish opponents was thus an
> intra-Jewish conflict (with the elite who represented the dominant
> ethos) about how to interpret the tradition. It was a hermeneutical
> struggle with sociopolitical consequences.[1]

> It was only when the implied challenge of the full ministry in
> Galilee was recognised for what it was, first by the scribes, but
> then also by the priestly aristocracy, that plans had to be made to
> have him removed, predictably in the Jerusalem setting, not the
> Galilean.[2]

HISTORICAL JESUS STUDIES TODAY, no longer preoccupied with the
existentialist theological questions of mid-century, pursue a more
refined tradition criticism, seek enlightenment through the excavations of
Palestinian archaeology, and search for the most appropriate conceptual
frameworks for understanding. Effective social interpretation depends
not only upon the textual and artifactual information available, but also
upon conceptual resources that condition our questions and amplify our
perceptions. This essay, working with social-systems models, urges a more
comprehensive and integrated approach to the social world of Jesus and
the interpretation of his historical activity.

---

1. Borg, "Portraits of Jesus," 13.

2. Freyne, *Galilee, Jesus and the Gospels*, 238.

SYSTEMS MODELS IN THE SOCIAL INTERPRETATION OF JESUS

All historians are conditioned by their contemporary social experience. This conditioning makes the social understanding of the past difficult. Inappropriate assumptions and analogies all too easily distort perceptions. The very different depictions of Galilee in Sanders and Horsley offer a case in point. Sanders sees no real basis for conflict under "the good Herods," while Horsley perceives a "spiral of violence."[33] Since both scholars draw upon virtually the same source material, their disagreement resides largely in their conceptual frameworks. Sanders' picture of a Galilee ruled by benevolent despots with enlightened tax policies seems influenced by unwarranted political assumptions. Horsley's use of peasant studies, and sensitivity to the political realities of a colonial situation, provides him with a very distinctive perspective on conditions under client rulers.

Historians too often promote generalizations based on anecdotal "evidence," without reaching clarity about larger social issues or contexts. Such inductive positivism, masquerading as an objective "social description," masks ideological bias and obscures conceptual basis for interpretation. Clear models help to overcome bias and social obfuscation by permitting critical examination of the conceptual frameworks into which historical data are summoned as evidence. Critically selected models allow data to speak in relationship to a larger picture, transforming it into compelling evidence. Further, potent models provide selectivity, aiding the interpreter in seeing what is most important or by highlighting social information that might otherwise be overlooked.[4]

An inductive positivist method in historical Jesus studies can be improved upon, therefore, through abductive procedures.[5] Abduction synthesizes both theoretical consciousness informed by the social sciences and historical data. A more sophisticated sociological imagination thus can inform social inquiry centered on the historical Jesus or Roman Galilee.

This is coming to be appreciated in recent scholarship. The cultural anthropology of the Mediterranean world (e.g., Gilmore) highlights key values and social arrangements in the largest socio-cultural environment of

---

3. E. P. Sanders, "Jesus in Historical Context"; idem, *The Historical Figure of Jesus*; Horsley, *Jesus and the Spiral of Violence*.

4. Elliott, *What Is Social-Scientific Criticism?*, 40–48.

5. Malina, "Interpretation"; Elliott, *What Is Social-Scientific Criticism?*, 48

Jesus and Galilee studies.[6] Malina and Rohrbaugh appropriately urge the ubiquitous importance of Mediterranean institutions like patronage for understanding the synoptic tradition.[7]

Likewise, the macrosociologies of Gerhard Lenski and John Kautsky offer important sounding boards.[8] Lenski identifies key features in the social stratification of agrarian societies. His theory also highlights the importance of power and privilege in relation to social structure. Despite his claim to mediate and move beyond functionalism and conflict theories, Lenski's schema is rather static and of somewhat limited significance in understanding historical dynamics in the social picture. His theory needs supplementation. Kautsky shows the prominence of politics in ancient societies, especially in the face of low productivity economies (where redistributive mechanisms are more significant than productive mechanisms).[9]

Macrocultural and sociological perspectives can be enhanced by systems perspectives. While systems theories are weak in the analysis of causation, and in some forms hinder conflict analysis, they help to elucidate the interrelationship of social phenomena. The powerful theoretical perspectives of Talcott Parsons can be of use in the model-building of this essay.[10] While Parsons' theories were developed largely with "modern societies" in mind, their abstraction lends them cross-societal value. Bellah shows the power of such a theoretical approach for understanding religious evolution in relation to social function.[11] Malina demonstrates the utility of Parsons' conceptions of generalized symbolic media for discussing early Christian

---

6. Gilmore, *Honor and Shame and the Unity of the Mediterranean.*

7. Malina and Rohrbaugh, *Social-Science Commentary on the Synoptic Gospels.*

8. Lenski, *Power and Privilege*; Lenski and Lenski, *Human Societies*; Horsley, *Jesus and the Spiral of Violence*; Saldarini, *Pharisees, Scribes and Sadducees*; idem, "Political and Social Roles of the Pharisees and Scribes in Galilee"; and Fiensy, *The Social History of Palestine in the Herodian Period* utilize Lenski in various ways. See the important discussion in Dennis C. Duling, "Matthew and Marginality," 649–52.

9. Kautsky, *The Politics of Aristocratic Empires.*

10. Parsons, *The Structure of Social Action*; idem, *Politics and Social Structure*; idem, *The System of Modern Societies.*

11. So Randall Collins, *Theoretical Sociology*, 57: "Parsons' system is extremely abstract, since it intends to supply basic components for the analysis of any society that has ever existed or might exist . . . ." Bellah, "Religious Evolution," shows the power of such a theoretical approach for understanding religious evolution in relation to social function.

developments.[12] For critical assessments of functionalist sociology, see Elliott and Horsley.[13]

Parsons' four-function model of the social system, employed strictly as an analytical framework, generates insight especially into how Mediterranean values were made operational in the political institutions of early Roman Palestine. A simplified version of the model looks like this:[14]

Figure 21: Parsons' Four-Function Model

External

Economy	Politics
Family	Community Law

Means   Ends

Education -----------Religion

Internal

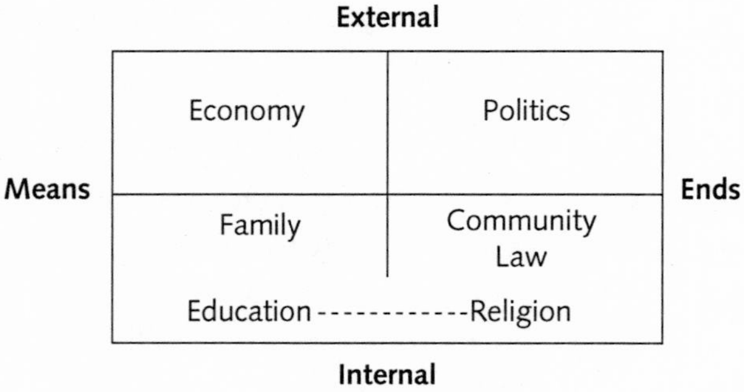

In real societies, the "quadrants" of the model usually do not exist discretely. Social domains interpenetrate one another; otherwise said, social domains can be embedded one within another. It is important to understand how one domain governs those that are inset.

The key social domain in Mediterranean societies, permeating all other institutional arrangements, is the family.[15] The most likely explanation for the preeminence of this social domain lies in the environmental adaptation demanded of peoples living in the circum-Mediterranean world. Life in a climate where rainfall is unpredictable, as well as life threatened repeatedly by encroaching mountain tribes, has socialized Mediterraneans to trust only those in firm interpersonal relationship.[16]

12. See Malina's important discussion of Generalized Symbolic Media (based upon Parsons) in *Christian Origins and Cultural Anthropology*, 68–97; also, idem, "Wealth and Poverty."

13. Elliott, ed., *Semeia*, Vol. 35: *Social-Scientific Criticism of the New Testament and Its Social World*; Horsley, *Sociology and the Jesus Movement*.

14. This graphical summary of Parson's four-function social theory is derived from chapter 2, "System Theories," in Collins, *Theoretical Sociology*, 58.

15. Malina, *The New Testament World* (1993²), 84, 119–26; (2001³), 82, 134–60; Pilch and Malina, *Biblical Social Values and Their Meaning*, 70, 139.

16. Crossan, *Historical Jesus*, 12.

Whatever the comprehensive causes of the primacy of family, even a cursory investigation of ancient literature will show how significant family was in autobiographical or biographical considerations. For instance, the first words of Josephus' *Life* are "my family" (*emoi de genos*). Likewise, Matthew's Gospel presents what the early church considered (from its placement in first rank) the authoritative story of Jesus. Matthew begins the story by reference to the putative genealogy of Jesus, tracing his lineage back to glorious ancestors of Israel.

As the first paragraphs of Josephus' *Life* also demonstrate, a first-century Judean stands within an extended family whose interests and values supply a basic point of reference for the social action of the individual.

The ancient family had its internal politics, with males over females, fathers over children and slaves, older over younger, etc. There would be a religious life of the clan, and its activities to feed, clothe, and provide amenities for its members could be labeled economic. The Greek word *oikonomia*, of course, means "household management." To understand the dominance of family-structure and the interpenetration of institutions, we talk about *domestic politics, domestic religion*, and *domestic economy*. The adjective underscores the linking of social dimensions.

What is often ignored in scholarly discussions of ancient societies is the primacy of power and prevalence of power-structured relationships throughout ancient institutions. When one clan or family deals with another, it does not do so on the basis of kinship but on the basis of power. As Marshall Sahlins has shown for tribal societies, family or quasi-familial relations are governed by reciprocity exchanges of one kind or another.[17] However, relations with strangers or enemies exhibit negative reciprocal characteristics. To do the stranger or enemy harm is the ordinary thing. Therefore, all social institutions of a public character in the ancient world have a political dimension that needs to be recognized and taken into account. Illustrious families strove to dominate others. To understand the peculiarities of ancient politics—patronage and enforcement, temples, and estates—we must speak of *political kinship, political religion*, and *political economy*. Again, the adjective underscores the linking of social dimensions.

Political kinship appears in faction members, clients, slaves, tenants, tax collectors, and the like. *Political religion* appears with the temple state

17. Sahlins, *Tribesmen*.

(with its own political kin organization), which is religiously rationalized into being "God's estate." The focus of political religion is the majesty and honor of the deity, i.e., worship. This worship demands appointments, so religious taxation (a rationalized political reality) is a necessity. *Political economy* identifies taxes, debts, forced extraction of goods and labor, production for redistribution (redistributive economy), and production for trade. Power relations govern all of these phenomena.

We need to be clear from the start, therefore, about the ranking of the socio-cultural (value) domains of Jesus' Mediterranean context: Kinship—Politics—Economy. Otherwise, we approach that social world inappropriately out of our own, where economy structures all other social institutions (even families) and where social institutions appear discrete and self-governing.

The comprehensive model for the work of this chapter grows out of the preceding reflections and building blocks.[18] The arrows in the following "Systems Model for the Social Interpretation of Jesus" attempt to indicate feedback and feedforward loops through attached pluses and minuses. A feedback loop indicates resistive or diminishing action; a feedforward loop indicates amplifying action.

The model highlights major values and interests involved in the social action of elites and non-elites. A macrosociological focus on power relations addresses concerns of conflict theory (social interests divide). However, a focus on the social system elucidates structural-functionalism's interest in operative social structures (which seek an integral system). Attention paid to values and symbols that motivate action brings in the emphasis of symbolic interactionists. The model attempts to integrate concerns of major theoretical camps.

The model does not focus directly on the domestic politics, religion, or economy. Domestic religion in the Jewish regions of Roman Palestine would perennially emphasize election motifs and intimacy with God. For elite Judeans, torah and temple symbolized election. The model, however, urges us to examine how institutions controlled by the upper 10% shaped the perspectives and behavior of the lower 90%. Elite religion serves political functions when legitimating social order and mandating taxes that flow to the elite. In terms of the actual society of Jesus, the Herodian-

---

18. Compare Oakman, "The Ancient Economy and St. John's Apocalypse," orig. 204 (chapter 6 above).

Figure 22: Systems Model for the Social Interpretation of Jesus

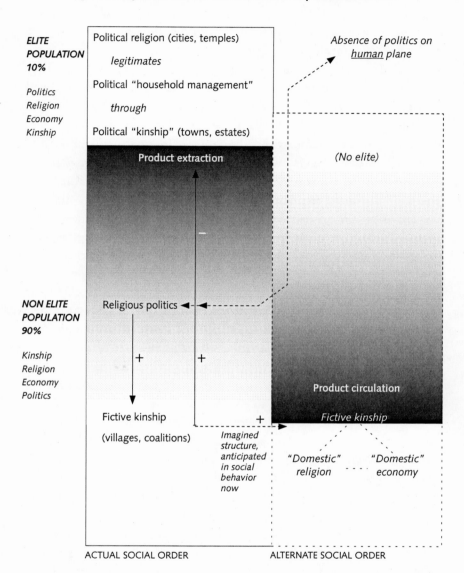

ELITE
POPULATION
10%

Politics
Religion
Economy
Kinship

Political religion (cities, temples)

legitimates

Political "household management"

through

Political "kinship" (towns, estates)

Product extraction

Absence of politics on
human plane

(No elite)

NON ELITE
POPULATION
90%

Kinship
Religion
Economy
Politics

Religious politics

+ +

Fictive kinship

(villages, coalitions)

Imagined
structure,
anticipated
in social
behavior
now

Product circulation

Fictive kinship

+

"Domestic"
religion

"Domestic"
economy

ACTUAL SOCIAL ORDER   ALTERNATE SOCIAL ORDER

Judean elite controlled the cities (Sepphoris, Tiberias, Jerusalem) and the
Jerusalem temple, i.e., the key political(-religious) institutions.

Political religion implies (feeds forward into) the need for political
kinship, represented strongly by groups in cities and towns. These "political kin" are responsible for the "political household management." They

are the enforcers and collectors for the system, responsible for actually entering the pressing installation to ensure the purity of oil and wine or going into the village to remove grain from the threshing floor. They are also the accountants for the system.

The Pharisees offer an interesting case study in this light. They emerged under John Hyrcanus when the Hasmonean dynast realigned himself politically with the Sadducees. Outright war between Pharisees and Hasmoneans ensued under Jannaeus. The Pharisees apparently represented a protest group from within the political kinship structure. Primarily lay, they formed fictive kingroups called *habûrôth*; members were *habērîm*. They emphasized the keeping of the whole law, even for laity. Thus, they embraced the purity regulations of the priests in daily life. Why did they do this? They were retainers of elite priests.[19] In their service of the temple, they became very familiar with the Mosaic legislation governing religious purity and taxation. They, therefore, came to know the laws even better than the priests and to distinguish themselves as a group by living according to the whole law, even though they were not priests. Throughout the first-century BCE, the Pharisees dared to criticize king and priest for their failure to adhere strictly to the law. The political repercussions of resistance or rebellion were predictable (Josephus, *Ant.* 13.288–291; 17.41–46).

From the non-elite side, a basic issue in a low-productivity, low-energy, semi-arid ecological adaptation (with elite structures as described) is whether there will be enough to eat. The non-elite provide the productive labor, only to see the produce carried off by tax collectors. When not much is produced anyway, hunger is a close relative.[20] The model indicates that *human political institutions* are a source of difficulty for the non-elite. Their strategies of resistance understandably tend to organize around the primary variable of kinship. Because of the need for concerted action, *fictive kinship* emerges, undergirded by religious warrant. The formation of fictive kin ties in villages and within coalitions represents a form of power; the politics of these groups tends to be sanctioned by deeply-held religious views. Therefore, non-elite politics tend to become *religious politics*. Non-elite leaders come to envision alternate social orders with two primary characteristics: The absence of politics, or of religiously sanctioned vio-

---

19. Saldarini, *Pharisees, Scribes and Sadducees*; idem, "Political and Social Roles."

20. Oakman, *Jesus and the Economic Questions of His Day*; Crossan, *Historical Jesus*, 43–46.

lence, on a human plane *and* the organization of society through fictive kinship with concomitant domestic religion and domestic economy.

How can the model help to understand first-century Galilee? Were Galilean Jews torah- and temple-loyal? Was there a distinctive Galilean theology bound up with specifiable social interests? A consideration of such questions especially in reference to Jesus of Nazareth must be deferred until we examine how archaeology can contribute to social understanding.

Social models, then, are not reality. They are symbolic simplifications of reality to aid in understanding strategic social features or processes.[21] The conceptual frameworks of this paper attempt to provide interpretive depth, like an old stereoscope, by linking several important perspectives, especially informed by macrocultural, macrosociological, and social-systems studies. The gain is an augmented understanding of politics as a key institutional and cultural variable and of struggles over social goals in the environment of Jesus. Herodian and Judean elite families dealt with non-elites through social institutions characterized by power and resource inequities. Non-elite politics and social action, conversely, were underwritten by culturally informed values that envisioned alternate institutions. Contemporary realities of power would shape non-elite imagination of a familial community without political economy.

GALILEAN ARCHAEOLOGY IN THE SOCIAL INTERPRETATION OF JESUS

Archaeological materials and interpretation are playing an increasingly important role in discussions of the social world of Jesus. For more precise understanding of first-century Galilee, archaeology needs to distinguish between cultural and social indices. Cultural indices ostensibly reflect the prevalent values of a people ("the Jews"), but are often urged or enforced by powerful elites (Jerusalem). These values may be shared formally by different social classes, though not necessarily understood in the same way. For first-century Judaism, such phenomena as aniconic coins and architecture could be viewed as "cultural" artifacts.[22]

21. De Raadt, *Information and Managerial Wisdom*, 9, defines a model as "a portion of knowledge set apart for a particular social purpose." The social purpose for the models in this essay is the understanding of the social purposes of Jesus of Nazareth. Carney, *The Shape of the Past*, 10.

22. In the now somewhat dated summary of Meyers and Strange, *Archaeology, the Rabbis, and Early Christianity*, cultural discussion predominates. The authors refer to

Archaeological social indices, however, must be of such a character that they can reliably identify social differentiation within a cultural group. The identification of social indices implies recognition of social "fault lines" introduced into material culture by inequities of power. Sometimes cultural indices can play a socio-interpretive role, for instance, when select Jewish groups might adopt Hellenistic coins embossed with pagan motifs. The archaeologist will want to shed light, so far as this is possible from the material record, upon where such coins were handled or how they were perceived by different social strata. The following reflections, therefore, are intended to be suggestive of the kinds of social information archaeologists might be seeking or examining to clarify the issues central to this paper.

Settlements

Most archaeology in Palestine up until recently was based upon work in ancient cities. This made sense in terms of historical investigations. "Biblical archaeology" correlated urban stratigraphic records with the literary record. Typological sequences of pottery were needed for determining archaeological periods. Coins aided in developing the basic chronologies required for future work.[23]

Even standard tools are limited by prevailing paradigms of interpretation. The regional articles in the *New Encyclopedia of Archaeological Excavations in the Holy Land* or the coverage of sites in the *Anchor Bible Dictionary*, for instance, more often provide perspectives on historical and cultural developments than information useful for sociological interpretation. However, as interest has grown in the social interpretation of the literary and archaeological records, a more extensive and comprehensive assessment of archaeological remains is needed. What seems called for are in-depth surveys of a wide variety of sites in Galilee, with special attention devoted to non-elite contexts. Only in this way will powerful social indices be identified.

"cultural indicators" (33), "cultural factors" (35), the pluralism of Galilean culture (38), etc., and generally treat of linguistic and "religious" indices. That these indices tend to reflect the interests of elites does not receive discussion. Again, Strange's recent article "Some Implications of Archaeology for New Testament Studies," 31–32, focuses on Rome's "urban overlay" upon "Jewish culture." There is no suggestion of similar "overlays" within Jewish culture.

23. The works of W. F. Albright or G. E. Wright come to mind. Moorey, *A Century of Biblical Archaeology*, chronicles the rise and decline of biblical archaeology, characterizing its basic weakness as "simplistic explanation" (175).

Archaeological method, of course, is also a critical factor. The Israeli method, often intent on exposing architecture, has seemed most useful for ascertaining cultural information. The American stratigraphic method, influenced as it is by general anthropology and concerns for total societal reconstruction, is best suited for refinement toward using the material culture for social interpretation.[24]

The following areas of archaeological inquiry might contribute further to the social interpretation of Galilee.[25]

Buildings

Some preliminary work is available for illustrating how settlement patterns and spatial organization can help us do social interpretation. David Fiensy provides a synthesis for supporting further work on the archaeology of the lower classes.[26] He demonstrates how building remains—isolated farms, houses, courtyards, alleys, villages—might provide significant social information. He thinks the early Roman *insulae* at Capernaum contribute evidence for an extended family organization of labor.[27] Could they also suggest the provision of housing by fishing contractors?

Social interpretation needs not only information from the cultural-political centers, the cities, but also now from towns and villages. Most of Jesus' contemporaries lived in villages; towns like Jotapata and Cana, Capernaum and Magdala, represented the domiciles of the "political kin" (see above on conceptual models) of the Herods and Judean elites. These sites will fill out our understanding of political economy in Galilee.

Monumental Structures, Waterworks, Roads

Archaeologists need to begin asking about the labor requirements involved in archaeological remains. Work of Dar and others, for instance, showed that each of the 962 stone towers in Samaria, weighing about 150 tons apiece and probably serving as artificial caves for estate wine production under the Ptolemies, were the result of 300–400 days of coordinated

24. The article of Shanks, "Dever's Sermon on the Mound," indicates some of the issues at stake; see the comments of Gottwald, *The Hebrew Bible*, 59, 63.

25. My experiences at Jotapata have informed these suggestions. Excavations began there in 1992 under the direction of Douglas Edwards, Mordechai Aviam, and David Adan-Bayewitz. Aviam and Adan-Bayewitz directed the second season (1993).

26. Fiensy, *The Land is Mine*, 119–46.

27. Ibid., 131–32.

labor.[28] These nearly 1000 years worth of petrified labor, extracted by Hellenistic overlords in less than a century's span, attest to the real political costs of the Greco-Roman period. What can be learned similarly from temples, roads, fortresses, and aqueducts? To what extent do these projects represent the accumulation of forced labor?[29]

Coins

As coins are excavated, archaeologists need to give more sustained attention to the social context of coin finds: Where are silver coins "contextualized"? Where are bronzes discovered? What types of hoards are found in cities, towns, or villages? Did these accumulations originate in commerce, taxation, loans, or rent extraction? A *desideratum* for social interpretation in Galilee would be a specialist publication that provided detailed coin profiles and maps detailing locations of discovery for all excavated and surveyed sites.

It is known that the temple tax was to be paid in Tyrian money (*m. Bek.* 8:7). Probably Herodian rents and taxes were paid in this currency as well, since the prevalence of Tyrian coins in towns of Lower Galilee and the Golan (Gamala, Chorazin, Bethsaida, Jotapata) is notable. It may reasonably be asked, therefore, how the presence of Tyrian coinage relates to political economy. Would the coin record bear out the thesis: Silver coinage, especially the Hellenistic types established at Tyre and Acco, supplied the basic money of the political economy—both in terms of taxation (Herodian realm, temple) and commerce (Tyre connection)? My suggestion is that Tyrian coinage reflects the political influence of Tyre, even in the domains of the Herodians and high priests. The text of Acts 12:20 is suggestive of the economic grounds for conflict between the Herods and Tyre. Since both taxation and commerce were elite pursuits, this conflict provides only an indirect index for village attitudes.

Would archaeological work also bear out the thesis of Polanyi that bronzes were token money intended only for rudimentary commodity exchanges or for conversion—with commissions (another form of

---

28. Fiensy, *The Land is Mine*, 32; Applebaum, "The Towers of Samaria"; Dar, *Landscape and Pattern*.

29. Horsley, *Jesus and the Spiral of Violence*, 6; Seeman, "The Urbanization of Herodian Galilee," offers some valuable suggestions about the adverse economic impact of the founding of Herod's two Galilean cities, Sepphoris and Tiberias.

taxation)—into silver by money-changers?[30] Consider the results of a concordance study of the New Testament: The silver *denarius* is strikingly associated with political economy, especially debt (Matt 18:28), estate payment (Matt 20:2, 10), taxation (Mark 12:15), and commerce (Luke 10:35; Rev 6:6). The non-elite are most likely familiar only with bronze coins: The two *lepta* of the widow (Mark 12:42); Jesus asking, probably not disingenuously, about the inscription and image on a silver coin (Mark 12:15).

The coins of the first revolt offer equally suggestive social information. Silver shekels of the first Jewish-Roman War have been discovered in connection with priestly effects.[31] These typically have the inscription "Jerusalem the Holy" (holiness a priestly interest) and were probably used to pay the temple tax. Bronze coins found elsewhere at Masada bear inscriptions "For the freedom of Zion" or "For the redemption of Zion," while a unique bronze type at Gamala is inscribed "For the redemption of Holy Jerusalem." Yadin remarks, "[The silver coins] must have been hidden by the defenders of Masada to prevent their falling into the hands of the Roman conquerors, unlike the bronze coins which were scattered all over the place."[32]

Of the bronzes Hengel observes, "It is a remarkable fact that 'freedom' does not, as it does in the case of the coins of the second revolt, refer predominantly to Israel, but is applied fundamentally to Zion."[33] The clear association of bronzes with a concern for Zion's freedom likely indicate a concern about temple taxation. The bronze revolt coins possibly mark as much a revolt against the temple establishment as against the Romans. The hidden silver coins at Masada indicate even there the conflicting ideologies and aims of the revolt.[34]

Archaeological work, it can be seen, needs to become precise enough to identify in the coin record differing circulation patterns and economic systems with quite different purposes. The vertical system of taxation and elite-commerce was by far the most significant. Thus, MacMullen's comment that local trade involved about "seventy-five percent" of total eco-

30. Polanyi, *Livelihood*, 116–19 and especially 258–64.

31. Yadin, *Masada*, 108.

32. Ibid.

33. Hengel, *The Zealots*, 118; for another accessible discussion of the coins, see Betlyon, "Coinage," 1087.

34. For a good discussion of these, see Price, *Jerusalem Under Siege*.

nomic exchange value in the Roman empire is a meaningless social statistic without some assessment of how much was controlled by elites.[35] Based on MacMullen, Edwards thinks that Galilean cities were not parasitic; however, this judgment ignores the political nature of Galilean economy.[36] A social interpretation alert to politics needs to suspect that regional commerce was not conducted on a level playing field and that perhaps up to seventy-five percent of system goods were moving vertically.

Bath Complexes

Up until now, *miqva'oth*, or ritual bath complexes, have been thought to be significant cultural indicators for a Jewish presence in the Galilee. For first and second-century Sepphoris, the excavations on the western side of the acropolis have uncovered significant evidence for a "Jewish quarter."[37] The presence there of private ritual baths, utility mosaic floors, and burials outside of the city precincts would show, in this interpretation, both a concern for ritual purity (baths) and aniconic sensitivities demonstrated through non-depiction of plants, animals, or humans on mosaic floors.[38]

A consideration of where *miqva'oth* appear in towns and outside cities gives pause to a simplistic cultural interpretation. As is well-known from the Mazar excavations at the temple mount and from Avigad's work in the Jewish Quarter of the Old City of Jerusalem, *miqva'oth* are clearly associated with concern for the purity of the temple and with the likely pre-70 CE domiciles of the high priestly families.[39] The Judean Essenes at Qumran clearly had concern for ritual bathing, attested both in the Scrolls and in the archaeological remains.[40] The bath complexes in the western palace of Herod at Masada may also indicate that monarch's concern to abide by Judean purity regulations. The wealthy and powerful could have these in domestic contexts.

What is striking about the *miqva'oth* in rural Judea is their association with agricultural installations, mostly pressing installations. These in-

35. MacMullen, "Market-Days," 333.

36. Edwards, "The Socio-Economic and Cultural Ethos of the Lower Galilee," 55.

37. Meyers, "Challenge of Hellenism," 88.

38. Meyers, "Roman Sepphoris," 325.

39. Results are conveniently summarized in Avigad, "How the Wealthy Lived in Herodian Jerusalem"; and Mazar, "Excavations Near Temple Mount Reveal Splendors of Herodian Jerusalem."

40. La Sor, "Discovering What Jewish Miqva'ot Can Tell Us About Christian Baptism."

stallations were provided by the estate owner for the workers to insure the ritual purity of the product. Ronny Reich's 1993 ASOR (Annual Meeting) presentation, "'*Miqwa'ot*' (Jewish Ritual Baths) in Rural Regions in the Second Temple Period," showed that purity baths were often part of Judean estate pressing installations.

In Galilee, the same pattern seems to hold outside the cities. At Gamala, a *miqveh* appears beside the oil press. At Chorazin, although probably from a much-later period, one finds *miqva'oth* near economic installations. Jotapata seems to show a similar configuration. Interestingly, pools at Nazareth do not seem associated with the oil/wine presses.[41] Plastered basins discovered under the Churches of the Annunciation and St. Joseph seem unrelated to the presses. The basins likely come from a time later than the early first century and show evidence of cultic functions. Could they be installations associated with the removal of the high priestly course to Nazareth after 70 CE? Otherwise, they might have been *loci* for Jewish Christian baptisms.[42] Their absence at installations associated with other Galilean Jewish villages would be a significant social index. Presses from this period in western Galilee appear to lack *miqva'oth* as well, but this is perhaps related to the dominance there of Acco.[43]

I suggest that for Jewish villagers in Lower Galilee *miqva'oth* were associated with political economy, and thus with *political* religion. Therefore, Galilean peasants had ample reason to detest purity concerns, along with the product extraction linked to them. Peasant anger compromised village loyalty to the temple, since it was the temple and levitical law that mandated such arrangements.

Pottery

The work of Adan-Bayewitz is noteworthy in pointing toward new ways of gleaning social information from the artifactual record. His tracing of pottery origins and distribution by detailed analysis of chemical profiles of pottery clay is a real step forward from simple morphological identifications. We accept Adan-Bayewitz's basic conclusions that Kefar Hananyah

41. Bagatti, *Excavations in Nazareth*, 1:52–57, 119–23, 219–33; Bellarmino Bagatti and Vassilios Tzaferis, "Nazareth," 1104.

42. See the discussion in Meyers and Strange, *Archaeology, the Rabbis, and Early Christianity*, 132, 136.

43. Frankel, "Some Oil Presses from Western Galilee."

and Kefar Shikhin manufactured the basic cooking wares and storage vessels respectively for Lower Galilee in the early Roman period.[44]

The discoveries of Adan-Bayewitz have seemed to support the notion that Lower Galilean society was well-integrated (low level of conflictual relations) and thoroughly commercialized, so that villagers could buy or trade pottery much as we would visit the store for dishware. It is at this point that the lack of an explicit model of agrarian societies in Adan-Bayewitz's work leads to an unlikely conclusion. For it is much more likely, given what we have looked at in this chapter, that powerful interests controlled the two pottery villages—especially when Shikhin was very close to Sepphoris and manufactured the basic vessel of liquid commerce—and that the distribution of these products reflects rather the outcome of monopoly than of a free market. Furthermore, one might ask whether other pottery manufacturing outlets could have existed *de facto* (given the necessary supplies of local clay), but did not *de jure* because of the prevailing socio-political arrangements. This is a matter that requires further inquiry. Furthermore, to speak of markets, as Adan-Bayewitz and Edwards do, is to ignore the results of comparative studies like Polanyi's that indicate "market" as we understand that word did not exist in antiquity; ancient markets were not price-markets; politics and "kinship" governed the dynamics of exchanges, distorting the purely economic rationality that modern people associate with markets.[45]

Archaeologists should give attention, in addition to formal pottery typologies and quantitative studies of pottery remains, to what types of vessels appear where. In towns, for instance, one might expect to find many storage jars and *pithoi* precisely because towns were the enforcement or collection points for rent and tax extraction. What kinds of volume do extant storage jar remains indicate? We will look below at the Unjust Steward parable of Jesus with precisely this question in mind.

Stone vessels, finally, like *miqva'oth*, are thought to be cultural indices of ritual purity concern (e.g., *m. Kelim* 10:1). These, not surprisingly, have been found in the wealthy area (Upper City) of ancient Jerusalem, at Qumran, and at Masada. They become social indices for political economy

---

44. Adan-Bayewitz and Perlman, "The Local Trade of Sepphoris in the Roman Period."

45. Polanyi et al., eds., *Trade and Market in the Early Empires*; Polanyi, *Livelihood*, 42–43, 126–42.

and political kinship contexts, i.e., they correlate well with the domiciles of the powerful or their agents.

Archaeology will have much to offer in the future for the social interpretation of Galilee. The interpretation of material artifacts is not exempt from the problems of textual interpretation. The interpreter has to have "some idea" of what is going on while approaching the material record. Social-systems modeling urges that archaeologists look for social indices that map social and economic structures and relations. As James F. Strange has noted, such modeling and interpretation will go hand in hand with work on the literary traditions.[46]

A PROPOSAL FOR THE SOCIAL INTERPRETATION OF JESUS

Conceptual models and archaeology can help to control the present discussion about the Jewishness (better: the Judean orientation) of Galilee and the meaning of the earliest Jesus movement. To this task we turn.

Burton Mack's recent analysis of Q provides a baseline for the ideas developed here.[47] He sees the earliest collection of Jesus' sayings in Galilee (Q^1, 40s CE) projecting an image of a cynic teacher. The Q tradents celebrate an ever-present kingdom of God through a playful, freedom-loving lifestyle. With the second stratum of Q (60s CE), clear marks of disappointment enter the picture. Besides the addition of material appealing to the "epic" tradition of Israel (Jonah, Solomon), Q^2 condemns "this generation" for rejecting the messages of John and Jesus, who are now envisioned in the line of Wisdom's emissaries. In Q^2, Jesus is understood in relationship to an imminent apocalyptic visit from the Son of Man. Q^3 completes the tradition before its assumption into the canonical Gospels of Luke and Matthew. In Q^3, Jesus quotes scripture to Satan and grieves over Jerusalem. Mack sees this stratum reflecting the aftermath of the Jewish-Roman war.

These results presuppose that Galilee, culturally speaking, was a highly Hellenized place and minimize the Judean orientation of Jesus. Mack indeed characterizes Galilee as a cosmopolitan area strongly permeated by Hellenistic culture.[48] He is also at pains to argue that "Judaism" in Galilee

46. Strange "Implications of Archaeology," 25.

47. Mack, *Lost Gospel.*

48. Ibid., chapter 4.

is like Samaritanism or Hellenized Judaism elsewhere. Only weak ties to Jerusalem or the temple are imagined.

This proposal can be evaluated as follows: It seems reasonable to say that some literate group, early on in urbanized northern Palestine, understood Jesus as a cynic sage. Mack and others have advanced arguments to make this perspective plausible.[49] However, this characterization has not shown that the historical Jesus is best understood in this way. Scholars like Freyne, Sanders, and Vermes raise important questions for Mack's portrait, because they see the historical Jesus in some definite relationship to the traditions of Israel. A further difficulty with Mack's theory: How could a so-thoroughly Hellenized Jesus and sayings-gospel be brought back so quickly into a certifiably Jewish domain in Q^2? What sociologically is going on? Why did not the Q tradition continue in its original "purely Hellenized" trajectory, so that Gospel of Thomas was its only legacy? This problem remains unresolved in Mack's presentation.

Mack rightly underscores, though, how difficult it may be to characterize the relationship between Jesus and Judaism. Jesus is not purely and simply a Judean, the way the Pharisees, Essenes, and Sadducees are Judeans. These three Judean groups known to us from Josephus, the Dead Sea Scrolls, and rabbinic traditions are all identifiable because of their intimate relationship to the temple. All three have measurable concerns for purity and for interpreting levitical traditions in Moses. The Jesus tradition shows uneasiness about simply fitting Jesus into temple and purity concerns without qualification. Crossan and Borg depict a Jesus in programmatic conflict with the temple system. The approach of Vermes is less persuasive in saying, e.g., that after the temple incident Jesus "calmed down" and remained temple-loyal, or that Jesus did not violate sabbath, food laws.[50]

As Mack observes, the Samaritans could give equal attention to Moses and no scholar today would call them "Jews." Should this designation be given to Galileans without further ado? Freyne and others have shown that *some* Galileans at least were devoted to the temple, if not overly to purity

49. Mack, *Lost Gospel*; Crossan, *Historical Jesus*, 72–88, 287–302; Vaage, *Galilean Upstarts*.

50. Vermes, *The Religion of Jesus the Jew*, 14 (after the temple incident Jesus "calmed down" and remained temple-loyal) and 22–26 (Jesus did not violate sabbath, food laws). Crossan *The Historical Jesus*, 322 shows a far more likely programmatic conflict with the temple system. Borg also lends strong support for a conflict perspective: *Conflict, Holiness and Politics in the Teachings of Jesus*; idem, *Jesus: A New Vision*; idem, "Portraits of Jesus."

concerns. Freyne has also suggested that some Galileans were descendants of Israelites.[51] Gary Rendsburg has proposed that "Israelians" continued in Galilee from 722 BCE through the time of the Mishnah, since there are clear linguistic contacts between Israelian Hebrew and Mishnaic Hebrew.[52] Second Chronicles 30 makes this suggestion quite persuasive, and it is an especially important text for the recognition of Israelians by Judeans at the time of Passover—a point we shall develop further.

We shall continue to call these Galileans "Jews," because of some measurable concern for both Jerusalem temple and Mosaic torah, with the proviso that we understand "Palestinian Judaism" in the first-century as a very broad and pluralistic designation and that we specify Jesus' Judaism in a way that does not fit neatly with Phariseeism, Essenism, or Sadduceeism. It is to a sketch of this relationship, and an attempt to account for why a Galilean Jew ends up crucified in Jerusalem, that we finally turn in this chapter.

Jesus and the Kingdom of God

Most recent Jesus studies have acknowledged Jesus' focus on "kingdom of God." For most of the twentieth century, the expression "kingdom of God" has been read against an apocalyptic Jewish background; in recent times that judgment has been contested.[53]

It seems remarkable in the light of our previously developed model that Jesus would pick a political metaphor to be central to his preaching.[54] As Jesus' articulation of non-elite Jewish aspirations in Galilee, it is our thesis that his central symbol signifies the removal of politics from the human plane, i.e., the elimination of political society entirely. The rule of God confers power to act differently, here and now, for the one who "enters it."

Crossan is surely correct in identifying healing and eating as central motifs of the Jesus movement. The exorcism of demons or the healing of bodies makes the kingdom real and present for the degraded, the

51. Freyne, *Galilee From Alexander the Great to Hadrian*, 38.

52. Rendsburg, "The Galilean Background of Mishnaic Hebrew," 227, 235.

53. Borg, "Portraits of Jesus," 1–2; Crossan *Historical Jesus*, 284, 292; Mack, *Lost Gospel*, 124; Evans, "From Public Ministry to the Passion"—all see a wisdom background. Sanders, "Jesus in Historical Context," 448, continues to hold out for the older Schweitzer view.

54. Horsley, *Jesus and the Spiral of Violence*, 170.

unclean, and the expendables (Lenski's bottom classes). These actions of Jesus represent not only healing of bodies but restoration of people to the community.[55]

Jesus' "open commensality," his eating with tax collectors, "sinners," and strangers, is surely one of the central metaphors for what kingdom means. The beautiful quote by Peter Brown sums up this connection to kingdom: "In the straitened Mediterranean, the kingdom of Heaven had to have something to do with food and drink."[56] As with the healing of bodies, so the feeding of people has to do centrally with community.

> Commensality was, rather, a strategy for building or rebuilding peasant community on radically different principles from those of honor and shame, patronage and clientage.[57]

However scholars may evaluate the last phrases—Bruce Malina would disagree on the "radically different principles"[58]—the emphasis on a communal outcome to feeding is very important. On these basic points, Crossan has offered very powerful arguments.

Concern for community in the historical Jesus undercuts the Mack approach in a fundamental way. For he (and those who would go along with him) sees "community formation" at a later point. Indeed, if Jesus was a cynic individualist, community formation was far from his aim. Mack's early Q stratum, then, offers support in his mind for a group of social dropouts. Crossan's instincts seem more to be correct, especially given that a Jewish Jesus will always imagine a community in response to God's reign.

We see, in terms of our elaborated model, that Jesus as an advocate of non-elite interests in Galilee envisions the emergence of an alternative social order under God's reign; this reign implies a community of fictive kinship. Its emergence, however, is hindered as long as the prevailing political order remains. There are indications in very ancient Jesus material of a critique of that political order.

55. Ibid.
56. Quoted in Crossan, *Historical Jesus*, 366.
57. Ibid., 344.
58. Malina, "Patron and Client."

Jesus' Critique of the Herodian-Judean Political Order

In the analysis by Crossan, Luke 9:57–58 is the only one of the so-called Son of Man sayings with multiple independent attestation. Crossan argues that the saying recollects an original Jesuanic idiom, when he occasionally used the semitic phrase to refer to humanity generally.[59] Crossan makes the prescient remark, "its meaning will demand much further context for final interpretation."[60]

This saying, in fact, makes eminent sense in a Galilean context. Its meaning within the formative stratum of Q could be used to support a cynic appreciation for natural living. In such a reading, foxes and birds would have their natural homes, but human beings have to build "un-natural dwellings." This gives a rather general sense to the *logion*, but one that might have been compelling to those who thought non-conformity meant a rejection of all social life.

A different reading emerges through familiarity with Jesus' old neighborhood. Nazareth stands near the location of ancient Sepphoris, Herod's capital city. Jesus is said to refer to Herod as "that fox" (Luke 13:31–33); Sepphoris derives from the Hebrew word for bird.[61] The natural image now receives a natural political referent: The "birds of the air," the Sepphoreans, control the villages and the product of the land. Such a reference to the elite receives support when one considers a saying of Tiberius Gracchus (Plutarch, *Tiberius Gracchus* 9.1)—a point first noticed by Arnold Toynbee.[62]

The large oil and wine presses, perhaps with their accompanying ritual baths, serve the elites. They are signs of the extraction of product, of its removal from profane or local use, and of its transfer far away. The tentacles of commercial Tyre and the temple system reach across the land. The Phoenician, Herodian, and Judean elites alike benefit from the Roman peace. The Herodian and Judean-oriented elite at Sepphoris have everything they need, but the ordinary person has nothing! The ordinary person meanwhile goes away hungry. "For to him who has will more be given; and from him who has not, even what he has will be taken away" (Mark 4:25 and par.). The *Foxes Have Holes* saying is critical of society, as

59. Crossan *Historical Jesus*, 255–56. Crossan includes this saying in Q¹ +1/2.
60. Ibid., 256.
61. Luke 13:32 is rated -3/1 by Crossan.
62. John Pairman Brown, "Prometheus, the Servant of Yahweh, Jesus," 113.

the Q tradents thought, but its original concern was blame of political society, not praise of nature.

A similar picture emerges from a study of Luke 16:1–7 (8). The steward (*oikonomos*) is situated somewhere within the political kinship structure of Jesus' Galilee. Perhaps the rich man lives in Sepphoris, while the steward oversees an estate in the fertile Beth Netofa Valley to the north. What hermeneutical possibilities does the systems perspective suggest for Luke 16:1–7 (8)?[63]

Here as in other parables of Jesus, the kingdom of God hovers behind the narrative. Does Jesus tell the story: 1) with sympathy for the master's interests and values? 2) to hold up the behavior of the steward as a negative or a positive example? 3) out of sympathy for the debtors?

Verse 8a, which is not considered by Crossan or Jeremias to be a part of the original parable of Jesus, would perhaps support hermeneutical Option 1 if included.[64] One possible reading of the parable in this form identifies the *kyrios* ("master," "lord") of verse 8 with the steward's master (verse 3). Scott advances literary arguments in favor of this identification.[65] Though the steward is labeled "dishonest" (*oikonomos tēs adikias*), the master finds the steward's shrewdness admirable. What the master particularly admires, we are probably to understand, is the steward's political wisdom; for by utilizing the master's resources yet once more to acquire a brood of clients, the steward's "benefactions" set him up royally for the near future.

This interpretation would overlook, however, the injury of the master's interests by the steward's behavior.[66] The following social consideration might urge that Jeremias is correct in rejecting v. 8 as a part of the original parable: The master typically would not have appreciated the steward's continuation of the ripoff. Columella (mid-first century) relates the advice of Cornelius Celsus (early first century):

63. Jeremias, *Parables*; Fitzmyer, "The Story of the Dishonest Manager (Luke 16:1–13)"; Scott, "Essaying the Rock"; and idem, *Hear Then the Parable*, 255–66, are basic for the following discussion. Crossan *Historical Jesus* does not discuss this parable, because it is not multiply attested. For one of the best discussions of the social import of this parable, see now Herzog, *Parables*, which came into my hands after this section on the Luke 16 parable had been completed. Herzog independently corroborates some of the conclusions reached here.

64. Crossan, *Sayings Parallels*, 17; Jeremias, *Parables*, 45–46.

65. Scott "Essaying the Rock, 38–41.

66. Kloppenborg, "The Dishonoured Master," 486.

> [Celsus] says that an [illiterate] overseer . . . brings money to his
> master oftener than he does his book, because, being illiterate, he
> is either less able to falsify accounts or is afraid to do so through a
> second party . . . .[67]

Matt 24:45–51/Luke 12:42–46 graphically depicts penalties for impropriety or malfeasance in a stewardship: The offending slave is cut in two (*dichotomeō*). Was the steward's meditation (Luke 16:3), therefore, designed to provoke laughter from Jesus' audience?[68] Kloppenborg sees rather the master on trial in the court of public opinion.[69]

It does not seem likely (at least to this writer) that Jesus' original intent was simply to evoke the audience's outrage or delight at the injury of the master's interests. Furthermore, it seems unlikely, on the basis of the previous considerations of this chapter, that Jesus told a simplistic morality story to justify the interests of the landlord class. Option 1, therefore, appears to be ruled out. In a similar vein, Jesus probably did not tell this parable strictly to hold the steward's action up for censure or blame (option 2a). Such a reading would only make sense from the master's point of view.

In favor of the view that Jesus portrays the steward as a hero (option 2b), Jeremias holds that verse 8a reflects a change of subject in the earliest Jesus tradition to bring out Jesus' own attitude toward the steward's behavior. In this reading, the Lord (Jesus) praises the shrewd action of the steward. The question then arises, what is praiseworthy about the steward's deed? Jeremias concludes simply that the steward acts resolutely in a crisis and that Jesus held this behavior up as exemplary in his eschatological message. Besides the objection that Jeremias' eschatological reading is outmoded, the trouble with this interpretation is that the hearer/reader of the parable is expected to suspend moral judgment on what transpires and to grasp simply that the "end" (the eschatological times) justifies the means (radical and apparently selfish behavior). The parable rather seems to invite moral judgment (in first-century terms) to come into play; the original hearers were undoubtedly captivated with the moral implications of such a story.[70]

---

67. Quoted from Lewis and Reinhold, eds., *Roman Civilization*, 171.
68. Scott, *Hear Then the Parable*, 263 has a similar idea.
69. Kloppenborg, "The Dishonoured Master," 489.
70. See also Danker, *Jesus and the New Age*, 173.

Proceeding to option 3, we might expect Jesus to be sympathetic to the victims of this story, namely, the people who were under both the master's and the steward's power. Jesus, of peasant origins, shared the values and outlook of the Palestinian peasantry to some extent. He took interest in the plight of victims.[71] The two central characters in Luke 16:1–8 are beneficiaries of the Galilean political economy that disenfranchised and disinherited so many small peasants. What does the parable mean when viewed from the underside of Jesus' society?

The nature and value of the debts involved in the story need to be discussed. The significance of the debt remission also requires consideration.

Jeremias offers the following suggestion about the nature of the debts:

> The debtors . . . are either tenants who have to deliver a specified portion (a half, a third, or a quarter) of the yield of their land in lieu of rent, or wholesale merchants, who have given promissory notes for goods received.[72]

Jeremias correctly sees private debts here. We are not to think of a public debt; the parable presents a different social situation from the one envisioned in Matt 18:23–34. On the other hand, it is probably unlikely that wholesale merchants are involved; the items in the Lukan text would more likely be "exported" from the estate by merchant middlemen in exchange for silver coinage.

That the debtors are tenants seems the most likely scenario. Are these then individual tenants? Examining the value of the debts may help to decide here. Jeremias, on the basis of the work of Dalman and others, thinks that 100 cors of wheat is the yield of 100 acres or 550 cwt. (= 27 short tons or 25 metric tons). An independent calculation, finds that 100 cors is 30 metric tons, over 1000 bushels of wheat, and the yield of 99.5 acres.[73] The *Mishnah* attests rents in the 10 cor per annum range (*m. B. Meṣ.* 9:7–10). The likelihood is that few small cultivators, who undoubtedly comprised the majority of tenants in early first-century Palestine, could have been responsible for the rent of 100 acres. Most tenants (and their families)

71. See my discussion of the Good Samaritan story, "Was Jesus a Peasant?" (chapter 12 above).

72. Jeremias, *Parables*, 181.

73. Using the computer program at the end of Oakman, *Jesus and the Economic Questions of His Day.*

farmed between 5 to 10 acres—a fact suggested by the late first-century report about the land holdings of Jesus' relatives: When summoned before Domitian, these relatives claimed 39 *plethra* (1 *plethron* = either 0.5 or 1 *iugerum* = either 0.3 or 0.6 acre; 39 *plethra* = either 6 or 12 acres) between two families.[74] Similarly, Jeremias notes that 100 baths of oil were the product of 146 olive trees or nearly 4000 liters of oil. Based upon the measurements in Adan-Bayewitz and Perlman, a typical Galilean storage jar held about 15 liters. 100 baths would amount to 267 jars of oil.[75] A typical peasant family probably could not care for so many trees or have so many jars of oil, but a village certainly could.

Hence, these debtors are representatives of tenant villages paying the (annual?) rent assessed against former village lands now part of a large estate somewhere in Galilee. The representatives, like the *kōmogrammateis* in early Hellenistic Palestine (Zenon Papyri), were the village tax accountants responsible to the landlord for the entire village obligation. As the story clearly indicates, these persons were literate (Luke 16:7).

How much were the debts worth? Jeremias calculates that the 100 cors of wheat were worth 2500 *denarii* and the 100 baths of oil, 1000 *denarii*, but since "oil was dearer than wheat" he sees a rough equality between the debt remissions.[76] In Galilee, the presumed original setting for Jesus' parable, the price of oil was extremely variable, because of the prevalence of olive orchards. The evidence for oil prices in Josephus and in rabbinic material indicates a fairly large range between the times oil was plentiful and the times oil was dear. A *denarius* might buy anything between 2 and 40 liters of oil.[77] Hence, Jeremias cannot be so sure that oil was dearer than wheat in the Galilean context. He is correct in saying that for both cases large debts were involved.

If this reading of the type of debt is correct, these debts were a heavy burden upon the local villages and representative of the changing social situation under the Romans. Not only were the debts burdensome, but their nature implies significant loss of local control over the product of the

74. Further discussion in Oakman, *Jesus and the Economic Questions of His Day*, 61; see also Fiensy *Social History of Palestine*, 93–95.

75. Adan-Bayewitz and Perlman "Local Trade of Sepphoris," 165.

76. Jeremias, *Parables*, 181.

77. Heichelheim, "Roman Syria," 184–85 conveniently gathers the major literary source material. Calculation again done with the computer program in Oakman, *Jesus and the Economic Questions of His Day*.

land. The reduction of the peasants' ties to the overlord to a relationship of economic exploitation would produce a great deal of resentment (Mark 12:1–12).

Does the steward's strategy of debt remission lead to a tactical power gain or is a fundamental change of relationship between the steward-enforcer of the political economy and the debtors envisioned? These two interpretive sub-options of hermeneutical Option 3 need to be explored for a moment.

There does not seem to be any indication within Jesus' narrative that the steward is in fact repentant of his former behaviors and that now a truly new behavior is in view. This consideration speaks against Fitzmyer's interpretation. He follows Derrett in thinking that the steward has simply foregone usury.[78] Kloppenborg provides additional arguments against these views.[79] The steward continues in his former behavior of embezzlement and acts in his own interests with the two debt remissions. Furthermore, as has been suggested already, the steward's self-interested benefactions put the debtors in his debt. Gift-giving in the ancient Mediterranean world brought with it the expectation of reciprocity; to give to someone else obligated them.[80] Surely the meaning of Jesus' similitude preserved by Luke at 11:5–8 hangs upon the same social assumption: A villager may not get up at midnight to provide for someone because he is a friend, but to keep the other in debt he certainly will. The meaning of the word *anaideian*, upon which this interpretation is hinged, is disputed, but the Egyptian papyri strongly urge the meaning "shameless desire for personal gain." The "friend" will make a loan at midnight on this basis.

The steward obviously counts on certain effects to follow his debt remission scheme. He is sure that his new friends will "welcome me into their houses" (v. 4). His tactics carefully demonstrate his new-found affections. He does not tell the debtors what they owe the master, as might be expected from the master's plenipotentiary, but asks each debtor what they owe. These presumably give a "low estimate." Then, the steward underbids even that low estimate. Finally, the debtors themselves are told to write their own contract. Would this be the normal course, or another opportunity for further reductions? The debtors are in his power, albeit

---

78. Fitzmyer, "Dishonest Manager," 176–77.
79. Kloppenborg, "Dishonoured Master," 481–86.
80. Discussion in Malina, *New Testament World*, 101, 103, and hint on 115.

a different kind of power than formerly. Malina and Rohrbaugh see the master also within the power of the steward, because the master's honor is also increased within the community by the steward's actions. The master cannot but praise the steward. Hence, Malina and Rohrbaugh find a good cultural reason to retain v. 8 as part of the original parable. Their interpretation, however, deflects attention slightly from the socio-political implications of the story.[81]

It is not easy to see how this message coalesces with Jesus' overall message of the kingdom of God. Perhaps the key to a genuinely new option within the situation lies in seeing the core element of debt forgiveness. The peasantry view the debt collection as "theft" and unjust. Rigorous enforcement of debt collection led to violence (again Mark 12:1–12). The story suggests that if folks can lower the debts even a little bit, and can live as friends—even if not under strictly mutual obligation—then the Galilean situation can improve, if only infinitesimally.

In reference to the kingdom, there is implied here a "lesser to the greater" moral argument. If the steward's dishonest personal machinations can have beneficial social effects, how much more will the debt forgiveness accomplish that is practiced under the conviction of the imminence of God's reign? Jesus is fascinated with the community-building possibilities of debt remission.[82] The story of Zacchaeus (Luke 19:1–10) also recalls this fascination. Kloppenborg considers the "swerve" in v. 8 to signify that the master is "'laughing' at his own honour and at the honour-shame codes with which the story has operated."[83] This interpretation is striking, but—like Malina and Rohrbaugh's—only indirectly offers critique of social-structural dynamics.

Jesus' story contains humor, irony, social critique, and the suggestion of new possibilities all rolled into one. While the original meaning remains uncertain, a combination of steward as hero and debt remission as a moral good gives the most satisfying result, since the parable focuses on the behavior of the steward but has implications for the debtors as well. Jesus' parable envisions the "conversion" of the political enforcers

81. Malina and Rohrbaugh, *Social-Science Commentary*, 373–75.

82. For further discussion of debt forgiveness, see Oakman, *Jesus and the Economic Questions of His Day*, 149–56. Herzog (*Parables*), though he contextualizes the parable scene somewhat differently, sees similar dynamics and suggests that the parable's import lies in the forgiveness of debts.

83. Kloppenborg, "The Dishonoured Master," 492.

of the Galilean economy to the alternate social order of fictive kinship under God's rule. With the undermining of enforcement or attraction of members of the enforcer (political kinship) class to his movement, Jesus was certainly going to come to the attention of the authorities and become a marked man.

The Galilean Life of Jesus and His Judean Death

Important suggestions have been offered recently about the relationship between Jesus' Galilean life and Judean death.[84] Mack, Miller, Seeley, and Crossan see the canonical passion narratives as substantially literary fictions, though Jesus' death in Jerusalem is accepted as fact.[85] Yet Mack's and Crossan's general views seem unable to account persuasively for the Judean interest of a Galilean "cynic" or for his death at the hands of the Jerusalem elite. Why would a cynic Jesus go to Jerusalem or be killed by the elite? Evans, rejecting Mack's "accidental" view, sees in Jesus' execution as "King of the Jews" a move to stop his proclamation of God's kingdom.[86]

While claims about historical fiction writing deserve serious consideration (the presence of creative elements in the passion narrative is indubitable), there are discernable weaknesses in them also. Refined tradition critical inquiries should be done, of course. But is it reasonable to see wholesale creation of crucial details, entirely unconstrained by communal memory? Crossan's insight into the general character of such creative work—that creative process and event are generally and substantively interrelated—can restrict radically deconstructive readings and help to recover the essential meaning of Jesus' death in relation to Passover.

Furthermore, important assumptions are made in specific arguments about historical fiction that deserve careful scrutiny. For instance, Miller's claim that Jesus' temple action is "implausible" rests upon the assumption that immediate arrest should have ensued.[87] Josephus recounts, though, that Jesus, son of Ananias, cried woe against the temple for seven years and five months, despite occasional arrest and opposition (*War* 6.302, 308;

---

84. Evans, "From Public Ministry to the Passion," supplies the title for this final section. I have also been stimulated by Evans, "Jesus' Action in the Temple"; and Richardson, "Why Turn the Tables," papers to which I responded at national meetings.

85. Mack, *A Myth of Innocence*; Robert J. Miller, "The (A)Historicity of Jesus' Temple Demonstration"; Seeley, "Jesus' Temple Act"; Crossan, *Jesus: A Revolutionary Biography*.

86. Evans, "From Public Ministry to the Passion."

87. Miller, "Jesus' Temple Demonstration," 248.

cf. Acts 4–5). Theissen's observation still retains force: The elites' concern over popular sentiment protected Jesus of Nazareth from immediate arrest.[88] Horsley has a variant of this view.[89] On another issue, Seeley simply assumes with E. P. Sanders and Jacob Neusner that all Jews in Jesus' day looked upon the Jerusalem temple as an "indispensable" and legitimate institution.[90] In light of the Elephantine papyri, the Egyptian temple of Onias IV (Josephus, *Ant.* 13.63), or even Qumran (Temple Scroll), this is clearly false for the Second Temple period.

Manifestly, Passover could become the focal point for alternative visions. In late Israelite times, observance of Passover clearly had political significance. Josiah's reform emphasized a centrally observed Passover service, probably as a potent symbol of liberation from Assyrian power (2 Kgs 23:21–23). During the Persian period, Passover was seen as an important time of pilgrimage in support of Judean interests (2 Chr 30). Passover had clearly political overtones during the Hellenistic period (Ezekiel the Tragedian), but liberation themes were coopted by elite interests.[91]

For the early Roman period, it is instructive to work through Josephus' explicit references to the Passover feast in order to make a judgment about his understanding of it. His usual habit is to characterize Passover by "the feast of unleavened bread" (*War* 2.10, 224, 244; 4.402; *not* 6.423; *Ant.* 18.90 or 20.106). It is at this feast that Archelaus slaughters those protesting Herod's murder of the men who had torn down the golden eagle (*War* 2.10; *Ant.* 17.213). Under Cumanus, a soldier's unseemly gesture leads to a riot (*War* 2.224; *Ant.* 20.106). Crossan notes that this event nearly provokes the Jewish-Roman war twenty years prematurely. Quadratus the Syrian Legate has to visit Jerusalem.[92] Likewise, Vitellius (*Ant.* 18.90) and Gallus visit Jerusalem at this feast (*War* 2.280). The Sicarii act at this time to raid Engeddi (*War* 4.402). John murders the partisans of Eleazar at the feast (*War* 5.99). It was at this time that omens appeared in the temple (*War* 6.290). And it is at this time that the catastrophic war against Rome broke out (*War* 6.421). Josephus makes it clear that Passover was a volatile time of year in Jerusalem.

88. Theissen, "Die Tempelweissagung Jesu," 149; cf. Mark 14:2.

89. Horsley, *Jesus and the Spiral of Violence*, 298.

90. Seeley, "Jesus' Temple Act," 265.

91. Finkelstein, "The Oldest Midrash"; idem, "Pre-Maccabean Documents in the Passover Haggadah" (2 parts).

92. Crossan, *Historical Jesus*, 184.

Antiquities 3.248 describes the institution of the *Pascha* sacrifice, "see-ing that in this month we were delivered from bondage to the Egyptians." This is as much as Josephus ever says about its meaning; he never explic-itly links Passover with contemporary aspirations. Both *Jewish War* and *Antiquities* emphasize that the people participate in the sacrifice *in groups* (*War* 6.423; *Ant.* 3.248).

The Samaritans desecrate the temple at Passover time (*Ant.* 18.30). This act is not simply a hostile jab against Judaism, but occurs after Judea (and Samaria in train) has become a Roman province (in the governorship of Coponius, 6–9 CE). Here the Samaritans perform a symbolic action in response to the perceived betrayal of the Mosaic tradition. A chapel of the Emperor is no better than a chapel of Pharaoh!

Passover is not mentioned at all in *Against Apion*. Here Josephus is content to counter the slanders of Manetho about the Exodus, the purpose of which in Josephus' mind was to found Jerusalem and the temple (*Ag. Ap.* 1.228). This probably states the normative meaning for the Jerusalem elite. Liberation readings of the Exodus are downplayed. Though it is a difficult fact to document directly, non-elites understand the liberation implications in the light of their own situation (just as African slaves in America). With the help of Josephus, Crossan can point to the several ma-gicians or prophet figures who led people into the wilderness to relive the conquest of the land.[93] Josephus, of course, downplays their significance and popularity. Nevertheless, these figures are important signs of libera-tion readings of Moses among the non-elites in Judea.

Surprisingly therefore, Brandon and Hengel make little of a Passover concern among the Zealots.[94] Hengel's statement,

> One can look in vain in the Old Testament, in the Book of Ecclesiasticus and in the Qumran documents for an equivalent to the Greek term *eleutheria* in its purely political meaning.
>
> The first appearance of the Hebrew concept for 'freedom' that can be precisely dated occurs significantly enough at the time of the Jewish War, when we find the word *hērûth* [on coins of the Jewish War][95]

---

93. Crossan, *Historical Jesus*, 160–67.
94. Brandon, *Jesus and the Zealots*; Hengel, *The Zealots*.
95. Hengel, *The Zealots*, 116.

is too narrowly focused on the linguistic evidence, ignoring important information about Passover disturbances in Josephus. Besides, the appearance of the word *hôrîn* in the Aramaic introduction to the Passover Haggadah is likely in a pre-70 tradition (see below). Hengel is nevertheless aware of what is at stake: "As soon as Israel's freedom came to be based, in the Haggadah, on the liberation from Egypt, the political question came to the surface . . . ."[96]

The Fourth Philosophy, "founded" by Judas of Gamala at the time of Judea's incorporation into the Roman provincial system (and of the census of Quirinius), had a simple tenet: God is the only Lord, and to pay Roman taxes was to admit to slavery. This was a radical reading of the implications of Exod 20:1–3 for the Galilean-Golan Jewish situation under the early empire. Later, Gamala was to make a desperate last stand against Titus (*War* 4.70–83). Horsley gives some account of the relationship between Judas and Exodus.[97]

And Horsley alone of our interpreters sees Jesus in relationship to Passover. He makes this connection several times without drawing the conclusion we are drawing.[98] He explicitly denies, though, that Jesus' frequent festive meals can be explained by the once-a-year Jewish Passover meal.[99]

Jesus' Death (However It Occurred) and Passover

Our model and previous discussion prompt us at last to explore how Jesus' non-elite vision coheres with the basic tradition of Israel. After benedictions, the Passover Seder begins:

> This is the bread of poverty which our forefathers ate in the land of Egypt. Let all who are hungry enter and eat; let all who are needy come to our Passover feast. This year we are here; next year may we be in the Land of Israel. This year we are slaves; next year may we be free men.[100]

---

96. Ibid., 119.

97. Horsley, *Jesus and the Spiral of Violence*, 82–83.

98. Ibid., 45, 50, 82, 93, 155, especially 189 (discussion of allusion to Exod 8:19 in Luke 11:20), and 300.

99. Ibid., 179.

100. Glatzer, ed., *The Passover Haggadah*, 20–21, conveniently supplies pointed text, English translation, and notes.

Segal makes no firm judgment on the antiquity of this part of the Haggadah, though he refers to Finkelstein's views that portions of the Haggadah are pre-70 CE.[101] Finkelstein makes no explicit statement about the Aramaic introduction, but sees pre-Maccabean material in the sections immediately following.[102] These, he stresses, make political accommodations to Ptolemaic or Seleucid sensitivities. Bokser, uninterested in political understandings of Passover, sees a great deal of anachronistic retrojection in the Seder.[103]

Glatzer regards the Aramaic introduction as beginning "one of the oldest parts of the Haggadah."[104] In light of a well known liturgical principle, the switch from Hebrew to Aramaic conservatively repristinates the ordinary speech of the Second Temple period. Especially important is the late-Hebrew word *ḥôr*. It referred originally to the elite of Judah (1 Kgs 21:8, 11; Jer 27:20; Neh 2:16; 4:8, 13; 5:7; 6:17; 7:5; 13:17). *Pace* Hengel, the Hebrew or Aramaic plural of the word following *bên* can represent the abstract noun.[105] It is assumed in the following, therefore, that the Aramaic introduction to the Passover Seder was known in similar (if not identical) form to the Jewish Jesus.

Crossan takes pains to show that Jesus' message, like cynicism, urges voluntary poverty, freedom, and kingdom. The freedom of the cynic philosopher grows out of his self-sufficiency. In this, the cynic finds freedom from social convention. As a free individualist, the cynic is his own king "Notice, in the flow of that passage [in Epictetus], the sequence from 'nothing' to 'free' to 'king,' the logic of poverty leading to freedom leading to royalty."[106] This is highly suggestive for the interpretation of Jesus, with his proclamation of kingdom, but Crossan (and Mack) decontextualize a Jewish Jesus in order to make the cynic philosophical connection.

The Aramaic introduction to the Passover Haggadah, as the more likely basis for making these points, shows that poverty (and its alleviation!), rule (over land), and freedom are equally hallmarks of Israelite-Jewish consciousness. Jesus leaves the issue of rule to God. He and his

101. Segal, *The Hebrew Passover*, 241.

102. Finkelstein, "Pre-Rabbinic Ideals and Teachings in the Passover Haggadah," and "Pre-Maccabean Documents in the Passover Haggadah."

103. Bokser, "Unleavened Bread and Passover, Feasts of," 764.

104. Glatzer, *Passover Haggadah*, 20.

105. GKC §124 d, e; BDB, 121, s. v. *bên* 8.

106. Crossan, *Historical Jesus*, 79.

followers practice domestic economy (eating) and religion (healing, "sons," "freedom") in response. Horsley thus appropriately links God's "politics" with feasting, healing, and freedom. Central in Jesus' strategy is fictive kinship, which Horsley calls "Renewal of Local Community."[107]

Furthermore, the Beatitudes, among the oldest and best Jesus traditions are concerned with just these matters. Consider the following table:

PASSOVER HAGGADAH	BEATITUDES
The bread of poverty	How honorable are you poor
Let all who are hungry	How honorable are the hungry
This year we are here	How honorable are those who mourn

The last element of the Aramaic introduction holds the words, "next year may we be free men" (*benê hôrîn*, lit. "sons of freedom"). In Matt 17:25–26 Jesus tells Peter, in relation to the temple tax, that "sons are free." In terms of Jesus' program of domestic religion, the alternate social order ("kingdom") of God does not involve political taxation as the Judean temple does. Horsley comes close to saying this: Jesus' temple action and words announce God's judgment against the Herodian temple-system. Jesus' vision grows out of the foundation story of Israel.[108]

In discussing Jesus' meal practices, Crossan claims:

> We have moved from, first, open commensality during the lifetime of Jesus through, second, general eucharistic meal without and then with a bread and wine (cup) emphasis and on, third, to specific passion remembrance, celebration, and participation.[109]

This judgment needs reconsideration. Crossan reaches it in a series of steps by asserting that Jesus' "open eating": 1) followed the standard Greco-Roman meal pattern of food/drink, 2) was not a distinctive sort of meal, 3) is still reflected apart from a Last Supper/Passover connection in *Didache* 10, and 4) only later was ritualized as such by Paul (1 Cor 11) and Mark (14).[110]

Crossan's case hinges on separating *Didache* 9–10. Kept together, these sections contain elements of a Jewish Passover meal with cup and

---

107. Horsley, *Jesus and the Spiral of Violence*, 170, 178 (feasting), 181 (healing), 188 (freedom); chapters 8–9 (community).

108. Ibid., 288, 300.

109. Crossan, *Historical Jesus*, 365.

110. Ibid., 360–64.

blessings before and after the meal.[111] The cup was the first element blessed (Greek: *eucharisteō*) in the Passover rite (*Did.* 9:1–2). The blessing of bread preceded the Passover meal proper (*Did.* 9:3; 10:1). Another blessing followed the meal, in conjunction with the third cup of wine, i.e., the "cup of blessing." This thanksgiving would properly dwell upon God's creative power and the gift of food and drink for humanity (*Did.* 10:3). Jeremias discussed *Didache* 9–10, but missed its real significance.[112] He thought it showed the separation of Lord's Supper from an Agape meal.

What it really shows is the consistent practice (Paul, Mark, *Didache*) of eating Jesus' meal as a Passover meal whenever (1 Cor 11:26) it was eaten! Crossan, downplaying Jesus' Jewishness as he does, has neglected to consider that Jesus' open table was founded upon the Passover meal and understood in that light even in Galilee. Saldarini and Behm insist that the Passover meal had to be eaten in Jerusalem.[113] They do not consider the political nature of this requirement: Exod 12:46 presumes household rites. Deut 16:2 is understood in later tradition, e.g., Tob 1:6, to refer to Jerusalem; Exod 23:15, 17 had not been so specific. Segal's discussion shows that *Jubilees* (49:16, 21) stresses the requirement to eat in Jerusalem, while Ezekiel the Tragedian does not mention it.[114] Thus, Mark 14 can be "true" as "process to event," recollecting Jesus' customary practice of (daily) Passover remembrance.

We are now in a position to summarize our proposal: If, as Evans argues and Crossan seems to accept, the death of Jesus was contingent upon his Galilean activity, we can now say that Jesus' Galilean table practices also included Passover bread and wine celebrations. That is, Jesus' meal-sharing was shaped at every point during his Galilean life by his understanding of the root tradition of Israel; therefore, even if early Christian process has shaped the passion narrative especially at the point of Last Supper, that process had to have included Jesus' understanding of his own tradition. This makes great sense if other northern Jews, like Judas of Gamala, understood their tradition as a liberation tradition. Therefore, the interpretations of Passover attributed to Jesus ("this bread is my body," "this wine is my blood of the covenant") should preeminently be understood as

111. Behm, "*klaō, ktl.*," 732–37; Jeremias, *Eucharistic Words*.

112. Jeremias, *Eucharistic Words*, 117–18.

113. Saldarini, *Jesus and Passover*, 32; Behm, "*klaō, ktl.*," 734.

114. Segal, *Hebrew Passover*, 20–25; Ezekiel the Tragedian, see Charlesworth, *OTP* 2: 815–16.

significations of the inner meaning of his Galilean activity. His healing as a social symbolization as well as his eating as a reconstitution of peasant community were both contributions to the covenant community that the Moses tradition evoked.

Jesus, therefore, is best not read against Judean levitical traditions. He was not as Schweitzer thought an apocalyptic prophet or a messianic futurist. Messiahs and apocalyptic prophets were Judean preoccupations. Samaritanism, the Fourth Philosophy, and Jesus' own Galilean Judaism found their fullest theological context within Exodus, not within Leviticus.

Systems thinking, a concern for archaeological social indices, and criticism of the Jesus traditions converge on the same interpretive result: The non-elite, Galilean Jesus made sense within broader Israelite tradition, was opposed to Herodianism and priestly Judeanism in Galilee on a principled basis, and finally went to his death for the sake of Passover freedom. Jesus' brief but enormously influential career might reasonably be understood as a non-elite midrash upon Israel's foundational story.

CHAPTER 16

Jesus the Tax Resister[1]

> Whenever you enter a town and they receive you, eat what is set before you; heal the sick in it and say to them, "The kingdom of God has come near to you." Q[1] 10:8–9

> Release us from debt, as we release those in debt to us. Q[1] 11:3

INTRODUCTION

IN CHAPTER 14 ON the Lord's Prayer, I attempted to state the original meaning of the prayer of Jesus and trace how the concrete material concerns of Jesus became abstract theological concerns of the later scribal tradents of the Jesus material and gospels. I argued that Jesus' prayer, presumably very closely tied to key interests behind his historical activity, articulated three concrete concerns in hunger, debt, and suborned justice. These were seen as internally related through the social situation of the early Jesus movement.[2]

Left undone in that essay, and continued here, is a more thorough investigation of the relationship between the concrete concerns of Jesus and earliest Q. As I suggested over a decade ago:

> literate followers of Jesus recorded and arranged his words. For these followers, whose literacy and experience moved them to a greater or lesser degree out of the predominately oral culture of

---

1. This chapter was originally delivered as a paper to the Q Section, at the National Meeting of the AAR/SBL, Denver, CO, November 2001. Several elements of the chapter were subsequently included in two public lectures in 2003 and 2004; those were published as "The Radical Jesus: You Cannot Serve God and Mammon."

2. "The Lord's Prayer in Social Perspective" (chapter 14 above).

the countryside, the meaning of the tradition shifted. Speaking from a different social "place," these early traditors [sic!] perceived the meaning of Jesus' appearance and words in more abstract and general terms (e.g. in relationship to the destiny of the whole people of Israel or as an appeal to the wise). . . . Yet as has been noted by others, the Jesus tradition is one of the few extant from antiquity where the "interface" between the ancient expressions of the lower classes in the countryside and the records of the literate is still relatively close.[3]

Abstract theological interests surely are at work in Q^1, but this tradition-stratum is as close as we get in a consistent body of early literary material to the historical interests and praxis of Jesus. The situation for a critical social appraisal of Q and Jesus is now stronger with the appearance of Kloppenborg Verbin's important book *Excavating Q* and *The Critical Edition of Q* from the International Q Project.[4]

As well, James C. Scott's comparative political studies of peasantry are increasingly appreciated in helping to articulate the meaning of Jesus.[5] Scott offers us a passage in *Domination and the Arts of Resistance* that will underwrite the explorations of this paper:

Malay paddy farmers, in the region in which I have conducted fieldwork, have resented paying the official Islamic tithe. It is collected inequitably and corruptly, the proceeds are sent to the provincial capital, and not a single poor person in the village has even received any charity back from the religious authorities. Quietly and massively, the Malay peasantry has managed to nearly dismantle the tithe system so that only 15 percent of what is formally due is actually paid. There have been no tithe riots, demonstrations, protests, only a patient and effective nibbling in a multitude of ways: fraudulent declarations of the amount of land farmed, simple failures to declare land, underpayment, and delivery of paddy spoiled by moisture or contaminated with rocks and mud to increase its weight.[6]

3. Oakman, "Rulers' Houses," orig. 110 (chapter 10 above).

4. Kloppenborg [Verbin], *Excavating Q*; Robinson, Hoffmann, and Kloppenborg, editors, *Critical Edition of Q*.

5. See Crossan, *Historical Jesus*; idem, *The Birth of Christianity*; Herzog, *Jesus, Justice, and the Reign of God*.

6. Scott, *Weapons of the Weak*, 89.

Recent Q studies and Scott's concept of peasant resistance help us to focus on certain basic facts about the early Jesus tradition. Q studies analyze the early sayings tradition into earlier and a later strata. We get even closer to the context in which Jesus' sayings were presumably translated from Aramaic and preserved, with attendant interests. Peasant resistance ("fraudulent declarations of the amount of land farmed, simple failures to declare land, underpayment, and delivery of paddy spoiled by moisture or contaminated with rocks and mud to increase its weight") provides a useful category to elucidate Jesus' activity.

This chapter pursues the thesis that Jesus advocated tax resistance as a concrete expression of the "kingdom of God." Jesus' historical activity attempted to facilitate the "eminent domain of God" by brokering the remission of debts and taxes through subversive resistance measures. He brokered remission by bringing together tax collector and tax payer in an attempt to alleviate tax burdens, by advocating dissimulation in representations of the tax situation (including manipulation of debt records), and by focusing his followers' praxis through prayer for such relief. For such reasons, Jesus would become a marked man in the eyes of the elites. The expected form of punishment meted out to tax resisters was crucifixion.

Jesus of Nazareth and Judas of Gamala

According to Josephus, the tax arrangements of the Roman imperium implemented when Judea became a Roman province in 6 CE were met with stiff resistance. Judas of Gamala (in Gaulanitis, the present-day Golan Heights to the east of the Galilean lake) and a certain Zaddok the Pharisee, insisting that there is no God but God and that paying taxes to Rome is a sign of servitude, advocated armed resistance.

> But a certain Judas, a Gaulanite from a city named Gamala, who had enlisted the aid of Saddok, a Pharisee, threw himself into the cause of rebellion. They said that the assessment carried with it a status amounting to downright slavery, no less, and appealed to the nation to make a bid for independence. (Josephus, *Ant.* 18.4 [Feldman, LCL])

> As for the fourth of the philosophies, Judas the Galilean set himself up as leader of it. This school agrees in all other respects with the opinions of the Pharisees, except that they have a passion for liberty that is almost unconquerable, since they are convinced

that God alone is their leader and master. (Josephus, *Ant.* 18.23 [Feldman, LCL])

The thesis that Jesus was a "zealot" or an armed insurrectionist, propounded by S. G. F. Brandon a generation ago, has been successfully questioned by Morton Smith, Richard Horsley, and others. However, one cannot but be struck by the proximity of Judas and Jesus, and the similarity of their messages. At the time of the census, Jesus would have been about ten years old and living only about 30 miles from Gamala. Moreover during the time of his historical activity, Jesus spent most of his time in the environs of the Galilean lake. Capernaum is within eyesight of Gamala, and vice versa.

That the central message of Jesus of Nazareth was the "kingdom of God" (in conventional translation) is among the most solidly accepted historical facts about him. The meaning of this term has been extensively debated over the years, but its similarity to the message of Judas and Zaddok has not gone unnoticed. Jesus of Nazareth was equally concerned about debt as Q^1 11:3 shows. An examination of very early Jesus traditions will demonstrate this to be a pervasive concern. Before turning to that task, though, some words are needed about the taxation system in Roman Galilee.

THE TAXATION SYSTEM IN ROMAN GALILEE

This section will eventually argue, though our evidence is more indirect than direct, that the client taxation system of Roman Galilee was burdensome and resented at the village level. The anti-tax sentiments of Judas attracted the notice of Josephus, a Judean writer; Josephus also mentions Jesus of Nazareth, but not in regard to taxation. One might urge, as does E. P. Sanders, that there was no taxation problem under the client rule of Herod Antipas. Sanders goes so far as to claim Antipas a "good tetrarch" and taxes at the time not "exorbitant."[7]

Obviously, the argument of this paper depends on an understanding of the impact of taxation in early Roman Palestine. Was it light and socially innocuous, or burdensome so as become an object of resistance? Several basic approaches have been taken. Lists of taxes have been compiled, and investigations of taxes (for instance) in Josephus conducted. Such is the approach of Sanders' student Fabian E. Udoh. After investigating "the evi-

7. E. P. Sanders, *The Historical Figure of Jesus*, 21.

dence" for early Roman period taxation (especially under Pompey, Julius Caesar, Herod, and the Judean temple), Udoh can make claims such as,

> The figures which Josephus gives for the income projected for Herod's successors are, we argued, inaccurate; nor is it clear how the revenues were broken up, for instance into direct and indirect taxes. It results that in spite of the sums which Josephus gives for Herod Antipas' annual income, we still cannot determine how he raised the revenues and how the Jews in Galilee were affected by the taxes he imposed from 4 B.C.E. to circa 39 C.E. And very little can be said of taxes under the *praefecti*.[8]

Udoh is convinced that Herod the Great, Herod Antipas' father, "opened the Jewish state to opportunities" and established "economic prosperity"; further, that "Herod's taxes were not as ruinous to his kingdom as is usually assumed."[9] Udoh in this follows the general lines of Sanders. He concludes that taxation levels and economic factors do not account for political developments in early Roman Palestine; these are left to vaguely specified ideological and political factors.

The older approach to taxation of Frederick C. Grant remains influential. Grant saw two competing tax systems up to 70 CE in Roman Palestine—the imperial and the temple. Since these operated somewhat independently, Grant saw their net effect as burdensome.[10]

Neither of these approaches incorporates the results of comparative social science. Studies of Lenski, Kautsky, and Sjøberg have been very influential lately in rethinking the social impact of taxation in agrarian contexts. Lists cannot begin to elucidate the social dynamics of agrarian taxation; competing social groups gets us closer to the truth. In my doctoral dissertation I incorporated such comparative perspectives, in addition to Eric Wolf's notions about the impact of exactions on peasant subsistence, to see a cultivator living on the edge. Subsistence and consumption needs were endangered in early Roman Palestine, and the appearance of overt revolts (4 BCE, 6 CE, 66 CE) and banditry corroborates. What lists and competing systems (of factions) cannot show, though, is the positive feedback arrangement of agrarian tax systems. Such systems do not have checks and balances to protect the cultivator.

Methodologically, a simple model will illustrate:

8. Udoh, "Tribute and Taxes in Early Roman Palestine," 335.
9. Ibid., 336.
10. Grant, *Economic Background of the Gospels*.

Figure 23: System of Taxation in Roman Palestine

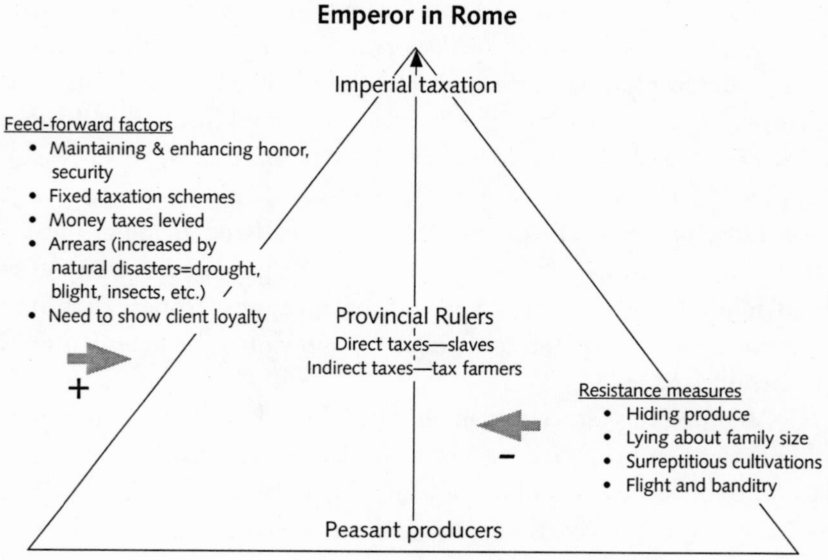

Emperor in Rome

Imperial taxation

Feed-forward factors
- Maintaining & enhancing honor, security
- Fixed taxation schemes
- Money taxes levied
- Arrears (increased by natural disasters=drought, blight, insects, etc.)
- Need to show client loyalty

+

Provincial Rulers
Direct taxes—slaves
Indirect taxes—tax farmers

Resistance measures
- Hiding produce
- Lying about family size
- Surreptitious cultivations
- Flight and banditry

–

Peasant producers

BRIEF EXPLANATION OF THE DIAGRAM:

Provincial elites must meet imperial demands for produce as well as demonstrate client loyalty; patron-client relations levy significant burdens (Augustus–Herod the Great); direct taxes collected by slaves (*oikonomoi*), indirect taxes collected through tax farming arrangements (*telōnai*). While the Q tradents were likely *kōmogrammateis* (see below), their association with the tax collection social stratum deeply reflects that ethos.

Early imperial taxes were fixed and levied in imperial silver. These were exacted from an agricultural base, hence had to be "converted" from in kind to species. Fixed or invariable taxes showed no respect for natural variance in product. Arrears or tax debt were tabulated in written records kept in royal and imperial archives.

Peasants had a number of means of ordinary resistance, though none of these did away with the systemic problem. Revolts were few and far between because of the perennial localism of peasants and the highly organized means of violence in the hands of elite groups. Not surprisingly, the Judean Revolt of 66–70 CE was accompanied by tax remedies.

JESUS' ASSOCIATIONS WITH "TAX COLLECTORS AND SINNERS"

A significant datum about Jesus of Nazareth in the early synoptic material is his association with "tax collectors and sinners" (Q both strata, and
Mark). The word *telōnēs* appears absolutely only in M and L (Matt 10:3;
Luke 3:12; 7:29; 18:10ff; 19:2). Otherwise, the word is paired with other
words *hamartōloi* (Q² 7:34; Mark 2:15; L 15:2), *ethnikos* (Q¹ 6:32 [see Q¹
6:34 and Matt 5:46–47]; M 18:17), or *pornēs* (M 21:31–32; L 18:11).
John Donahue thus can summarize: "The word is never found outside
the Synoptic Gospels and, in them, only in the pre-Jerusalem setting of
Jesus' ministry, usually in the framework of controversy stories. Thus from
a source critical viewpoint, 'toll collectors and sinners,' is found as a set
phrase in Mark and Q."[11]

Although this association might be evaluated as "literary invention"
or invective by opponents,[12] the criterion of embarrassment would argue
against both (since it would be difficult to imagine why the early tradents
would invent or preserve this material). Kloppenborg's observations about
the locus of early Q as "wisdom" give significant reason for considering
this information as positive historical data:

> If one asks, who would be in a position to frame the Sayings Gospel
> as it has been framed, the answer would appear to be village and
> town notaries and scribes. . . . There is ample evidence from Egypt
> to indicate the presence of a variety of scribes, of varying educa-
> tional levels, in towns and villages, some serving in the appartus of
> the provincial administration and others functioning as freelance
> professionals. The *kōmogrammateus* (village scribe) was concerned
> with tax and census matters.[13]

What has not happened yet given this insight is a move toward the political significance of this association. As Kloppenborg's own discussion of
recent Q scholarship testifies, most interpretations of the material depend
upon assumptions about their alleged philosophical or religious concern.[14]
The following commentary explores the significance in a very different

---

11. Donahue, "Tax Collectors and Sinners," 55.

12. On *telōnēs* as a stock term in invective, see MacMullen, *Roman Social Relations*,
Appendix B, "The Lexicon of Snobbery."

13. Kloppenborg, *Excavating Q*, 200–201.

14. Ibid., 166–213. Kloppenborg and Piper have moved the discussion in a more social
direction. I hope soon to review the work of Arnal.

direction. For one must ask why Jesus associated as of central concern with village scribes, "tax collectors," and "sinners."

Jesus was attempting to mitigate the situation of the indebted ("sinner") by promoting the subversion of the imperial tax system in Galilee. This subversion would have operated both in terms of tax evasion and distortion of the tax records.

EARLIEST Q RECENSION: WHAT THE TAX COLLECTORS HEARD

This selective commentary on Q material limits itself to Kloppenborg's Q[1] stratum, though parts are jettisoned to concord with the new critical text of Q.[15] At the end, "resonances" in other early Jesus traditions are also noted.

As I have argued, Q[1] perhaps began to be set down in Jesus' own lifetime, by scribal groups around the Lake associated with the Tiberian archives. These were transferred back to Sepphoris under Agrippa II (ca. 54 CE); hence, Q[2] represents a "Judean recension" of Q incorporating prophetic and Deuteronomic interests of scribes hostile to the temple and Pharisees.[16] Q[1] is notably distant from Judean issues, and more directly concerned with the political situation under Antipas.

The First Early Q Discourse:
God's Patronage as Liberating Eminent Domain

The first sayings collection of early Q reflects on the ethos and largesse of God's eminent domain. With roots in Passover meditation, and perhaps the example of Moses in mind (Exod 2:11–12), these sayings inculcate a wisdom of higher liberative purpose.

Q 6:20b–23

I have argued elsewhere that these words allude to some form of the first-century Passover Haggadah.[17] Thus, they bespeak a concern at the be-

---

15. Our mini-commentary depends on Kloppenborg's analysis of Q[1] in *The Formation of Q*, Appendix 2.

16. Oakman, "The Lord's Prayer in Social Perspective," orig. 147–48 (chapter 14 above).

17. Most extensively in Oakman, "Models and Archaeology in the Social Interpretation of Jesus," orig. 128–31 (chapter 15 above). The first two sayings appear separately in *Gos. Thom.* 54 and 69b, and *Gospel of Thomas* has no parallel to the third saying. While it could be argued that the Q tradents have provided the conjunction of the sayings, they are much closer to the original context of meaning. Thus in my view, the sphere of meaning provided

ginning of the very earliest Jesus material a concern for liberation in the Mosaic mold. They also corroborate the connection made between Jesus of Nazareth and Judas of Gamala.

Q 6:27–28

Early Q immediately takes up the theme "love for enemies." A series of four descriptors is given:

> *tous echthrous, tois misousin, tous katarōmenous, tōn epēreazontōn.*

These descriptors indicate severely conflictual relations as would obtain when the tax collector appears. Regarding "abuse," cf. 1 Pet 3:16; Josephus, *Ant.* 16.160, 170, Jews of Cyrene complain to Marcus Agrippa "that they are abused by certain informers, and, under pretense of taxes which were not due, are hindered from sending them."

Q 6:29–30

Non-retaliation for a dishonorable slap to the cheek, permitting the seizure of both outer- and under-garments indicate a quite different set of relations between tax collector and tax payer. No longer are goods seized in the name of the Galilean Crown, but now goods are redistributed in the name of God's eminent domain.

Possibly Q: Matt 5:41

The appearance of the important word *angareusei* deserves comment. *Angareuein* was the word regularly used in the Roman East (with roots back into the Hellenistic period, as shown by Josephus, *Ant.* 13.52 and the Egyptian papyri) to denote service compelled by the Crown. The doubling of the service is an acted parable of God's eminent domain.

Q 6:31

The "Golden Rule" is understood not as a generalized ethical norm, but as a reversal of the normal dynamics of imperial taxation.

Q 6:32

The interpretation of this saying hinges on the meaning of *hamartōloi*. To put the matter as clearly as possible, the word is usually understood to refer

---

by Israelite tradition and Judas of Gamala is much more salient. The *Thomas* tradents, whether in Syria or Egypt, were clearly not interested in Passover connections.

to those whose relations with God are disordered either through impurity or ethical infraction. Matthew Black and others, however, long ago called attention to the ambiguity of the Aramaic *ḥôbâ*.[18] As a translation of the Aramaic *ḥôbin*, the word could just as well refer to the condition of those in irretrievable indebtedness. Matthew's *telōnai* is surely redactional (shifting the meaning in the direction of moral and theological disorder); however, *telōnai* were also in debt and so *hoi hamartōloi* could be understood to refer generally to "those indebted." Given this understanding, the saying sharply highlights the ordinariness of conventional morality when even the indebted practice balanced reciprocity. God's eminent domain will call forth a more radical ethic commensurate with debt- and tax-forgiveness.

Probably in Q: 6:34

The word *danisēte* (subjunctive "[if] you loan") has in view the handling of money loans. This would be the prerogative of someone in elite circumstances, or perhaps of a moneychanger ("banker," the main role of whom was to exchange politically weak coinage into authorized coinage). Concessions to change money were farmed, hence could fall into the realm of the *telōnēs*.

Q 6:36–(38)

Oiktirmosunē is practiced specifically as *mē krinete kai mē katadikazete*. The *oikonomos* and *telōnēs* are not to execute against the debtor. The aphorism about measuring resonates within the framework of in-kind taxation.

The Second Early Q Discourse: The Praxis of God's Eminent Domain

The so-called "Mission Discourse" is almost universally discussed as though it were a description of either wandering itinerants or cynic-like missionaries of the Jesus movement. In other words, this sayings collection is treated as though it were "religious" or "philosophical," in line with the ideology of high imperial culture. These sayings assume a quite different aspect when they are understood to reflect the tax-resistance praxis of Jesus!

The sayings about "following" take up the implications of movements and action in the name of the Crown.

---

18. Black, *An Aramaic Approach to the Gospels and Acts*, 140.

Q 9:58

These words reflect the life of the elites at Sepphoris (Aram. *ṣipôrîn* = birds) with their extensive storehouses, and appeal to the *oikonomoi* and *telōnai* to consider the lifestyle attendant to a representative of the Crown ("Son of the Man").[19]

Q 9:59–60

The image is one of hyperbole, but reflects the social disruption of the Crown's compulsory demands. Like other sayings of Jesus, this is not a literal description of his "discipleship," but a sarcastic characterization of his social circumstances (cf. Q² 19:26).

Q 10:2

Irony continues in this statement. *Hoi ergatai* and *ho kyrios* refer not to religious missionaries of God, but to the customary tax collectors and the Crown. Irony comes in because Jesus and his audience know that *hoi ergatai* now operate under the eminent domain of God to make sure more of the harvest remains in the village and the Crown is deprived of its due.

Q 10:3

In a reversal of the expected image (tax payers are the sheep fleeced by the wolves), the tax collectors supporting Jesus' cause and praxis are the ones in danger.

Q 10:4

Would tax collectors literally have traveled this way in their official capacities? A staff is associated with *telōnai*. As this text could also allude to a Passover liturgy (see *Ezek. Trag.* 181–184), it reminds that the praxis is liberative in the same way that the Israelites departed Egypt. The tax collectors give up their customary demands in a symbolic exodus from their imperial role.

Q 10:5–6

"Entry into a house" (*eiserchomai*) has the appearance of the customary intrusive access of the tax collector. Verb forms *eperchomai* and *epeiserchomai*

---

19. "Son of the Man" as a throne rival: Oakman, "Rulers' Houses, Thieves, and Usurpers," orig. 117 (chapter 10 above); Sepphoris: "Models and Archaeology in the Social Interpretation of Jesus," orig. 120 (chapter 15 above).

appear in the Egyptian papyri in conjunction with forced entry by tax collectors. The Talmud too uses the phrase "entry of a house" regularly in this connection.[20] The greeting of peace may reflect customary practices (with extreme irony again intended), but in this context suggests subversively the surprise that comes with God's eminent domain. The householder may not accept the "peace," not wanting to run the risk of punishment for tax-evasion, which probably means that the tax collector has to play the usual coercive role.

Q 10:7–8

But if the envoy is accepted and fed, and the tax and debt remissions are effected (God's patronage), no additional exactions are to be requested or accepted (see Luke 3:13). A conventional proverb endorses these arrangements (v. 7).

Q 10:9

Just as the tax collectors metaphorically are "laborers," so also metaphorically are they "physicians." They heal by reducing the tax load and ease the pressure against the subsistence margin. Hence, their "medical practice" is an expression of God's eminent domain (v. 9b).

The Third Early Q Discourse: God's Patronage and Debt Remission

Q 11:2–4

The conclusions of Oakman 1999 regarding the prayer of Jesus have already been indicated. However, they are modified slightly in this connection. Perhaps the most convincing evidence for this paper's thesis is found in Q 11:3. For now, the petition is resonant in other ways:

> Release us (tax collectors) from debt, as we release those in debt to us (those who owe taxes).

Who would have collected taxes? Would such people have done this willingly? Direct taxes were gathered by slaves or agents of the responsible provincial elites. Farmed taxes (e.g., tolls) were apparently collected by the "free," but these people were indebted (provided sureties) for the amount. We know of three prominent *telōnai* in early Roman Palestine: John of

---

20. Donahue, "Tax Collectors and Sinners," 50 lists examples from *m. Ṭehar.* 7:6 and *m. Ḥag.* 3:6.

Caesarea, John of Gischala, and Bar Mayan. An interesting comparative instance from Pompeii:

> Holograph [acknowledgment] of Privatus, public slave of the colony of Veneria Cornelia, on receipt of 1,652 sesterces for the fullers' tax of the first year. . . . I, Privatus, slave of the colony, hereby declare in writing that I received from Lucius Caecilius Jucundus 1,652 sesterces for the fullers' tax from the balance of the first year.[21]

A municipal tax has been farmed to Jucundus, who provides collateral for the tax and pays it in installments. The collection is done by the slave Privatus. The roles of the imperial tax-collection systems are occupied by people under various forms of compulsion.

Q 11:9–10

"Asking," "searching," and "knocking" are activities related to on-site evaluation of the tax situation.

Q 11:11–13

These rhetorical questions illuminate the situation of need for the village tax-payer. They do not need a written tax receipt, or money, but real consumption goods. As I have argued earlier in this volume [chapter 7], peasants cannot eat a token [coinage], but require real goods.

The Fourth Early Q Discourse: Fearless Action and the Danger of Delation

Rostovtzeff comments on the frequency during the Hellenistic period of *mēnutai*–those who turn in royal opponents (including tax-evaders):

> [In Ecclesiastes, under Ptolemy II] The spies of Ptolemy, who are so ubiquitous that "a bird of the air shall carry the voice" of him who cursed the king in secret, were presumably both fiscal and political *mēnutai*.[22]

The same pattern perdures into the Roman period with the phenomenon of *delatio*. Irony again frames the following Q-words (with God's eminent domain finessing Herod's royal or Roman imperial prerogatives).

21. *CIL*, 4: 3,340, cxli, quoted in Lew and Reinhold, ed., *Roman Civilization*, 333.
22. Rostovtzeff, *SEHHW*, 350.

Q 12:2–3

Nothing can remain secret.

Q 12:4–5

So there is no need to fear. The authorities only have power over the individual body, but not the movement's power.

Q 12:6–7

Nothing gets sold in the market without the Sovereign's knowledge. All is subject to the tax! (God's observation and accounting is even more rigorous than the taxation system.)

Q 12:11–12

The synagogue here is the place of public assembly and examination. The hippodrome at Tarichaeae can play a similar function when Josephus is accused of treason by Jesus, son of Sapphias and chief magistrate of Tiberias (*Life* 132). Josephus addresses assemblies at the stadium in Tiberias (*Life* 92, 331).

The Fifth Early Q Discourse: God's Patronage and Subsistence Anxiety

Subsistence security is tied to "seeking first God's eminent domain" (Q 12:31). A selection of concerns related to our theme is highlighted here.

Q 12:24

The storehouse economy is contrasted now with the economy of the kingdom. The birds recall those of 12:6–7 (objects of royal/imperial taxation) and 9:58 (allegorically, the elites of Sepphoris), but these now are enemies of the sown. They steal from the crown as expression of God's eminent domain. *A minori ad maius*, Jesus' associates are far more important in the scheme of the kingdom.

Q 12:27

The "lilies" are weeds, again proliferating against the sown.[23]

---

23. In earlier work, I discussed these plant images as drawing an analogy between weeds and the power of the kingdom (chapter 9). This is a new application of that idea.

The Sixth Early Q Discourse:
How Difficult for the Powerful-Rich to Enter God's Domain

Early Q ends with a warning that underscores the difficulty of Jesus' praxis
for the powerful-rich and for those concerned about family.

Q 13:24

The narrow gate is difficult of access. Such is Jesus' praxis. Is there a palace
image here, suggestive of privileged access? Mark 10:25 makes a similar
point. Matthew expands the saying in the direction of the conventional
two ways of wisdom.

Q 14:26

Hatred of family members (understood ironically) implies that one's actions for the sake of God's eminent domain put family members at grave
risk. Besides the implications of Matt 18:25, there is the story told by
Philo about the actions of an Egyptian tax collector:

> Recently a man was appointed tax collector among us. When some
> of those who were supposed to owe taxes fled because of poverty
> and in fear of unbearable punishment, he carried off by force their
> wives, their children, the parents, and the rest of their families,
> striking them, and insulting them, and visiting all manner of out-
> rages upon them in an effort to force them either to inform against
> the fugitive or else to make payment in his stead.[24]

Q 14:27

This saying provides the crux of the whole argument. For it indicates very
clearly Jesus' consciousness of the political consequences deriving from his
praxis (see next section). The presence of this saying can hardly be understood as an invention of the Q tradents (who say hardly a word otherwise
about Jesus' death). If it is hyperbole, why would it be associated with
family and bodily danger? The saying's literal meaning must then be taken
seriously on the very lips of Jesus.

Q 17:33
Recalls Q 12:31.

---

24. Philo, *Spec. Laws*, 2.19.92–94, quoted in Lewis and Reinhold, ed., *The Empire*,
400.

Q 14:34–35

The final image is from the simple courtyard oven. It cannot be fired without the catalyst of salt.[25] Just so, God's eminent domain, the "oven," will not fire without the catalyst, praxis such as Jesus': See Q¹ 12:28. The image of fire gets taken further in Q² (3:9; 12:49).

Evidence From Other Early Jesus Material

Interesting corroborations of these interpretations are found in other good early Jesus material. Here only a few instances are reviewed.

M/Matt 18:34

The remission of enormous tax debt here is noteworthy. The slaves are expected to follow suit.

Q2/Luke 16:1–8

In a very different light, now, the political significance of this parable lies open for scrutiny. An *oikonomos* manipulates debt (tax?) records in his own interests and against those of the *kyrios*. These manipulations are viewed positively (v. 8), and the Steward anticipates "being welcomed into their [villagers'] houses."

Whether Mark 12:17 might be invoked in support of the argument is debatable, though it shows the liveliness and danger of the tax question. Evidence may be selectively preserved even at the level of the evangelists, since in Luke 23:2 Jesus is accused before Pilate of advocating tax evasion. The M/Matt 17:26b saying is also noteworthy.

JESUS' DEATH AS A *LĒSTĒS*

The fact of Jesus' crucifixion is the most certain historical datum we have. Q, of course, is silent about Jesus' death, but Mark reports that Jesus was crucified with two other *lēstai*. The cross was the Roman punishment reserved for seditious provincials.

Tacitus, *Annals* 1.72–73: "Tiberius gave new impetus to the law of treason. This law had the same name in olden times, but other matters came under its jurisdiction—betrayal of an army, or inciting the plebs to

25. Pilch, *The Cultural Dictionary of the Bible*, 4–5.

sedition, in short, any public malfeasance which diminished the majesty of the Roman people."[26]

Justinian's *Digest* indicates that these actions were considered treasonable: "men are gathered together for seditious purposes . . . a person . . . knowingly makes or cites a false entry in the public records . . . Moreover, the Julian Law on Treason directs that a person who injures the majesty of the state is liable to prosecution . . . by whom with malice aforethought anyone is bound by oath to act against the state . . . if a person is accused of treason under any other section of the Julian Law, his death extinguishes the charge."[27]

Paulus *Opinions* 5.22–24 indicates disposition in capital crimes (though only Roman citizens receive "capital punishment," i.e. decapitation): "Instigators of sedition and riot or rousers of the people are, according to the nature of their rank, either crucified, thrown to wild beasts, or deported to an island. . . . humble persons . . . are either crucified or thrown to wild beasts."[28]

All of this gives historical basis for asserting that Jesus of Nazareth suffered crucifixion ca. 30 CE for *crimen maiestatis Romanorum*, viz. as this paper has argued, for conspiring to subvert the Roman taxation system within the client realm of Herod Antipas.

CONCLUSION: THE MEANING OF RESISTANCE AND THE RESISTIVITY OF MEANING IN THE JESUS TRADITIONS

The activity of historical Jesus, reflected not only in earliest Q but also in other important Jesus materials, signified tax subversion in the name of the eminent domain of God's ruling power. The meaning of Jesus' resistance has not been obliterated by later scribal interests in the gospels, so the resistivity of meaning is a noteworthy feature in the tradition (given prevelant post-modern suspicions about such historical judgments).

Jesus' historical activity was essentially about politics, and the restructuring of society, and not about religion or theology. Jesus was a conservative in relation to the traditions of Israel; like Judas of Gamala, Jesus accepted the basic themes of Exodus in the Israelite scriptures. Both men applied their understandings to the concrete social problems of their

26. Quoted in Lewis and Reinhold, *The Empire*, 93.
27. Ibid., 30.
28. Ibid., 548.

Golan/Galilean context. Judas and Zadok, however, advocated violent resistance to Rome; Jesus was not a follower of the Fourth Philosophy in that respect. But he agreed with the Fourth Philosophy regarding the eminent domain of God, its implications for tax resistance, and the servile condition of indebtedness.

Clarity about this result can only come with the aid of the social sciences. This is not "reductionism," if by that is meant an obliteration of Jesus' on-going significance; rather, this result represents a clarity about the deepest historical significance of Jesus' work—tied as it was to the interests of the little people and their subsistence ethic. To continue to discuss the meaning of historical Jesus in terms of German idealism or anachronistic Euro-American experience runs the danger of great historic obfuscation. While Jesus' historical resistance to imperial and colonial realities left its traces in his traditions, it is also true that the canonical gospels of the New Testament shifted Jesus' focus from social relations to relations between human beings and God. In this sense, the New Testament made an early contribution to obscuring the meaning of Jesus' resistance.

CHAPTER 17

Jesus, Q, and Ancient Literacy
in Social Perspective[1]

THE Q SECTION OF the 2004 national SBL meeting in San Antonio heard papers arguing that Q should not be thought of as a document with two or three recensions, but as a product of oral culture and performance—thus challenging in key ways the foundational hypothesis of James M. Robinson, John S. Kloppenborg, and the International Q Project.

Kloppenborg's well-known Q hypothesis posits a document in Greek, which passed through at least two recensions (an earlier characterized by the wisdom instruction form and deliberative reasoning, a later characterized by prophetic pronouncements and chreiai), and which was incorporated in slightly different forms into Matthew and Luke after the first Judean-Roman War. The critical reconstruction of the Q text has thus pursued the methodological procedure of separating out Q by systematically removing the redactional treatments respectively of Matthew/Luke.

These recent challenges to written-Q, represented among others by Werner H. Kelber, Richard A. Horsley, Jonathan A. Draper, and now James D. G. Dunn, while slightly different in their bases and interests, all seem to claim that Q held a fluid form in oral tradition until very late in its first-century existence. It is not always clear whether this means that Matthew and Luke drew upon an oral Q, or that Q was written down before Matthew and Luke and used in different ways by the two synoptic

1. Presented as a paper first to the Northwest Regional AAR/SBL Meeting, Seattle University, Seattle, WA, April 2005 and then to the International St. Petersburg/Context Group Conference "Interpreting the Bible and the Biblical Communities in Their Social and Cultural Contexts," St. Petersburg Christian University, June 2005; this chapter has not otherwise been published.

evangelists. Horsley and Draper, for instance, following terminology of John Miles Foley, refer to Q as an "oral-derived text," with the following characterization: "Q would appear to be closest to a scribal transcript of a 'text' that had been regularly performed in a movement or community. Matthew and Luke appear to have used the same transcribed text of Q (or very similar ones)."[2] Alan Kirk, whose fine paper at that same AAR/SBL meeting inspired some aspects of this discussion, concludes that "Q is best understood as an artifactualization of a tradition of oral moral exhortation" intended to support multiple performances.[3]

My argument in this chapter, really only a very rough sketch at this point, aims to suggest that the precise characterization of written Jesus traditions, and their relationship to Jesus' oral culture, must be interposed between results of third-quest historical Jesus studies and contemporary gospel research as well as put into firmer political and social-structural perspective (in terms both of social location of writing and social location and development of the written synoptic tradition). Consider for a moment the following points and questions:

1. Ancient literacy was highly restricted, and recent discussions of ancient literacy are increasingly important for the question of written Jesus traditions. Why and how did oral Jesus material get written down? Or, was Jesus "written up"? In whose interests was inscription of his words (initially)? What were the social factors involved? And what at bottom do we imagine is really going on in this process of tradition?

2. It is clear that for written Jesus traditions to emerge in the first century, there must have been sponsoring scribal groups. Their interests and identity for the most part must be inferred from internal evidence within Jesus traditions. Their reasons for writing, however, can generally have stretched along a spectrum from "unsympathetic" to "sympathetic." The predominant assumption of scholarship through many proposals has been that Jesus-sympathizers inscribed his words, probably from Aramaic oral exemplars, into written Greek. This assumption in

2. Horsley and Draper, *Whoever Hears You Hears Me*, 167.

3. Kirk, "Administrative Writing, Oral Tradition, and Q." I am grateful to Professor Kirk for sharing the text of his paper and allowing me to cite it here briefly.

some respects might profitably be challenged. Is it correct to presume, for instance, that written Jesus traditions were solely inscribed by sympathizers?

3. The question of Jesus' native tongue, or the native language of his sayings, has been vigorously debated. However, it seems that the common language of village and town in Roman Palestine was Aramaic. Unless Jesus regularly spoke Greek, translation of Jesus' sayings from Aramaic into Greek must have taken place. There is some evidence for this within the synoptic tradition, but a written Aramaic collection of Jesus-sayings behind Q seems entirely ruled out. So, would this translation have been done from oral Aramaic to written Greek? Or from oral Aramaic to oral Greek to written Greek?

4. How can the matter of written traditions be assessed in relation to Jesus' own interests, or the interests of the Jesus movement? What needs to be perceived from a social perspective in this inscription process?

These issues are now examined in a bit more detail, after which the essay concludes by suggesting how the Sower parable and the Q material about Good and Bad Trees illustrate the crucial divide between Jesus' oral critique of political economy, probably originally in Aramaic, and the subsequent development of a quite different theological critique in written Greek.

ANCIENT LITERACY IN ROMAN GALILEE

The work of William V. Harris is considered the standard treatment now of ancient literacy. Harris concluded that no more than 10–15% of the Greco-Roman population could read and write. Obviously, the literate would have been among the ancient elites. Catherine Hezser, building on Harris, has recently provided a more nuanced discussion about literacy in Roman Palestine. She concludes that there were a number of types of literacy there within a largely oral culture—from the full reading and writing literacy necessary to create rich literary texts to semi-literacy of scribes who played mere functionary roles within administrative structures to illiteracy even of wealthy folks like Babatha who had to have a *hypographeus* sign her name for her.[4]

Since literacy was extremely limited in the ancient world, discerning differing types of literacy (and their social locations) is very important to the whole question. For the purposes of this exploration, ancient literacy involved differential abilities in relation to reading, writing, or both. We might distinguish a) villagers entirely unable to read or write, living out lifetimes within communities of memory and oral culture; b) craft literacy involving limited ability to read and/or write relative to the task at hand; c) scribes of restricted administrative literacy who could read or write standardized legal documents; and d) well-educated people who possessed ability to read or write to a high literary degree. Hezser states, "The most complex and difficult type of written material were literary texts, whereas accounts, lists, and labels stood at the other end of the scale."[5] Figure 24 illustrates some of the possibilities.

Figure 24: A Model of Ancient Literacy

	Reading ability—weakest to strongest ⟶			
Writing ability—weakest to strongest	*Oral Culture*	Craft literacy	Administrative documents	Literary works
	Craft literacy			
	Administrative documents	*"The most complex and difficult type of written material were literary texts, whereas accounts, lists, and labels stood at the other end of the scale."* —Catherine Hezser		
	Literary works			

Q, LITERACY, AND THE ADMINISTRATION OF HERODIAN TERRITORY

The Q tradition reflects a fairly high degree of literacy, but in two directions: The Greco-Roman ideal is manifest in the creation of eudaimonistic wisdom arguments out of various Jesus-instructions; the Judean ideal is manifest in the shaping of Jesus material in light of Israel's great tradi-

4. Hezser, *Jewish Literacy*, 487.
5. Ibid., 476.

tion, especially prophetic pronouncements and chreiai influenced by deuteronomistic perspectives, and eventually quotations of Torah in the Q temptation.

It seems reasonable to assume that two different "catchment basins" for Jesus material are in view (see Figure 25). Material reflected in the Greco-Roman stratum is the product of non-Judean village and town scribes in the Herodian administration of Galilee, as has been suggested by Kloppenborg and Arnal.[6] Because of references to Bethsaida, Capernaum, and Chorazin, Arnal is of the opinion that Q was entirely composed in or near Capernaum.[7] His early dating of Deuteronomic-Q to the 40s, however, is not entirely persuasive because it involves accepting 1 Thess 2:14–16 as authentically Pauline.[8] Paul's theological outlook was hardly deuteronomic!

Figure 25: Scribes of The Kingdom

Galilean and Judean "Scribal Catchment Basins"

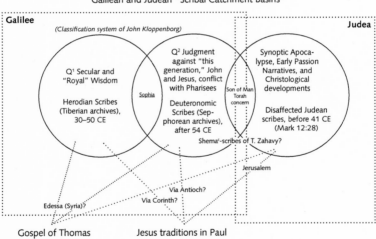

I myself have thought the earliest Q material was gathered during the time the imperial archives were housed in Tiberias—up to the early 50s CE. Under the Judean Agrippa II and Nero (according to Josephus, *Life* 9), the archives passed back to Sepphoris.[9] The Sepphorean scribes were more

6. Kloppenborg, *Excavating Q*, 200–201; Arnal, *Jesus and the Village Scribes*, 168.

7. Arnal, *Jesus and the Village Scribes*, 162.

8. Ibid., 247 n. 15.

9. Josephus, *Life* 9 (Thackeray, LCL): "Justus, son of Pistus, the ring-leader of the third party, while feigning hesitation on the subject of hostilities, was really eager for revolution,

within the Judean socio-political orbit, and if recent work of Overman, and now Aaron Gale, is correct, perhaps even the Gospel of Matthew was composed in Sepphoris.[10] The material of Tiberian Q was not necessarily collected by sympathizers, but perhaps originated as intelligence about the Jesus movement (along the lines suggested by Andreas in Gerd Theissen's *Shadow of the Galilean*). Yet already in the early rhetorical elaborations of Tiberian Q, we probably see the work of sympathizers; certainly by the time of Sepphorean Q, the material expresses the positive sentiments of Judean scribes toward Jesus.

In preliminary appraisal, the oral-Q hypothesis may not reckon sufficiently with written phenomena evidenced within Q (especially repeated rhetorical elaborations or chreiai) or with the nature of the socio-political process by which Jesus traditions were inscribed. At the very least, discussions about how Jesus traditions came to be written down, and by whom, must be solidly connected with discussions about the spectrum of ancient literacies and the social origins of the Jesus movement.

JESUS' NATIVE LANGUAGE AND WRITTEN GREEK SOURCES

Jesus himself was either illiterate (unable to read or write at all), or possessed at best a craft literacy. His native tongue would have been Aramaic, the language of the village in Herodian Galilee; however, Jesus may have spoken some Greek.[11] Despite Luke 4:17–18, it is not likely that Jesus could read literary works. And there is no credible ancient evidence that he could write. Jesus traditions were written down early by more "secular" administrative scribes in Herodian Galilee (associated with the archives of Tiberias) and at some point (probably later) by those better acquainted with

---

reckoning that a change of government would bring him into power. So he came forward and endeavoured to instill into the people that their city had always been the capital of Galilee, at least under its founder, Herod the tetrarch, whose intention was that the city of Sepphoris should be subordinate to Tiberias; and that even under King Agrippa the elder they had not lost this primacy, which had continued until Felix became procurator of Judaea. Now, however, he continued, they had had the misfortune of being handed over by Nero as a present to Agrippa the younger; Sepphoris, by submission to Rome, had forthwith become the capital of Galilee and the seat of the royal bank and the archives"; see Oakman, "The Lord's Prayer in Social Perspective" (chapter 14 above).

10. Overman, *Matthew's Gospel and Formative Judaism*; idem, *Church and Community in Crisis*; Gale, *Redefining Ancient Borders*.

11. Hezser, *Jewish Literacy*, 240: "Greek was the language of the politically powerful administration officials and the aristocracy of the Greek cities . . . [non-Jewish Greek-speakers] will have felt little need and incentive to learn the native population's Aramaic."

the traditions of Israel (both in Sepphoris and Jerusalem). The two types of scribal material are juxtaposed in Q. If originally spoken in Aramaic, it is probable that Jesus' sayings were directly translated into written Greek by more literate town scribes. The literary level of Q in all strata, as well as Mark, would already indicate a high level of literacy in early written Jesus traditions. Arnal observes: the "literacy [of Q scribes] was more than merely functional . . . [but] Alongside extended historical writings, developed biographies, or apocalypses, Q can appear rather disorganized, simplistic, or primitive."[12]

Jesus' key interest in the kingdom of God must be considered in relation to the question of how his words came to be written down. Jesus' political concerns, understood either as interest in political economy or religious politics, were paramount. Historical Jesus was largely a political figure, someone who disturbed the existing order, which is why he was crucified as well as received elite notice in the pages of Josephus; the scribal tradents of the Jesus traditions eventually reinterpreted him through Judean political religion (for instance, in terms of christology) and turned his words into material of theological and eschatological critique directed against the leadership of Judean religion (somewhat along the lines of the Dead Sea Scrolls).

I suggested quite awhile ago that Jesus used parables and double-meanings to hide political critique.[13] Jesus' distinctive penchant for parabolic and figurative language, as well as his likely communication in Aramaic, was rooted in his concern to address pressing social needs without attracting unwanted elite attention. Whether we are ever successful at reconstructing any original Aramaic Jesus-words, we have to assume that some of the social meaning of Jesus has been preserved in early Jesus material. If Jesus regularly spoke in the language of the Galilean village to hide his political aims, however, at least some evidence must be preserved in the early Greek Jesus traditions: we might recall here the "birds of the air" and "son of man" references in Q 9:58, which I have taken as veiled references to Sepphoris and Galilean commoners.[14] However, the matter can more

12. Arnal, *Jesus and the Village Scribes*, 170; for Mark, see Rohrbaugh, "The Social Location of the Marcan Audience," 115–16.

13. Oakman, "Rulers' Houses, Thieves, and Usurpers," orig. 112 (chapter 10 above).

14. Oakman, "The Archaeology of First-Century Galilee and the Social Interpretation of the Historical Jesus," orig. 235–36; also in idem, "Models and Archaeology in the Social Interpretation of Jesus" (chapter 15 above).

readily be discussed in this brief article in terms of Jesus' use of parables and similitudes. In a moment, we'll examine a couple of those.

JESUS' CENTRAL PREOCCUPATION WITH "GOD'S EMINENT DOMAIN"

All contemporary Jesus scholars believe that his central message had to do with the kingdom of God; however, the meaning for Jesus of this symbol has been debated by scholars for well over a century. Johannes Weiss and Albert Schweitzer believed that Jesus was an apocalyptic preacher, so "kingdom of God" would have meant for him what it meant in numerous Judean apocalyptic writings. Almost all twentieth-century interpreters followed them.

Attention to Jesus in Galilean context has raised serious questions about this standard view and reopened the discussion in fruitful ways. As was argued in chapter 16, "Jesus the Tax Resister," Jesus' central symbol was consistently connected to mundane issues of village subsistence and the problem of debt and taxation that deprived many of Jesus' contemporaries of the means of life. Peasant religion is universally connected with concerns about subsistence and political economy as well as magical ideas about overcoming injustice and hunger. Jesus' central symbol was rooted in Israel's Exodus traditions, such that freedom from hunger, debt, injustice, or concern with Israel's Passover meal, could saliently become Jesus' concerns. This Passover bread is my body, he is remembered to have said; this Passover cup is my blood. "Kingdom of God," in this understanding, refers to God's eminent domain, God's power to liberate from Egypt, God's power to reclaim the goods of life distrained by the powerful wealthy or locked up in their storehouses. The illiterate Jesus was not a learned eschatologist like the scribes of Qumran or Jerusalem, or those who later preserved his deeds and words; rather like any peasant through the ages, Jesus was concerned about daily subsistence and the immediate power of God to challenge the oppression and unjust arrangements of Rome and its Herodian administration. Jesus understood God's kingdom as the power to seize for purposes of sustaining life; God's eminent domain was God's *angareia*, and the practice was explicitly remembered in Mark 11:3 ("The Lord has need of it."). Not surprisingly, Roman agents eventually took notice of Jesus as a rebel against the Roman order and meted out to him the punishment regularly reserved for such rebels.

Mark's Sower and Q's Good and Bad Trees

The central referent of Jesus' parables and similitudes, thus, holds political significance. The Sower parable is connected with God's kingdom, God's eminent domain, but how? The similitude indicates the fate of four types of seed: that which falls along the path to be eaten by birds, that which falls among the rocks to be scorched by the sun, that which falls into the thorns to be eaten by worms, and that which falls upon "good soil" to bear fruit. In the conventional interpretation of the twentieth century, Jesus' original point rested with the dramatic contrast between the lost seeds and the final harvest from the good soil. Jeremias discussed the meaning of the Sower under the "Great Assurance" that God's eschatological purposes will be realized. Jeremias writes, "out of the most insignificant beginnings, invisible to human eye, God creates his mighty Kingdom, which embraces all the peoples of the world."[15] Brandon Scott traces the "originating oral structure" through three independent instances of Mark, Luke, and Thomas to conclude that the contrast is not so dramatic and "[i]n failure and everydayness lies the miracle of God's activity."[16] Interestingly, William R. Herzog does not find in the Sower apparently any "subversive speech," since he does not discuss the parable.

What commentators have overlooked is the possibility that Jesus' point lies not in the good soil and the harvest, but in the seeds sown upon the path, rocks, thorns. In this novel view, much seed (perhaps up to 75%) is sown under conditions that cannot be taxed (unlike the harvest from the good soil) and therefore in situations that stand ready to manifest the eminent domain of God, to provide food free for the taking! The path, the rocks, the thorns provide a "tax shelter," and the seed there must be rescued from the birds, the sun, the worms, and the thorns. Act quickly, Jesus says. Whoever has ears, let them hear! God's kingdom has come near, God's eminent domain is effective.

The Q tradition of the Good and Bad Trees can be approached in a similar way. The pericope exists in both Q and Thomas, but Thomas lacks the comparison of the two trees. Both Q and Thomas have the statements about figs and grapes, though Q and Thomas reverse the association with thorns and thistles:

15. Jeremias, *Parables*, 149.
16. Bernard Brandon Scott, *Hear Then the Parable*, 350–52, 358, 362.

Q 6:44		Gos. Thom. 45:1	
Figs	thorns	Grapes	thorns
Grapes	thistles	Figs	thistles

Both pericopes conclude by referring to good and evil people/treasures. Both also connect the good/evil behaviors with the heart. In each case, the respective tradents drew some ethical moral from these sayings. Arnal, following Ronald A. Piper, in fact emphasizes that Jesus' radical statements are domesticated, so to speak, through the structures of Q's rhetorical clusters. Arnal writes, "The [early Q] compositions, then, were organized with a view toward subsuming these radical or inversionary sayings into coherent and persuasive arguments that asserted fairly commonplace conclusions . . . ."[17]

Another interpretive possibility emerges with the connection to God's eminent domain. Thorns and thistles were everywhere in Roman Galilee, the bane of the ancient farmer. But under their pervasive "cover" could be hidden stands of grapes or young fig trees (which could bear after seven years). As John Pairman Brown notes, "The fig takes years to mature, and a grown tree testifies to decades of peace."[18] The tax collector is not going to be looking in the thorns and thistles. Neither will the tax collector expect much from "bad trees," but hungry villagers might still glean bare sustenance even from trees with rotting fruit (reconsider in this light the parable in Luke 13:6–9).

Reference to good and evil treasures, *pace* the moralistic purposes of the Q scribes, plausibly fits with Jesus' critique of the storehouse economy of Roman Galilee and the arrangements of mammon which the powerful-wealthy trusted to the detriment of the many.[19] God's "treasury" is seen in the gracious providence of the natural environment that provides gleanings for birds and hungry villagers. In these last words may originally have been reference to secret underground galleys that peasants also dug to hide produce from the tax collectors. Perhaps in these words also, Jesus made an appeal even to sympathetic tax collectors and their accountants, to "have a heart," to look the other way to the advantage of the many Galilean villag-

17. Arnal, *Jesus and the Village Scribes*. 187.

18. John Pairman Brown, *Israel and Hellas*, 2:12. For details about Mediterranean fig trees, see Hepper, *Baker Encyclopedia of Bible Plants*, 110; or United Bible Societies, *Fauna and Flora of the Bible*, 118.

19. Oakman, "The Radical Jesus."

ers ekeing out a meager existence under the Herodian-Roman administration. The Q 12 discourse about anxiety, or parables such as the Rich Fool (Luke 12) and the Unjust Steward (Luke 16) give corroborating evidence elsewhere for such critique or appeal.

CONCLUSION

In summary, what attracted the notice of the powerful-wealthy to Jesus (mediated in part we suppose through scribal informants) was his subversive political-economic agenda, legitimated by his appeal to God's eminent domain, which advocated the cultivation of "tax shelters" in the wilds or the sharing of secreted goods. The cross was the normal provincial punishment for anyone caught subverting the Roman taxation system.

Jesus' subversive sayings, originally Aramaic words blowing upon the Galilean winds, were written down, perhaps initially as evidence for indictment. However, in time, or perhaps even during Jesus' own lifetime, the scribes of the Greek sayings of Jesus became sympathizers—a process we already see completed in earliest Q. But what was originally in the Jesus movement a social critique of Herodian Galilee becomes in later written Jesus tradition an indictment of Judean political religion (critique of Pharisees, judgment against "this generation"). Ironically in this understanding of developments, the words of the original indictment against Jesus are turned into his indictments of others. This transformation—from Jesus' religious politics in the interests of Galilean peasantry to the political religious contest between the nascent Christian movement and rabbinic Judaism (as we see in Matthew)—depended centrally upon a palimpsest Jesus, an illiterate peasant whose own interests were roughshod overwritten by those of the scribes of the kingdom.

Abbreviations

/	A slant between synoptic passages indicates close parallel material.
AAR	American Academy of Religion
AB	Anchor Bible
ABD	*Anchor Bible Dictionary.* 6 vols. Edited by David Noel Freedman. New York: Doubleday, 1992
Ag. Ap.	Josephus, *Against Apion*
ANRW	*Aufstieg und Niedergang der römischen Welt*
'Arak.	Tractate *'Arakin* (Mishnah or Talmud)
b.	Babylonian Talmud (*Babli*); in names, Hebrew *ben*, "son of"
BAGD	Bauer, Walter, William F. Arndt, F. Wilbur Gingrich, and Frederick W. Danker. *A Greek English Lexicon of the New Testament and Other Early Christian Literature,* 2d ed.
BASOR	*Bulletin of the American Schools of Oriental Research*
BAR	*Biblical Archaeology Review*
BDB	Francis Brown, S. R. Driver, and Charles A. Briggs, *A Hebrew and English Lexicon of the Old Testament*
BDF	Friedrich Blass, Albert Debrunner, and Robert W. Funk, *A Greek Grammar of the New Testament and Other Early Christian Literature*
B. Meṣ.	Tractate *Baba Meṣi'a* (Mishnah or Talmud)
Bek.	Tractate *Bekorot* (Mishnah or Talmud)
Ber.	Tractate *Berakot* (Mishnah or Talmud)
BTB	*Biblical Theology Bulletin*
cf.	confer, compare
CBQ	*Catholic Biblical Quarterly*
CD	Damascus Rule
CIL	Corpus inscriptionum latinarum
Did.	*Didache*
Eccl. Hist.	Eusebius, *Ecclesiastical History*

'Ed.	Tractate *'Eduyyot* (Mishnah or Talmud)
f., ff.	following page, following pages
Forum	*Foundations and Facets Forum*
GKC	*Gesenius' Hebrew Grammar*
Git.	Tractate *Giṭṭin* (Mishnah or Talmud)
Gos. Thom.	*Gospel of Thomas*
Ḥag.	Tractate *Ḥagigah* (Mishnah or Talmud)
HTR	*Harvard Theological Review*
IDB	*Interpreter's Dictionary of the Bible.* Edited by George A. Buttrick. Nashville: Abingdon, 1962
IEJ	*Israel Exploration Journal*
IESS	*International Encyclopedia of the Social Sciences.* 17 vols. Edited by David L. Sills. New York: Macmillan, 1968
Int	*Interpretation*
JBL	*Journal of Biblical Literature*
JJS	*Journal of Jewish Studies*
JNTS	*Journal of New Testament Studies*
JPS	*Journal of Peasant Studies*
JRS	*Journal of Roman Studies*
JSJ	*Journal for the Study of Judaism*
JSNT	*Journal for the Study of the New Testament*
JSNTSup	Journal for the Study of the New Testament Supplement Series
JSOT	*Journal for the Study of the Old Testament*
JSOTSup	Journal for the Study of the Old Testament Supplement Series
Jub.	*Jubilees*
Ketub.	Tractate *Ketubboth* (Mishnah or Talmud)
LCL	Loeb Classical Library
LSJ	Liddell, H., R. Scott, and H. Jones. *A Greek English Lexicon with A Supplement*
Life	Josephus, *The Life*
Listening	*Listening: Journal of Religion and Culture*
m.	*Mishnah*
Ma'aś.	Tractate *Ma'aśerot* (Mishnah or Talmud)
Menaḥ	Tractate *Menaḥot* (Mishnah or Talmud)
M. Qaṭ	Tractate *Mo'ed Qaṭan* (Mishnah or Talmud)
n., nn.	note, notes
Nat. Hist.	Pliny, *Natural History*
Ned.	Tractate *Nedarim* (Mishnah or Talmud)
NovT	*Novum Testamentum*
NRSV	New Revised Standard Version of the English Bible

NTOA	Novum Testamentum et Orbis Antiquus
NTS	*New Testament Studies*
NTTS	New Testament Tools and Studies
OGIS	*Orientis graeci inscriptiones selectae.* 2 vols. Edited by W. Dittenberger. Leipzig: Hirzel, 1903–1905
OTP	*The Old Testament Pseudepigrapha.* 2 vols. Edited by James H. Charlesworth. Garden City, NY: Doubleday, 1983–1985
par.	parallel(s)
Peʾah	Tractate *Peʾah* (Mishnah or Talmud)
PEQ	*Palestine Exploration Quarterly*
POxy	Oxyrhynchus Papyrus
Rab.	*Midrash Rabbah*
RB	*Revue biblique*
RSV	Revised Standard Version of the English Bible
SBL	Society of Biblical Literature
SBT	Studies in Biblical Theology
SEHHW	Michael Rostovtzeff, *Social and Economic History of the Hellenistic World*
SEHRE	Michael Rostovtzeff, *Social and Economic History of the Roman Empire*
Sheb.	Tractate *Shebiʿit* (Mishnah or Talmud)
Sheqal.	Tractate *Sheqalim* (Mishnah or Talmud)
Sib. Or.	*Sibylline Oracles*
SNTSMS	Society of New Testament Studies Monograph Series
Spec. Laws	Philo, *On the Special Laws*
Str-B.	Hermann L. Strack and Paul Billerbeck. *Kommentar Zum Neuen Testament Aus Talmud und Midrasch*
SUNT	Studien zur Umwelt des Neuen Testaments
t.	*Tosefta*
Taʿan.	Tractate *Taʿanit* (Mishnah or Talmud)
Ṭehar.	Tractate *Ṭeharot* (Mishnah or Talmud)
TJT	*Toronto Journal of Theology*
TDNT	*Theological Dictionary of the New Testament.* 10 vols. Edited by Gerhard Kittel and Gerhard Friedrich. Translated by Geoffrey Bromiley. Grand Rapids: Eerdmans, 1964–1976
ʿUq.	Tractate *ʿUqsin* (Mishnah or Talmud)
v., vv.	verse, verses
War	Josephus, *Jewish War*
WUNT	Wissenschaftliche Untersuchungen zum Neuen Testament

y.	Jerusalem Talmud (*Yerushalmi*)
Yeb.	Tractate *Yebamot* (Mishnah or Talmud)
ZNW	*Zeitschrift für die neutestamentliche Wissenschaft und die Kunde der älteren Kirche*

Bibliography

Adan-Bayewitz, David, and Isadore Perlman. "The Local Trade of Sepphoris in the Roman Period." *IEJ* 40 (1990) 91–100.

Aland, Kurt. *Synopsis Quattuor Evangeliorum.* Stuttgart: Württembergische Bibelanstalt, 1973.

Amiran, D. H. K. "The Pattern of Settlement in Palestine." *IEJ* 3 (1950) 65–78.

Applebaum, Shimon. "Economic Life in Palestine." In *The Jewish People in the First Century: Historical Geography, Political History, Social, Cultural and Religious Life and Institutions*, edited by S. Safrai and M. Stern, 2:631–700. Compendia Rerum Iudaicarum Ad Novum Testamentum, section 1. Philadelphia: Fortress, 1976.

———. "Judaea as a Roman Province; Countryside as a Political and Economic Factor." In *ANRW* II.8:355–96. Berlin: de Gruyter, 1977.

———. "The Towers of Samaria." *PEQ* 110 (1978) 91–100.

Arav, Rami. "Bethsaida." *IEJ* 38 (1988) 187–88.

———. "Bethsaida." *IEJ* 39 (1989) 99–100.

———. "Bethsaida." *IEJ* 41 (1991) 184–85.

———. "Bethsaida." *IEJ* 42 (1992) 252–54.

Aristotle, *The Nicomachean Ethics.* Translated by W. D. Ross. In *Aristotle: II*, edited by Robert Maynard Hutchins, 9:339–436. The Great Books of the Western World. Chicago: Encyclopaedia Britannica, 1952.

Arnal, William E. *Jesus and the Village Scribes: Galilean Conflicts and the Setting of Q.* Minneapolis: Fortress, 2001.

Austin, M. M., and P. Vidal-Naquet. *Economic and Social History of Ancient Greece.* Berkeley: University of California Press, 1977.

Aviam, Mordechai. "Galilee: The Hellenistic to Byzantine Periods." In *The New Encyclopedia of Archaeological Excavations in the Holy Land*, edited by Ephraim Stern, 2:453–58. New York: Simon & Schuster, 1993.

Avigad, Nachman. "How the Wealthy Lived in Herodian Jerusalem." *BAR* 2/4 (1976) 1, 22–35.

Avi-Yonah, Michael, editor. *Encyclopedia of Archaeological Excavations in the Holy Land.* 4 vols. Englewood Cliffs, NJ: Prentice-Hall, 1976.

———. *The Holy Land: From the Persian to the Arab Conquest (536 B.C.–A.D. 640).* Rev. ed. Grand Rapids: Baker, 1977.

Badian, E. *Publicans and Sinners: Private Enterprise in the Service of the Roman Republic.* Ithaca, NY: Cornell University Press, 1972.

Bagatti, Bellarmino. *Excavations in Nazareth*. Vol. 1: *From the Beginning till the XII Century*. Studium Biblicum Franciscanum 17. Jerusalem: Franciscan Printing Press, 1969.

Bagatti, Bellarmino, and Vassilios Tzaferis. "Nazareth." In *The New Encyclopedia of Archaeological Excavations in the Holy Land*, edited by Ephraim Stern, 3:1103–5. New York: Simon & Schuster, 1993.

Bagnall, Roger, and Peter Derow. *Greek Historical Documents: The Hellenistic Period*. Sources for Biblical Study 16. Chico, CA: Scholars, 1981.

Bailey, Kenneth E. *Poet and Peasant: A Literary Cultural Approach to the Parables in Luke*. Grand Rapids: Eerdmans, 1976.

———. *Through Peasant Eyes: More Lucan Parables, Their Culture and Style*. Grand Rapids: Eerdmans, 1980.

———. ""Agriculture," "Clothing," "Crafts," "Houses," "Furniture," "Utensils," "Trade and Transport"." In *The Oxford Companion to the Bible*, 18–19, 125–26, 139–40, 293–99, 748–49. Oxford: Oxford University Press, 1993.

Balz, Horst, and Gerhard Schneider. *Exegetisches Wörterbuch Zum Neuen Testament*. 3 vols. Stuttgart: Kohlhammer, 1983.

Bandstra, Andrew J. "The Original Form of the Lord's Prayer." *Calvin Theological Journal* 16 (1981) 15–37.

Baron, Salo. "Population." In *Encyclopaedia Judaica*, edited by Cecil Roth and Geoffrey Wigoder, 13:866–72. Jerusalem: Keter, 1971.

———. *A Social and Religious History of the Jews*. 18 vols. 2d ed. New York: Columbia University Press, 1952–1983.

Barr, James. "Abba Isn't Daddy." *Journal of Theological Studies* 39 (1988) 28–47.

Barrett, C. K. *The Gospel according to St. John*. 2d ed. Philadelphia: Westminster, 1978.

Barrois, A. "Debt, Debtor." In *IDB* 1:809–10.

Barton, Bruce. *The Man Nobody Knows*. Indianapolis: Bobbs-Merrill, 1925.

Batey, Richard. *Jesus and the Forgotten City*. Grand Rapids: Baker, 1992.

Bauer, Walter. *A Greek English Lexicon of the New Testament and Other Early Christian Literature*. Translated by William F. Arndt, F. Wilbur Gingrich and Frederick W. Danker. 2d ed. Chicago: University of Chicago Press, 1979.

Bauer, Walter, and Frederick W. Danker. *A Greek English Lexicon of the New Testament and Other Early Christian Literature*. Based on Walter Bauer's Griechisch-deutsches Wörterbuch zu den Schriften des Neuen Testaments und der frühchristlichen Literatur, 6th ed., edited by Kurt Aland and Barbara Aland, with Viktor Reichmann and on previous English editions by William F. Arndt, F. Wilbur Gingrich, and Frederick W. Danker. 3d ed. Chicago: University of Chicago Press, 2000.

Baumgardt, David. "Kaddish and Lord's Prayer." *Jewish Bible Quarterly (Dor LeDor)* 19 (1991) 164–69.

Behm, Johannes. "*Klaō, ktl.*" In *TDNT* 3 (1965) 726–43.

Bellah, Robert N. *Beyond Belief: Essays on Religion in a Post-Traditional World*. New York: Harper & Row, 1970.

———. *Beyond Belief: Essays on Religion in a Post-Traditional World*. Berkeley: University of California Press, 1991.

Belo, Fernando. *A Materialist Reading of the Gospel of Mark*. Translated by Matthew J. O'Connell. Maryknoll, NY: Orbis, 1981.

Ben-Tor, Amnon. "Qiri, Tel." In *The New Encyclopedia of Archaeological Excavations in the Holy Land*, edited by Ephraim Stern, 4:1228–29. New York: Simon & Schuster, 1993.

Benoît, Pierre, Józef T. Milik, and Roland de Vaux. *Les Grottes de Murabbaʿat*. 2 vols. Discoveries in the Judean Desert 2. Oxford: Clarendon, 1961.

Beteille, A. *Social Inequality*. Baltimore: Penguin, 1969.

Betlyon, John W. "Coinage." In *ABD* 1:1085–89.

Betz, Hans Dieter. *The Sermon on the Mount*. Hermeneia. Minneapolis: Fortress, 1995.

Birnbaum, Philip, editor. *Daily Prayer Book*. Hebrew Publishing Company, 1949.

Black, Matthew. *An Aramaic Approach to the Gospels and Acts*. 3d ed. Reprinted, with an Introduction by Craig A. Evans. Peabody, MA: Hendrickson, 1998.

Blackman, Philip. *Mishnayoth*. 7 vols. 2d ed. New York: Judaica, 1964.

Blass, Friedrich, Albert Debrunner, and Robert W. Funk. *A Greek Grammar of the New Testament and Other Early Christian Literature*. Chicago: University of Chicago Press, 1961.

Blau, Ludwig. "Der Prosbol im Lichte der griechischen Papyri und der Rechtsgeschichte." In *Festschrift zum 50 jährige Bestehen der Franz-Josef-Landesrabbinerschule in Budapest*, edited by Ludwig Blau, 96–151. Budapest: Alexander Kohut Memorial Foundation, 1927.

Booth, William James. *Households: On the Moral Architecture of the Economy*. Ithaca: Cornell University Press, 1993.

Borg, Marcus J. *Conflict, Holiness and Politics in the Teachings of Jesus*. SBEC 5. New York: Mellen, 1984.

————. *Jesus: A New Vision*. San Francisco: Harper & Row, 1987.

————. "Portraits of Jesus in Contemporary North American Scholarship." *HTR* 84 (1991) 1–22.

Botha, F. J. "Recent Research on the Lord's Prayer." *Neotestamentica* 1 (1967) 42–50.

Brandon, S. G. F. *Jesus and the Zealots: A Study of the Political Factor in Primitive Christianity*. New York: Scribner, 1967.

Braudel, Fernand. *The Mediterranean and the Mediterranean World in the Age of Philip II*. 2 vols. Translated by Siân Reynolds. 2d ed. New York: Harper & Row, 1972–1973.

————. *The Structures of Everyday Life*. 3 vols. New York: Harper & Row, 1981.

Brooke, George J. "The Lord's Prayer Interpreted Through John and Paul." *Downside Review* 98 (1980) 298–311.

Broshi, M. "La Population de L'Ancienne Jerusalem." *RB* 82 (1975) 5–14.

————. "The Population of Western Palestine in the Roman-Byzantine Period." *BASOR* 236 (1980) 1–10.

Broshi, M., and R. Gophna. "The Settlements and Population of Palestine During the Early Bronze Age II–III." *BASOR* 253 (1984) 41–53.

————. "Middle Bronze Age II Palestine: Its Settlements and Population." *BASOR* 261 (1986) 73–90.

Broughton, T. R. S. "Roman Asia Minor." In *An Economic Survey of Ancient Rome*, edited by Tenney Frank, 4:503–916. 6th ed. Patterson, NJ: Pageant, 1959.

Brown, Francis, S. R. Driver, and Charles A. Briggs. *A Hebrew and English Lexicon of the Old Testament*. London: Oxford University Press, 1907.

Brown, John Pairman. "Techniques of Imperial Control: The Background of the Gospel Event." In *The Bible and Liberation: Political and Social Hermeneutics*, edited by Norman K. Gottwald, 357–77. Maryknoll, NY: Orbis, 1983.

———. "Prometheus, the Servant of Yahweh, Jesus: Legitimation and Repression in the Heritage of Persian Imperialism." In *The Bible and the Politics of Exegesis: Essays in Honor of Norman K. Gottwald on His Sixty-Fifth Birthday*, edited by David Jobling, Peggy L. Day and Gerald T. Sheppard, 109–25. Cleveland: Pilgrim, 1991.

———. *Israel and Hellas*. 3 vols. Berlin: de Gruyter, 1995–2001.

———. *Ancient Israel and Ancient Greece: Religion, Politics, and Culture*. Minneapolis: Fortress, 2003.

Brown, Raymond E. "The Pater Noster as an Eschatological Prayer." In *New Testament Essays*, 217–53. Milwaukee: Bruce, 1965.

———. *The Death of the Messiah: From Gethsemane to the Grave. A Commentary on the Passion Narratives in the Four Gospels*. 2 vols. New York: Doubleday, 1994.

Brown, Raymond E., Joseph A. Fitzmyer, and Roland E. Murphy, editors. *The New Jerome Biblical Commentary*. Englewood Cliffs, NJ: Prentice-Hall, 1990.

Brueggemann, Walter. *The Prophetic Imagination*. Philadelphia: Fortress, 1978. 2d ed., 2001.

———. "Trajectories in Old Testament Literature and the Sociology of Ancient Israel." *JBL* 98 (1979) 161–85.

Bruggen, Jacob van. "The Lord's Prayer and Textual Criticism." *Calvin Theological Journal* 17 (1981) 78–87.

Brunt, Peter. *Social Conflicts in the Roman Republic*. New York: Norton, 1971.

———. "Josephus on Social Conflicts in Roman Judaea." *Klio* 59 (1977) 149–53.

Büchler, Adolph. "The Economic Conditions of Judaea after the Destruction of the Second Temple." London: Jews College, 1912. Reprinted in *Studies in Jewish History: Adolph Büchler Memorial Volume*, edited by I. Brodie and J. Rabbinowitz. London: Oxford University Press, 1956.

Bultmann, Rudolf. *Jesus and the Word*. Translated by Louise Pettibone Smith and Erminie Huntress Lantero. New York: Scribner, 1958.

———. *History of the Synoptic Tradition*. Rev. ed. Translated by John Marsh. New York: Harper & Row, 1963.

———. "*Aphiēmi, ktl.*" In *TDNT* 1 (1964) 509–12.

Byatt, A. "Josephus and Population Numbers in First Century Palestine." *PEQ* 105 (1973) 51–60.

Cancian, Frank. "Economic Behavior in Peasant Communities." In *Economic Anthropology*, edited by Stuart Plattner, 127–70. Stanford: Stanford University Press, 1989.

Carney, Thomas F. *The Economies of Antiquity: Controls, Gifts and Trade*. Lawrence, KS: Coronado, 1973.

———. *The Shape of the Past: Models and Antiquity*. Lawrence, KS: Coronado, 1975.

Case, Shirley Jackson. *The Millennial Hope: A Phase of War-Time Thinking*. Chicago: University of Chicago, 1918.

Cassidy, Richard J., and Philip J. Scharper, editors. *Political Issues in Luke–Acts*. Maryknoll, NY: Orbis, 1983.

Cassirer, Ernst. *Language and Myth*. Translated by Susanne K. Langer. New York: Dover, 1946.

Charlesworth, James H., editor. *The Old Testament Pseudepigrapha*. Vol. 1: *Apocalyptic Literature and Testaments*. Garden City, NY: Doubleday, 1983.

———. *The Old Testament Pseudepigrapha*. Vol. 2: *Expansions of the "Old Testament" and Legends, Wisdom and Philosophical Literature, Prayers, Psalms, and Odes, Fragments of Lost Judeo-Hellenistic Works*. Garden City, NY: Doubleday, 1985.

———. "A Caveat on Textual Transmission and the Meaning of *Abba*: A Study of the Lord's Prayer." In *The Lord's Prayer and Other Prayer Texts from the Greco-Roman Era*, edited by James H. Charlesworth et al., 1–14. Valley Forge, PA: Trinity, 1994.

Childe, V. Gordon. *What Happened in History?* With a new foreword by Professor Grahame Clark. New York: Penguin, 1964.

Childers, Norman F. *Modern Fruit Science: Orchard and Small Fruit Culture*. 2d ed. New Brunswick, NJ: Horticultural Publications, Rutgers University, 1961.

Chilton, Bruce. *The Temple of Jesus: His Sacrificial Program within a Cultural History of Sacrifice*. University Park: The Pennsylvania State University Press, 1992.

Cicero, Marcus Tullius. *De officiis*. Translated by Walter Miller. LCL. Cambridge: Harvard University Press, 1956.

Clark, Colin, and Maurine Haswell. *The Economics of Subsistence Agriculture*. 4 ed. New York: St. Martin's, 1970.

Collins, Adela Y. *Crisis and Catharsis: The Power of the Apocalypse*. Philadelphia: Westminster, 1984.

Collins, John J. "Early Jewish Apocalypticism." In *ABD* 1:282–88.

———. "Sibylline Oracles." In *OTP* 1:317–472. Garden City, NY: Doubleday, 1983.

Collins, Randall. *Theoretical Sociology*. San Diego: Harcourt Brace Jovanovich, 1988.

Coote, Robert B., and Mary P. Coote. *Power, Politics, and the Making of the Bible: An Introduction*. Minneapolis: Fortress, 1990.

Correns, Dietrich. *Schebiit. Vom Sabbatjahr: Text, Übersetzung und Erklärung*. Die Mischna: Text Übersetzung und ausführliche Erklärung. Berlin: Töpelmann, 1960.

Countryman, L. William. *The Rich Christian in the Church of the Early Empire: Contradictions and Accommodations*. Texts and Studies in Religion 7. New York: Mellen, 1980.

Cranfield, C. E. B. *The Gospel according to Saint Mark*. Cambridge: Cambridge University Press, 1959.

Crawford, Michael. "Money and Exchange in the Roman World." *JRS* 60 (1970) 40–48.

Cross, Frank M. "Reconstruction of the Judean Restoration." *JBL* 94 (1975) 4–18.

Crossan, John Dominic. *In Parables: The Challenge of the Historical Jesus*. San Francisco: Harper and Row, 1973.

———. *In Fragments: The Aphorisms of Jesus*. San Francisco: Harper and Row, 1983.

———. *Sayings Parallels: A Workbook for the Jesus Tradition*. Foundations and Facets. Philadelphia: Fortress, 1986.

———. *The Historical Jesus: The Life of a Mediterranean Jewish Peasant*. San Francisco: HarperSanFrancisco, 1991.

———. *Jesus: A Revolutionary Biography*. San Francisco: HarperSanFrancisco, 1993.

———. *The Birth of Christianity Discovering What Happened in the Years Immediately after the Execution of Jesus*. San Francisco: HarperSanFrancisco, 1998.

Cyster, R. F. "The Lord's Prayer and the Exodus Tradition." *Theology* 64 (1961) 377–81.

Dalman, Gustaf. *Die Worte Jesu*. 2d ed. Leipzig: Hinrichs, 1930.

———. *Arbeit und Sitte in Palästina.* 7 vols. 1928–1939. Reprinted, Hildesheim: Olms, 1964.

Daly, Herman, and John B. Cobb, Jr. *For the Common Good: Redirecting the Economy Toward Community, the Environment, and a Sustainable Future.* 2d ed. Boston: Beacon, 1994.

Danby, Herbert. *The Mishnah: Translated from the Hebrew with Introduction and Brief Explanatory Notes.* Oxford: Oxford University Press, 1933.

Danker, Frederick W. *Jesus and the New Age: A Commentary on St. Luke's Gospel.* St. Louis: Clayton, 1972.

———. *Luke.* Proclamation Commentaries. Philadelphia: Fortress, 1976.

———. *Jesus and the New Age: A Commentary on St. Luke's Gospel.* 2d ed. Philadelphia: Fortress, 1988.

Dar, Shimon. *Landscape and Pattern.* Oxford: BAR, 1986.

Davies, W. D., and Dale C. Allison. "Excursus: The Lord's Prayer: Matthew 6.9–13 = Luke 11.2–4." In *Matthew,* 590–617. International Critical Commentary. Edinburgh: T. & T. Clark, 1988.

Deissmann, Adolf. *Light From the Ancient East: The New Testament Illustrated by Recently Discovered Texts from the Graeco-Roman World.* Rev. ed. Translated by L. R. M. Strachan. 1927. Reprinted, Eugene, OR: Wipf & Stock, 2004.

———. *Bible Studies.* Translated by Alexander Grieve. 1909. Reprinted, Winona Lake, IN: Alpha, 1979.

Derrett, J. Duncan M. "Law in the New Testament: The Parable of the Unjust Judge." *NTS* 18 (1971) 178–91.

de Ste. Croix, G. E. M. *The Class Struggle in the Ancient Greek World: From the Archaic Age to the Arab Conquests.* Ithaca, NY: Cornell University, 1981.

Dickey, Samuel. "Some Economic and Social Conditions of Asia Minor Affecting the Expansion of Christianity." In *Studies in Early Christianity,* edited by Shirley Jackson Case, 393–416. New York: Century, 1928.

Dio Chrysostom. Translated by H. L. Crosby. LCL. Cambridge: Harvard University Press, 1962.

Dobrowolski, Kazimierz. "Peasant Traditional Culture." In *Peasants and Peasant Societies,* edited by Teodor Shanin, 277–98. Harmondsworth, UK: Penguin, 1971.

Donahue, John. "Tax Collectors and Sinners: An Attempt at an Identification." *CBQ* 33 (1971) 39–61.

———. "Recent Studies on the Origin of 'Son of Man' in the Gospels." *CBQ* 48 (1986) 484–98.

Donaldson, T. L. "Rural Bandits, City Mobs and the Zealots." *JSJ* 21 (1990) 19–40.

Duling, Dennis C. "Matthew and Marginality." In *Society of Biblical Literature 1993 Seminar Papers,* edited by Eugene H. Lovering, Jr., 642–71. Atlanta: Scholars, 1993.

———. *The New Testament: History, Literature, and Social Context.* 4th ed. Belmont, CA: Wadsworth/Thomson, 2003.

Duling, Dennis C., and Norman Perrin. *The New Testament: Proclamation and Parenesis, Myth and History.* 3d ed. Fort Worth, TX: Harcourt Brace College Publishers, 1994.

Duncan-Jones, Richard. *The Economy of the Roman Empire: Quantitative Studies.* 2d ed. Cambridge: Cambridge University Press, 1982.

———. *Money and Government in the Roman Empire*. Cambridge: Cambridge University Press, 1994.

Dundes, Alan. *Study of Folklore*. Englewood Cliffs, NJ: Prentice-Hall, 1965.

Edwards, Douglas R. "First Century Urban/Rural Relations in Lower Galilee: Exploring the Archaeological and Literary Evidence." In *Society of Biblical Literature 1988 Seminar Papers*, edited by David J. Lull, 169–82. Atlanta: Scholars, 1988.

———. "The Socio-Economic and Cultural Ethos of the Lower Galilee in the First Century: Implications for the Nascent Jesus Movement." In *The Galilee in Late Antiquity*, edited by Lee I. Levine, 53–73. New York: Jewish Theological Seminary of America, 1992.

Eissfeld, Otto. *The Old Testament: An Introduction*. Translated by Peter R. Ackroyd. Harper & Row, 1965.

Elliott, John H., editor. *Semeia*. Vol. 35: *Social-Scientific Criticism of the New Testament and Its Social World*. Decatur, GA: Scholars, 1986.

———. *A Home for the Homeless: A Social-Scientific Criticism of 1 Peter, Its Situation and Strategy*. 2d ed. 1990. Reprinted, Eugene, OR: Wipf & Stock, 2005.

———. *What Is Social-Scientific Criticism?* Guides to Biblical Scholarship. Minneapolis: Fortress, 1993.

———. "Jesus the Israelite was Neither a 'Jew' nor a 'Christian': On Correcting Misleading Nomenclature." *Journal for the Study of the Historical Jesus* 5.2 (2007) 119–54.

Eppstein, Victor. "The Historicity of the Gospel Account of the Cleansing of the Temple." *ZNW* 55 (1964) 42–58.

Esler, Philip F., editor. *Modelling Early Christianity: Social-Scientific Studies of the New Testament in Its Context*. London: Routledge, 1995.

———. "Models, Context and Kerygma in New Testament Interpretation." In *Modelling Early Christianity*, 1–20.

Eusebius. *Ecclesiastical History*. Translated by Kirsopp Lake and J. E. L. Oulton. LCL. Cambridge: Harvard University Press, 1973–1975.

Evans, Craig A. "Jesus' Action in the Temple and Evidence of Corruption in the First-Century Temple." In *Society of Biblical Literature 1989 Seminar Papers*, edited by David J. Lull, 522–39. Atlanta: Scholars, 1989.

———. *Life of Jesus Research: An Annotated Bibliography*. NTTS 13. Leiden: Brill, 1989.

———. "From Public Ministry to the Passion: Can a Link Be Found Between the (Galilean) Life and the (Judean) Death of Jesus." In *Society of Biblical Literature 1993 Seminar Papers*, edited by Eugene H. Lovering, Jr., 460–74. Atlanta: Scholars, 1993.

———. *Life of Jesus Research: An Annotated Bibliography*. Rev. ed. NTTS 24. Leiden: Brill, 1996.

Fiensy, David A. *The Social History of Palestine in the Herodian Period: The Land is Mine*. SBEC 20. Lewiston, NY: Mellen, 1991.

Finegan, Jack. *The Archaeology of the New Testament: The Life of Jesus and the Beginning of the Early Church*. Rev. ed. Princeton: Princeton University Press, 1992.

Finkelstein, Louis. "The Oldest Midrash: Pre-Rabbinic Ideals and Teachings in the Passover Haggadah." *HTR* 31 (1938) 291–317.

———. "Pre-Maccabean Documents in the Passover Haggadah." *HTR* 35 (1942) 291–332.

———. "Pre-Maccabean Documents in the Passover Haggadah." *HTR* 36 (1943) 1–38.

Finley, Moses I. *The Ancient Economy*. Sather Classical Lectures 43. Berkeley: University of California Press, 1973.

Fitzmyer, Joseph A. "The Story of the Dishonest Manager (Luke 16:1–13)." In *Essays on the Semitic Background of the New Testament*, 161–84. Sources for Biblical Study 5. Missoula, MT: Scholars, 1974.

————. *The Gospel according to Luke*. 2 vols. AB 28, 28A. Garden City, NY: Doubleday, 1981–1985.

Foerster, W. "*Epiousios*." In *TDNT* 2 (1964) 590–99.

Ford, Josephine M. "Yom Kippur and the Matthean Form of the Pater Noster." *Worship* 41 (1967) 609–19.

————. *Revelation*. AB 38. Garden City, NY: Doubleday, 1975.

Foster, George M. "Introduction: What is a Peasant?" In *Peasant Society: A Reader*, edited by J. Potter, M. Diaz, and G. M. Foster, 2–14. Boston: Little, Brown, and Co., 1967.

————. "Peasant Society and the Image of the Limited Good." In *Peasant Society: A Reader*, edited by J. Potter, M. Diaz, and G. M. Foster, 300–323. Boston: Little, Brown, and Co., 1967.

Frank, Tenney, editor. *An Economic Survey of Ancient Rome*. 6 vols. 6th ed. Patterson, NJ: Pageant, 1959.

Frankel, Rafael. "Some Oil Presses from Western Galilee." *BASOR* 286 (1992) 39–71.

Freedman, H., and M. Simon. *Midrash Rabbah*. New York: Soncino, 1939.

Freyne, Seán. *Galilee from Alexander the Great to Hadrian 323 B.C.E. to 135 C.E.* Wilmington, DE: Michael Glazier, 1980.

————. *Galilee, Jesus and the Gospels: Literary Approaches and Historical Investigations*. Philadelphia: Fortress, 1988.

Funk, Robert. "The Looking-Glass Tree Is for the Birds." *Int* 27 (1973) 3–9.

————. *New Gospel Parallels*. 2 vols. Philadelphia: Fortress, 1985.

————. "Poll on the Parables." *Forum* 2,1 (1986) 54–80.

Funk, Robert W., Bernard B. Scott, and James R. Butts. *The Parables of Jesus: Red Letter Edition*. Jesus Seminar Series. Sonoma, CA: Polebridge, 1988.

Funk, Robert W., Roy W. Hoover, and The Jesus Seminar. *The Five Gospels: What Did Jesus Really Say?* San Francisco: HarperSanFrancisco, 1993.

Furnish, Victor Paul. *Theology and Ethics in Paul*. Nashville: Abingdon, 1968.

Gale, Aaron M. *Redefining Ancient Borders: The Jewish Scribal Framework of Matthew's Gospel*. New York: T. & T. Clark, 2005.

Garnsey, Peter, and Richard Saller. *The Roman Empire: Economy, Society and Culture*. Berkeley: University of California, 1987.

Geertz, Clifford. "Village." In *IESS* 16:318–22.

Georgi, Dieter. *Remembering the Poor: The History of Paul's Collection for Jerusalem*. Nashville: Abingdon, 1992.

Gerth, H. H., and C. W. Mills. *From Max Weber: Essays in Sociology*. New York: Oxford University Press, 1946.

Gesenius' Hebrew Grammar. edited and enlarged by E. Kautzsch. Translated by A. E. Cowley. 2d. ed. Oxford: Clarendon, 1919.

Gilmore, David D. *Honor and Shame and the Unity of the Mediterranean*. Special Publication of the American Anthropological Association 22. Washington: American Anthropological Association, 1987.

Ginzberg, E. *Studies in the Economics of the Bible.* Philadelphia: Jewish Publication Society, 1932.

Glatzer, Nahum, editor. *The Passover Haggadah. with English Translation Introduction and Commentary. Based on the Commentaries of E. D. Goldschmidt.* 3d ed. New York: Schocken, 1979.

Goodman, Martin. "The First Jewish Revolt: Social Conflict and the Problem of Debt." *JJS* 33 (1982) 417–27.

———. *State and Society in Roman Galilee, A.D. 132–212.* Totowa, NJ: Rowman & Allanheld, 1983.

———. *The Ruling Class of Judaea: The Origins of the Jewish Revolt Against Rome A.D. 66–70.* Cambridge: Cambridge University Press, 1987.

Goodspeed, Edgar J. *The New Testament: An American Translation.* Chicago: University of Chicago Press, 1923.

———. *As I Remember.* New York: Harper, 1953.

Gottwald, Norman K. *The Tribes of Yahweh: A Sociology of the Religion of Liberated Israel, 1250–1050 BCE.* Maryknoll, NY: Orbis, 1979.

———. *The Hebrew Bible: A Socio-Literary Introduction.* Philadelphia: Fortress, 1985.

Gouldner, Alvin. "The Norm of Reciprocity." In *Friends, Followers, and Factions: A Reader in Political Clientelism*, edited by Steffen W. Schmidt et al., 28–43. Berkeley: University of California, 1977.

Grant, Frederick C. *The Economic Background of the Gospels.* London: Oxford University Press, 1926. Reprint, New York: Russell & Russell, 1973.

———. *Ancient Roman Religion.* The Library of Religion 8. New York: Liberal Arts, 1957.

Grondin, Jean. *Introduction to Philosophical Hermeneutics.* Foreword by Hans-Georg Gadamer. Translated by Joel Weinsheimer. Yale Studies in Hermeneutics. New Haven: Yale University Press, 1994.

Gutman, Shmaryahu. "Gamala." In *The New Encyclopedia of Archaeological Excavations in the Holy Land*, edited by Ephraim Stern, 2:459–63. New York: Simon & Schuster, 1993.

Haenchen, Ernst. *John 1.* Translated by Robert W. Funk. Hermeneia. Philadelphia: Fortress, 1984.

Hamburger, Herbert. "Money, Coins." In *IDB* 3:423–35.

Hamel, Gildas. "Poverty and Charity in Roman Palestine." Ph. D. diss., University of California, Santa Cruz, 1983.

———. *Poverty and Charity in Roman Palestine, First Three Centuries C.E.* Near Eastern Studies 23. Berkeley: University of California Press, 1990.

Hamilton, Neill Q. "Temple Cleansing and Temple Bank." *JBL* 83 (1964) 365–72.

Hammond, N. G. L., and H. H. S. Scullard, editors. *The Oxford Classical Dictionary.* 2d ed. Oxford: Clarendon, 1970.

Hanson, K. C. "'How Honorable!' 'How Shameful!' A Cultural Analysis of Matthew's Makarisms and Reproaches." *Semeia* 68 (1994[96]) 81–111.

———. "The Economy of Galilean Fishing and the Jesus Tradition." *BTB* 27 (1997) 99–111.

————. "Jesus and the Social Bandits." In *The Social Setting of Jesus and the Gospels,* edited by Wolfgang Stegemann, Bruce J. Malina, and Gerd Theissen, 283–300. Minneapolis: Fortress, 2002.

————, and Douglas E. Oakman. *Palestine in the Time of Jesus: Social Structures and Social Conflicts.* Minneapolis: Fortress, 1998.

Hanson, P. D., A. K. Grayson, and J. J. Collins. "Apocalypses and Apocalypticism." In *ABD* 1:279–88.

Harper, George McLean, Jr. "Village Administration in the Roman Province of Syria." *Yale Classical Studies* 1 (1928) 105–68.

Harrington, Daniel. "Mark." In *The New Jerome Biblical Commentary,* edited by Raymond E. Brown, Joseph A. Fitzmyer and Roland E. Murphy, 596–629. Englewood Cliffs, NJ: Prentice-Hall, 1990.

Harris, William V. *Ancient Literacy.* Cambridge: Harvard University Press, 1989.

Hauck, F. "*Mamōnas.*" In *TDNT* 4 (1967) 388–90.

————. "*Opheilō, ktl.*" *TDNT* 5 (1967) 559–66.

Heichelheim, F. M. "Roman Syria." In *An Economic Survey of Ancient Rome,* edited by Tenney Frank, 4:121–257. Baltimore: Johns Hopkins University Press, 1938.

Heilbroner, Robert. *The Making of Economic Society.* 7th ed. Englewood Cliffs, NJ: Prentice-Hall, 1985.

Hemer, Colin J. "*Epiousios.*" *JSNT* 22 (1984) 81–94.

————. *The Letters to the Seven Churches of Asia in Their Local Setting.* JSOTSup 11. Sheffield: University of Sheffield, 1986.

Hengel, Martin. *Judaism and Hellenism: Studies in Their Encounter in Palestine During the Early Hellenistic Period.* 2 vols. Translated by John Bowden. Philadelphia: Fortress, 1974.

————. *The Zealots: Investigations Into the Jewish Freedom Movement in the Period from Herod I Until 70 A.D.* WUNT 10. Edinburgh: T. & T. Clark, 1989.

Hennecke, Edgar. *New Testament Apocrypha.* 2 vols. Edited by Wilhelm Schneemelcher. Translated by R. McL. Wilson. Philadelphia: Westminster, 1963.

Hepper, F. N. *Baker Encyclopedia of Bible Plants.* Grand Rapids: Baker, 1992.

Herskovits, Melville. *Economic Anthropology: The Economic Life of Primitive Peoples.* 2d ed. New York: Knopf, 1952.

Herzog, William R. II. *Parables as Subversive Speech: Jesus as Pedagogue of the Oppressed.* Louisville: Westminster John Knox, 1994.

————. *Jesus, Justice, and the Reign of God a Ministry of Liberation.* Louisville: Westminster John Knox, 2000.

Hesiod: The Works and Days, Theogony, The Shield of Herakles. Translated by Richmond Lattimore. Ann Arbor: University of Michigan Press, 1959.

Hezser, Catherine. *Jewish Literacy in Roman Palestine.* Texts and Studies in Ancient Judaism 81. Tübingen: Mohr/Siebeck, 2001.

Hiers, Richard H. "Purification of the Temple: Preparation for the Kingdom of God." *JBL* 90 (1971) 82–90.

Hobsbawm, Eric. *Primitive Rebels.* New York: Norton, 1959.

————. "Peasants and Politics." *Journal of Peasant Studies* 1 (1973) 3–22.

————. *Bandits.* Rev. ed. New York: Pantheon, 1981.

Hollenbach, Paul. "Liberating Jesus for Social Involvement." *BTB* 15 (1985) 151–57.

The Holy Bible Containing the Old and New Testaments. Newly edited by the American Revision Committee. Standard Edition. New York: Nelson, 1901.

Hopkins, Ian. "The City Region in Roman Palestine." *PEQ* 112 (1980) 19–52.

Horsley, Richard A. "Popular Messianic Movements Around the Time of Jesus." *CBQ* 46 (1984) 471–95.

———. "Like One of the Prophets of Old." *CBQ* 47 (1985) 435–63.

———. *Jesus and the Spiral of Violence: Popular Jewish Resistance in Roman Palestine*. San Francisco: Harper & Row, 1987.

———. *Sociology and the Jesus Movement*. New York: Crossroad, 1989.

———. "Jesus, Itinerant Cynic or Israelite Prophet?" In *Images of Jesus Today*, edited by J. H. Charlesworth and W. P. Weaver, 68–97. Valley Forge, PA: Trinity, 1994.

———. *Galilee: History, Politics, People*. Valley Forge, PA: Trinity, 1995.

———. *Archaeology, History, and Society in Galilee: The Social Context of Jesus and the Rabbis*. Valley Forge, PA: Trinity, 1996.

Horsley, Richard A., and John S. Hanson. *Bandits, Prophets, and Messiahs: Popular Movements at the Time of Jesus*. San Francisco: Harper & Row, 1985.

Horsley, Richard A., and Jonathan A. Draper. *Whoever Hears You Hears Me: Prophets, Performance, and Tradition in Q*. Harrisburg, PA: Trinity, 1999.

Hoselitz, Bert F. *A Reader's Guide to the Social Sciences*. New York: Free Press, 1959.

Houlden, J. L. "The Lord's Prayer." In *ABD* 4:356–62.

Hug, August. "*PANDOKEION.*" In *Pauly's Realencyclopädie der Classischen Altertumswissenschaft*, edited by K. Ziegler, vol. 18.3:520–29. 2d ed. Munich: Druckenmüller, 1983.

Hunt, A., and C. Edgar. *Select Papyri*. Vol. 2: *Non-literary Papyri*. LCL. Cambridge: Harvard University Press, 1956.

Hunzinger, Claus-Hunno. "*Sinapi.*" *TDNT* 7 (1971) 287–91.

———. "*Sykē, ktl.*" *TDNT* 7 (1971) 751–59.

Idelsohn, A. Z. *Jewish Liturgy*. New York: Schocken, 1960.

Jackson, F. J. Foakes, and Lake Kirsopp. *The Beginnings of Christianity: The Acts of the Apostles*, Vol. 2: *Prolegonmena II: Criticism*. Reprint. Grand Rapids: Baker, 1979.

Jacobson, Arland D. *The First Gospel: An Introduction to Q*. 1992. Reprint, Eugene, OR: Wipf & Stock, 2005.

Jastrow, Marcus. *Dictionary of the Targumim, the Talmud Babli and Yerushalmi, and the Midrashic Literature*. 2 vols. 1903. Reprint, New York: Pardes, 1950.

Jeremias, Joachim. "The Lord's Prayer in Modern Research." *Expository Times* 71 (1960) 141–46.

———. "*Ēl(e)ias.*" In *TDNT* 2 (1964) 928–41.

———. *Abba: Studien zur neutestamentlichen Theologie und Zeitgeschichte*. Göttingen: Vandenhoeck & Ruprecht, 1966.

———. *The Eucharistic Words of Jesus*. Translated by Norman Perrin. 1966. Reprint, Philadelphia: Fortress, 1977.

———. *The Prayers of Jesus*. SBT 2/6. Naperville, IL: Allenson, 1967.

———. *Jerusalem in the Time of Jesus*. Translated by F. H. Cave and C. H. Cave. Philadelphia: Fortress, 1969.

———. *New Testament Theology*. Vol. 1: *The Proclamation of Jesus*. Translated by John Bowden. New York: Scribner, 1971.

————. *The Parables of Jesus.* Translated by S. H. Hooke. 2d ed. New York: Charles Scribner's Sons, 1972.

————. *The Lord's Prayer.* Translated by John Reumann. Philadelphia: Fortress, 1980.

Jeske, Richard L., and David L. Barr. "The Study of the Apocalypse Today." *Religious Studies Review* 14 (1988) 337–44.

Jones, A. H. M. "Taxation in Antiquity." In *The Roman Economy; Studies in Ancient Economic and Administrative History*, edited by P. A. Brunt, 151–85. Oxford: Blackwell, 1974.

Josephus. *Josephus in Nine Volumes.* Translated by H. St. J. Thackeray. LCL. Cambridge: Harvard University Press, 1976.

Kaplan, David, and Robert Manners. *Culture Theory.* Englewood Cliffs, NJ: Prentice-Hall, 1972.

Karris, Robert J. "Poor and Rich: The Lukan Sitz Im Leben." In *Perspectives on Luke-Acts*, edited by Charles H. Talbert, 112–25. Danville, VA: Association of Baptist Professors of Religion, 1978.

Kautsky, John H. *The Politics of Aristocratic Empires.* Chapel Hill, NC: University of North Carolina Press, 1982.

Kearsley, R. A. "Asiarchs." In *ABD* 1:495–97.

Kiley, Mark. "The Lord's Prayer and Other Prayer Texts from the Greco-Roman Era: A Bibliography." In *The Lord's Prayer and Other Prayer Texts from the Greco-Roman Era*, edited by James H. Charlesworth et al., 101–257. Valley Forge, PA: Trinity, 1994.

Kippenberg, Hans von. *Religion und Klassenbildung Im Antiken Judäa.* SUNT 14. Göttingen: Vandenhoeck & Ruprecht, 1978.

Kirk, Alan. "Administrative Writing, Oral Tradition, and Q." Unpublished paper: Q Section, AAR/SBL national meeting, San Antonio, TX, 2004.

Klausner, Joseph. *Jesus of Nazareth: His Life, Times, and Teaching.* Translated by Herbert Danby. New York: Macmillan, 1925.

Kloppenborg (Verbin), John S. "Q 11:14–20: Worksheets for Reconstruction." In *Society of Biblical Literature 1985 Seminar Papers*, edited by Kent Harold Richards, 133–51. Atlanta: Scholars, 1985.

————. *Q Parallels: Synopsis, Critical Notes, and Concordance.* Foundations and Facets. Sonoma, CA: Polebridge, 1988.

————. "The Dishonoured Master (Luke 16,1–8a)." *Biblica* 70 (1989) 474–95.

————. "Alms, Debt and Divorce: Jesus' Ethics in Their Mediterranean Context." *TJT* 6 (1990) 182–200.

————. "Literary Convention, Self-Evidence and the Social History of the Q People." In *Semeia*, Vol. 55: *Early Christianity, Q, and Jesus*, edited by John S. Kloppenborg and Leif E. Vaage, 77–102. Atlanta: Scholars, 1992.

————. "The Sayings Gospel Q: Recent Opinion on the People Behind the Document." *Currents in Research: Biblical Studies* 1 (1993) 9–34.

————. *Excavating Q: The History and Setting of the Sayings Gospel.* Minneapolis: Fortress, 2000.

Kloppenborg, John S., and Leif E. Vaage. "Early Christianity, Q and Jesus: The Sayings Gospel and Method in the Study of Christian Origins." In *Semeia*, Vol. 55: *Early Christianity, Q, and Jesus*, edited by John S. Kloppenborg and Leif E. Vaage, 1–14. Atlanta: Scholars, 1992.

Koester, Helmut. *Introduction to the New Testament.* 2 vols. Philadelphia: Fortress, 1982.

Koffmahn, E. *Die Doppelurkunden aus der Wüste Juda*. Leiden: Brill, 1968.

Kreissig, Heinz. "Die Landwirtschaftliche Situation in Palastina vor dem Judaischen Krieg." *Acta Antiqua* 17 (1969) 223–54.

———. *Die Sozialen Zusammenhänge Des Judäischen Krieges: Klassen und Klassenkampf Im Palästina Des 1. Jahrhunderts v. u. Z*. Berlin: Akademie, 1970.

———. *Wirtschaft und Gesellschaft Im Seleukidenreich: Die Eigentums- und die Abhängigkeitsverhältnisse*. Berlin: Akademie, 1978.

Kreitzer, Larry J. *Striking New Images: Roman Imperial Coinage and the New Testament World*. JSNTS 134. Sheffield: Sheffield Academic, 1996.

La Sor, William S. "Discovering What Jewish Miqva'ot Can Tell Us about Christian Baptism." *BAR* 13,1 (1987) 52–59.

Lachs, Samuel Tobias. "The Lord's Prayer." In *A Rabbinic Commentary on the New Testament*, 117–24. Hoboken, NJ: Ktav, 1987.

Lake, Kirsopp. *Apostolic Fathers*. 2 vols. LCL. Cambridge: Harvard University Press, 1976–1977.

Landsberger, Henry A. "Peasant Unrest; Themes and Variations." In *Rural Protest: Peasant Movements and Social Change*, edited by Henry A. Landsberger, 1–64. Publications of the International Institute for Labour Studies New York: Macmillan, 1974.

Leach, Maria. "Anthropomorphism." In *Standard Dictionary of Folklore Mythology and Legend*, edited by Maria Leach and Jerome Fried, 1:64–65. New York: Funk & Wagnalls, 1949.

Lenski, Gerhard E. *Power and Privilege: A Theory of Social Stratification*. New York: McGraw-Hill, 1966.

———. *Power and Privilege: A Theory of Social Stratification*. 2d ed. Chapel Hill: University of North Carolina Press, 1984.

Lenski, Gerhard E., and Jean Lenski. *Human Societies: An Introduction to Macrosociology*. 2d ed. New York: McGraw-Hill, 1974.

———. *Human Societies: An Introduction to Macrosociology*. 5th ed. New York: McGraw-Hill, 1987.

Levine, Lee I., editor. *The Galilee in Late Antiquity*. New York: Jewish Theological Seminary of America, 1992.

Lewis, Naphtali, and Meyer Reinhold, editors. *Roman Civilization: Selected Readings*. Vol. 2: *The Empire*. New York: Columbia University Press, 1955.

Liddell, H., R. Scott, and H. Jones. *A Greek English Lexicon with A Supplement*. Oxford: Clarendon, 1968.

Lightfoot, John. *A Commentary on the New Testament from the Talmud and Hebraica*. 4 vols. 1859. Reprint, Grand Rapids: Baker, 1979.

Ma`oz, Zvi Uri. "Golan: Hellenistic Period to the Middle Ages." In *The New Encyclopedia of Archaeological Excavations in the Holy Land*, edited by Ephraim Stern, 2:534–46. New York: Simon & Schuster, 1993.

Mack, Burton L. *A Myth of Innocence: Mark and Christian Origins*. Philadelphia: Fortress, 1988.

———. *The Lost Gospel: The Book of Q and Christian Origins*. San Francisco: HarperSanFrancisco, 1993.

Mack, Burton L., and Vernon K. Robbins. *Patterns of Persuasion in the Gospels*. Foundations and Facets. Sonoma, CA: Polebridge, 1989.

MacMullen, Ramsay. *Enemies of the Roman Order: Treason, Unrest, and Alienation in the Empire.* Cambridge: Harvard University Press, 1966.

———. "Market-Days in the Roman Empire." *Phoenix* 24 (1970) 333–41.

———. *Roman Social Relations: 50 B.C. to A.D. 284.* New Haven: Yale University Press, 1974.

Macro, Anthony D. "The Cities of Asia Minor under the Roman Imperium." In *ANRW* II. 7.2, 658–97. Berlin: de Gruyter, 1980.

Malbon, Elizabeth Struthers. "The Jewish Leaders in the Gospel of Mark: A Literary Study of Marcan Characterization." *JBL* 108 (1989) 259–81.

Malina, Bruce J. *The New Testament World: Insights from Cultural Anthropology.* Louisville: Westminster, 1981.

———. *Christian Origins and Cultural Anthropology: Practical Models for Biblical Interpretation.* Atlanta: John Knox, 1986.

———. "Wealth and Poverty in the New Testament and Its World." *Int* 41 (1987) 354–67.

———. "Patron and Client: The Analogy Behind Synoptic Theology." *Forum* 4,1 (1988) 2–32.

———. "Interpretation: Reading, Abduction, Metaphor." In *The Bible and the Politics of Exegesis: Essays in Honor of Norman K. Gottwald on His Sixty-Fifth Birthday,* edited by David Jobling, Peggy L. Day and Gerald T. Sheppard, 253–66. Cleveland: Pilgrim, 1991.

———. *The New Testament World: Insights from Cultural Anthropology.* Rev. ed. Louisville: Westminster John Knox, 1993.

———. *The Social World of Jesus and the Gospels.* London: Routledge, 1996.

———. *The New Testament World: Insights From Cultural Anthropology.* 3d ed. Louisville: Westminster John Knox, 2001.

Malina, Bruce J., and Richard L. Rohrbaugh. *Social-Science Commentary on the Synoptic Gospels.* Minneapolis: Fortress, 1992.

———. *Social-Science Commentary on the Synoptic Gospels.* 2d ed. Minneapolis: Fortress, 2003.

Malinowski, B. *Argonauts of the Western Pacific.* New York: Dutton, 1961.

Malter, Henry. *The Treatise Ta'anit of the Babylonian Talmud.* The JPS Library of Jewish Classics. Philadelphia: Jewish Publication Society of America, 1956.

Manson, T. W. *The Sayings of Jesus.* London: SCM, 1949.

———. *The Teaching of Jesus: Studies of Its Form and Content.* Cambridge: Cambridge University Press, 1959.

Marcuse, Herbert. *One-Dimensional Man: Studies in the Ideology of Advanced Industrial Society.* Boston: Beacon, 1964.

Marshall, I. Howard. *The Gospel of Luke.* New International Greek Testament Commentary. Grand Rapids: Eerdmans, 1978.

Martínez, Florentino García. *The Dead Sea Scrolls Translated: The Qumran Texts in English.* Translated by Wilfred G. E. Watson. 2d ed. Leiden: Brill, 1996.

Matthews, Victor H. *Manners and Customs in the Bible: An Illustrated Guide to Daily Life in Bible Times.* Rev. ed. Peabody, MA: Hendrickson, 1991.

Mazar, Benjamin. "Excavations Near Temple Mount Reveal Splendors of Herodian Jerusalem." *BAR* 6, 4 (1980) 44–59.

McCasland, S. V. "Will of God." In *IDB* 4:844–48.

McEvedy, C., and R. Jones. *Atlas of World Population History*. New York: Penguin, 1978.

McKenzie, J. "The Gospel According to Matthew." In *The Jerome Biblical Commentary*, edited by Raymond E. Brown, Joseph A. Fitzmyer and Roland E. Murphy. Englewood Cliffs, NJ: Prentice-Hall, 1968.

Meeks, Wayne A. *The First Urban Christians: The Social World of the Apostle Paul*. New Haven: Yale University Press, 1983.

Meier, John P. "Jesus." In *The New Jerome Biblical Commentary*, edited by Raymond E. Brown, Joseph A. Fitzmyer and Roland E. Murphy, 1316–28. Englewood Cliffs, NJ: Prentice-Hall, 1990.

———. *A Marginal Jew: Rethinking the Historical Jesus*. Vol. 1: *The Roots of the Problem and the Person*. The Anchor Bible Reference Library. New York: Doubleday, 1991.

———. *A Marginal Jew: Rethinking the Historical Jesus*. Vol. 2: *Mentor, Message, and Miracles*. The Anchor Bible Reference Library. New York: Doubleday, 1994.

Meshorer, Yaakov. "Jewish Numismatics." In *Early Judaism and Its Modern Interpreters*, edited by Robert A. Kraft and George W. E. Nickelsburg, 211–20. The Bible and Its Modern Interpreters 3: Atlanta: Scholars, 1986.

Metzger, Bruce M. *A Textual Commentary on the Greek New Testament: A Companion Volume to the United Bible Societies' Greek New Testament*. 3d ed. London: United Bible Societies, 1975.

Meyers, Eric M. "The Challenge of Hellenism for Early Judaism and Christianity." *Biblical Archaeologist* 55 (1992) 84–91.

———. "Roman Sepphoris in Light of New Archeological Evidence and Recent Research." In *The Galilee in Late Antiquity*, edited by Lee I. Levine, 321–38. New York: The Jewish Theological Seminary of America, 1992.

Meyers, Eric M., and James F. Strange. *Archaeology, the Rabbis, and Early Christianity*. Nashville: Abingdon, 1981.

Michel, Otto. "*Telōnēs*." In *TDNT* 8 (1972) 88–105.

Miller, Robert J. "The (A)Historicity of Jesus' Temple Demonstration: A Test Case in Methodology." In *Society of Biblical Literature 1991 Seminar Papers*, edited by Eugene H. Lovering, Jr., 235–52. Atlanta: Scholars, 1991.

———, editor. *The Complete Gospels: Annotated Scholar's Version*. 3rd ed. Sonoma, CA: Polebridge, 1995.

Miller, Stuart S. *Studies in the History and Traditions of Sepphoris*. Studies in Judaism in Late Antiquity 37. Leiden: Brill, 1984.

Mintz, Sidney. "A Note on the Definition of Peasantries." *Journal of Peasant Studies* 1 (1973) 91–106.

Monson, James M., et al. *Student Map Manual*. Grand Rapids: Zondervan, 1979.

Moor, Johannes C. de. "The Reconstruction of the Aramaic Original of the Lord's Prayer." In *The Structural Analysis of Biblical and Canaanite Poetry*, edited by W. van der Meer and J. C. de Moor, 397–422. JSOTSup 74. Sheffield: JSOT Press, 1988.

Moorey, P. R. S. *A Century of Biblical Archaeology*. Louisville: Westminster John Knox, 1991.

Moulton, James H., and Wilbert F. Howard. *A Grammar of the New Testament Greek*. Vol. 2: *Accidence and Word Formation, with an Appendix on Semitisms in the New Testament*. Edinburgh: T. & T. Clark, 1920.

Moulton, James H., and George Milligan. *The Vocabulary of the Greek Testament.* 1930. Reprint, Grand Rapids: Eerdmans, 1985.

Moxnes, Halvor. *The Economy of the Kingdom: Social Conflict and Economic Relations in Luke's Gospel.* Overtures to Biblical Theology. Philadelphia: Fortress, 1988.

Myers, Ched. *Binding the Strong Man: A Political Reading of Mark's Story of Jesus.* Maryknoll, NY: Orbis, 1988.

Nash, Manning. "Economic Anthropology." In *IESS* 4:359–65.

Netzer, Ehud. "Masada." In *The New Encyclopedia of Archaeological Excavations in the Holy Land,* edited by Ephraim Stern, 3:973–85. New York: Simon & Schuster, 1993.

Neusner, Jacob. *From Politics to Piety: The Emergence of Pharisaic Judaism.* 1973. Reprinted, Eugene, OR: Wipf & Stock, 2003.

Neyrey, Jerome H., editor. *The Social World of Luke-Acts: Models for Interpretation.* Peabody, MA: Hendrickson, 1991.

Nicholas, Barry. *An Introduction to Roman Law.* Clarendon Law Series. Oxford: Clarendon, 1962.

Nineham, Dennis. *St. Mark.* Pelican New Testament Commentaries. New York: Penguin, 1963.

Oakman, Douglas E. "Jesus and Agrarian Palestine: The Factor of Debt." In *Society of Biblical Literature 1985 Seminar Papers,* edited by Kent Harold Richards, 57–73. Atlanta: Scholars, 1985.

———. *Jesus and the Economic Questions of His Day.* SBEC 8. Lewiston, NY: Mellen, 1986.

———. "The Buying Power of Two Denarii: A Comment on Luke 10:35." *Forum* 3,4 (1987) 33–38.

———. "Rulers' Houses, Thieves, and Usurpers: The Beelzebul Pericope." *Forum* 4,3 (1988) 109–23.

———. "BTB Readers Guide: The Ancient Economy in the Bible." *BTB* 21 (1991) 34–39.

———. "'All the Surrounding Country': The Countryside in Luke-Acts." In *The Social World of Luke-Acts: Models for Interpretation,* edited by Jerome H. Neyrey, 151–79. Peabody, MA: Hendrickson, 1991.

———. "Was Jesus a Peasant? Implications for Reading the Samaritan Story (Luke 10:30–35)." *BTB* 22 (1992) 117–25.

———. "Purposiveness/End-Orientation, Self-Sufficiency." In *Biblical Social Values and Their Meaning: A Handbook,* edited by Bruce J. Malina and John J. Pilch, 153–55, 159–60. Peabody, MA: Hendrickson, 1993.

———. "The Ancient Economy and St. John's Apocalypse." *Listening* 28 (1993) 200–214.

———. "Cursing Fig Trees and Robbers' Dens: Pronouncement Stories Within Social-Systemic Perspective (Mark 11:11–25 and Parallels)." In *Semeia,* Vol. 64: *The Rhetoric of Pronouncement,* edited by Vernon K. Robbins, 253–72. Atlanta: Scholars, 1993.

———. "The Archaeology of First-Century Galilee and the Social Interpretation of the Historical Jesus." In *Society of Biblical Literature 1994 Seminar Papers,* edited by Eugene H. Lovering, Jr., 220–51. Atlanta: Scholars, 1994.

———. "The Ancient Economy." In *The Social Sciences and New Testament Interpretation,* edited by Richard L. Rohrbaugh, 126–43. Peabody, MA: Hendrickson, 1996.

———. "The Lord's Prayer in Social Perspective." In *Authenticating the Words of Jesus*, edited by Bruce Chilton and Craig A. Evans, 137–86. NTTS 28.1. Leiden: Brill, 1999.

———. "Economics of Palestine." In *Dictionary of New Testament Background*, edited by Craig A. Evans and Stanley E. Porter, 303–8. InterVarsity, 2000.

———. "Galilee." In *The Eerdmans Dictionary of the Bible*, edited by David Noel Freedman, 478–80. Grand Rapids: Eerdmans, 2000.

———. "Models and Archaeology in the Social Interpretation of Jesus." In *Social-Scientific Models for Interpreting the Bible: Essays by the Context Group in Honor of Bruce J. Malina*, edited by John J. Pilch, 102–31. Biblical Interpretation Series 53. Leiden: Brill, 2001.

———. "Money in the Moral Universe of the New Testament." In *The Social Setting of Jesus and the Gospels*, edited by Wolfgang Stegemann, Bruce J. Malina, and Gerd Theissen, 335–48. Minneapolis: Fortress, 2002.

———. "Die Rolle des Geldes im Moralischen Universum des Neuen Testaments." In *Jesus in Neuen Kontexten*, edited by Wolfgang Stegemann, Bruce J. Malina, and Gerd Theissen, 158–66. Translated by Anselm Hagedorn. Stuttgart: Kohlhammer, 2002.

———. "The Radical Jesus: You Cannot Serve God and Mammon." *BTB* 34 (2004) 122–29.

———. "The Promise of Lutheran Biblical Studies." *Currents in Theology and Mission* 32,1 (2004) 40–52.

———. "Das Verhältnis von Kultur, Gesellschaft und 'eingebetteter' Religion in der Antike." In *Was Begegnet Sich im Christlich-Jüdischen Dialog?*, edited by Gabriella Gelardini and Peter Schmid, 13–33. Translated by Andrea Haüser. Judentum und Christentum. Stuttgart: Kohlhammer, 2004.

———. "Culture, Society, and Embedded Religion in Antiquity." *BTB* 35 (2005) 4–12.

———. "Il denaro nell' universo etico del Nuovo Testamento." *Il nuovo Gesù storico*, edited by Wolfgang Stegemann, Bruce J. Malina, and Gerd Theissen, 203–15. Introduzione allo studio della Bibbia, Supplementi 28. Brescia: Paideia, 2006.

———. "The Radical Jesus: You Cannot Serve God and Mammon." *From Biblical Interpretation to Human Transformation: Reopening the Past to Actualize New Possibilities for the Future. A Festschrift Honoring Herman C. Waetjen*, 218–30. Salem, OR: Chora-Strangers, 2006.

———. "Biblical Hermeneutics: Marcion's Truth and a Developmental Perspective." *Ancient Israel: The Old Testament in Its Social Context*, edited by Philip F. Esler, 267–82. Fortress, 2006.

———. "Batteries of Power: Coinage in the Judean Temple System." In *In Other Words: Essays on Social Science Methods and the New Testament in Honor of Jerome H. Neyrey*, edited by Anselm C. Hagedorn, Zeba A. Crook, and Eric Stewart, 171–85. Social World of Biblical Antiquity 1. Sheffield: Sheffield Phoenix, 2007.

Oster, Richard. "Numismatic Windows into the Social World of Early Christianity." *JBL* 101 (1982) 195–223.

Overman, J. Andrew. "Who Were the First Urban Christians? Urbanization in Galilee in the First Century." In *Society of Biblical Literature 1988 Seminar Papers*, edited by David J. Lull, 160–68. Atlanta: Scholars, 1988.

———. *Matthew's Gospel and Formative Judaism: The Social World of the Matthean Community*. Minneapolis: Fortress, 1990.

———. *Church and Community in Crisis: The Gospel according to Matthew*. Valley Forge, PA: Trinity, 1996.

Parsons, Talcott. *The Structure of Social Action*. New York: McGraw-Hill, 1937.

———. *Politics and Social Structure*. Glencoe, IL: Free Press, 1969.

———. *The System of Modern Societies*. Englewood Cliffs, NJ: Prentice-Hall, 1971.

Patterson, Stephen J. *The God of Jesus: The Historical Jesus and the Search for Meaning*. Harrisburg, PA: Trinity, 1998.

Pearson, L. C. *Principles of Agronomy*. New York: Rheinhold, 1967.

Perkins, Pheme. "Taxes in the New Testament." *Journal of Religious Ethics* 12 (1984) 182–200.

Perrin, Norman. *Rediscovering the Teaching of Jesus*. New York: Harper & Row, 1976.

Petuchowski, J. J., and M. Brocke, editors. *The Lord's Prayer and Jewish Liturgy*. New York: Seabury, 1978.

Pilch, John J. *The Cultural Dictionary of the Bible*. Collegeville, MN: Liturgical, 1999.

Pilch, John J., and Bruce J. Malina, editors. *Biblical Social Values and Their Meaning: A Handbook*. Peabody, MA: Hendrickson, 1993.

Pilgrim, Walter. "Universalism in the Apocalypse." *Word & World* 9 (1989) 235–43.

Piper, Ronald A. *Wisdom in the Q-Tradition: The Aphoristic Teaching of Jesus*. SNTSMS 61. Cambridge: Cambridge University Press, 1989.

———. "Wealth, Poverty and Subsistence in Q." In *From Quest to Q: Festschrift James M. Robinson*, edited by Jon Ma Asgeirsson et al., 219–64. BETL 146. Leuven: Leuven University Press, 2000.

Plato. *Laws*. Translated by Benjamin Jowett. In *Plato*, edited by Robert Maynard Hutchins, vol. 7:640–799. The Great Books of the Western World. Chicago: Encyclopaedia Britannica, 1952.

Plattner, Stuart, editor. *Economic Anthropology*. Stanford: Stanford University Press, 1989.

Pliny the Elder. *Natural History*. Translated by H. Rackham. 10 vols. LCL. Cambridge: Harvard University Press, 1938–1963.

Plutarch. *Lives*. Translated by Bernadotte Perrin. 11 vols. LCL. Cambridge: Harvard University Press, 1914–1926.

Polanyi, Karl. *The Great Transformation: The Political and Economic Origins of Our Time*. Introduction by R. M. MacIver. Boston: Beacon, 1957.

———. *The Livelihood of Man*. Edited by Harry W. Pearson. Studies in Social Discontinuity. New York: Academic, 1977.

———, Conrad M. Arensberg, and Harry W. Pearson, editors. *Trade and Market in the Early Empires: Economies in History and Theory*. Glencoe, IL: Free Press, 1957.

Poole, L., editor. *Practical Basic Programs: IBM Personal Computer Edition*. Berkeley: Osborne/McGraw-Hill, 1981.

Preisigke, Friedrich. *Fachwörter des öffentlichen Verwaltungsdienstes Ägyptens in den griechischen Papyrusurkunden der ptolemäisch-römischen Zeit*. Göttingen: Vandenhoeck & Ruprecht, 1915.

Price, Jonathan. *Jerusalem under Seige: The Collapse of the Jewish State, 66–70 C.E.* Brill's Series in Jewish Studies 3. Leiden: Brill, 1992.

Pritchard, James. *Ancient Near Eastern Texts Relating to the Old Testament.* 3d ed. Princeton: Princeton University Press, 1969.

———. *The Ancient Near East.* Princeton: Princeton University Press, 1958.

Raadt, J. D. R. de. *Information and Managerial Wisdom.* Pocatella, ID: Paradigm, 1991.

Rad, Gerhard von. *Old Testament Theology.* Translated by D. M. G. Stalker. 2 vols. New York: Harper & Row, 1962–1965.

Räisänen, Heikki. *Marcion, Muhammad and the Mahatma: Exegetical Perspectives on the Encounter of Cultures and Faiths.* The Edward Cadbury Lectures at the University of Birmingham, 1995–1996. London: SCM, 1997.

———, editor. *Reading the Bible in the Global Village.* Atlanta: Society of Biblical Literature, 2000.

Rapoport, Anatole. "Rank-Size Relations." In *IESS* 13:319–23.

Redfield, Robert. *Peasant Society and Culture.* Chicago: University of Chicago Press, 1956.

———. "The Social Organization of Tradition." In *Peasant Society: A Reader*, edited by J. Potter, M. Diaz, and G. M. Foster, 25–34. Boston: Little, Brown, and Co., 1967.

Reich, Ronny. "More on Miqva'ot." *BAR* 13.6 (1987) 59–60.

———. "The Great Mikveh Debate." *BAR* 19.2 (1993) 52–53.

Rendsburg, Gary. "The Galilean Background of Mishnaic Hebrew." In *The Galilee in Late Antiquity*, edited by Lee I. Levine, 225–37. New York and Jerusalem: Jewish Theological Seminary of America, 1992.

Richardson, Peter. "Why Turn the Tables? Jesus' Protest in the Temple Precincts." In *Society of Biblical Literature 1992 Seminar Papers*, edited by Eugene H. Lovering, Jr., 507–23. Atlanta: Scholars, 1992.

Riesner, Rainer. "Bethany Beyond the Jordan." In *ABD* 1:703–5.

Robbins, Vernon K. *Exploring the Texture of Texts: A Guide to Socio-Rhetorical Interpretation.* Valley Forge, PA: Trinity, 1996.

Robertson, R. G. "Ezekiel the Tragedian." In *The Old Testament Pseudepigrapha*, edited by James H. Charlesworth, Vol. 2: *Expansions of the "Old Testament" and Legends, Wisdom and Philosophical Literature, Prayers, Psalms and Odes, Fragments of Lost Judeo-Hellenistic Works.* Garden City, NY: Doubleday, 1985.

Robinson, James M. "The Mission and Beelzebul: Pap. Q 10:2–16; 11:14–23." In *Society of Biblical Literature 1985 Seminar Papers*, edited by Kent Harold Richards, 97–99. Atlanta: Scholars, 1985.

Robinson, James M., Paul Hoffmann, and John S. Kloppenborg. *The Critical Edition of Q.* Hermeneia Supplements. Minneapolis: Fortress, 2000.

Rohrbaugh, Richard L. *The Biblical Interpreter: An Agrarian Bible in an Industrial Age.* Philadelphia: Fortress, 1978.

———. "Models and Muddles: Discussions of the Social Facets Seminar." *Forum* 3,2 (1987) 22–33.

———. "A Peasant Reading of the Parable of the Talents/Pounds: A Text of Terror?" *BTB* 23 (1993) 32–39.

———. "The Social Location of the Marcan Audience." *BTB* 23 (1993) 114–27.

———. *The New Testament in Cross-cultural Perspective.* Matrix. Eugene, OR: Cascade, 2007.

Roseberry, William. "Peasants and the World." In *Economic Anthropology*, edited by Stuart Plattner, 108–26. Stanford: Stanford University Press, 1989.

Rostovtzeff, Michael. *A Large Estate in Egypt in the Third Century B.C.* University of Wisconsin Studies in the Social Sciences and History 6. Madison: University of Wisconsin Press, 1922.

———. *The Social and Economic History of the Hellenistic World.* 3 vols. Oxford: Clarendon, 1941.

———. *The Social and Economic History of the Roman Empire.* 2 vols. Oxford: Clarendon, 1957.

Rousseau, John J., and Rami Arav. *Jesus and His World: An Archaeological and Cultural Dictionary.* Minneapolis: Fortress, 1995.

Royce, James R. "A Philonic Use of *Pandocheion.*" *NovT* 23 (1981) 193–94.

Safrai, S., and M. Stern, editors. *The Jewish People in the First Century: Historical Geography, Political History, Social, Cultural and Religious Life and Institutions.* Compendia Rerum Iudaicarum Ad Novum Testamentum. 2 vols. Philadelphia: Fortress, 1974–1976.

Safrai, Zeev. *The Economy of Roman Palestine.* London: Routledge, 1994.

Sahlins, Marshall. *Tribesmen.* Englewood Cliffs, NJ: Prentice-Hall, 1966.

Saldarini, Anthony J. *Jesus and Passover.* New York: Paulist, 1984.

———. *Pharisees, Scribes and Sadducees: A Sociological Approach.* Wilmington, DE: Glazier, 1988.

———. "Political and Social Roles of the Pharisees and Scribes in Galilee." In *Society of Biblical Literature 1988 Seminar Papers*, edited by David J. Lull, 200–209. Atlanta: Scholars, 1988.

Salisbury, E. J. *Weeds and Aliens.* New Naturalist. London: Collins, 1961.

Sanders, E. P. *Jesus and Judaism.* Philadelphia: Fortress, 1985.

———. "Jesus in Historical Context." *Theology Today* 50 (1993) 429–48.

———. *The Historical Figure of Jesus.* London: Penguin, 1993.

Sanders, Irwin T. *Rural Society.* Foundations of Modern Sociology Series. Englewood Cliffs, NJ: Prentice-Hall, 1977.

Sawicki, Marianne. *Crossing Galilee: Architectures of Contact in the Occupied Land of Jesus.* Harrisburg, PA: Trinity, 2000.

Schmidt, Thomas E. "Taxes." In *Dictionary of Jesus and the Gospels*, edited by Joel B. Green, Scot McKnight, and I. Howard Marshall, 804–7. Downers Grove, IL: InterVarsity, 1992.

Schottroff, Luise, and Wolfgang Stegemann. *Jesus von Nazareth—Hoffnung der Armen.* 2d ed. Stuttgart: Kohlhammer, 1981.

———. *Jesus and the Hope of the Poor.* Translated by Michael J. O'Connell. Maryknoll, NY: Orbis, 1986.

Schrenk, Gottlob. "*Boulomai.*" In *TDNT* 1 (1964) 629–37.

———. "*Thelēma.*" In *TDNT* 3 (1965) 52–62.

Schweitzer, Albert. *The Quest of the Historical Jesus: A Critical Study of Its Progress From Reimarus to Wrede.* Translated by W. Montgomery. London: A. and C. Black, 1910.

———. *The Quest of the Historical Jesus.* First complete ed. Edited by John Bowden. Translated by W. Montgomery, J. R. Coates, Susan Cupitt, and John Bowden. Fortress Classics in Biblical Studies. Minneapolis: Fortress, 2001.

Scott, Bernard Brandon. "Essaying the Rock: The Authenticity of the Jesus Parable Tradition." *Forum* 2,1 (1986) 3–63.

———. *Hear Then the Parable: A Commentary on the Parables of Jesus.* Minneapolis: Fortress, 1989.

Scott, James C. *The Moral Economy of the Peasant: Rebellion and Subsistence in Southeast Asia.* New Haven: Yale University Press, 1976.

———. *Weapons of the Weak: Everyday Forms of Peasant Resistance.* New Haven: Yale University Press, 1985.

———. *Domination and the Arts of Resistance: Hidden Transcripts.* New Haven: Yale University Press, 1990.

Scroggs, Robin. "The Sociological Interpretation of the New Testament: The Present State of Research." *NTS* 26 (1980) 164–79.

Seeley, David. "Jesus' Temple Act." *CBQ* 55 (1993) 263–83.

Seeman, Christopher. "The Urbanization of Herodian Galilee as an Historical Factor Contributing to the Emergence of the Jesus Movement." Unpublished M.A. Thesis. Graduate Theological Union, Berkeley, CA, 1993.

Seesemann, H. *"Peira."* In *TDNT* 6 (1968) 23–36.

Segal, J. B. *The Hebrew Passover: From the Earliest Times to A.D. 70.* London Oriental Series 12. London: Oxford University Press, 1963.

Shanks, Hershel. "Dever's Sermon on the Mound." *BAR* 13.2 (1987) 54–57.

Sherwin-White, A. N. *Roman Society and Roman Law in the New Testament.* The Sarum Lectures 1960–1961. Grand Rapids: Baker, 1963.

———. *Roman Foreign Policy in the East: 168 B.C. to A.D.1.* Norman: University of Oklahoma Press, 1983.

Sjøberg, Gideon. *The Preindustrial City: Past and Present.* New York: Free Press, 1960.

Smith, B. T. D. *The Parables of the Synoptic Gospels: A Critical Study.* Cambridge: Cambridge University Press, 1937.

———. "Lord's Prayer." In *IDB* 3:155.

Sorokin, Pitirim Aleksandrovich, and Charles Josiah Galpin. *A Systematic Source Book in Rural Sociology.* 3 vols. Edited by Carle Clark Zimmerman. Minneapolis: University of Minnesota Press, 1930–1932.

Spiegel, M. *Probability and Statistics.* Schaum's Outline Series in Mathematics. New York: McGraw-Hill, 1975.

Stählin, Gustav. *"Xenos, ktl."* In *TDNT* 5 (1967) 1–36.

———. *"Xēra."* In *TDNT* 9 (1974) 440–65.

Stegemann, Ekkehard S., and Wolfgang Stegemann. *The Jesus Movement: A Social History of Its First Century.* Translated by O. C. Dean Jr. Minneapolis: Fortress, 1999.

Stegemann, Wolfgang. *The Gospel and the Poor.* Translated by Dietlinde Elliott. Philadelphia: Fortress, 1984.

Stendahl, Krister. "Matthew." In *Peake's Commentary on the Bible*, edited by Matthew Black and H. H. Rowley. London: Nelson, 1962.

Strabo. *Geography.* Translated by Horace Leonard Jones. 8 vols. LCL. Cambridge: Harvard University Press, 1917–1933.

Strack, Hermann L., and Paul Billerbeck. *Kommentar zum Neuen Testament aus Talmud und Midrasch.* 6 vols. Munich: Beck, 1922–1961.

————. *Kommentar zum Neuen Testament aus Talmud und Midrasch.* 6 vols. 9th ed. Munich: Beck, 1986.

Strange, James F. "Some Implications of Archaeology for New Testament Studies." In *What Has Archaeology to Do with Faith?*, edited by James H. Charlesworth and Walter P. Weaver, 23–59. Faith and Scholarship Colloquies. Philadelphia: Trinity, 1992.

Strickert, Fred. "Coins as Historical Documents." In *Jesus and His World: An Archaeological and Cultural Dictionary*, edited by John J. Rousseau and Rami Arav, 61–68. Minneapolis: Fortress, 1995.

Tarn, W. W., and G. T. Griffith. *Hellenistic Civilisation.* 3d ed. London: Arnold, 1959.

Taussig, Hal. "The Lord's Prayer." *Forum* 4,4 (1988) 25–41.

Taylor, Vincent. *The Gospel according to St. Mark.* New York: Macmillan, 1953.

————. *The Gospel according to St. Mark.* 2d ed. Thornapple Commentaries. Grand Rapids: Baker, 1966.

Telford, William R. *The Barren Temple and the Withered Tree: A Redaction-Critical Analysis of the Cursing of the Fig-Tree Pericope in Mark's Gospel and Its Relation to the Cleansing of the Temple Tradition.* JSNTSup 1. Sheffield: JSOT Press, 1980.

Theissen, Gerd. "Die Tempelweissagung Jesu: Prophetie Im Spannungsfeld von Stadt und Land." *Theologische Zeitschrift* 32 (1976) 144–58.

————. *Sociology of Early Palestinian Christianity.* Translated by John Bowden. Philadelphia: Fortress, 1978.

————. *The Social Setting of Pauline Christianity: Essays on Corinth.* Translated and edited with an introduction by John H. Schütz. Philadelphia: Fortress, 1982.

————. *The Shadow of the Galilean: The Quest of the Historical Jesus in Narrative Form.* Translated by John Bowden. Minneapolis: Fortress, 1987.

————. *Lokalkolorit und Zeitgeschichte in den Evangelien.* NTOA 8. Göttingen: Vandenhoeck & Ruprecht, 1989.

————. *The Gospels in Context: Social and Political History in the Synoptic Tradition.* Translated by Linda M. Maloney. Minneapolis: Fortress, 1991.

Thompson, Leonard L. *The Book of Revelation: Apocalypse and Empire.* New York: Oxford University Press, 1990.

Thomson, Stith. *Motif-Index of Folk-Literature.* 6 vols. Bloomington: Indiana University Press, 1932–36.

Thorner, D. "Peasantry." In *IESS* 11:503–11.

Thucydides, *The History of the Peloponnesian War.* Translated by Richard Crawley. Revised by R. Feetham. In *Herodotus, Thucydides.* Edited by Robert Maynard Hutchins, 6:349–593. The Great Books of the Western World. Chicago: Encyclopaedia Britannica, 1952.

Thurnwald, Richard. *Economics in Primitive Communities.* London: Oxford, 1932.

Trevor, J. C. "Fig Tree, Fig." In *IDB* 2:267.

Turner, Nicholas. *A Grammar of New Testament Greek.* Edinburgh: T. & T. Clark, 1963.

Udoh, Fabian Eugene. "Tribute and Taxes in Early Roman Palestine (63 BCE–70 CE): The Evidence from Josephus." Ph.D. dissertation, Duke University, 1996.

————. *To Caesar What Is Caesar's: Tribute, Taxes and Imperial Administration in Early Roman Palestine (63 B.C.E.–70 C.E.).* Brown Judaic Studies 343. Providence, RI: Brown Judaic Studies, 2005.

United Bible Societies. *Fauna and Flora of the Bible.* Helps for Translators 11. London: United Bible Societies, 1980.

United Nations. "World Urbanization Prospects." United Nations, 2005. <http://www.un.org/esa/population/publications/WUP2005/2005wup.htm>. Accessed June 10, 2007.

———. "UN Report Says World Urban Population of 3 Billion Today Expected to Reach 5 Billion by 2030." United Nations, March 25, 2004. <http://www.unis.unvienna.org/unis/pressrels/2004/pop899.html>. Accessed June 10, 2007.

Vaage, Leif. *Galilean Upstarts: Jesus' First Followers according to Q.* Valley Forge, PA: Trinity, 1994.

Vaux, Roland de. *Ancient Israel.* 2 vols. Translated by John McHugh. 1965. Reprinted, Grand Rapids: Eerdmans, 1997.

Vermes, Geza. *The Religion of Jesus the Jew.* Minneapolis: Fortress, 1993.

Viviano, Benedict T. "The Gospel according to Matthew." In *The New Jerome Biblical Commentary,* edited by Raymond E. Brown, Joseph A. Fitzmyer and Roland E. Murphy, 630–74. Englewood Cliffs, NJ: Prentice Hall, 1990.

Waetjen, Herman C. *A Reordering of Power: A Socio-Political Reading of Mark's Gospel.* Minneapolis: Fortress, 1989.

Walker, William O. "Jesus and the Tax Collectors." *JBL* 97 (1978) 221–38.

———. "The Son of Man: Some Recent Developments." *CBQ* 45 (1983) 584–607.

Warriner, Doreen. *The Economics of Peasant Farming.* 2d ed. New York: Barnes & Noble, 1965.

Weber, Max. *Ancient Judaism.* Translated by Hans H. Gerth and Don Martindale. Glencoe: Free Press, 1952.

———. *General Economic History.* Translated by Frank H. Knight. New York: Collier, 1961.

———. *The Sociology of Religion.* Introduction by Talcott Parsons. Translated by Ephraim Fischoff. Boston: Beacon, 1963.

———. *The Agrarian Sociology of Ancient Civilizations.* Translated by R. I. Frank. London: NLB, 1976.

———. *Economy and Society.* 2 vols. Edited by Guenther Roth and Claus Wittich. Translated by Ephraim Fischoff. Berkeley: University of California Press, 1978.

Westcott, B. F., and F. J. A. Hort. *Introduction to the New Testament in the Original Greek, With Notes on Selected Readings.* New York: Harper, 1882.

White, K. D. *Roman Farming.* Ithaca, NY: Cornell University Press, 1970.

———. *Country Life in Classical Times.* Ithaca, NY: Cornell University Press, 1977.

Wittvogel, Karl A. *Oriental Despotism: A Comparative Study of Total Power.* New Haven: Yale University Press, 1957.

Wolf, Eric R. *Peasants.* Edited by Marshall D. Sahlins. Foundations of Modern Anthropology Series. Englewood Cliffs, NJ: Prentice Hall, 1966.

———. "The Hacienda System and Agricultural Classes in San Jose, Puerto Rico." In *Social Inequality: Selected Readings,* edited by André Béteille, 172–90. Penguin Modern Sociology Readings. Baltimore: Penguin, 1969.

Wright, Addison G. "The Widow's Mites: Praise or Lament?" *CBQ* 44 (1982) 256–65.

Yadin, Yagael. *Masada: Herod's Fortress and the Zealot's Last Stand.* Translated by M. Pearlman. New York: Random House, 1966.

Yeivin, Zeev. "Chorazin." In *The New Encyclopedia of Archaeological Excavations in the Holy Land*, edited by Ephraim Stern, 1:301–4. New York: Simon & Schuster, 1993.

Young, Brad. *The Jewish Background to the Lord's Prayer*. Austin, TX: Center for Judaic-Christian Studies, 1984.

Zahavy, Tzvee. *Studies in Jewish Prayer*. Studies in Judaism. Lanham, NY: University Press of America, 1990.

Zipf, George K. *Human Behavior and the Principle of Least Effort*. Cambridge: Addison-Wesley, 1949.